European Administrative Governance

The series maps the range of disciplines addressing the study of European public administration. In particular, contributions to the series will engage with the role and nature of the evolving bureaucratic processes of the European Union, including the study of the EU's civil service, of organization aspects of individual institutions such as the European Commission, the Council of Ministers, the External Action Service, the European Parliament, the European Court and the European Central Bank and of inter-institutional relations among these and other actors. The series also welcomes contributions on the growing role of EU agencies, networks of technical experts and national officials, and of the administrative dimension of multilevel governance including international organizations. Of particular interest in this respect will be the emergence of a European diplomatic service and the management of the EU's expanding commercial, foreign, development, security and defence policies, as well as the role of institutions in a range of other policy areas of the Union. Beyond this strong focus of EU administrative governance, the series will also include texts on the development and practice of administrative governance within European states. This may include contributions to the administrative history of Europe, which is not just about rules and regulations governing bureaucracies, or about formal criteria for measuring the growth of bureaucracies, but rather about the concrete workings of public administration, both in its executive functions as in its involvement in policy-making. Furthermore the series will include studies on the interaction between the national and European level, with particular attention for the impact of the EU on domestic administrative systems. The series editors welcome approaches from prospective contributors and are available to contact at t.christiansen@maastrichtuniversity.nl and s.vanhoonacker@maastrichtuniversity.nl for proposals and feedback.

More information about this series at
http://www.palgrave.com/gp/series/14977

Marie De Somer

Precedents and Judicial Politics in EU Immigration Law

palgrave
macmillan

Marie De Somer
University of Leuven
Leuven, Belgium

European Administrative Governance
ISBN 978-3-030-06763-2 ISBN 978-3-319-93982-7 (eBook)
https://doi.org/10.1007/978-3-319-93982-7

Softcover re-print of the Hardcover 1st edition 2019

Cover credit: Andrew Paterson / Alamy Stock Photo

Printed on acid-free paper

This Palgrave Macmillan imprint is published by the registered company Springer Nature Switzerland AG
The registered company address is: Gewerbestrasse 11, 6330 Cham, Switzerland

Contents

1 Introduction 1
1.1 The EU Court of Justice and European Integration Processes 1
1.2 Precedents and Judicial Politics 2
1.3 Testing Strategies 4
1.4 Outline and Structure 6
References 8

2 The Court's Role in Processes of European Integration 11
2.1 Introduction 11
2.2 The Origins: The Contextualist Legal Scholarship of the 1980s 12
2.3 The Role of the CJEU in Processes of European Integration: A Classic *Debate* 16
2.3.1 The Early 1990s: Intergovernmentalist Vs. Neofunctionalist Readings 16
2.3.2 The Mid-1990s: Other Scholars Join In 23
2.4 An Ongoing *Debate: Developments Since 2000* 29
2.4.1 Qualitative Research Continued 29
2.4.2 Quantitative Methods Added 39
2.5 In Sum—A Long-Lasting *Debate: Taking Stock of Theoretical and Methodological Divides* 48
References 54

3 Precedents and Judicial Politics 61
3.1 Introduction 61
3.2 Precedents and Judicial Interlocutors 67
3.3 Precedents and Non-judicial Interlocutors (Member States) 74
3.4 Conclusion 82
References 85

4 Case Selection and Data 89
4.1 Family Reunification Immigration: A Least-Likely Case 89
4.2 Data Collection: EU Family Reunification Law, Case Law and Self-Citation Activity 92
4.2.1 EU Family Reunification Law 93
4.2.2 EU Family Reunification Case Law 98
4.2.3 Self-Citation Activity 100
References 101

5 Identifying Member States' Interests 107
5.1 Identifying Member States' Interests: A Benchmark for Judicial Autonomy 107
5.2 Drafting Family Reunion Rights under Free Movement Law 111
5.2.1 The Early Instruments 111
5.2.2 The Citizenship Directive 112
5.3 Drafting Family Reunion Rights under EU Immigration Law 119
5.3.1 Preceding Legislative Efforts 119
5.3.2 The Family Reunification Directive 120
5.4 Conclusion: A Contested Personal Scope 140
References 143

6 Quantitatively Structuring Precedents 151
6.1 Introduction 151
6.2 A Self-Citation Sequencing Model 153
6.2.1 Step 1: Citation Scores 153
6.2.2 Step 2: Relative Citation Scores 154
6.2.3 Step 3: Dominant Scores—Citation Structures 160
6.3 Self-Citation Structures in CJEU Case Law on Family Reunification Immigration 161

6.3.1 *Quantitative Structuring* 161
6.3.2 *Numerical Observations* 165
6.4 *Conclusion* 169
References 169

7 Qualitatively Charting Precedents 173
7.1 *Introduction* 173
7.2 *The Mid 1970s—Early 1990s: Derived Rights and the Internal Rule* 175
7.3 *The 1990s: The Internal Rule, 'Effet Utile', Fundamental Rights and EU Citizenship* 180
7.4 *The 2000s: Further Refinements* 200
7.4.1 *The* Akrich *and* Jia *Cases* 201
7.4.2 Zhu & Chen, Eind *and* Metock 209
7.4.3 EPvCouncil *and* Chakroun 232
7.5 *The 2010s: A New Paradigm and Its Fine-Tuning* 244
7.5.1 Zambrano, McCarthy *and* Dereci 244
7.5.2 Iida, O&S, Ymeraga *and* Alopka 261
7.6 *Recent Developments:* O&B *and* S&G 274
7.7 *Conclusion* 280
References 280

8 Precedents and Judicial Politics: Analytical Findings 287
8.1 *Introduction* 287
8.2 *Judicial Autonomy* 287
8.2.1 *Member State Preferences* 287
8.2.2 *Judicial Outcomes* 290
8.3 *Precedents and Judicial Interlocutors* 294
8.3.1 *Cue-Taking* 294
8.3.2 *Steering Through Precedent* 298
8.4 *Precedents and Member States* 302
8.4.1 *Cue-Taking* 302
8.4.2 *Camouflaging Through Precedent* 305
8.5 *Conclusion* 310
References 310

9 Conclusions and Suggestions for Further Research 313
9.1 The Court of Justice and European Integration 313
9.2 Precedents and Judicial Politics: Key Findings 314
9.2.1 Precedents and Judicial Interlocutors 315
9.2.2 Precedents and EU Member States 318
9.3 Limitations and Suggestions for Further Research 320
References 323

Appendix 325

References 329

Index 353

List of Abbreviations

AG	Advocate General
CFREU	Charter of Fundamental Rights of the European Union
CJEU	Court of Justice of the European Union
COREPER	Committee of Permanent Representatives
CRC	UN Convention on the Rights of the Child
EC	European Community
ECHR	European Convention on Human Rights
ECtHR	European Court of Human Rights
ECJ	European Court of Justice
EP	European Parliament
EU	European Union
FRA	European Union Agency for Fundamental Rights
ICCPR	International Covenant on Civil and Political Rights
JHA	Justice and Home Affairs
MEP	Member of the European Parliament
OEIL	European Parliament Legislative Observatory
QMV	Qualified Majority Voting
SCIFA	Strategic Committee on Immigration, Frontiers and Asylum
SEA	Single European Act
TEU	Treaty on European Union
TFEU	Treaty on the Functioning of the European Union

CHAPTER 1

Introduction

1.1 The EU Court of Justice and European Integration Processes

This is a study into the Court of Justice of the European Union (CJEU) and its role in European integration processes. Enquiries of this kind hold a long lineage within academic literature. In social science, to begin with, since the first political scientists who famously 'discovered' the Court in the early 1990s advanced opposing readings of its role as either "faithfully implementing the preferences of national governments" (Garrett, 1992, p. 558), or—instead—"systematically overriding member states' true preferences" (Mattli & Slaughter, 1995, p. 184), competing conceptions of the Court's autonomy have stirred much contention. Arguably, few scholars would nowadays still frame their conceptions of the Court's role in such antagonistic terms (although see Carruba, Gabel, & Hankla, 2012 versus Stone Sweet & Brunell, 2012). Nevertheless, differing perceptions on the interpretative leeway which the EU judiciary enjoys relative to the preferences of the Union's political actors continue to, at its core, divide political science scholarship on the CJEU.

Questions of this kind also occupy debates within legal scholarship. Beginning with Stein's (1981) ground-breaking survey of the political implications attaching to the Court's jurisprudence, observations of case law outcomes that, to greater or lesser extents, reverberate beyond the

M. De Somer, *Precedents and Judicial Politics in EU Immigration Law*, European Administrative Governance,
https://doi.org/10.1007/978-3-319-93982-7_1

strictly legal sphere and questions on how to appraise such outcomes have formed the backbone to legal scientist debates on the Court's legitimacy (e.g., Adams, De Waele, Meeusen, & Straetmans, 2013), or whether or not it is activist (De Witte, Dawson, & Muir, 2013, Goldner-Lang, 2018).

1.2 Precedents and Judicial Politics

The current study provides new perspectives on these questions by adopting a long-term analytical approach that looks into the workings and effects of reasoning by precedent. As bears mentioning at the outset, precedents, in this context, are not conceptualized in terms of the formally binding nature they are known to hold in the framework of common law systems. Instead, they are construed more broadly as referring to the Court's practice of deciding new cases with reference to decisions reached in earlier proceedings.

Practices of this kind are frequently observed within both political science and legal scholarship. In both sets of literature, scholars also generally and repeatedly attest to the need of analysing CJEU rulings in the context of earlier judgments, or in the light of the implications these rulings may come to hold for follow-up litigation.

Within legal scholarship, first, commentaries on the high-profile, 2011 *Zambrano* ruling for instance provide ample illustrations of such observations. Pointing at the "open formulations" by means of which the Court expounded this decision, Hailbronner and Thym (2011, p. 1257) for example refer to the possibility that the CJEU deliberately left room "for later refinement" which would then allow it "to take on board political and academic criticism". Dawson (2014, pp. 428–429) similarly linked the judgement, and its later refinements in *McCarthy* and *Dereci* to what he called strategic discursive "repeat games" by means of which the Court could set down an "integrationist principle" but "limit its temporal or material impact" so as to reserve "the ability to fine tune, rescind or even expand" depending, amongst others, on the "attitudes and levels of 'resistance' emerging from governments". Lenaerts (2015, p. 3), who sat on the case as a judge, described the "stone-by-stone approach" taken in *Zambrano* and its follow-up judgments as stemming from a perceived need of "judicial prudence" in contexts touching on "politically sensitive questions". By adopting an open-ended reasoning in the first case, it could be left to future cases to decide whether the Court would opt for an either "strict or broad interpretation" of *Zambrano*.

Similar observations have featured in political science writings on the Court's role since the earliest beginnings. In fact, the perspective that precedents matter and may hold a politico-strategic advantage, constitutes one of the single consensual understandings on the Court's role that emerged out of the earliest, polarized debates in the 1990s referred to above. Where Garrett (1995, p. 178) had originally posited that the Court's behaviour would be "conditioned by its expectations about the likely responses of member governments", he later conceded, with reference to the arguments of his academic opponents (Mattli & Slaughter, 1995), that "precedent greatly concerns the ECJ". Amongst others, precedents were found to enable the Court to "embed decisions with potentially important long-term consequences for EU jurisprudence in relatively uncontroversial cases" so as to first entrench its positions (Garrett, Kelemen, & Schulz, 1998, pp. 157–168). At a later time, the Court could then modify its interpretation.

Similar perspectives have also featured centrally in later political science writings. Amongst others, in her seminal 'Masters of the Treaty' article, Alter (1998, pp. 130–131) advanced that one of the key explanations for the Court's power related to the manner in which the Court could play off the shorter time horizons of politicians. As she stated, the Court expanded its power "by establishing legal principles but not applying those principles to the case at hand". In that manner, it could make sure that the immediate political impact was minimal. However, what were in first instance marginal decisions, politically speaking, would later turn out to hold "revolutionary" implications. Taking examples from the more recent literature, in her "Justice Contained" monograph, Conant (2002, pp. 39–41) advanced that "prudent judgment", by means of which the CJEU adopts an "incremental approach" to the interpretation of EU law has played a critical role in the construction of the European legal order. It enabled the Court to "project neutrality" and on that basis hide the controversial implications attaching to its decisions. Most recently, Blauberger and Schmidt similarly mention processes of jurisprudential "fine-tuning" whereby the Court is observed to "curtail the demands" of its rulings (Schmidt, 2014, p. 773) when it becomes "sensitized to domestic concerns" (Blauberger, 2012, p. 123).

In spite of these recurring and mirroring observations in both political science and legal scholarship, neither of the two disciplines has thus far invested much efforts to uncover the precise mechanisms that underpin the observed dynamics and their eventual effects. In what follows, the present study draws on these different sets of related observations, made across the disciplinary divides that separate law and political science, and engages in a systematic review of precedent-based patterns within the Court's case law and the implications of such patterns for the Court's role in a broader institutional setting. The study argues that, by strategically engaging with precedent, the Court is able to, in the long run, strengthen the interpretative leeway and autonomy that it enjoys vis-à-vis the Union's political actors, most notably the Member States.

1.3 Testing Strategies

The research question guiding the evaluation of the above argument is *whether* and *how* precedent-based reasoning strengthens the Court's autonomy relative to the preferences of the Member States. Given that the extent to which the Court enjoys such an autonomy vis-à-vis the Member States remains, as indicated above, contested in the literature, examining the first *whether* question is a precondition before being able to meaningfully engage with the second *how* question.

The analysis is conducted against the Court's case law on family reunification immigration. The choice for this case law record is grounded in two considerations. First, EU family reunification law is considered to be a particularly politically sensitive area of law and, on that basis, a 'least-likely case' for observing a strong or increasing judicial autonomy. More specifically, as this area of law touches on questions of border control and the entry and residence of foreigners, and inasmuch as family reunification generally accounts for one of the numerically largest legal migration inflows into the European Union (Eurostat, 2017), it is a highly sovereignty-sensitive and politicized issue area. In that light, Member States are expected to be least likely to lower their guards in respect of case law outcomes that depart from their political preferences. Rather, any judicial developments of this kind are expected to be closely watched by the Union's political actors. On that basis as well, if the Court generally stays close to dominant political preferences it should be especially prone (or obliged) to do so in an area of law as sensitive as family reunification migration. In that light, and in line with the traditional rationale for adopting a least-likely case study design (George & Bennett, 2005), if findings of autonomous Court behaviour can be substantiated in this sensitive area, they are expected to offer a strong basis for generalizing to other areas of EU law as well. As the second consideration, EU family reunification immigration law was selected over other, potentially similarly politically sensitive areas on account of the particularly long track record of CJEU jurisprudence in this field. As questions on family reunion are partially embedded within EU free movement legislation as gradually established from the late 1960s onwards (a particularity sometimes overlooked in the literature), the CJEU's case law on such questions can be traced back as far as the 1976 *Kermaschek* ruling (C-40/76). The long timespan of this case law record, spanning four decades, is essential for gaining access to the long-term, cumulative dynamics that are expected to underpin precedent-based reasoning processes as well as define their broader effects.

The empirical analysis is conducted in three steps. The three sets of enquiries, taken together, combine both qualitative and quantitative orientations granting the research overall the character of a 'mixed methods' design. In a first step, Member States' political preferences on EU family reunion law are mapped by means of detailed reviews of the interest-articulation voiced by national governments during the drafting of the relevant legal provisions. This first analysis provides for an *ex ante* benchmark of dominant political preferences against which to assess, in the two subsequent stages, *whether* and *how* the Court was able to develop judicially autonomous decisions, that is, decisions that are independent from the identified preferences. By means of this *ex ante* benchmark, the analysis also seeks to gain leverage on the problem of observational equivalence. Observational equivalence relates to the difficulty of empirically distinguishing scenarios in which the Court acts autonomously from those in which, conversely, it is constrained by the preferences of the Member States but rationally adapts its behaviour beforehand so that no political antagonism or retaliation measures will appear. As is detailed in the next chapter, this methodological challenge has hindered judicial politics' analyses of the Court's role from the very outset (see Garrett & Weingast, 1993; Alter, 2008; Carruba, Gabel, & Hankla, 2008; Stone Sweet & Brunell, 2012). By benchmarking Member States' interests prior to the relevant jurisprudential developments, such observational difficulties can be overcome.

In a second empirical step, the study proceeds with a quantitative structuring of observations on CJEU self-citation practices, that is, observations of Court citations to its own prior rulings. More precisely, on the basis of a numerically grounded comparison, this second part of the analysis provides an overview of the self-citation structures that appear most prominent for the long-term development of the CJEU's case law on family reunification as a whole. The need for such a quantitative exercise is connected to the study's explicitly longitudinal outlook which calls, as observed above, for a dataset of Court rulings that spans a sufficiently long time period and is, by consequence, voluminous. The quantitative structuring serves to facilitate and systematize the further analytical engagement with the sizeable dataset. In addition, by structuring the data on the basis of objective, numerical criteria, the quantitative exercise also shields these further analyses from selective case sampling on the dependent variable (*in casu*, autonomous Court behaviour) which has been a subject of academic charges and counter-charges in the context of preceding qualitative literature.

The quantitative findings provide a roadmap on the basis of which, in a third and final empirical step, the study proceeds with qualitative and contextualized reviews of the discourses defining the numerically identified patterns. In so doing, this third step uncovers the more fine-grained causal mechanisms, of mostly a discursive nature, that are theoretically expected to underpin the workings and effects of reasoning by precedent. To the extent that these reviews enable collecting the empirical evidence necessary for corroborating context-dependent causal mechanisms, they also shield the study from reproducing binary 'grand theory' constructs on the Court's role which, although largely abandoned within qualitative scholarship, are still found to hinder opportunities for consensus-building in contemporary quantitative studies (Carruba et al., 2012; Stone Sweet & Brunell, 2012). In all, by combining both quantitative and qualitative orientations the study seeks, in line with the traditional argument for conducting mixed methods research (Creswell & Clark, 2010), to combine the strengths of each approach whilst simultaneously offsetting their respective weaknesses.

1.4 Outline and Structure

The study is composed of nine chapters. After this initial sketch of the research agenda, Chap. 2 surveys prior political science engagements with questions on the CJEU's role and autonomy. The chapter traces these engagements from their origins in 1980s contextualist legal literature, over their meta-theoretical phases during the 1990s, up onto the most recent writings. By now, social scientists have produced more research on the CJEU and its political impact than on any other court in the world, with the single exception of the US Supreme Court (Stone Sweet, 2010).

Whilst debates on the CJEU's role have been declared "closed" or "resolved" at various stages over this long time period (see e.g., Ibid., p. 22; Mattli & Slaughter, 1998), claims and counter-claims on the interpretative leeway which the Court enjoys relative to the EU Member States continue to date to claim the attention of the field. The chapter's concluding section retraces the different sets of hindrances of both a theoretical and methodological nature that account for the striking perseverance of these academic divides. The findings on these theoretical and methodological hindrances constitute the background against which the theoretical perspectives and methodological strategies of the present study are presented in detail.

Drawing on insights from both legal theory and political science, Chap. 3 advances a theoretical framework on the nature and long-term, cumulative effects of reasoning by precedent. Chapter 4 presents the data collection.

The next three chapters embed the empirical analyses. Chapter 5, to begin with, traces Member States' interest articulations during the negotiations on EU family reunification law. In that manner, it provides an *ex ante* benchmark of Member States' political preferences against which the further analytical stages set out to review *whether* and *how* autonomous judicial outcomes can be observed. Chapter 6 presents the quantitative analyses and the systematization of the data achieved on that basis. The quantitative findings provide the structure that guides the analytical focus of the qualitative reviews that form the subject of Chap. 7. Chapter 8 brings together the findings on Member States' political preferences as collected at the beginning of the analysis with those on the long-term implications deriving from the Court's precedent-based reasoning as examined in the further analyses. On that basis, this chapter presents the study's overall analytical findings on *whether* and *how* precedent-based patterns strengthen the Court's autonomy. Chapter 9 concludes by reflecting on these findings, evaluating their limits and offering avenues for further research.

References

Primary Sources

CJEU Case Law

Case C-34/09 *Gerardo Ruiz Zambrano v Office national de l'emploi (ONEM)* [2011] ECR I-1177.

Case C-434/09 *Shirley McCarthy v Secretary of State for the Home Department* [2011] ECR I-3375.

Case C-256/11 *Murat Dereci and Others v Bundesministerium für Inneres* [2011] ECR I-11315.

Other Sources

Eurostat. (2017). *Residence Permit Statistics.* Retrieved December 28, 2017, from http://ec.europa.eu/eurostat/statistics-explained/index.php/Residence_permits_statistics

Literature

Adams, M., De Waele, H., Meeusen, J., & Straetmans, G. (2013). *Judging Europe's Judges: The Legitimacy of the Case Law of the European Court of Justice.* Oxford: Hart Publishing.

Alter, K. (1998). Who are the Masters of the Treaty? European Governments and the European Court of Justice. *International Organization, 25*(1), 125–152.

Alter, K. (2008). Agents or Trustees? International Courts in Their Political Context. *European Journal of International Relations, 14*(1), 33–63.

Blauberger, M. (2012). With Luxembourg in Mind…The Remaking of National Policies in the Face of ECJ Jurisprudence. *Journal of European Public Policy, 19*(1), 109–126.

Carruba, C., Gabel, M., & Hankla, C. (2008). Judicial Behavior under Political Constraints: Evidence from the European Court of Justice. *American Political Science Review, 102*(4), 435–452.

Carruba, J., Gabel, M., & Hankla, C. (2012). Understanding the Role of the European Court of Justice in European Integration. *American Political Science Review, 106*(1), 214–223.

Conant, L. (2002). *Justice Contained: Law and Politics in the European Union.* Ithaca, NY: Cornell University Press.

Creswell, J., & Clark, V. (2010). *Designing and Conducting Mixed Methods Research.* Thousand Oaks, CA: SAGE Publications.

Dawson, M. (2014). How Does the European Court of Justice Reason? A Review Essay on the Legal Reasoning of the European Court of Justice. *European Law Journal, 20*(3), 423–435.

De Witte, M., Dawson, M., & Muir, E. (2013). *Judicial Activism at the European Court of Justice Causes, Responses and Solutions.* Cheltenham: Edward Elgar Publishing.

Garrett, G. (1992). International Cooperation and Institutional Choice: The European Community's Internal Market. *International Organization, 46*(2), 533–560.

Garrett, G. (1995). The Politics of Legal Integration in the European Union. *International Organization, 49*(1), 171–181.

Garrett, G., Kelemen, R. D., & Schulz, H. (1998). The European Court of Justice, National Governments, and Legal Integration in the European Union. *International Organization, 52*(1), 149–176.

Garrett, G., & Weingast, B. (1993). Ideas, Interests and Institutions: Constructing the European Community's Internal Market. In J. Goldstein & R. Keohane (Eds.), *Ideas and Foreign Policy: Beliefs, Institutions, and Political Change* (pp. 173–206). Ithaca, NY: Cornell University Press.

George, A., & Bennett, A. (2005). *Case Studies and Theory Development in the Social Sciences.* Cambridge, MA: MIT Press.

Goldner-Lang, I. (2018, January 24). Towards 'Judicial Passivism' in EU Migration and Asylum Law? Preliminary Thoughts for the Final Plenary Session of the 2018 Odysseus Conference. *Blogpost on EU Immigration and Asylum Law and Policy.* Retrieved from http://eumigrationlawblog.eu/towards-judicial-passivism-in-eu-migration-and-asylum-law-preliminary-thoughts-for-the-final-plenary-session-of-the-2018-odysseus-conference/

Hailbronner, K., & Thym, D. (2011). Comment on *Zambrano. Common Market Law Review, 48*, 1253–1270.

Lenaerts, K. (2015). EU Citizenship and the European Court of Justice's 'Stone-by-Stone' Approach. *International Comparative Jurisprudence, 1*, 1–10.

Mattli, W., & Slaughter, A.-M. (1995). Law and Politics in the European Union: A Reply to Garrett. *International Organization, 49*(1), 183–190.

Mattli, W., & Slaughter, A. M. (1998). Revisiting the European Court of Justice. *International Organization, 52*(1), 177–209.

Schmidt, S. (2014). Judicial Europeanisation: The Case of Zambrano in Ireland. *West European Politics, 37*(4), 769–785.

Stein, E. (1981). Lawyers, Judges, and the Making of a Transnational Constitution. *The American Journal of International Law, 75*(1), 1–28.

Stone Sweet, A. (2010). The European Court of Justice and the Judicialization of EU Governance. *Living Reviews in European Governance, 5*(2), 1–50.

Stone Sweet, A., & Brunell, T. (2012). The European Court of Justice, State Noncompliance, and the Politics of Override. *American Political Science Review, 106*(1), 204–213.

CHAPTER 2

The Court's Role in Processes of European Integration

2.1 Introduction

> Tucked away in the fairyland Duchy of Luxembourg and blessed, until recently, with benign neglect by the powers that be and the mass media, the Court of Justice of the European Communities has fashioned a constitutional framework for a federal-type structure in Europe. (Stein, 1981, p. 1)

This famous first sentence of Stein's seminal "The Making of a Transnational Constitution" has, since its appearance in 1981, featured in many accounts on the Court's role in processes of European integration. Rightly so, as this first sentence (and Stein's account generally), epitomized a turn in the literature on the CJEU—at the time, exclusively legal scholarship—away from previous legalist formalist approaches which had studied EU law as determinate constructs devoid of any socio-political dimension (see on this early scholarship Arnull, 2008 or Neergaard & Wind, 2012). Stein's article set the stage for what was, in hindsight, termed a new contextualist approach to EU law. This contextualist legal scholarship would, in turn, pave the way for the political science discovery of the CJEU in the early 1990s and inform much of its early research agenda.

In what follows, this first chapter traces the long lineage of political science debates on the Court's role in processes of European integration, starting off with their origins in the contextualist legal scholarship of the 1980s (Sect. 2.2). The next Sect. (2.3) details, first, how the competing

M. De Somer, *Precedents and Judicial Politics in EU Immigration Law*, European Administrative Governance,
https://doi.org/10.1007/978-3-319-93982-7_2

claims of 1990s pioneering political scientists established the conceptual groundworks of an academic discussion that was to become a classic as over time new generations of scholars enlisted at either side of the opposing propositions. By now, social scientists have produced more research on the CJEU than on any other court in the world, with the single exception of the US Supreme Court (Stone Sweet, 2010, p. 5). Section 2.4 examines how the debate's original fault lines still divide current political science works as both qualitative scholarship (2.4.1) and quantitative analyses (2.4.2) continue to engage with the research topics and questions defined in the early 1990s; albeit separately, that is, within distinct sub-pockets of research.

In spite of significant refinements introduced over the course of more than three decades of sustained academic analysis, both theoretically as methodologically, competing conceptions on the autonomy of the CJEU relative to the Member States continue to claim the attention of the field. The chapter's concluding Sect. (2.5) retraces the different sets of hindrances of both a theoretical and methodological nature that account for the striking perseverance of these academic divides. The findings on these hindrances constitute the background against which the theoretical and methodological perspectives guiding the present study are presented.

2.2 The Origins: The Contextualist Legal Scholarship of the 1980s

Following on from its famous "Tucked away" opening line, Stein's account proceeded with a critical review of a number of the Court's landmark decisions. Particular attention was paid to the manner in which these decisions interrelated with and impacted on the Community's broader political processes. Amongst others, Stein coined the argument that the Court's "fashioning" of a "constitutional framework" had been built on the judicial establishment of first, the principle of direct effect in *Van Gend en Loos* (C-26/62) and, second, the doctrine of EU law supremacy following *Costa vs. ENEL* (C-6/64). The interaction of these two doctrines was presented as having transformed the EU legal order from what was originally a set of legal arrangements between sovereign states, into a vertically integrated, 'higher-law' constitutional regime that from then onwards effectively conferred individual rights which could be enforced before domestic tribunals. The net effect of these constitutionalizing developments, Stein emphasized, was also to enable the Court to "arrogate to itself the ultimate authority to draw the line between Community law and national law" (Ibid.). Of importance, and what further set his writings apart from his legalist predecessors, in developing this 'constitutionalization narrative', he undertook to assess to what extent the Court had accommodated for the policy preferences of Member States. By comparing the arguments which governments submitted in their written observations to the Court with the final disposition of the cases, he concluded that the CJEU had developed its constitutionalizing case law in the face of "consistent opposition to increased integration from the part of the member governments" (Ibid., p. 25).

Following Stein, an increasing number of legal scholars was to move beyond the prior 'black letter' approach to EU law and extend their analytical focus to the interaction of the Court's jurisprudence with broader processes of European integration. In that manner, Stein's 'constitutionalization narrative' was ever more fleshed out over the decade that followed. Works regularly cited in relation to this new 'contextualist' literature include, amongst others, those of Weiler (1981, 1982, 1991), Rasmussen (1986), Mancini (1989), and Lenaerts (1990, 1992).

Writing but one year later, Weiler (1982) for instance advanced a strong plea for political scientists to start engaging with Community law, given that the Court's increased legal output had played, and was playing, an important role in the evolution of the Community's political structure. Starting off on the basis of Stein's findings, his work provided a further evaluation of the Court's expansionary, constitutionalizing doctrines with particular emphasis on their ramifications for Community decision-making processes. This, so as to highlight the relevant 'points of contact' for future political scientist works on judicial processes. In his later, influential "The Transformation of Europe", Weiler (1991) further expanded on these contentions, providing additional detail to the documentation of the Court's constitutionalizing jurisprudence. Amongst others, it was in this paper that he put forward the much-quoted observation that, on account of the Court's establishment of the doctrine of direct effect, "(e)ffectively, individuals in real cases and controversies (usually against state public authorities) became the principal "guardians" of the legal integrity of Community law" (Ibid., p. 2414). Weiler's account further described how, in combination with the supremacy principle and other constitutionalizing doctrines (e.g., implied rights, human rights) an incrementally accelerating process of legal integration was set in motion as ever growing numbers of individual rights claims were invoked before national courts which—through the preliminary reference procedure—fed into the CJEU's docket.

Featuring strongly in Weiler's work, and in many of the contextualist writings of the time, is an engagement with questions relating to the federal character of the EU polity, and in particular the authority of the CJEU to administer the vertical division of powers between the supranational ('federal') and national ('federated') levels of governance. The starting point for these enquiries being, as also pointed out by Stein, that the net effect of the constitutionalization of the EU legal order had been a self-appropriation of authority from the part of the CJEU to draw the line between national and Community competences. Besides Weiler, other notable contributions to this topic were provided by Lenaerts (1990, 1992). Amongst others, Lenaerts (1990) reviewed a number of Court rulings that had already amounted to *de facto* pronouncements on the fault line between national and EU law. This judicial 'umpiring' of the balance of powers between the EU and its Member States was, he asserted, the CJEU's proper function given that, as the findings of a comparative assessment of federal judiciaries around the world revealed, this was nothing but customary practice of supreme courts in federations everywhere. In a later 1992 article, these lines of reasoning re-appeared in the context of a broader review of the interaction between the Community's judicial structures and its political processes (Lenaerts, 1992). According to the author, in spite of what could at first sight appear to be a "one-way street in which the former pushed the latter", the Court had in fact responded to the expectations of the political processes (Ibid., p. 133). That is, a number of judgments that may have originally been perceived as "excesses of judge-made law" were to later serve as catalysts for moving Community political processes forwards. In freeing political decision-makers from a number of difficult decisions, the Court enabled them to move beyond political gridlocks towards a higher level of effectiveness. The Court's establishment of the principle of mutual recognition in *Cassis de Dijon* (C-120/78) and the ensuing incorporation of this principle in the Single European Act (SEA), was cited as a case in point. In all, the Court helped safeguarding the effectiveness and continued development of European integration. In the end, therefore, it was ultimately the Community's political processes that emerged as the 'true winners' of the Court's innovative jurisprudence.

Similar considerations around the ultimately positive boost that the CJEU's integrationist case law provided to the EU's political processes could also be found in the writings of Mancini (1989) who was, like Lenaerts, a judge in Luxembourg at the time of writing. In his depiction of the Court's constitutionalizing jurisprudence, he readily admitted that the CJEU's "judicial creativeness" had, at times, met with "bitter opposition" in certain quarters. However, with time, the resulting "wounds" to the Court's legitimacy had healed and the scars were left barely visible as many came to realize that the alternative to the Court's expansive rulings would have been an erosion of the Community, "a possibility that nobody really envisaged, not even the most intransigent custodians of national sovereignty" (Ibid., pp. 600–603; p. 614).

A more critical perspective was provided by Rasmussen's (1986) broad-gauge study on "judicial policy-making". Although recognisant of the fact that the European judiciary safeguarded the Community experiment at an early stage of its development, he nevertheless famously ended his review of the Court's constitutionalizing rulings with the warning that the "judicial activism running wild", as displayed over the course of the 1960s and 1970s, could in time be met with court-curbing, or even court-destroying initiatives from the part of countervailing powers (Ibid., p. 513). The ensuing loss of legitimacy and authority of its judicial institution could eventually prove fatal to the Community which does not possess effective means of its own for the enforcement of its laws (Ibid., pp. 8–9).

It would not take long before these striking claims and findings around the political dimensions of the Court's jurisprudence were picked up by political scientists as Weiler (1982) had advocated for. In fact, the questions engaged with by these early contextualist legal scholars, and their differing evaluations of the exact political leeway available to the Court strongly resonated with the sort of analyses that were in vogue around the same time in political science scholarship. That is, following the reinvigoration of political and economic integration processes post-SEA (1986), renewed attention had gone out to contending 'grand theory' explanations of European integration processes (Nugent, 2010). At their core, and put in the most basic terms, these metatheories divided on whether either the rational behaviour of nation states primarily accounted for the pace and substance of integration processes (intergovernmentalist perspectives), or whether instead these processes principally resulted from the interactions of sub- and supra-state actors who, responding to demands for further cooperation stemming from earlier harmonization efforts ('spillover effects'), continuously pushed integration further, even beyond Member States' political preferences (neofunctionalist models). The EU judiciary, however, had not yet been included in these discussions. Rather, and remarkably similar to the perspectives of the earlier formalist legal approach to EU law, the Court and its activities were perceived as pertaining to a politically-neutral, technical domain, the study of which was the province of legal scholarship exclusively. This, in sharp contrast to the state of affairs in US political science scholarship, where the study of judicial politics in relation to the US Supreme Court had already become part and parcel of mainstream political science. Not surprisingly, as remarked by Dyevre (2010), the first political scientists to start analysing the role of the EU's Court all hailed from American universities. As first, Garrett (1992), and next Burley and Mattli (1993), took up on the findings of the contextualist legal scholarship and framed them within contending European integration paradigms, a debate was instigated that—as the next sections outline—has continued fuelling academic discussions to date.

2.3 The Role of the CJEU in Processes of European Integration: A *Classic* Debate

2.3.1 The Early 1990s: Intergovernmentalist Vs. Neofunctionalist Readings

The first work to pick up on the constitutionalization narrative was Garrett's (1992) account of the evolution of European integration since the SEA (Garrett, 1992). His rational choice explanation of these developments specifically included an evaluation of the judicial oversight to common rules provided by the CJEU. Citing in his argumentation amongst others the writings of Stein and Weiler, he conceded that the Court held a remarkable authority to impose EC law on Member States and constrain their behaviour, even in areas that "impinge directly on the traditional authority of national governments" (Garrett, 1992, p. 555). This was puzzling from a rational choice perspective and led him to question why sovereign states would abide by Court dictates when these are detrimental to their interests. The answer, he asserted, and reminiscent of Lenaerts' and Mancini's evaluations, resided in the fact that the judicial enforcement of the EC legal system was ultimately consistent with Member States' broader interests in having a functioning common market.

Garrett went on to explain this 'seemingly paradoxical' assessment by pointing out, first, that the Court's judicial monitoring is helpful in providing information on compliance with commonly agreed rules. Without it, uncertainty over other members' behaviour would reign and incentives for defecting from the agreements would be high. In other words, judicial oversight helped to alleviate problems of 'incomplete information'. Second, and in connection, given that it is impossible to make exhaustive agreements that anticipate every possible application of the common rules to all specific situations that may arise, the CJEU also assisted in mitigating what are known as 'incomplete contracting' problems. In that light, Garrett asserted that the power of the Court was not to be overstated. Ultimately aware of its servient role, and the fact that its authority and legitimacy are contingent upon the continued acquiescence of Member States, the Court, he stated, was careful to make decisions that "faithfully implement the collective internal market preferences of national governments" (Ibid., p. 558).

Garrett supported these arguments, first, by highlighting the control and sanctioning mechanisms retained by Member States; that is, legislative override (through secondary legislation or, at the extreme, Treaty revision) and control over the processes of judges' appointment. Second, he argued that a number of seemingly contra-national rulings were in fact congruent with the economic trade liberalization preferences of powerful Member States, most notably those of Germany and France. Following this logic, observations of government-sanctioning Court rulings that were ultimately complied with did not discard his evaluation as it was to be expected that the CJEU would at times issue sanctioning rulings when this was required to strengthen the efficacy of the common market. In doing so, however, the Court would always act strategically and only rule against a Member State when it anticipated that its decisions would not provoke a political reaction, as the affected government would consider the broader economic benefits gained from the ruling to outweigh the losses suffered in the short-run. Empirically, this claim was supported by a review of the Court's *Cassis de Dijon* decision. This seminal judgment was considered exemplary of the CJEU's practice to cater to the interests of France and Germany. Although the Court sanctioned German protectionist measures, overall, the outcomes of the ruling helped opening up European markets to foreign trade by dismantling non-tariff barriers which was ultimately in line with Germany and France's broader economic interests. Of importance, in so doing, the Court was careful not to venture into those areas of economic activity that these powerful Member States deemed central to their domestic economic performance (e.g., industrial policies).

This delegation-centred line of reasoning also returned in a co-authored work with Weingast (Garrett & Weingast, 1993). Although the authors did not explicitly avow to this themselves, by emphasizing the importance of state interests and rejecting the capacity of a supranational Court to generate outcomes that counteract national governments' interests, their writings were to become associated with intergovernmentalist theories of European integration. The two-fold delegation-centred explanation around (i) incomplete information and (ii) incomplete contracting was to become an evergreen of subsequent works that, in their footsteps, reviewed the role of the Court from an intergovernmental, state-centred perspective. In addition, the labelling of their work as intergovernmentalist may also have been inspired by the fact that the writings that most forcefully came to criticize Garrett (and Weingast) strongly avowed to a neofunctionalist reading of European integration processes.

These were the writings of Burley and Mattli who, shortly after, presented an entirely contrasting interpretation of the Court's judicial autonomy (Burley & Mattli, 1993). Like Garrett and Weingast, the authors also started off on the basis of the remarkable recording of the Court's authority presented by the contextualist 'constitutionalization' narrative. Legal scholarship on this constitutionalization process had however, in their view, failed to provide an explanation that was convincing to political scientists. In attributing aggregate motives and interests to the institutions involved and failing to specify causal mechanisms, this literature lacked microfoundations and was therefore unsatisfactory from a theoretical point of view. On the other hand, the explanations that had been offered by political scientists—that is, at the time of writing only those of Garrett and Weingast—were "simply wrong" (Ibid., p. 51). Amongst others, the authors strongly criticized the empirical support Garrett and Weingast had adduced in support of their contentions. This consisted of no more than one single judgment, *Cassis de Dijon*, which, Mattli and Burley stated, was selectively chosen and of which—in addition—the outcomes had been incorrectly explained so as to fit the authors' claims.

The deficiencies to both sets of literature, legal scholarship and political science alike, could be remedied by truthfully integrating the insights from the first in a theoretical framework acceptable to the latter. Such a framework was found in Haas' (1958) neofunctionalist theory. The application of this theoretical model to the contextualist legal literature's findings would lead the authors to conclusions that diametrically opposed those of Garrett and Weingast. That is, the Court's jurisprudence was said to have generated 'supranational' outcomes that went beyond the intentions of national governments. These results came about, and could be explained—following neofunctionalist predictions—by the converging of interests of a number of sub- and supra-state actors who joined forces across national boundaries in the pursuit of their own aims and ambitions and who, in doing so, further added to the 'integrative momentum' at the expense of nation states' sovereignty.

In the context of legal integration, the Court had largely created those opportunities itself with its constitutionalizing judgments in *Van Gend en Loos* (direct effect) and *Costa v. Enel* (supremacy of EU law). By that token, these judgments were in and of themselves examples of a supra-state actor promoting its own self-interest, that is, extending its mandate to have a more influential say in Community affairs. These Court decisions were also the pre-conditions that would, next, allow for the co-opting of sub-state interests by providing personal incentives for individual litigants, national courts, lawyers and the wider legal academic community to participate in the construction of an expanding EU legal system. Following an argumentation similar to that presented by Weiler (1991) and others in the contextualist legal literature, the pronunciation of direct effect was credited for having transformed citizens into a new constituency of rights-holders to whom, henceforth, EU law represented an opportunity structure for the advancement of their own goals. If need be, by holding their own governments accountable to their EU obligations before domestic tribunals. This, also in line with the logics established by Weiler (1991), Lenaerts (1992) and others, encouraged further use of the preliminary reference procedure and in that way granted national courts a stake in the Community law game. That is, to national courts, EU law came to represent an opportunity structure for the enhancement of their own judicial power vis-à-vis their governments; or in the case of lower courts vis-à-vis higher tribunals. On account of these interconnected processes, lawyers and legal academics also gained an interest in the furtherance of EU law. Particularly academics were said to have wilfully exploited this interest by providing apologetic, legitimizing descriptions of the Court's expansionary case law so as to burnish the prestige of the institution to which they were themselves professionally connected.

With time, the different interests for whom EU law represented an opportunity structure started converging and would come to reciprocally empower one another. The processes of continued integration which their interactions sustained were further buttressed by the (neofunctionalist) dynamics of functional spillover, according to which cooperation in one area creates the need for action in a related sector, which in turn creates a further need for action, and so on. Such dynamics could, amongst others, be identified in the CJEU's habit of portraying its expansionary decisions as filling in legal interstices that were merely a logical follow-up of the parts of the legal structure already built. In addition, the authors identified political spillover effects of adaptive behaviour in the incremental acceptance of CJEU discourses by Member States who, although originally overtly hostile to a certain decision, at a later point in time would come to accept that Court's pronouncement as a statement of law and proceed to make arguments from that benchmark in subsequent litigation. This also served as an illustration of how, in all of this, the role of governments was reduced to one of being, at best, "creatively responsive" (Ibid., p. 54).

Overarching their entire line of argumentation is the oft-cited assertion that "law functions as a mask for politics". That is, the neofunctionalist dynamics described were enabled by the apparent separation of law from politics, or, by the nominally non-political nature of legal dictates. As Haas had originally foreseen for the field of economics, the Court could indirectly penetrate the realm of the political by clothing its decisions in the purportedly neutral, technical language of the law so as to camouflage the potentially controversial political ramifications of its decisions. Such political ramifications would nevertheless eventually be felt. However, given that judicial decisions were framed as legal observations, contending political interests that would react in follow-up could no longer attack them but by a 'battle of proxy'. That is to say, they had to frame their political objections as legal objections, which then relegated these objections back into the sphere where the Court holds the last word. In that sense, law functioned not only as a 'mask', but also as a 'shield'. Like the writings of Garrett and Weingast which they challenged, the lines of reasoning advanced by Mattli and Burley were to become evergreens of scholarly works that, in their footsteps, rejected a portraying of the Court as merely a validator of Member States' interests but instead supported the claim that the CJEU held sufficient autonomy to engender independent, supranational outcomes.

In spite of the critique they had voiced on Garrett and Weingast's methodology, Burley and Mattli's line of reasoning was similarly supported by no more than a few scant citations to Court decisions which served mostly as illustrations to the arguments made. In essence, they repeated Garrett and Weingast's narrow sampling on the dependent variable. That is, where Garrett and Weingast discussed cases they viewed as axiomatic of Court's responsiveness to Member State interests, Burley and Mattli similarly selected cases they considered exemplary of—conversely—Court autonomy. To add to the problem, and oddly enough, the same *Cassis de Dijon* judgment featured in both of the contending accounts, albeit with entirely contrasting readings as either (i) a judgment that furthered Member States' interests (Garrett & Weingast) or, conversely, (ii) one that counteracted those interests (Mattli & Burley).

Garrett retaliated (1995), and so did Mattli and Burley (by then Slaughter) in sequence (Mattli & Slaughter, 1995). Both nuanced their theoretical contentions in the process, but did not depart from their central claims and cause for disagreement, that is, their differing views on the extent to which the Court takes account of States' interests. The (limited) theoretical refinement was not matched by progress on the methodological plane however. To the contrary, in the newer contributions, the methodological discrepancies were brought even stronger to the fore and became new points of contention in and of themselves. Both pairs of authors would come, in parallel, to challenge the other study's empirical strategies around a two-fold set of comparable shortcomings. This dual set of methodological hindrances would later on resurface in much of the political science literature on the CJEU that was to follow.

First, as Mattli and Burley had already done in their earlier review, each study criticized the case selection strategies that were employed in the rivalling account. Along similar lines, these were said to be both biased, as well as too narrow to constitute a representative sample of the Court's activities and hence allow for a generalisation of the respective findings to the CJEU's case law as a whole. Additionally, and in connection, the small-n case study evidence adduced did not allow for disproving contending propositions as each Court ruling cited in support of either Member State or Court autonomy could—in turn—be counterchecked by the opposing study with references to a next, different decision more supportive of the opposite scenario. These are, of course, familiar methodological obstacles of qualitative case study research generally speaking. They are particularly problematic, however, against the background of an empirical environment as heterogeneous and idiosyncratic as the CJEU's case law. Given that each single Court judgment is highly issue-specific and context-dependent, numerous case law shifts can be observed over the course of time depending on such factors as the issue matters under review, the precise legal provisions invoked, the wording of the questions raised, and many more aspects unique to the proceedings at hand. Such contingencies then create opportunities for the analyst to, depending on the rulings selected, either observe decisions that appear reminiscent of Member State interests, or—conversely—rulings in which the Court apparently did little to accommodate for such political interests. Further exacerbating this problem, given that proceedings before the CJEU usually consist of multiple legal issues—over which the Court does not necessarily always favour the same side—even within a single Court decision evidence can be marshalled to support competing claims, depending on which issues in the judgement are singled out for observation. In the discussions between Garrett, Mattli and Burley, *Cassis de Dijon* continued to take centre stage in that regard as both accounts—in taking turns—continued to subject this landmark ruling to ever more intricate interpretations meant to either prove, or disprove, its compatibility with Member State interests.

A second methodological problem to hinder these first discussions relates to what is more generally known in delegation literature as the problem of 'observational equivalence'. That is, scenarios in which institutions with delegated powers (*in casu*, the Court) operate independently from their delegators (*in casu*, the Member States) can be 'observationally equivalent' to their opposing others, i.e., scenarios in which the entity with delegated powers is in fact constrained by the policy preferences of its delegators but anticipates the delegators' reactions and rationally adapts its behaviour beforehand in order to avoid provoking costly retaliations. Following such logics of rational anticipation, if threats of political sanctions (e.g., legislative override) are effective, they need not be used and there will, accordingly, not be anything for the analyst to observe. Consequently, observations of the absence or rarity of Member State sanctions in response to Court rulings cannot discriminate between opposing views as they are consistent with scenarios of both Court autonomy as well as Member State control, albeit for different reasons (this methodological problem in the context of the CJEU is discussed further below, Sect. 2.4.2; see for a more general discussion in the context of delegation literature, Pollack, 2002). Along such lines, Garrett and Weingast's 'rational anticipation' evaluation also discarded the evidence on the rarity of

Member State sanctions which Mattli and Burley had adduced. As contended by Garrett and Weingast: "The fact that a court's decisions are neither overturned nor the subject of considerable controversy does not demonstrate that it exercises real discretion. The opposite conclusion is also consistent with the same observation." (Garrett & Weingast, 1993, p. 202; see also Garrett, 1995; pp. 180–181).

2.3.2 *The Mid-1990s: Other Scholars Join In*

The theoretical divides and methodological obstacles of these earliest political science writings on the Court were to set the stage for much of the political science to come. Among the first to pick up on the assertions put forward was Alter. In her seminal 1996 paper "The European Court's Political Power" she furthered Mattli and Slaughter's argument (originally deriving from the contextualist legal scholarship of such authors as Weiler (1991) and Lenaerts (1992)), that the Court's ability to advance legal integration against Member States' interests rested to a significant extent on the successful co-opting of national courts. On the basis of a review of the different responses by differently ranked domestic courts to the CJEU's declaration of the supremacy doctrine depending on their respective hierarchical ranking within national legal systems, she argued that the gradual penetration of EU law into such national legal systems had been significantly facilitated by inter-court competitive dynamics. That is, lower courts were more inclined to accept the doctrine of supremacy, start applying EU law, and refer preliminary questions than higher courts. Used to having a higher hierarchical court above them, such lower courts had lesser concerns in having their decisions rewritten by another tribunal. In addition, for such lower courts the application of EU law also represented an opportunity structure to circumvent potentially restrictive jurisprudence of domestic higher courts, or to re-open legal debates that had been closed with an outcome that was not to their liking. The CJEU encouraged these dynamics by giving serious evaluations to the referred questions and dismissing higher court refutations of their own authority. As the inflow of preliminary questions continued increasing, so did the opportunities for the CJEU to expand its jurisprudence and jurisdiction. Eventually, as EU law started touching on ever more issues of domestic law, and so many lower courts were following the CJEU's lead, the potential opposition to the application of EU law by higher courts lost its effectiveness. Once co-opted, the support of national courts greatly enhanced the CJEU's authority as its decisions became binding not only on the basis of its own jurisdiction, but also on the basis of that held by domestic tribunals. This then significantly changed the political realities associated with non-compliance. Whereas ignoring CJEU decisions could have been a feasible strategy for national governments previously, disobeying their own domestic tribunals would have very different political implications.

In a later article, "Who are the Masters of the Treaty", Alter would come to more clearly join the counter-Garrett and Weingast side (Alter, 1998). She repeated her argumentation on the authority enhancement that the co-opting of national courts entailed, and then added two further lines of explanation to account for the Court's remarkable power. To begin with, drawing on theoretical explanations on European integration developed by Pierson (1996), the Court, she argued along the lines of Mattli and Slaughter's 'mask and shield' argument, had successfully played off the inherently shorter time horizons of politicians by carefully and gradually developing legal doctrines that, although significant in the long term, were first announced in materially unimportant cases in order to evade immediate political reactions. However, "(t)he doctrinal precedents stuck into the Court's benign legal decisions were in fact formidable institutional building blocks that would be applied in the future to more polemic cases" (Ibid., p. 135). In so doing, the Court could successfully exploit politicians' fixation on the short-term material consequences of legal decisions and instead focus on expanding its authority in the long run. In addition, Alter took issue with Garrett's and Weingast's delegation-centred arguments by positing, in contrast, that the control mechanisms available to Member States did not constitute a 'credible threat' to the CJEU. Governed by the logics of 'joint-decision traps' (Scharpf, 1988), it was very difficult for Member States to find a uniform consensus to override Court decisions through legislative changes, let alone to mobilize sufficient political support to change the situation through Treaty amendment. Moreover, unified control through appointment processes was equally improbable, considering the fact that career paths of high judicial officials strongly diverge from Member State to Member State. Like the preceding literature with which she engaged, Alter's arguments were empirically supported, predominantly, by qualitative analyses of 'fitting' case law.

Alter's challenge of the delegation-centred framework is indicative of another trend that would come to run through the debate. Following on from Garrett's narration of limited Court influence on account of the delegated nature of its powers, others were to similarly formulate their rebuttals of this account in political science 'Principal-Agent constructs', albeit emphasizing—conversely—the weakness of Member States as Principals to control their Agent the Court. Criticizing, like Alter, the effectiveness of Member States' sanctioning mechanisms, such works would claim that the CJEU in fact operates in an unusually permissive environment which offers many opportunities for agent "shirking" or "slippage" (e.g., Pollack, 1997a; Tallberg, 2000a, 2000b).

Other notable works to join the neofunctionalist side included the writings of Stone Sweet and Brunell (1998) who tested neofunctionalist predictions of ever expanding legal integration processes against a comprehensive dataset of preliminary reference proceedings covering a period of three decades. On the basis of, first, a quantitative statistical analysis they reported a positive correlation between, on the one hand, growing transnational trade within the EU and, on the other, growing litigation on EU law. This increasing interdependence of transnational exchange and judicial activity would lead to ever more 'spill-over effects' as litigants came to identify and put pressure on new barriers to cross-national exchanges. This first set of dynamics then propelled a self-reinforcing process that pushed for the progressive expansion of supranational governance. In addition, a more detailed, qualitative review of jurisprudential developments in the areas of free movement of goods and social provisions led them to the conclusion that such self-reinforcing progressive dynamics were in no manner congruent with the preferences of dominant states. In respect of the freedom of movement of goods, first, they identified a disproportionate amount of 'integrative' case law outcomes in litigation that targeted those countries with markets of high interest to cross-national traders (with Germany as the most notable example), indicating how free trade litigants—not governments—were in the driving seat of integration. With regard to social provisions legislation, second, in-depth reviews of the case law indicated that the CJEU had primarily attacked precisely those national rules and practices that represented the lowest common denominator position adopted by the Council. At times the Court even used its judicial fiat to re-enact provisions that had previously been vetoed by one or more Member States during Council negotiations. Following Mattli and Burley's depiction, governments' overall role was portrayed as limited to being 'reactive', not 'proactive' in integration processes.

Following up on the findings of Stone Sweet and Brunell, Cichowski (1998) tested a range of similar neofunctionalist predictions against data on preliminary reference rulings in the area of EU environmental protection legislation. She found broad support for the claim that preferences of powerful governments do not constrain the Court on the basis of an analysis in which she reviewed (i) first, how many times the CJEU ruled to declare the national rule as consistent or inconsistent with EU law obligations and (ii) second, how these judicial outcomes related to the written observations submitted by Member States prior to the ruling. In line with Stone Sweet and Brunell's conclusions, Cichowski's findings revealed, for the first question (i) that the Court had often ruled to declare national rules 'inconsistent' with EU law and, second (ii) that the relation of these rulings to the written observations refuted the intergovernmentalist premise that the preferences of powerful Member State governments systematically constrain the Court. The paper further specified, in a subsequent qualitative analysis, how the Court's decisions had, over time, cumulatively engendered expansive outcomes that progressively shifted policy authority away from Member State control to the supranational level. In addition, in this article, and more clearly in later analogous works on gender equality legislation (Cichowski, 2001, 2004), Cichowski also called attention to the role of civil society interest groups who increasingly started using EU law litigation as a forum for promoting their interests. Questions regarding this additional role of public interest litigation in supporting the build-up of the Court's authority and the expansive outcomes of its case law, were also notably explored in the writings of Wincott (1995), Pollack (1997b) or Alter and Vargas (2000).

A final addition to the neofunctionalist line of reasoning that deserves mention is the work of Schmidt (1998, 2000), who outlined how a dynamic of mutual strategic co-opting between the Commission on the one hand, and the Court on the other, explained the remarkable authority of these two supranational institutions over the policy preferences and legislative actions of the Council of Ministers. According to her account, the Commission strategically initiated and followed up on Court rulings as a means to either change the legislative preferences of some Member States by singling them out for targeted infringement proceedings, or coax the Council as a whole into taking legislative action by tactically initiating a series of strategic infringement proceedings within a certain specific policy area.

Returning to the intergovernmentalist side, although the claims of Garrett and Weingast appear to have generated more challenges than support, intergovernmentalist readings of the Court's role were not left unattended in the meantime.[1] Garrett himself remained the most forceful defender of his own account. In a later game theoretic analysis, co-authored with Kelemen and Schulz, he reinforced his statement that the Court is a strategic actor in that it must take account of, and is restrained by, the reactions of member governments (Garrett, Kelemen, & Schulz, 1998). Responding however to criticisms on the earlier work, these contentions were strongly qualified in comparison to the previous versions in that the authors accepted the argument voiced by, amongst others, Mattli and Slaughter (1995) that the Court's authority is also dependent on it being seen as an impartial arbiter of the law. As a result, the authors conceded, the Court is at times cross-pressured as it must weigh considerations on anticipated Member State reactions against the requirement to respect legal consistency by taking account of case law precedents. This could explain the outcomes of some Court decisions that Member States arguably would not support as, in cases where precedent is clear, the CJEU would feel compelled to issue adverse rulings in order to maintain the requirement of legal consistency. In response to criticisms regarding the empirical grounding of the previous accounts, the new, more nuanced version was based on qualitative analyses of a range of CJEU decisions in three different policy areas (agricultural trade, gender equality and state liability) although, arguably, the criticism of selective sampling of Court decisions on the dependent variable still applied.

In a next article with Tsebelis, Garrett re-visited the Principal-Agent framing of Member State-Court relations that had, in follow-up to his indirect usage of these constructs in the earlier articles, spurred a range of scholarship on the Court that made use of the same paradigm (Tsebelis & Garrett, 2001). On the basis of an elaborate game theoretical model of institutional interactions at EU level and the rules set up to govern those interactions, the authors argued that Court rulings—even when appearing

[1] Remarkably, even within intergovernmentalist circles, Garrett's state-centred account of the CJEU's role was not unequivocally supported. Moravcsik, one of the leading exponents of intergovernmentalist theory at the time, for instance conceded that the CJEU represented an "anomaly" for his functional explanation of national governments' delegation of power to the supranational level. He instead accepted—with reference to Mattli and Burley's work—that the Court's decisions transcended what was foreseen and desired by most national governments (Moravcsik, 1993, pp. 513–514).

to move beyond the legislative intent of the Council—were often still located at a policy position within the 'core area' of what Member States would deem acceptable.

Over the years, as ever more scholars took up on the different claims that underpinned the initial, competing accounts of Garrett, Mattli and Burley, contributing new insights and new data, the debate as a whole acquired more nuance and gradation. Explanatory variables were further specified, or newly added, and tested against empirics from ever more diverse issue areas. With time, this generated more support for nuancing ideas that, in the end, both legal and political considerations matter when accounting for the role of the Court. By the end of the 1990s, few scholars would still subscribe to the stark, binary claims as originally advanced in the pioneering accounts, including those authors themselves who came to mutually recognize the added value of integrating the insights from the opposing versions into their own frameworks (see Garrett et al., 1998; Mattli & Slaughter, 1998). Scholars would also take pains to situate their narratives of the Court's role in what were perceived as more nuanced theoretical frameworks. Alter (1998, see also 2009), for instance, would come to label her arguments as historical institutionalist because such a theoretical approach was seen as offering a more open framework that dealt better with contingency and could capture important contextual elements that neofunctionalist framings could miss. Stone Sweet framed his arguments within a revised 'institutionalist' neofunctionalism (Stone Sweet & Sandholtz, 1997; Stone Sweet & Caporaso, 1998). Other works asserted that their more nuanced theoretical approaches allowed for a straddling of the paradigmatic divides in the literature. Amongst these for instance Garrett et al.'s (1998) game theoretic analysis of the Court-Member States strategic environment, Garrett and Tsebelis' institutionalist explanations (Tsebelis & Garrett, 2001) or Tallberg's use of an 'extended' Principal-Agent model (Tallberg, 2000b). In their third and final contribution to the discussions, Mattli and Slaughter even set out to "close the books" on the neofunctionalist-intergovermentalist debate they had themselves initiated. A new generation of scholarship and empirical puzzles, they asserted, would have to focus on working towards the development of 'midrange hypotheses' regarding the conditions under which the CJEU enjoys either more or less autonomy relative to the Member States (Mattli & Slaughter, 1998, pp. 178–179).

In spite of these efforts however, the 'books' were not 'closed'. Whilst growing cross-engagement between the different theoretical foci led to a more nuanced portrayal of claims and findings, it did little more than that. In essence, and as documented, the writings of the late 1990s could still with ease be positioned at either side of the conceptual divides that had been drawn up in Mattli, Burley and Garrett's original accounts; i.e., stressing either Court autonomy or, conversely, Member State control. In addition, although the increased scholarly interest and output led to a broadening of the empirical data on which different claims rested, the strategies for evaluating these data were not necessarily updated much in parallel. With the exception of Stone Sweet and Brunell's (1998) mixed quantitative-qualitative research design and the work of Cichowski (1998), analyses continued to rely predominantly on traditional, qualitative case study approaches. As a result, essentially the same, two-fold set of methodological obstacles that had hindered the pioneering discussions of the early 1990s resurfaced in the follow-up literature. First, the small-n case study approaches continued raising questions in regard of case selection and the representativeness of that selection and, second, this evidence could not generally control for the invisible effects of possible 'rational anticipation' behaviour by the Court (in line with the problem of 'observational equivalence').

In all, the core point of contention—that is, the extent to which the Court can make decisions independent of Member States' preferences—carried over into the next decade with some theoretical refinement, but little to no progress as regards methodological testing strategies. As will be elaborated on next, this central question has continued to permeate much of recent political science on the CJEU's role, as both qualitative (2.4.1.) and quantitative (2.4.2.) works continue to seek to account for either Member State control or Court autonomy.

2.4 An *Ongoing* Debate: Developments Since 2000

2.4.1 Qualitative Research Continued

The 2000s and 2010s saw, to begin with, the continuation and accumulation of qualitative case study research on the role and autonomy of the CJEU. The tendency to move away from the meta-theoretical, binary paradigms of the early accounts, already instigated at the close of the 1990s, was generally carried on after the turn of the century. That is, instead of framing their enquiries in the frameworks of 'grand' European integration theories, a new generation of scholars focused on midrange hypotheses that allowed for more precision and nuance. As a result, and in order to do justice to these developments, the below sketching out of the fault lines in the more recent political science research on the Court's role also no longer accords to the neat black-and-white image that could be drawn for the 1990s but is instead necessarily more nuanced as well.

To begin with, and a research theme that was clearly carried on from the 1990s, relates to evaluations of the role of national courts and the extent to which their strategic interaction with the CJEU assists this latter in enacting a pro-integrative agenda. Nyikos has for instance widened the focus of such enquiries by reviewing in two subsequent works, (i) first, what happens *after* the CJEU has ruled on a preliminary reference question in terms of the implementation of that judgment by national courts and, (ii) second, what happens *prior* to such a preliminary reference in terms of the potential strategic leveraging of the CJEU's authority by lower national tribunals. The findings of her first study revealed an overall tendency of national courts to faithfully implement the CJEU's guidelines once it has pronounced its verdict (Nyikos, 2003). This tendency, in turn, strongly affected litigation strategies of private parties at the national level. The more secure litigants felt that national courts would follow the CJEU's ruling, the more likely they were to desist from the national proceedings. Instead they then chose to jointly apply the CJEU's rulings themselves as a means to save money and time. This practice, Nyikos asserts, can be regarded as lending further legitimacy to the CJEU as its authority commands respect not only at the elite judicial level but also amongst litigants facing on-the-ground legal disputes. In the second article, Nyikos (2006) built on the earlier findings of Alter regarding the strategic co-opting of the CJEU by domestic courts. She critically analysed the procedure whereby domestic courts and—in line with Alter's findings—particularly lower ones, send 'preemptive opinions' along with their preliminary references. Her findings revealed that domestic courts strategically use such prior opinions as a means to signal their substantive legal preferences to the EU judiciary and steer the CJEU's interpretation towards their own preferred positions.

Further new insights into the nature of CJEU-national court relations were provided in Conant's seminal, broad-gauge study on interest mobilization dynamics in litigation on EU law (Conant, 2002). Amongst others, the data she collected on EU-related case law from French, German and UK tribunals revealed that the large majority of domestic court rulings on questions of EU law are in fact decided upon without a reference to the CJEU. This, at the very least, calls for an attenuation of the importance attached to national court-CJEU strategic interactions. Davies (2012) points to a similar "overstatement" of the CJEU's influence in national litigation contexts as, he argues, national judges in fact enjoy considerable margins of interpretative discretion when ruling on the merits of cases concerning EU law or when deciding on whether or not to refer a question to the EU judiciary.

Conant's work also contributed, more specifically, to research on the role of societal interest groups in organizing and sustaining the judicial enforcement of EU rights, a second research theme that was continued from the 1990s. Amongst others, Conant called attention to the fact that integrationist or innovative Court rulings do not exert an automatic policy influence in and of themselves. Rather, her argument goes, they typically remain 'contained' to Member States' compliance with only the smaller, more detailed and specific requirements of a judgment as they apply to the facts of the case. In order for the ramifications of a judgment to move beyond such narrow 'containment' and acquire a broader policy relevance, she argued, sustained mobilization efforts are indispensable. In their absence, evasive political or administrative responses that seek, above all, to dilute the broader consequences of a Court decision will prevail. Mobilization efforts can consist of strategies such as, for instance, filing new, related legal claims ('copycat cases'), or lobbying elected representatives and government officials. Given the high resources needed to sustain such mobilization efforts however, those societal interests that command the strongest organizational and/or financial capital are also most likely to see their strategic EU law litigation campaigns translate into broader policy outcomes. Börzel (2006) and Slepcevic (2009) have reached similar conclusions in related studies, with Börzel synthesizing her findings on private enforcement litigation around EU environmental law as "paradoxically, the empowerment of the already powerful" (Börzel, 2006, p. 130).

Further notable recent contributions to this area of research have been provided by Cichowski (2004, 2007). Building on her earlier findings, and in staying close to her original neofunctionalist orientations, she put forward a comprehensive conceptualization of public interest litigation around EU law as consisting of multiple processes, involving a multitude of actors and institutions, whose evolving dynamic interactions are causally connected by means of 'feedback effects'. According to her evaluation, civil society organizations and the CJEU come to mutually, and in taking turns, empower one another. Every CJEU decision offers the potential for filing new claims, and every new legal claim in follow-up to a Court ruling in turn reinforces that judgment and enables the CJEU to continue clarifying and constructing its case law. These arguments were supported by mixed methods research designs within which reviews of large-N datasets on preliminary references in the areas of gender equality legislation (Cichowski, 2004, 2007) and environmental protection (Cichowski, 2007) were supplemented with in-depth qualitative analyses of important Court decisions. In all these works, the earlier as well as the later ones, Cichowski (1998, 2004, 2007) employed a similar coding scheme to structure data on Court rulings as either 'consistent' (no violation of EU law) or 'adverse' (a violation). This information was then assessed against Member States' preferences as recorded in written observations submitted to the CJEU prior to the ruling. For both policy areas under review, the exercise led her to conclude that the expansionary feedback effects of societal interest litigation around EU law resulted in an expansion of EU competences "often in the face of Member State opposition" (Cichowski, 2004, p. 508; 2007, p. 91, 136).

Strongly embedded in this literature on societal interest litigation lies, as a third example of a sustained research topic, a clear acknowledgment of the importance of individual rights' claims for furthering the influence and authority of the CJEU's jurisprudence. As in the preceding 1990s literature, or the even earlier contextualist legal scholarship, this has continued to be a central theme underpinning many recent research agendas on the role of the CJEU. The importance of individual rights' claims has either been related to other, connected research interests (such as above, in the literature on civil society litigation), or has featured as a topic of interest in and of itself. Examples of such latter enquiries include the writings of Stone Sweet and Stranz (2012) or, in that same special journal issue, Scharpf (2012), who have argued in similar ways that the continued and even strengthened emphasis on individual rights (*e.g.*, on account the conferral of binding legal effect on the EU Charter of Fundamental Rights in the Lisbon Treaty) predicts a continued, or even strengthened, Europeanization of national law. Considerations along these lines also feature prominently in Kelemen's assertion that EU governance is increasingly taking on characteristics of an American style 'adversial legalism' (Kelemen, 2003, 2006, 2011). That is, according to his analyses, EU law and law-making are marked by a growing rule-orientation, a rising emphasis on formal and adversial enforcement of legal norms and—on the other hand—a declining importance of originally more cooperative, informal means of achieving regulatory objectives. Indications of the emergence of such a "European variant of American regulatory style" include, for instance, the increased use of a 'language of rights' in EU policy-making processes (although see Kagan, 2007, for a more sceptical take on whether an increased legalization indeed indicates a move towards American 'adversial legalism').

A further example of a current research theme of which the analytical origins can be traced back to the 1990s relates to evaluations of practices by which other supranational institutions 'co-opt' the CJEU's judicial authority for their own purposes. This field of enquiry has been notably reinforced by contributions of, amongst others, McCown (2003), Jupille (2004) or, more recently, Blauberger and Weiss (2013). McCown has for instance critically reviewed legal basis disputes initiated by the European Parliament (EP) under Art. 236 TFEU as part of a broader strategy aimed at strengthening its own institutional involvement in the EU's decision-making processes. Typically, judicial questions raised in such disputes seek to secure an answer from the Court that would institutionalize a preference for a legal basis that prescribes, for instance, the co-decision procedure over a legal basis requiring merely consultation with the EP. McCown's findings show that these strategies tend to be successful. The Council saw its margin of political discretion over the choice of Treaty base shrink over the years as it had to continuously adjust its workings to a growing body of CJEU case law which contained dictates on the criteria to be used when making such choices. Recently, Blauberger and Weiss (2013) argued, along the lines of Schmidt's (2000) contentions reviewed above, that the smooth adoption of the defence procurement directive in 2009 can be attributed to the Commission's strategic use of the CJEU's jurisprudence. The Commission deliberately induced new case law through infringement proceedings and interpreted the implications of earlier Court jurisprudence expansively so as to alert and threaten Member States with the possibility of leaving further harmonization in this sensitive area 'uncontrolled' in the hands of CJEU judges. At the same time these 'negative incentives' were combined with the 'positive incentive' of proposed draft legislation which offered an opportunity to 'restore political control'. On the whole, by strategically engaging in judicial politics, the Commission was able to both 'push' and 'pull' originally recalcitrant Member States into legislative agreement.

Furthermore, the continued interest around delegation-centred, Principal-Agent models of CJEU-Member State relations deserves mention as well.

Tallberg (2002) and Pollack (2003) have for instance continued refining their earlier accounts of the Court as an Agent which enjoys an extraordinarily large zone of discretion vis-à-vis its Principals, the Member States. They base this assertion, amongst others, on a comparative assessment of the Court's discretion relative to that which has been granted to the Commission. Most recently, Davies (2016) has further extended on these premises by arguing that the zone of discretion which the Court enjoys is so large that the Principal-Agent relationship should in fact be construed conversely, that is, as the Court being the 'Principal' and the Union legislature the 'Agent'.

Alter (2008) has similarly continued extending her earlier line of delegation-centred arguments to reach the conclusion that the Court's autonomy vis-à-vis the Member States is of such an extraordinary size that it surpasses the perimeters of standard Principal-Agent constructs. As she argues, the relation between the CJEU and national governments is better conceived of as corresponding to the logics of 'Trusteeship' as developed, amongst others, by Majone (2001). According to such logics, delegating relations are not to be thought of as singular in nature, but rather, 'dual' in that they may consist of either (i) those installed for the purpose of reducing decision-making costs, which accord to 'traditional' Principal-Agent relations, or (ii) those introduced to enhance the credibility of long-term policy commitments, which are better conceived of as relations of 'Trusteeship'. In this second type of delegation, the Principal accords powers to the 'delegate-trustee' with the specific aim of enhancing the trustworthiness of its policy commitments in the long run. This can be necessary vis-à-vis powerful civil society actors or large economic interests whose cooperation is required for achieving the desired policy goals. Such type of delegation tends to be applied particularly to those issue matters for which optimal long-term policy strategies conflict with what would seem profitable from a short-run perspective as, in such situations, incentives for policy-makers to renege on prior policy commitments may be high. Similarly, 'trusteeship delegation' can also be advisable for those policy contexts in which it is uncertain whether the next legislature would still abide by the (long-term) policy choices made by the current one. In such situations it is a necessary condition that the delegate-trustee is awarded with sufficient autonomy to pursue the course of action that it deems most appropriate according to its own professional standards and expertise, even when these differ from the dominant political preferences of the day. It is even in the Principal's interest to ensure that the delegate-trustee's preferences are not always perfectly aligned with those it holds itself as such would defy the purpose of the trustee delegation act in the first place (Majone, 2001, p. 110; Alter, 2008, pp. 38–44).

'Lock-in' arguments of this kind are of course no novelty to studies on the role and autonomy of courts (see e.g., the discussion in Staton & Moore, 2011). Alter specifically applied them to the context of the CJEU however, as she also strongly emphasized in later work (Alter, 2009), with the goal of laying to rest a personally held academic frustration with the methodological problem of 'observational equivalence'. In her understanding, this problem was a product of flawed rationalist interpretations of the Court's role which subscribed to the tautological reasoning that: "the mere fact that states do not sanction the ECJ is assumed to be proof that the state sought, or realized they actually desired, the outcome they got" (Ibid., p. 13). Given their tautological nature, such presumptions could not be empirically falsified. Or, by adopting an imagery of Member States acting as 'hidden puppet masters' through the threat of contractual sanctioning, such logics placed a burden of proof on contending academic claims that could not possibly be met. Her application of the Trusteeship model to the CJEU's context was aimed at breaking new ground in this respect by destabilizing the epistemological underpinnings of such rationalist Principal-Agent conjectures (Ibid.; Alter, 2008).

A further topic that informs recent literature on the Court's role relates to what appears as a new wave of academic interest in tracing the outcomes of Court rulings up to their factual, on-the-ground implications. Of course, evaluations of the impact of Court decisions have always been a central concern of political science on the Court's role. In the past however, such evaluations often remained limited to comparing the outcomes of Court rulings with stated (or assumed) Member State preferences. This does not surprise when considering the vast empirical ground that has to be covered in order to grasp the range of possible on-the-ground effects that Court rulings can have across the European Union. Nevertheless, in a number of recent works, scholars have precisely started to pave the way towards a deeper understanding of the *de facto* domestic impacts of CJEU judicial rule-making. Many of these new research puzzles are informed by Conant's earlier (2002) "justice contained" thesis as they set out to review whether, and to what extent, CJEU rulings indeed tend to remain limited ("contained") to their immediate, first-hand legal consequences or under which conditions broader policy implications can be discerned.

Wasserfallen (2010) for instance built on Conant's argumentation to review when and how Court decisions gain traction beyond their immediate "court room relevance". More specifically, he critically assessed the ability of Court rulings to influence the adoption of secondary legislation at EU level by means of a process-tracing analysis of the manner in which the seminal *Grzelczyk* (C-184/99) judgment reverberated in EU negotiations on the then to-be-adopted Citizenship Directive (2004/38/EC). His findings revealed that, in instances where there is little consensus amongst Member States in the Council or amongst EU institutions, the Court's pro-integration doctrines hold a significant sway on legislative decision-making processes by strengthening the power brokerage of the more integrationist actors in the discussions. However, the point to be taken away from the analysis, Wasserfallen posited, is that in spite of salient policy impacts, "activist Court decisions cannot by themselves effectively influence Europeans' everyday lives". Instead, "they need explicit support of some member states and other relevant actors in the legislation process" (Ibid.; pp. 1142–1143).

Also starting off from Conant's 'contained compliance' thesis, Blauberger (2012) reviewed the strategies available to national governments to defend their regulatory autonomy in the face of adverse CJEU rulings. Pointing at the high consensus requirements that hinder attempts at jointly redressing Court decisions through legislative action at EU level, he argued that more attention needed to go out to the ways in which Member States instead respond unilaterally through legislative adjustments at national level. His analysis of such domestic reforms showed that they differ from Member State to Member State depending on such factors as 'adjustment costs' or 'resonance with domestic political culture'. Often governments will find themselves cross-pressured to both comply with CJEU judgments in order to avoid further legal challenges, whilst at the same time remaining responsive to domestic constituencies that call for the preservation of the regulatory *status quo ante*. Eventually, given that Court rulings hardly ever prescribe specific policy responses, but rather "circumscribe a legal corridor within which member states can remake their policies in various EU-compatible ways" (Ibid., p. 111), governments tend to be able to preserve their original legislation to a considerable extend whilst making it 'CJEU-proof' by adopting a variety of either more or less intrusive reregulation strategies.

In a next, 2014 article these logics were further explored (Blauberger, 2014). Seeking to shed further light on the conflict in theoretical arguments around, on the one hand, the 'contained' impact of Court rulings as posited by Conant (2002) and others and, on the other, empirical records of broad policy reforms engendered by Court decisions, he went on to evaluate two opposing theoretical expectations. The first positing that Member State governments may opt for a strategy of 'contained compliance' when ambiguities in CJEU case law create 'loopholes' for minimising broad domestic consequences. The second advancing that ambiguities in CJEU case law may, on the other hand, also provide opportunities for interested litigants to pressure national policy-makers to enact broader policy reforms in order to avoid sustained legal conflicts. Empirically, the broad domestic reforms enacted in response to CJEU decisions in the context of 'posted workers' cases were compared to the limited legislative adjustments that had taken place in response to Court jurisprudence on free movement of capital ('golden shares' cases). The exercise revealed that governments' strategic calculations to either 'contain' compliance or, instead, engage in broader policy reforms differed depending on how the burden of legal uncertainty was distributed. Where this burden rested mostly on the shoulders of those seeking to challenge the regulatory status quo, for instance because they did not command the necessary resources to engage in new Court proceedings, strategies of 'contained compliance' were likely to prevail. Where, conversely, governments carried the burden of legal uncertainty themselves as the likelihood of follow-up legal action was high or undermined political planning capacity, broader legislative reforms were more likely to be enacted.

Against the background of a related research agenda, Martinsen (2011) evaluated how the principle of proportionality (as a general principle of EU law) has served as a powerful instrument for the CJEU to engage in 'judicial policy-making'. That is, judicial scrutiny around whether or not national provisions are 'proportionate to a legitimate aim pursued', allow the CJEU to target exactly those policy practices or administrative barriers set up in domestic bureaucratic arenas to restrict the reach of EU law. As she documented for the sovereignty-sensitive areas of immigration and social welfare, CJEU activities built around proportionality tests led to a dismantling of administrative requirements that functioned as barriers to filter the access to EU-granted rights. Her analysis further demonstrated that such judicial interventions subsequently resulted in discernible, on-the-ground policy effects in both areas.

Schmidt (2014) has similarly reviewed the effects of CJEU case law on national policy practices regarding the granting of residence rights to third-country national family members of EU citizens. Taking issue with the academic assumption that "member states only reluctantly embrace the requirements of case law", with reference to Conant (2002) and Wasserfallen's (2010) works, she evaluated Member State responses in the aftermath of the CJEU's controversial *Zambrano* decision (C-34/09). Her analysis revealed a patchwork of different policy adjustments that often moved beyond the case's factual issue matters or even the state concerned as politicians, national courts or administrative bodies across the Union's multilevel system engaged in many different modifications to factor in the *Zambrano* outcome. Such proactive reactions took place, even in the absence of strong political mobilisation pressures. Given their plurality however, and because such adjustments tend to get absorbed into new administrative practices that become daily routine without necessarily receiving much public attention, it may be difficult for the analyst to observe them. Overall, however, Schmidt concluded, the implications of CJEU rulings may be difficult to trace, but they are real and more far-reaching than the literature suggests. In all, "there does not seem to be a 'justice contained'" (Ibid., pp. 781–782).

On the whole, Schmidt's conclusion goes against the 'justice contained' thesis of Conant (2002) and the follow-up findings by Wasserfallen (2010). Martinsen's (2011) insights are, similarly, not congruent with the perspective that CJEU decisions exert little *de facto* influence in the absence of explicit political mobilisation. Such competing propositions are not exclusive to this last sub-area of enquiry. Rather, incongruences of this kind can be found running through the larger body of post-2000 qualitative scholarship on the CJEU's role and autonomy. Similar issues for instance plague the literature on national courts-CJEU interactions. Where Nyikos' (2003, 2006) research continues to bestow a strong importance to the support that national judiciaries provide for the CJEU's authority, findings put forward by Conant (2002) and Davies (2012) throw such views into question. Conant's (2002) findings regarding the role of societal interest groups highlight the limits to CJEU influence, whilst Cichowski (2004, 2007)—conversely—puts forward a conceptualisation of mutually strengthening dynamics between the CJEU and civil society groups whose interactions, through feedback effects, result in ever widening, judicially-enforced EU rights entitlements. It is possible to go on.

In all, discrepancies of this kind limit the amount of definitive conclusions this qualitative scholarship produces. Although the meta-theoretical focus has decisively made way for one on midrange hypotheses regarding the 'degree of', or the 'conditions under which', this has not led to a synthetic understanding of the Court's role in processes of European integration. Instead, as before, different scholars continue to reach different conclusions, albeit in a less conflictual language, on whether or not—or, rather, in the more recent writings 'the extent to which'—the Court can exert autonomous policy outcomes independent of Member States' preferences. In addition, in spite of significant theoretical advancements, little attention has gone out to updating methodological testing strategies alongside. To be sure, progress was made as new issue areas were opened up to empirical enquiry, datasets were widened, and some works complemented their qualitative analyses with descriptive statistics (e.g., Kelemen, 2006, 2011; Conant, 2002; Cichowski, 2004, 2007). Generally however, the orientation towards traditional, small-n case study research was sustained. Against the backdrop of an empirical environment as heterogeneous and multifaceted as the Court's developing jurisprudence (and, even more so, the on-the-ground policy implications of this developing jurisprudence), this has continued allowing, as before, for marshalling empirical evidence in support of competing conceptions of the Court's autonomy relative to the Member States depending on the cases, issue areas or on-the-ground implications singled out for review. In addition, as registered in the context of the delegation-centred literature, the problem of observational equivalence has also continued to stir emotions.

2.4.2 *Quantitative Methods Added*

Faced with these methodological obstacles and in light of the more general difficulties to closing the academic ranks, a second strand of post-2000 scholarship has concentrated their analyses around quantitative testing strategies. As referred to in most of these works, the more specific aim has been two-fold. To begin with, recent quantitative analyses have sought to gain traction on the problem of observational equivalence. Second, these analyses have sought to move beyond problems related to selective case selection and questions around generalisability as registered in prior small-n case study approaches. By employing large-n statistical methods that allow for both (i) the systematic juxtaposition and evaluation of competing claims across (ii) a large range of Court decisions, such studies have sought to generate evidence that can both (i) discriminate between rival theoretical perspectives and (ii) produce findings that can be generalized to speak for the Court's activities as a whole.

For the purposes of employing such large-n testing strategies, however, these quantitative works have displayed a tendency to return to the binary, 'grand theory' conjectures of the early 1990s. These earlier, meta-theoretical paradigms offer neatly opposing, mutually exclusive theoretical expectations that, in addition, are pitched at high levels of abstraction facilitating their operationalisation in the context of large-n analyses. Accordingly, and in sharp contrast to the increased conceptual refinement and nuance marking the works of their qualitative counterparts, recent quantitative scholarship has revived the binary 'intergovernmentalist-neofunctionalist' divides of the early 1990s.

On the whole, two main approaches can be distinguished in quantitative scholarship on the CJEU's role. The first consists of using written observations submitted by national governments prior to the CJEU's rulings as proxies for *ex ante* assessing Member State preferences on the outcome of the case. By comparing these Member States' briefs with the Court's eventual disposition of the case, analysts seek to gain leverage on the problem of observational equivalence. More precisely, the 'before and after' comparative design can be used to uncover whether the Court indeed proved responsive to previously articulated Member States' preferences or whether, instead, no such judicial deference to Member States' concerns could be identified. As noted by Stone Sweet (2010), this analytical method in fact holds its roots in Stein's (1981) pioneering account on "The Making of a Transnational Constitution" in which the latter author established that the CJEU had issued its 'constitutionalizing' rulings against "the consistent opposition to increased integration on the part of the member governments". This claim was supported by observations of Member States' briefs in which governments had argued against the outcomes of such cases as *Van Gend en Loos*, *Costa v. Enel*, *Lütticke* (C-57/65), *Defrenne* (C-43/75) and others. The method also found its application in Cichowski's (1998, 2004, 2007) work on public interest litigation in the areas of gender equality and environmental protection reviewed above. Its operationalization in recent quantitative scholarship will be discussed at further length below.

The second approach originated from Stone Sweet and Brunell's (1998) method of juxtaposing data on the incidence of preliminary references sent to the CJEU with figures on transnational trade activity as a means to test the validity of neofunctionalist predictions against contending intergovernmentalist claims (*cf.* Sect. 2.3.2). More precisely, the positive relationship between the levels (and increase) of intra-EU trade on the one hand and the levels (and increase) of preliminary reference questions on EU law on the other, were taken to provide evidence of self-reinforcing, neofunctionalist processes progressively moving European integration forward. Or, as demonstrating that increasing levels of transnational interaction generated demands for further supranational governance which then instigated further transnational activity, as such reinitiating the cycle again. Stone Sweet and Brunell's statistical correlations, and the methods they used, have been reviewed and updated by numerous others.

First, Stone Sweet updated his own 1998 account in collaboration with Fligstein (Fligstein & Stone Sweet, 2002). Adding the activities of lobby groups to the explanatory variables reviewed and using a more extensive dataset, further regression analyses confirmed the 1998 claim that economic transnational activity and EU law litigation are causally connected and through self-sustaining feedback loops contribute to the expansive growth of the EU market and polity. Around the same time, Pitarkis and Tridimas (2003) equally subjected Stone Sweet and Brunell's (1998) findings to further review. Taking issue with the unclear direction of causality between the number of preliminary references and intra-EU trade in Stone Sweet and Brunell's original assessments, they went on to widen the datasets on both references and trade figures. These were subsequently tested using a different type of regression analysis said to better allow for reviewing the causality structure between the identified relationships. Their empirical results confirmed Stone Sweet and Brunell's causal link between national court references and trade ratio, albeit with a causality running from references to trade and not necessarily the other way around. Put differently, this implied support for the view that legal integration is an important force in driving economic integration, but not necessarily for the further neofunctionalist perspective that increased economic integration also drives legal integration.

Tridimas and Tridimas (2004) similarly took up on the claims of Stone Sweet and Brunell (1998) and integrated them within a broader public choice spatial model. The findings of their study presented the process of European legal integration as the equilibrium outcome of optimising behaviour on the part of three different groups of decision-makers, (i) litigants who have an economic stake deriving from integration and demand preliminary rulings and interact with (ii) national courts, who seek strengthened judicial authority and (iii) the CJEU itself which has its own set of pro-integration policy preferences. Transnational economic activity was included in the model as one of the factors possibly affecting the self-interested behaviour of private litigants. Overall, their findings confirmed the convergence of self-interested behaviour of sub-and supra-state actors operating above and below and the state. Although strongly aligned with neofunctionalist premises, the authors themselves interpreted these conclusions as neither according to neofunctionalism nor intergovernmentalism, but instead as providing an "eclectic view" (Ibid., p. 143).

The scholar who has proven most critical of Stone Sweet and Brunell's analysis, and the claims derived on that basis, is Carruba. In a first paper, however, co-authored with Murrah (Carruba & Murrah, 2005), the challenges to Stone Sweet and Brunell's work remained embedded within a larger research set-up and, overall, moderate. The authors took issue with the fact that the literature had, more generally, produced many theoretical explanations on the relation between the EU's legal system and processes of European integration but had not managed to reach consensus on the relative importance of different sets of explanatory variables vis-à-vis one another as "systematic empirical work has lagged behind" (Ibid., pp. 399–400). They went on to note that: "Although numerous possible motivations have been posited and substantial empirical evidence has been collected to support the various arguments, no tests have been performed that also control for alternative explanations" (Ibid.). In order to remedy this situation they proceeded with a series of extended statistical analyses on the basis of Stone Sweet and Brunell's original, longitudinal dataset. Aside from reviewing the volume of preliminary references in relation to transnational trade activity (in line with Stone Sweet and Brunell's design), they additionally controlled for the explanatory power of such factors as 'public opinion in relation to EU integration', 'the public's political awareness', and differences in legal culture. The results of their regression analyses generated strong support for Stone Sweet and Brunell's predictions that numbers and variations in the use of the preliminary reference system are correlated with differences in the levels of intra-EU trade. Carruba and Murrah pointed out, however, that this positive correlation could also be explained, following a more simple logic, by the fact that the majority of EU law in fact relates to the creation of the common market; or, as followed, by the fact that transnational trade actually conditions the opportunity for conflict over EU law to arise. Consequently, a positive correlation could be expected even in the absence of Stone Sweet and Brunell's 'virtuous circles' according to which the expansion of EU law opens up opportunities for transnational activity, which then leads to demands for further EU regulation and so on. The grit of the authors' challenge with Stone Sweet and Brunell's work (and the literature more generally), however, revolved around the charge that the latter had been too myopic in focusing solely on one explanatory variable, transnational activity, when accounting for increasing EU law litigation. Instead, they posited, legal integration cannot be explained by single, mono-causal arguments, but should be examined by incorporating and controlling for all steps in the legal process, from case generation to actual reference. As their empirical tests revealed, not only economic activity affected the number of preliminary references, significant positive relations could also be identified for the other causal variables that had been included (i.e., public opinion, political awareness, legal culture).

In a single-authored paper, later that year, Carruba (2005) engaged with the methodological problem of 'observational equivalence' that troubled the literature on the power of courts more generally. Using the EU and its judiciary to illustrate his arguments, he put forward a game theoretic account that was aimed at further clarifying why "one cannot infer from observing high rates of compliance with a court's rulings that the court is a powerful body, capable of ruling against governments" (Ibid., p. 686). That is, as the predictions generated by his model demonstrated, such observations would also be consistent with the opposite story in which the judicial ability to enforce compliance is dependent on, and limited by, the willingness of other governments to enforce the Court's rulings, and in which—in anticipation—the Court only rules against Member States when it foresees that a government's non-compliance with its decisions will be punished by the other governments. In such a scenario, courts can help sustain agreements between states, but they cannot promote "deeper" cooperation than governments are implicitly willing to enforce (Ibid., p. 687). On that basis, he went on to assert that the "emerging consensus in the literature over the European Court's ability to promote further integration"—based on observations of Member States' complying with CJEU rulings—was "premature" as the supporting empirical proof was uninformative (Ibid., pp. 682–686).

These lines of reasoning were further elaborated on in a next, broad-gauge project in collaboration with Gabel and Hankla (Carruba, Gabel, & Hankla, 2008). The research was specifically set up with the aim of providing the "first discriminating test of member state-government influence" over the Court's rulings that could move beyond the "observational equivalence problem" (Ibid., p. 436). On the basis of a new longitudinal dataset the authors coded for a large range of CJEU decisions whether the Court ruled in favour of the plaintiff or the defendant. Next, and applying the method of using Member States' written observations as proxies for governments' preferences, this information on pro-plaintiff or pro-defendant decisions was compared to the arguments filed by governments in their written observations prior to the rulings. Each written observation was additionally weighted against the national vote shares that each respective government held in the Council. In that manner, the study sought to control for differences in the expected political pressure that Member States could exert in case of a disliked outcome. The general hypothesis directing their enquiries stated that, the more Member States filed briefs with convergent policy positions on the issue at hand, the stronger the likelihood that the Court would expect these Member States to either (i) not punish another government for not complying with a disliked ruling or (ii) produce a sufficiently large coalition to pursue a legislative override. As the results of different probit models indicated both the threats of (i) non-compliance and (ii) legislative override systematically shaped judicial decisions as increases in numbers of observations either pro-plaintiff or pro-defendant affected the probability of the Court deciding in favour of, respectively, either the plaintiff or the defendant. The authors pointed out that these results were "exactly the opposite" of the conclusions reached in some of Stone Sweet's (2004) work and that of Cichowski (2004) who, employing essentially the same analytical set-up (*i.e.*, using written observations as proxies for Member States' preferences), had found that governments' written observations are in fact not influential on (Stone Sweet), or even negatively associated with (Cichowski), Court rulings. These discrepancies, they speculated, were most likely to be ascribed to differences in sampling or in statistical methods employed. Overall, they concluded, the evidence provided by their study was "more consistent with the intergovernmentalist argument that political constraints should have large, systematic, and substantively significant effects on judicial decision making, rather than with neofunctionalist arguments that (…) the court has the latitude to pursue an agenda independent of and contrary to member-state governments' interests" (Ibid., p. 449).

Stone Sweet and Brunell (2012) took strong issue with the project. In their response, they sharply refuted the research's theoretical foundations as well as its empirical analyses and findings. With regard to first, the theoretical considerations, these were said to wrongly revive myopic intergovernmentalist perspectives on the role of the Court that the literature had in fact already largely abandoned. In addition, and more specifically, Carruba et al.'s ideas on the 'political threats' of legislative override and noncompliance were theoretically nonplausible for a number of reasons. Amongst others, Stone Sweet and Brunell claimed that the history of European integration did not provide for a single instance of a successful legislative override of, or noncompliance with, Court decisions. Moreover, in respect of noncompliance threats, they emphasized, these do not emanate from national governments but instead derive from domestic judiciaries who are factually at the receiving end of most CJEU rulings (preliminary references) and get to take the authoritative decisions on whether 'to comply' or 'not to comply' with the CJEU's interpretation. The empirical analyses, second, were similarly charged with a number of flaws. Whilst in general recognisant of the need to find ways in which analysts could gain leverage on the problem of 'observational equivalence', Carruba et al.'s empirical strategies to this purpose were erroneous for a number of reasons. Amongst others, Stone Sweet and Brunell criticized the manner in which these authors had operationalized their hypotheses and governments' net weighted written observations as a means to test the Court's responsiveness to political threats. For one, they identified that for 90% of Carruba et al.'s cases the decision-making rule governing legislative reversal would have been unanimity and not qualified majority voting (QMV) which rendered the relevance of 'weighting' government observations per vote share in the Council of questionable merit. As one of the most important critiques, Stone Sweet and Brunell asserted that Carruba et al. had not made it credible that in cases where the Court followed a line found in one of the written observations, that it could be inferred that this outcome derived from the existence of political constraints. In addition, as the results of their own statistical modelling of written observations revealed, these government briefs were generally of such a low volume that Member States did not come close to reaching a qualified majority, let alone unanimity, in any systematically meaningful way. Carruba et al.'s claims around the existence of threats of legislative override were therefore "inexplicable" (Ibid., p. 208). In a second part of their rebuttal, Stone Sweet and Brunell proceeded with a further pitting of intergovernmentalist theory against contending neofunctionalist perspectives. Using Carruba et al.'s "own preferred constructions of integration theory", they set out to review the extent to which the Court appeared responsive to the interests of 'transnational elites' as neofunctionalist theory would predict, relative to its responsiveness to the political preferences of Member State governments as intergovernmentalist perspectives would hold. These binary, opposing theoretical hypotheses were further operationalized as a test around the degree to which the CJEU sided with the written observations submitted by the European Commission compared to those put forward by Member States. As the results of their tests showed, in instances where the briefs of Member States opposed the position taken by the Commission, the Commission's perspectives prevailed more than two-thirds of the time. This, they asserted, constituted a "landslide" victory in the "head-to-head showdown between intergovernmentalism and neofunctionalism" (Ibid., p. 204).

Carruba, Gabel, and Hankla (2012) rebutted these charges in the same journal issue. To begin with, on the theoretical plane, they contested the interpretation of their earlier findings (Carruba et al., 2008) as an effort to adjudicate between intergovernmentalism and neofunctionalism as Stone Sweet and Brunell had portrayed them. Next, on the empirical level, they strongly refuted Stone Sweet and Brunell's challenges of their earlier analyses, as well as the subsequent tests these latter had performed to substantiate contending claims. First, they provided a number of examples of both successful legislative overrides as well as instances of noncompliance with Court rulings so as to bolster the plausibility of their theoretical expectations. However, as they made sure to emphasize, such examples were in fact not material to their argument as—returning to the realm of the 'observational equivalence' conundrum—in case their claims on the CJEU's responsiveness to threats of override and noncompliance held, not many instances of such override or noncompliance should be expected given that the Court would temper its rulings in anticipation. They then provided further justifications for the weighting of Member State observations, amongst others by referring to processes of logrolling in EU decision-making processes. Most importantly, they refuted Stone Sweet and Brunell's statistical tests and the conclusions arrived at on that basis. To begin with, the testing methods employed by Stone Sweet and Brunell were said to not provide appropriate measures of the hypotheses that had been advanced in the first account (Carruba et al., 2008). Amongst others, the original hypotheses had sought to specifically review the relations between increases in the numbers of observations submitted (pro-plaintiff or pro-defendant) and the likelihood of the Court deciding in favour of either one or the other side. Stone Sweet and Brunell's 'dichotomous tests' failed to capture these continuous effects that had been central to the original claims. Next, Carruba et al. (2012) proceeded with additional tests aimed at revisiting the original claims whilst simultaneously controlling for the charges of Stone Sweet and Brunell. To that purpose, they introduced further measures on the effect of Commission observations. In addition, they also included the positions adopted by the CJEU's Advocate Generals (AG) as a proxy with which to control for the 'legal merits' of a case. In that manner, they sought to respond to Stone Sweet and Brunell's challenge that observations on correlations between the arguments submitted in government briefs and the final disposition of the case did not provide evidence of anticipatory Court behaviour in response to political threats. That is, by accounting for plausible alternative explanations for the observed correlation, i.e. that government briefs may simply substantiate the side with the strongest 'legal merits', the odds that the analysis suffered from these problems were minimized. In that way, the new tests were also said to provide for a 're-analyzation' of Stone Sweet and Brunell's neofunctionalist hypotheses. This was required as Stone Sweet and Brunell had failed to control for possible alternative explanations that could account for the correlations between Court judgements and Commission briefs. The results of Carruba et al.'s more "appropriate statistical models" revealed that Member State briefs, as well as Commission observations and AG opinions, all held important and independent effects on the direction of CJEU rulings. Consequently, a "landslide" in favour of any one single theoretical explanation could not be sustained (Ibid., p. 222).

Arguably, these quantitative attempts to move beyond the two-fold set of empirical impasses that hindered qualitative research in order to, on that basis, generate conclusive findings, did not meet their purpose. Certainly, significant progress was made as, first, the larger datasets allowed for travelling beyond the specifics of individual cases and, second, new perspectives were advanced in respect of how to gain leverage on the problem of observational equivalence. Nevertheless, as recorded, this did not settle academic disputes, rather to the contrary.

Where qualitative works could be found charging contending accounts around the selective sampling of cases, quantitative scholars, when accommodating for differences in phrasing, accused contending analyses around selective sampling of the 'appropriate' statistical methods. Furthermore, authors were also generally not able to reach consensus on what constituted reliable proxies for Member State preferences or how such proxies were to be operationalised in a manner accurately reflecting political and institutional realities. Adding to these discussions, by having anchored their analyses in the mutually exclusive, 'grand theory' frameworks of the early 1990s, any discrepancies in the findings resulting from the application of such different statistical models, datasets or proxies were, by implication, presented as mutually exclusive and in binary opposition to one another. In all, the literature appears to have come full circle as the divides in the most recent debates reviewed—that is, the discussions between Stone Sweet and Brunell and Carruba et al.—dovetail with those that marked the original debates of the early 1990s.

2.5 In Sum—A *Long-Lasting* Debate: Taking Stock of Theoretical and Methodological Divides

Twenty-five years of sustained enquiries did not yield much consensual understandings on the Court's role and autonomy in processes of European integration. In short, where problems of a methodological nature continued obstructing qualitative scholarship as it gradually moved away from the meta-theoretical stalemates of the early 1990s, those same theoretical stalemates resurfaced in the quantitative research that sought precisely to overcome the methodological issues troubling the qualitative scholarship. In all, the literature appears to have come full circle as the most recent discussions reviewed, those of Stone Sweet and Brunell (2012) versus Carruba et al. (2012), strand on the same conceptual battleground as that which was marked out by the competing claims of the pioneering works that had 'discovered' the CJEU more than two decades earlier (through the striking claims of the even earlier contextualist legal scholarship of the 1980s).

To be sure, these theoretical divides did experience significant modifications over the course of sustained academic enquiry. By the end of the 1990s already, qualitative scholarship had largely abandoned the 'grand theory' precepts that had fuelled polemics at the beginning of the decade. As increasing numbers of scholars enlisted at either side of the contending 'intergovernmentalist-neofunctionalist' divides drawn up in the works of respectively, Garrett and co-authors (1992, 1993, 1998); Burley and Mattli (1993) and Mattli and Slaughter (1995), the accumulation of new insights and data generated ever more support for qualifying perspectives that both sets of frameworks had to be widened in order to accommodate for the findings generated at the other side of the divide. With time, the meta-theoretical preoccupations of the pioneering accounts made way for a focus on midrange hypotheses around such questions as 'how' or the 'conditions under which' the CJEU enjoys either more or less autonomy relative to the Member States.

These theoretical refinements and rapprochements notwithstanding, different perspectives continued to be advanced, albeit in a softened language, within the qualitative literature as it evolved. As the theoretical advancements had generally not been paired with parallel attention to methodological innovation, the two types of methodological hurdles that already hindered the earliest discussions resurfaced in the later literature and obstructed opportunities at generating discriminating empirical evidence. First, in an empirical context as heterogeneous and idiosyncratic as the Court's developing case law, small-n case study findings could not easily be generalised to speak for the Court's activities as a whole. In connection, on account of the same idiosyncrasy, depending on the rulings (or aspects within the rulings) selected for review, empirical evidence could be marshalled in support of contending points of view. Second, on account of the problem of observational equivalence, evidence on the rarity or absence of Member State sanctions in response to adverse CJEU rulings could not discriminate between opposing views on either Court autonomy or Member State control. That is, on account of invoked logics of anticipatory Court behaviour, such evidence could also be consistent with scenarios in which Member States effectively retained control through threats of override or noncompliance but, given the effectiveness of these threats and through rational anticipation by the Court, such sanctioning measures never needed to be executed.

After the turn of the century, further progress was made with regard to problems of a theoretical nature, in qualitative literature, and with regard to methodological difficulties, in quantitative scholarship. The two sets of literature have, however, insufficiently engaged with each other's advancements which to a large extent explains why questions on the Court's role have continued claiming the attention of the field. Whilst qualitative research sustained earlier commitments at introducing ever more conceptual gradation, the methodological advances introduced in this literature have been few. Accordingly, as differently selected cases (or aspects of such cases) have continued allowing for garnering support for competing claims, the conclusions produced by this literature as a whole are difficult to summarize. On the other hand, where quantitative research has introduced new, large-n testing methods which offer opportunities at moving beyond issues related to selective case sampling or the problem of observational equivalence, differences in testing strategies or the operationalisation of data and proxies have also resulted in differing results. As the theoretical conjectures guiding these quantitative analyses largely reproduce the meta-theoretical, mutually exclusive propositions of the early 1990s, such differing results have in parallel, and by implication, been presented as incommensurable with one another.

In light of these observations, the present study aims to further efforts towards more nuanced, midrange theoretical insights regarding the Court's role and autonomy whilst, simultaneously, paying attention to methodological problems related to selective case sampling or observational equivalence. The study's theoretical perspectives and methodological strategies are presented in short in what follows and linked to the findings of the above literature overview. They then receive further detail in, respectively, Chaps. 3 and 4.

Theoretically, to begin with, the study aims to provide new insights on the workings and effects of strategic precedent-based reasoning by the CJEU. Whilst practices of precedent-based reasoning are frequently referred to in writings on the Court's role and the need to evaluate CJEU decisions in the light of its earlier judgments is often recognized, the incidence and workings of precedents have to date not been subject to much systematic scholarly analysis. The theoretical hypotheses guiding the study's enquiries are set up in such a way as to align with recent advances in the qualitative literature. As will be set out in detail in Chap. 3, the conceptual approaches adopted explicitly take account of context-dependent and issue-specific variables. By adopting a midrange level of theoretical abstraction, the study's propositions seek alliance with the above identified commitment to increased conceptual refinement and nuance.

The study's methodological strategies are grounded in a mixed-methods research design, i.e., a design that combines both quantitative and qualitative orientations. On that basis, and in line with the traditional argument for conducting mixed methods research (see Creswell & Clark, 2010), the study aims to combine the strengths of each approach whilst, simultaneously, offsetting their respective weaknesses. The qualitative analyses, first, aim at providing the type of in-depth and fine-grained empirical observations necessary for evaluating theoretical hypotheses which, as indicated above, are framed at a low level of abstraction and seek to account for context-dependent variables. The quantitative strategies allow, on the other hand, for systematising the data on the basis of objective, empirical criteria which helps mitigating problems related to selective case sampling and generalisability. In addition, specific attention has gone out to the problem of observational equivalence. For the purpose of ruling out that the outcomes of the Court's case law were possibly in line with what Member States' preferred, and similar to the above identified strategies, an *ex ante* benchmark of Member States' preferences was adopted. Different from the above identified strategies, however, the study has not defined such preferences on the basis of written observations submitted to Luxembourg prior to the rulings. As documented in the above literature review, such benchmarking has in the past given rise to a number of challenges. Amongst others, benchmarks based on written observations are rarely grounded on a representative sample of the interests held by Member States across the Union as the number of written observations submitted is usually low (ranging from one or two, to maximum a dozen) as well as unevenly spread across the Union (Granger, 2004). Instead, and as outlined in further detail in Chap. 5, a new benchmarking strategy is advanced which, as an alternative, takes stock of the interests and preference-led demands voiced by Member States during EU negotiations on the legal provisions that, at later stages, became the subject of Court rulings. To the extent that this alternative, negotiations-based benchmark takes account of a context within which Member States operate collectively, it controls for such representativeness issues.

As an additional set of considerations, the present research is also set up in such a way as to deliver on calls to combine insights from different disciplinary approaches on the Court, most notably, from law and political science. Such pleas hold a long lineage in the context of studies on the CJEU. They can be traced back all the way to the 1980s contextualist literature from which the political science 'discovery' of the CJEU was to later originate (e.g., Weiler, 1982). From there they have resurfaced over the course of the 1990s (e.g., Joerges, 1996; Mattli & Slaughter, 1998), up to the most recent scholarship (e.g. Alter, Dehousse, & Vanberg, 2002; de Búrca, 2005; Neergaard & Wind, 2012). Both the sizeable volume of these calls, as their recurrence, hold little surprise in light of the subject matter which, by its very nature, straddles the disciplinary boundaries of political science and legal scholarship.

The challenge however resides, as most of these calls also attest to, in how, or the extent to which to integrate the methods or theoretical affinities of the different disciplines. As is clear, wholly 'synthetic' approaches (that fully, and to equal extents, integrate both approaches) are neither feasible, nor necessarily desirable (e.g., Joerges, 1996; Alter et al., 2002).

Instead, as with interdisciplinary works generally, a variety of different approaches that combine different sets of multidisciplinary techniques, data or concepts can be discerned along a "continuum ranging from lesser to greater degrees of synthesis" (Vick, 2004, p. 165). As follows, there is also little to no interdisciplinary scholarship within which information traffic flows even-handedly into, and out of, each implicated discipline. Rather, different endeavours to cross-pollinate analyses on the Court's role with multiple disciplinary perspectives tend to remain, predominantly, within the core discipline from which the researcher(s) originally depart(s). Novel interdisciplinary insights become refracted through the pre-existing disciplinary matrices and serve to improve upon these, but not to change their core scientific identity (Ibid.). In Alter's phrasing: "(W)e straddle the divide whilst remaining within our own disciplines (…). At the end of the day it is always clear who is the political scientist and who is the lawyer" (Alter et al., 2002, p. 122).

The present work is not an exception. It is inscribed, principally, within political science paradigms which are complemented with insights from legal scholarship. In injecting law into the social scientist enterprise, however, particular attention went out to making sure that this was done in a way that also provides meaning from the perspective of legal scholarship. In this manner, the study seeks to respond to an often-voiced criticism on multi-disciplinary political science efforts to engage with EU legal developments. That is, that such efforts, in line with political science's general quest for parsimonious explanatory frameworks, tend to buy into oversimplified and ill-informed constructions of law. Often, these works are said to portray EU law in overly narrow, instrumentalist ways as either a functional tool through which the Court constructed a pro-integration agenda or, instead, as an instrument at the command of powerful, intergovernmental actors. Such conceptualizations have been faulted by legal scholars for failing to take account of the law's more complex, interpretative dimensions and normative qualities (e.g., Joerges, 1996; Armstrong, 1998; de Búrca, 2005).[2]

[2] Note that, the other way around, interdisciplinary legal works engaging with political science have also been met with charges of, for instance, not fully considering the "theoretical spectrum on offer in the field of political science" (Joerges, 1996, p. 108), or of treating these "as a residual category that only comes into play where law and legal reasoning fall short" leading to "an impoverished view of the role of politics in legal decision-making" (Alter et al., 2002, p. 117).

In an acclaimed commentary, Joerges (1996) for instance posited early on that the interdisciplinary writings on the CJEU of his days had to start making more meaningful efforts at "taking the law seriously". More specifically, political science analyses had to move away from instrumentalist views that failed to "acknowledge the Law's normative logic and discursive power" and that viewed "the routines of legal argument with suspicion" (Ibid., p. 105; p. 107). As he emphasized, his was not a call for the removal of disciplinary boundaries. Social scientists were not to start engaging in a "*lege artis* type of intra-legal discourse", but their explanations had to be conceptualised "in such a way that normative discourse maintains significance" (Ibid., p. 119). Similar critiques were provided by Armstrong who, replicating the opening sentence of Mattli and Slaughter's (1998) third and final contribution to the debate, asked: "Political science has discovered the European Court of Justice (ECJ). But has it discovered law?" (Armstrong, 1998, p. 155). In analogy to Joerges' plea, the way forward, he posited, was to develop "a more critical approach to law, in which the normative dimension of law and its role in EU governance are interrogated beyond assumptions of simple instrumentality" (Ibid., p. 172). More recently, de Búrca also chided political science works on legal developments for not being prepared to consider the law's more complex and social dimensions, "whether for fear that it would render less parsimonious the explanatory theory developed, or simply because it is more difficult to subject to empirical investigation" (de Búrca, 2005, p. 323). Along similar lines, Shapiro has noted that court specialists among political scientists, in focusing their efforts towards "revealing judicial discretion and judicial lawmaking", have paid insufficient attention to considering how this judicial discretion is both "expressed in legal language" as well as "closely confined by legal rules" (Shapiro, 2008, p. 772).

The present focus on precedent-based discourses delivers on these points of concern in that it grants an independent causal role to the law's normative dimensions, and its interpretative and discursive nature. In order to gain access to these more complex normative and interpretative aspects, and engage with them in a way that also provides meaning when judged through the lenses of legal analyses, the study's premises take account of legal scholarship insights on judicial reasoning. This is done in a manner that allows for the legal perspectives to speak not only to the theoretical concepts that inform the enquiry, but also to the empirical methods advanced to evaluate these.

First, with regard to theory-building, the law's "normative logic and discursive power" (Joerges, 1996, p. 105) are given analytical primacy within the causal structures hypothesized to underpin the workings of precedents. More in particular, and as will be set out in detail in the next chapter, they are conceived of as pre-conditions for explaining the autonomy-enhancing effects that precedent-based discourses are expected to engender. Intra-legal discursive interactions and elements such as the "routines of legal argument" (Ibid., p. 107), the manner in which "judges express their discretion in legal language" (Shapiro, 2008, p. 772), or how law is a "normative social practice, an explicitly interpretive enterprise" (de Búrca, 2005, p. 318) are all centrally implicated in the propositions put forward.

Second, with regard to the empirical strategies, the analysis consciously uses multiple testing means of which, in particular, the qualitative phase allows for infusing the political science methodological orientations with inference logics important to traditional doctrinal, legal exegesis. For this purpose, critical interpretative techniques were borrowed from legal scholarship. More specifically, through "prolonged exposure" to the conceptual constructs and parameters within which and through which the Court's judges conceptualize and articulate legal problems, the analysis' qualitative section aims at reaching the sort of "intimate familiarity" and discursive fluency that legal scholars strive for when deconstructing and evaluating judicial reasoning (Lasser, 2009, pp. 3–26; Vick, 2004). In that way, on the basis of close readings that engage with doctrinal detail, the study aims to provide for empirical findings that reflect the high degree of empirical nuance and context-validity that provides meaning from the perspective of legal analyses.

References

Primary Sources

EU Law

Directive 2004/38/EC of the European Parliament and of the Council on the Right of Citizens of the Union and their Family Members to Move and Reside Freely Within the Territory of the Member States [2004] O.J. L 158/77.

CJEU Case Law

Case C-26/62 *NV Algemene Transport- en Expeditie Onderneming van Gend & Loos v Netherlands Inland Revenue Administration* [1963] ECR 13.
Case C-6/64 *Flaminio Costa v E.N.E.L.* [1964] ECR 585.
Case C-57/65 *Alfons Lütticke GmbH v Hauptzollamt Sarrelouis* [1966] ECR 205.
Case C-43/75 *Gabrielle Defrenne v Société anonyme belge de navigation aérienne Sabena* [1976] ECR 455.
Case C-120/78 *Rewe-Zentral AG v Bundesmonopolverwaltung für Branntwein* [1979] ECR 649.
Case C-184/99 *Grzelczyk v Centre public d'aide sociale d'Ottignies-Louvain-la-Neuve* [2001] ECR I-6193.
Case C-34/09 *Gerardo Ruiz Zambrano v Office national de l'emploi (ONEM)* [2011] ECR I-1177.

Literature

Alter, K. (1998). Who are the Masters of the Treaty? European Governments and the European Court of Justice. *International Organization, 25*(1), 125–152.
Alter, K. (2008). Agents or Trustees? International Courts in Their Political Context. *European Journal of International Relations, 14*(1), 33–63.
Alter, K. (2009). *The European Court's Political Power*. Oxford: Oxford University Press.
Alter, K., Dehousse, R., & Vanberg, G. (2002). Law, Political Science and EU Legal Studies. An Interdisciplinary Project? *European Union Politics, 3*(1), 113–136.
Alter, K., & Vargas, J. (2000). Explaining Variation in the Use of European Litigation Strategies: European Community Law and British Gender Equality Policy. *Comparative Political Studies, 33*(4), 452–482.
Armstrong, A. (1998). Legal Integration: Theorizing the Legal Dimension of European Integration. *Journal of Common Market Studies, 36*(2), 156–174.
Arnull, A. (2008). The Americanization of EU Law Scholarship. In A. Arnull, P. Eeckhout, & T. Tridimas (Eds.), *Continuity and Change in EU Law: Essays in Honour of Sir Francis Jacobs* (pp. 415–431). Oxford: Oxford University Press.
Blauberger, M. (2012). With Luxembourg in Mind…The Remaking of National Policies in the Face of ECJ Jurisprudence. *Journal of European Public Policy, 19*(1), 109–126.
Blauberger, M. (2014). National Responses to European Court Jurisprudence. *West European Politics, 37*(3), 457–474.

Blauberger, M., & Weiss, M. (2013). 'If You Can't Beat Me, Join Me!' How the Commission Pushed and Pulled Member States into Legislating Defence Procurement. *Journal of European Public Policy, 20*(8), 1120–1138.
Börzel, T. (2006). Participation through Law Enforcement. *Comparative Political Studies, 39*(1), 128–152.
Burley, A.-M., & Mattli, W. (1993). Europe before the Court: A Political Theory of Legal Integration. *International Organization, 47*(1), 41–76.
Carruba, C. (2005). Courts and Compliance in International Regulatory Regimes. *The Journal of Politics, 67*(3), 669–689.
Carruba, C., Gabel, M., & Hankla, C. (2008). Judicial Behavior under Political Constraints: Evidence from the European Court of Justice. *American Political Science Review, 102*(4), 435–452.
Carruba, C., & Murrah, L. (2005). Legal Integration and Use of the Preliminary Ruling Process in the European Union. *International Organization, 59*(2), 399–418.
Carruba, J., Gabel, M., & Hankla, C. (2012). Understanding the Role of the European Court of Justice in European Integration. *American Political Science Review, 106*(1), 214–223.
Cichowski, R. (1998). Integrating the Environment. *Journal of European Public Policy, 5*(3), 387–405.
Cichowski, R. (2001). Judicial Rulemaking and the Institutionalization of EU Sex Equality Policy. In A. Stone Sweet, W. Sandholtz, & N. Fligstein (Eds.), *The Institutionalization of Europe*. Oxford: Oxford University Press.
Cichowski, R. (2004). Women's Rights, the European Court, and Supranational Constitutionalism. *Law & Society Review, 38*(3), 489–512.
Cichowski, R. (2007). *The European Court and Civil Society: Litigation, Mobilization and Governance*. Cambridge: Cambridge University Press.
Conant, L. (2002). *Justice Contained: Law and Politics in the European Union*. Ithaca, NY: Cornell University Press.
Creswell, J., & Clark, V. (2010). *Designing and Conducting Mixed Methods Research*. Thousand Oaks, CA: SAGE Publications.
Davies, G. (2012). Activism Relocated. The Self-restraint of the European Court of Justice in its National Context. *Journal of European Public Policy, 19*(1), 76–91.
Davies, G. (2016). The European Union Legislature as an Agent of the European Court of Justice. *Journal of Common Market Studies, 54*(4), 1–16.
De Búrca, G. (2005). Rethinking Law in Neofunctionalist Theory. *Journal of European Public Policy, 12*(2), 310–326.
Dyevre, A. (2010). Unifying the Field of Comparative Judicial Politics: Towards a General Theory of Judicial Behavior. *European Political Science Review, 2*(2), 297–327.

Fligstein, N., & Stone Sweet, A. (2002). Constructing Polities and Markets: An Institutionalist Account of European Integration. *American Journal of Sociology, 107*(5), 1206–1243.

Garrett, G. (1992). International Cooperation and Institutional Choice: The European Community's Internal Market. *International Organization, 46*(2), 533–560.

Garrett, G. (1995). The Politics of Legal Integration in the European Union. *International Organization, 49*(1), 171–181.

Garrett, G., Kelemen, R. D., & Schulz, H. (1998). The European Court of Justice, National Governments, and Legal Integration in the European Union. *International Organization, 52*(1), 149–176.

Garrett, G., & Weingast, B. (1993). Ideas, Interests and Institutions: Constructing the European Community's Internal Market. In J. Goldstein & R. Keohane (Eds.), *Ideas and Foreign Policy: Beliefs, Institutions, and Political Change* (pp. 173–206). Ithaca, NY: Cornell University Press.

Granger, M.-P. (2004). When Governments Go to Luxembourg…: The Influence of Governments on the Court of Justice. *European Law Review, 29*(1), 3–31.

Haas, E. (1958). *The Uniting of Europe*. Stanford, CA: Stanford University Press.

Joerges, C. (1996). Taking the Law Seriously: On Political Science and the Role of Law in the Process of European Integration. *European Law Journal, 2*(2), 105–135.

Jupille, J. (2004). *Procedural Politics: Issues, Influence and Institutional Choice in the European Union*. Cambridge: Cambridge University Press.

Kagan, R. (2007). Globalization and Legal Change: The 'Americanization' of European Law? *Regulation & Governance, 1*(2), 99–120.

Kelemen, D. (2003). The EU Rights Revolution: Adversial Legalism and European Integration. In T. Börzel & R. Cichowski (Eds.), *The State of the European Union* (pp. 221–235). Oxford: Oxford University Press.

Kelemen, D. (2006). Suing for Europe: Adversial Legalism and European Governance. *Comparative Political Studies, 39*(1), 101–127.

Kelemen, D. (2011). *Eurolegalism: The Transformation of Law and Regulation in the European Union*. Cambridge, MA: Harvard University Press.

Lasser, M. D. S.-O.-L.'. E. (2009). *Judicial Deliberations: A Comparative Analysis of Judicial Transparency and Legitimacy*. Oxford: Oxford University Press.

Lenaerts, K. (1990). Constitutionalism and the Many Faces of Federalism. *American Journal of Comparative Law, 38*(2), 205–263.

Lenaerts, K. (1992). Some Thoughts about the Interaction Between Judges and Politicians. *University of Chicago Legal Forum, 1992*(1), 93–133.

Majone, G. (2001). Two Logics of Delegation. Agency and Fiduciary Relations in EU Governance. *European Union Politics, 2*(1), 103–122.

Mancini, G. F. (1989). The Making of a Constitution for Europe. *Common Market Law Review, 26*, 595–614.

Martinsen, D. S. (2011). Judicial Policy-Making and Europeanization: The Proportionality of National Control and Administrative Discretion. *Journal of European Public Policy, 18*(7), 944–961.

Mattli, W., & Slaughter, A.-M. (1995). Law and Politics in the European Union: A Reply to Garrett. *International Organization, 49*(1), 183–190.

Mattli, W., & Slaughter, A.-M. (1998). Revisiting the European Court of Justice. *International Organization, 52*(1), 177–209.

McCown, M. (2003). The European Parliament before the Bench: ECJ Precedent and EP Litigation Strategies. *Journal of European Public Policy, 10*(6), 974–995.

Moravcsik, A. (1993). Preferences and Power in the European Community: A Liberal Intergovernmentalist Approach. *Journal of Common Market Studies, 31*(4), 473–524.

Neergaard, U., & Wind, M. (2012). Studying the EU in Legal and Political Sciences Scholarship. In U. Neergaard & R. Nielsen (Eds.), *European Legal Method: In a Multi-level EU Legal Order* (pp. 263–292). Copenhagen: Djof Publishing.

Nugent, N. (2010). *The Government and Politics of the European Union*. Basingstoke: Palgrave Macmillan.

Nyikos, S. (2003). The Preliminary Reference Process: National Court Implementation, Changing Opportunity Structures and Litigant Desistment. *European Union Politics, 4*(4), 397–419.

Nyikos, S. (2006). Strategic Interaction Among Courts within the Preliminary Reference Process—Stage 1: National Court Preemptive Opinions. *European Journal of Political Research, 45*(4), 527–550.

Pierson, P. (1996). The Path to European Integration: A Historical Institutionalist Perspective. *Comparative Political Studies, 29*(2), 123–163.

Pitarkis, J.-Y., & Tridimas, G. (2003). Joint Dynamics of Legal and Economic Integration in the European Union. *European Journal of Law and Economics, 16*(3), 357–368.

Pollack, M. (1997a). Delegation, Agency, and Agenda Setting in the European Community. *International Organization, 51*(1), 99–134.

Pollack, M. (1997b). Representing Diffuse Interests in EC Policy-Making. *Journal of European Public Policy, 4*(4), 572–590.

Pollack, M. (2002). Learning from the Americanists (Again): Theory and Method in the Study of Delegation. *West European Politics, 25*(1), 200–219.

Pollack, M. (2003). *The Engines of European Integration: Delegation, Agency and Agenda-Setting in the EU*. Oxford: Oxford University Press.

Rasmussen, H. (1986). *On Law and Policy in the European Court of Justice: A Comparative Study in Judicial Policymaking*. Dordrecht: Martinus Nijhoff Publishers.

Scharpf, F. (1988). The Joint-Decision Trap: Lessons from German Federalism and European Integration. *Public Administration, 66*(Autumn), 239–278.

Scharpf, F. (2012). Perpetual Momentum: Directed and Unconstrained? *Journal of European Public Policy, 19*(1), 127–139.

Schmidt, S. (1998). *Following up on Judicial Politics: How the European Commission Uses the Court of Justice to Pressure the Member States.* Paper prepared for the Annual Meeting of the American Political Science Association, 3–6 September, Boston, MA.

Schmidt, S. (2000). Only an Agenda-Setter? The European Commission's Political Power over the Council of Ministers. *European Union Politics, 1*(37), 37–61.

Schmidt, S. (2014). Judicial Europeanisation: The Case of Zambrano in Ireland. *West European Politics, 37*(4), 769–785.

Shapiro, M. (2008). Law and Politics: The Problem of Boundaries. In K. Whittington, D. Kelemen, & G. Caldeira (Eds.), *The Oxford Handbook of Law and Politics* (pp. 767–774). Oxford: Oxford University Press.

Slepcevic, R. (2009). The Judicial Enforcement of EU Law through National Courts: Possibilities and Limits. *Journal of European Public Policy, 16*(3), 378–394.

Staton, J., & Moore, W. (2011). Judicial Power in Domestic and International Politics. *International Organization, 65*(3), 553–587.

Stein, E. (1981). Lawyers, Judges, and the Making of a Transnational Constitution. *American Journal of International Law, 75*(1), 1–27.

Stone Sweet, A. (2004). *The Judicial Construction of Europe.* Oxford: Oxford University Press.

Stone Sweet, A. (2010). The European Court of Justice and the Judicialization of EU Governance. *Living Reviews in European Governance, 5*(2), 1–50.

Stone Sweet, A., & Brunell, T. (1998). Constructing a Supranational Constitution: Dispute Resolution and Governance in the European Community. *American Political Science Review, 92*(1), 63–81.

Stone Sweet, A., & Brunell, T. (2012). The European Court of Justice, State Noncompliance, and the Politics of Override. *American Political Science Review., 106*(1), 204–213.

Stone Sweet, A., & Caporaso, J. (1998). From Free Trade to Supranational Polity: The European Court and Integration. In W. Sandholtz & A. Stone Sweet (Eds.), *European Integration and Supranational Governance* (pp. 92–134). Oxford: Oxford University Press.

Stone Sweet, A., & Sandholtz, W. (1997). European Integration and Supranational Governance. *Journal of European Public Policy, 4*(3), 297–317.

Stone Sweet, A., & Stranz, K. (2012). Rights Adjudication and Constitutional Pluralism in Germany and Europe. *Journal of European Public Policy, 19*(1), 92–108.

Tallberg, J. (2000a). The Anatomy of Autonomy. An Institutional Account of Variation in Supranational Influence. *Journal of Common Market Studies, 38*(5), 843–864.

Tallberg, J. (2000b). Supranational Influence in EU Enforcement. *Journal of European Public Policy, 7*(1), 104–121.
Tallberg, J. (2002). Delegation to Supranational Institutions: Why, How and with What Consequences? *West European Politics, 25*(1), 23–46.
Tridimas, G., & Tridimas, T. (2004). National Courts and the European Court of Justice: A Public Choice Analysis of the Preliminary Reference Procedure. *International Review of Law and Economics, 24*(2), 125–145.
Tsebelis, G., & Garrett, G. (2001). The Institutional Foundations of Intergovernmentalism and Supranationalism in the European Union. *International Organization, 55*(2), 357–390.
Vick, D. (2004). Interdisciplinarity and the Discipline of Law. *Journal of Law and Society, 31*(2), 163–193.
Wasserfallen, F. (2010). The Judiciary as Legislator? How the European Court of Justice Shapes Policy-making in the European Union. *Journal of European Public Policy, 17*(8), 1128–1146.
Weiler, J. (1981). The Community System: The Dual Character of Supranationalism. In F. Jacobs (Ed.), *Yearbook of European Law* (pp. 267–280). Oxford: Oxford University Press.
Weiler, J. (1982). Community, Member States and European Integration: Is the Law Relevant? *Journal of Common Market Studies, 21*(1), 39–56.
Weiler, J. (1991). The Transformation of Europe. *Yale Law Journal, 100*, 2403–2483.
Wincott, D. (1995). The Role of Law or the Rule of the Court of Justice? An Institutionalist Account of Judicial Politics in the European Community. *Journal of European Public Policy, 2*(4), 583–602.

CHAPTER 3

Precedents and Judicial Politics

3.1 Introduction

Referring to 'precedent' in the context of the EU is bound to raise questions with an informed reader. He or she will be aware that—unlike in common law systems—precedent holds no formally binding authority in EU law. In the context of this study, however, precedent is conceptualized in a way that does not confine its meaning to the common law doctrine of *stare decisis*, i.e., as conferring binding legal effect on prior court decisions. It is instead construed more broadly as referring to the practice of the Court to decide new cases with reference to decisions made in earlier proceedings.

This conceptualization accords to what has long been described in legal theory as a standard decision-making practice of courts everywhere; in judiciaries operating at both state and supra-state level, and in common and civil law systems alike.[1] Within those systems where prior decisions are not formally binding, precedents generally take on, not necessarily a law-making character in the formal sense of the phrase—i.e., as laying down a binding rule for the resolution of future cases—but come to exert a more

[1] The standard volume in this regard is that of MacCormick and Summers (1997) who provide a comparative overview of precedents across European legal systems. More recent enquiries into the subject have been provided by Komarek (2009, 2013). See also Pelc (2014) or Lupu and Voeten (2012) on precedent-formation in international law systems.

M. De Somer, *Precedents and Judicial Politics in EU Immigration Law*, European Administrative Governance,
https://doi.org/10.1007/978-3-319-93982-7_3

broad, normative influence, setting out interpretative guidelines that pave the way for a uniform interpretation of legal norms and principles in upcoming proceedings (Bankowski, MacCormick, Morawski, & Ruiz Miguel, 1997).

Reasons for the wide use of precedents by courts everywhere, whether or not in a formally binding sense, are manifold. To begin with, on an ideological, deontological level, as has long been an insight of legal theory, the practice of referring to earlier decisions is intimately connected to some of the most cardinal notions of justice. A first, and easily perceptible connection can be made with the core maxim of 'justice as fairness' which requires 'like cases to be decided alike' (Schauer, 1987; Golding, 1984; Bankowski et al., 1997). Precedent also relates closely to such other core rule of law requirements as 'coherence' of the legal order as a whole, or 'consistency' in the relation of different court decisions vis-à-vis one another. Further keystone notions of legality often associated with the formation of precedent include, amongst others: impartiality or the prohibition of arbitrariness, generality, predictability and the protection of reasonable expectations. Adherence to precedent is said to strengthen respect for all these notions, and as a result, to also enhance the perception of judges acting in line with what is expected of them. That is, deciding cases in line with earlier decisions allows courts to both bolster the perception of consistency of singular rulings vis-à-vis one another, as well as, concomitantly, showcase the internal coherence of the overall body of law they administer. This then helps in fending off potential challenges by strengthening the perception of cases having been decided, not whimsically in line with whatever preferences judges may have personally held, but—instead—on the basis of pre-existing, general and transparent legal standards that apply to each individual equally.

In addition to these considerations of a deontological nature, authors have also highlighted precedents' more practical function of boosting the efficiency of the judicial effort. This, first, by limiting or avoiding the unnecessary repetition of litigation through signalling the appropriate interpretative approach to prospective parties or lower courts. Furthermore, precedents also help economizing judges' individual decision-making efforts by providing standard templates and argumentation patterns, and allowing for less reconsideration of issues or questions already dealt with in the context of previous proceedings (Schauer, 1987; Bankoswski et al., 1997).

In this light it does not surprise that adherence to precedent can also be observed before the CJEU. The first appearance of precedent practices has been traced back to the Court's constitutionalizing jurisprudence of the 1960s (Tridimas, 2012; Beck, 2012). From their sporadic use during the 1970s they are reported to have grown more prevalent over the course of the 1980s as the Court's corpus of decisions that could function as models for later proceedings grew more articulate and dense (Barceló, 1997; Tridimas, 2012). By the 1990s, adherence to precedent had developed into "standard practice" (Tridimas, 2012, p. 309). At current, Beck notes, there is hardly any case the CJEU decides "in which it does not refer to its previous case law at least a few times in the course of the judgment" (Beck, 2012, p. 440). Jacob similarly observes that "it is almost impossible nowadays to read a decision by the Court and not come across a reference to an earlier decision" (Jacob, 2014, p. 92). His dataset of Grand Chamber judgments rendered in the year 2010 reveals that each new judgment invokes, on average, nineteen precedents, and that some judgments even surpass fifty such references (Ibid.).

In explaining this strong penchant for precedent in the Court's case law, in spite of the absence of a binding legal doctrine to that effect in EU law, legal scholarship on the CJEU's reasoning has adduced reasons that run parallel to those outlined in legal theory on the role of precedent in legal systems more generally. With regard to practicality and efficiency, first, Jacob has for instance noted that "(P)erceived benefits of arguing by precedent revolve around system maintenance. For one, precedents can increase efficiency and save time when used as convenient shorthand, polished phrases or ready-made building blocks in later reasoning processes. They bring an element of industrialisation to dispute settlement through standardised argumentation patterns" (Jacob, 2014, p. 14). Second, on the deontological plane, Bengoetxea, MacCormick, and Moral Soriano (2001) have connected the "strong theory of precedent that operates within the EU judicial system", to the rule of law requirements of handing down decisions in a manner that is 'consistent' and 'coherent'; i.e. decisions that are mutually compatible and that can be conceived of as part of a legal order that makes sense as a whole. Maduro has similarly observed that: "The authority which the Court itself recognises to its previous decisions is a consequence of the need to guarantee the values of coherence, uniformity and legal certainty inherent to any legal system". As he added, in the "framework of a decentralised system of enforcement such as that of the EU", these values "are particularly important" (Maduro, 2007, p. 14).

A strengthened coherence and consistency of the CJEU's jurisprudence enables the plurality of actors that together comprise the EU legal order, and that may stem from different judicial traditions, to more easily engage with, and apply, the Court's rulings (Ibid.; see also Beck, 2012).

Authors have also reasoned on from such observations to connect the use of precedent to broader notions relating to the legitimacy or persuasiveness of the Court's decisions. That is, by considering how a strengthened perception of coherence and consistency, and hence, neutrality, in the Court's jurisprudence feeds into the overall reception of this case law. Beck for instance writes: "Judicial authority and legitimacy (…) rest on the perceived impartiality of the judiciary. If the courts, in their decisions, simply ignored (…) rationality expectations which underlie the basic fabric of judicial legitimacy, the courts themselves would begin to lose wider credibility and legitimacy as their decisions would no longer be perceived to be the logical consequences of legal rules, but the results of political choices or personal preferences or whims. The capital of judicial authority would be eroded, just as it would be if similar cases were openly and without distinguishing reasons decided differently and thus seemingly randomly by the same or even different judges" (Beck, 2012, p. 33). Jacob's study of 'Precedents and Case-Based Reasoning' at the CJEU explicitly engages with the notion of precedent as a "tool" for the Court to "bolster its legitimacy and acceptance and to fend off outside challenges". "While there are also other potential reasons for case citations", he writes, "the Court above all refers to past decisions to resolve cases, demonstrate the coherence of EU law and thus enhance its credibility vis-à-vis other actors in the European legal space, notably the Member States (and in particular their courts)" (Jacob, 2014, p. 7).

These are precisely the sort of considerations that are also at the heart of the political science works that have reviewed the workings of precedent before the CJEU, and that further inform the present analysis. To date, only a limited number of such works can be identified however. In spite of the ample academic attention that has gone out to the Court within political science generally speaking (*cf.* the preceding chapter), the strategic nature of the Court's reasoning and the role of precedent therein have, thus far, not been subject to much systematic scholarly treatment. Four studies of note can be cited as exceptions to this general observation.

First, McCown's (2003) study on EP litigation strategies (*cf.* Chap. 2), has explicitly been built around the theoretical expectation that precedent-based practices, as they accumulate over time, induce ever more support for the Court's dicta amongst both litigants and national courts, as well as, eventually, Member States. Second, along similar lines, Stone Sweet's (2004) monograph, 'The Judicial Construction of Europe', conceptualizes precedents as "argumentation frameworks" which operate within EU adjudication processes, and which shape to ever increasing extents—on the basis of the CJEU's leads—the manner in which different EU law actors frame their discourses and engage with each other's arguments. In developing this conceptualization Stone Sweet built strongly on an earlier study, which had appeared in a co-authored volume with Shapiro, on the path-dependent, longitudinal discursive influence that precedents bear in legal systems more generally (Shapiro & Stone Sweet, 2002). In addition, and fourth, Schmidt's (2012) work on the path-dependent nature of CJEU rulings, whilst not explicitly framed around a conceptualization of precedent, resonates in many ways with the theoretical premises that guide the writings of Stone Sweet, Shapiro and Stone Sweet, and McCown. As will be set out in what follows, the insights of these studies inform the conceptual premises that ground the present study.

In addition, in spite of the limited express engagement with the role of precedent, a number of the most prominent political science studies on the CJEU have nevertheless highlighted that the Court's legitimacy is contingent on the extent to which it conveys its decisions in the neutral, technical language of the law or, more specifically, on the Court deciding new cases with reference to its holdings in earlier, related proceedings. Of particular interest, such considerations have cropped up at both sides of the theoretical fault lines that, as identified in the preceding chapter, divide the academic debates in this body of this literature. The present study's conceptualization will further draw on perspectives relating to the strategic nature of arguing by precedent that have been advanced in the works of Mattli and Burley/Slaughter (1993, 1995, 1998), Garrett, Kelemen, and Schulz (1998) and Alter (1998, 2008) (but see also Conant, 2002; Cichowski, 2007; Blauberger, 2012; Schmidt, 2014).

Third, the findings from these political science works are complemented and merged with insights from legal scholarship on the Court's reasoning, in general, and the role of precedent therein more specifically. Generally, and as has been pointed out by a number of commentators, much like political science, legal scholarship has, to date, not paid much attention to the CJEU's legal reasoning when compared to the wealth of literature that addresses the Court's jurisprudence broadly speaking (though see Bengoetxea, 1993; see for comments, de Búrca, 2001; Lasser, 2009;

Jacob, 2014). Most recently a shift seems to be taking place however as, over the past few years, four monographs on the subject have appeared (Lasser, 2009; Conway, 2012; Beck, 2012; Jacob, 2014), alongside a number of article-length reviews (Komarek, 2009; Itzcovich, 2009; Tridimas, 2012; Lenaerts, 2015). Particularly the monographs of Beck (2012) and Jacob (2014) offer perspectives that supplement the understandings of the political science literature.

As a starting point, two analytical foci can be discerned. They feature in each of the four identified political science works that have specifically reviewed the workings of precedent before the Court (McCown, 2003; Shapiro & Stone Sweet, 2002; Stone Sweet, 2004; Schmidt, 2012). First, the perception that the strategic value of precedent is longitudinal in nature. That is, it does not—or at least not most significantly—relate to the legitimating influence that one singular precedent holds on a next case, but rather, reveals itself in the manner by which precedent-based patterns, over different lines of cases, come to progressively shape and structure the argumentative environment within which the Court's decisions are received and evaluated. A second and connected analytical observation relates to the perception that this long-term strategic value of precedent does not play out in a vacuum, but rather, materializes only to the extent that it enhances the Court's legitimacy in the eyes of its external interlocutors. This is an obvious, but as will be set out in the below, by no means trivial observation.

Two different categories of external interlocutors can be identified. First, 'judicial actors' whose professional operations take place, predominantly, within the legal-judicial sphere. Most notably, in the CJEU's context, (i) litigants or their lawyers and (ii) national courts. Second, 'non-judicial' actors, or actors whose professional activities take place, mostly, outside of the legal-judicial sphere. In the CJEU's setting this relates most pertinently to the EU Member States. In what follows, the legitimacy-enhancing workings of reasoning by precedent, and the longitudinal nature thereof, are explored, in turn, for each of the two categories of external interlocutors.[2] This two-fold structure is reproduced in the

[2] Further categories of interlocutors can of course be identified. To begin with, in the legal-judicial sphere, precedent-based reasoning can also bolster the legitimacy of the Court's reasoning vis-à-vis academics (see on CJEU-legal scholars' interactions e.g., Schepel & Wesseling, 1997). Relying on precedent can also be expedient in the context of interactions with other supra-state courts, most notably the ECtHR (see on discursive interactions between the CJEU and the ECtHR for instance Schimmelfennig, 2006). Furthermore, it is

study's concluding chapter (Chap. 8) which presents the overall analytical findings.

The theoretical perspectives adduced in the two sections run parallel to one another. Each subsection discusses first, generally, the manner in which adherence to precedent aids the Court in cultivating well-functioning, cooperative relations with each set of interlocutors and how this strengthens the overall positive reception of the Court's activities by these interlocutors. Next, the sections both turn to review how precedents' legitimating influence, over time, moves beyond the context of singular cases to start operating within the broader, long-term development of these relations. As will be outlined, the sections are also interlinked in that the autonomy-enhancing dynamics vis-à-vis the two sets of interlocutors mutually strengthen each other's workings and effects. That is, the autonomy-strengthening effects of precedent-based reasoning vis-à-vis judicial interlocutors feed into precedents' autonomy-strengthening workings in the non-judicial sphere, and *vice versa*. A final, concluding section summarizes the main conceptual premises and expectations put forward.

3.2 Precedents and Judicial Interlocutors

First, and at its most apparent, the Court interacts with litigant parties who invoke claims under EU law and, second, with national courts who—through the Art. 267 TFEU preliminary ruling procedure—transmit these claims to the EU judiciary's bench. Such preliminary references make up the overwhelming majority of the CJEU's caseload (Court of Justice of the European Union, 2017). In a number of ways, reasoning by precedent can facilitate both (i) the Court's task of clearly communicating its decisions vis-à-vis these legal actors, as well as, (ii) bolster the likely positive reception and persuasiveness of those decisions vis-à-vis these interlocutors.

To begin with, this results from the coherence and consistency-strengthening workings of reasoning by precedent referred to above, and—in connection—from the manner in which a strengthened coherence

plausible that precedent-based reason-giving could be of use, not only in relation to 'external' interlocutors, but also vis-à-vis 'internal' interlocutors, that is, fellow judges. By grounding their arguments in previously approved Court decisions, judges may find it easier to convince their peers of the appropriateness of their reasoning (see e.g., Jacob, 2014, for suggestions along these lines). These additional categories of interlocutors, however, fall outside of the scope of the research questions guiding the present study.

and consistency feeds into the perception of judicial neutrality and impartiality. With regard to litigants, first, as Alter has for instance pointed out in her work on trusteeship, "the noble lie of judicial neutrality is a necessary fiction" developed and reinforced by judges to convince the losing party in the case that they had a fair chance at winning, and that the ruling was not subjective" (Alter, 2008, p. 45). Lupu and Voeten similarly write in the context of precedent formation before the ECtHR that "(d)emonstrating the consistency of a decision with past decisions may alleviate the losing party's potential to claim that a decision was whimsical or motivated by non-legal considerations" (Lupu & Voeten, 2012, p. 419). Second, precedent-based practices, and the extent to which they strengthen the coherence and consistency of the Court's case law, are also likely to appeal to the professional norms and hermeneutics of national judges. This both to the extent that they help bolster the perception of respect for the maxim of judicial neutrality and, in addition, inasmuch as they are likely to dovetail with those judges' own standard practices in deciding cases (see for a similar line of argumentation e.g., Weiler, 1994).

Moreover, precedent-based reasoning also allows the Court to emit clear(er) signals and guidelines as to how EU law is to be interpreted. As has been set out by Stone Sweet, arguing by precedent enables the CJEU to make conscious, strategic choices as to which elements of justification it wishes to emphasize as important in its reasoning (Stone Sweet, 2004; Shapiro & Stone Sweet, 2002). More specifically, by reinforcing certain arguments rather than others, over different lines of case law, the Court can signal, over time, the weight that it attaches to certain arguments rather than others. In Stone Sweet's phrasing, "the social function of precedent is to organize legal arguments" (Ibid., p. 32).

Litigators and national courts, from their part, are usually keen to take cues from these signals as this enables them to maximize the effectiveness of their own legal strategies. First, with regard to litigants, given the costs of adjudication, parties in a dispute tend to only take matters up before a court when they, or at minimum one of them, expects the costs incurred by the proceedings to be outweighed by the returns of an anticipated favourable ruling (Stone Sweet, 2004). By clearly signalling which sort of factors or arguments it considers authoritative, on the basis of strategically repeated reinforcements, the Court enables litigant parties (or the lawyers that advise them) to better assess their chances of success through court proceedings. Typically, Court decisions, or elements of these decisions, only get followed up on in subsequent litigation to the extent that they expand the opportunities or benefits of litigating for certain categories of individuals (Stone Sweet, 2004, p. 35; Schmidt, 2012; see in this context also Conant, 2002 and Cichowski, 2004 on societal interest litigation). In addition, once cases have entered the adjudication stage, the CJEU's argumentative patterns will constitute the basic templates upon which litigant parties will model their own discourses. In order to secure a favourable outcome for their clients, litigators will seek to advance what they consider to be the most effective argumentative strategies in the court room. This usually implies presenting arguments within the discursive structures through which the Court articulates its decisions, putting forward considerations that were deemed important in earlier proceedings, and generally demonstrating expert knowledge of the law and its correct (prior) interpretation (McCown, 2003; Shapiro & Stone Sweet, 2002; Schmidt, 2012).

In relation to national courts, second, similar "orienting functions" of precedent (Schmidt, 2012, p. 21) can be outlined. To begin with, to the extent that precedent-based practices enhance the consistency and coherence of CJEU decisions, they also enable domestic courts to take cues in respect of how to apply this case law independently at the national level (Ibid.; see also Maduro, 2007; Bobek, 2013), or to (more) accurately filter out those EU law questions that need further elucidation and are hence to be referred to the EU judiciary. In addition, to the extent that national courts are concerned about communicating the referred questions as clearly as possible and avoid talking at cross-purposes with the CJEU, they are also likely to take cues from the Court's discourses in terms of how to discursively model their own submissions.

Political scientists have connected these cue-taking practices of litigators and courts that inhere in adjudication processes, and that are facilitated by adherence to precedent, to concepts of "feedback loops" or "increasing returns" deriving from historical institutionalist literature on path-dependency (Shapiro & Stone Sweet, 2002; Stone Sweet, 2004; Schmidt, 2012; with reference to the work of, most prominently, Pierson, 2000). As each of these works notes, not all Court decisions are equally likely to provoke such 'feedback effects', or at least not all to the same extent. First, as already referred to, Court cases that open up opportunities for new rights claimants to bring a case before the CJEU, or strengthen their legal claims, are more likely to be followed up on. In addition, Stone Sweet's (2004) work also indicates that some types of legal provisions or Court pronouncements are more likely than others to generate feedback effects. First, he mentions: "normative statements that (a) announce general rules and then justified exceptions to those rules and (b) govern how conflicting legal interests ought to be balanced, or how the conflict between two otherwise applicable norms is to be resolved" (Stone Sweet, 2004, p. 34). Second, he points out that the relative hierarchical ranking of a norm within its legal order also has consequences for the extent to which it will favour "increasing return logics" in the context of precedent-based developments (Ibid., pp. 36–37; Shapiro & Stone Sweet, 2002, pp. 120–121). These two expectations are addressed in turn and connected to additional scholarly insights.

To begin with, in relation to the first set of perspectives, it has long been an axiom of legal theory that the relative degree of precision or otherwise of a legal act is proportional to an either greater or lesser degree of discretion for the judicial interpreter (see e.g., Hart, 1994). Beck's (2012) study on the "Legal Reasoning of the Court of Justice of the EU" has transferred these understandings to the EU legal system. As he observes, the CJEU's "discretion expands and contracts with the degree of legal uncertainty" of the legal norms relevant to the specific legal problems it is asked to resolve (Ibid., pp. 8–9). Generally speaking, given that EU legislation is often characterized by high degrees of "value pluralism" and "conceptual vagueness", Beck posits, the Court frequently enjoys considerable "interpretative freedom" with regard to key questions on the scope and depth of EU law (see in this regard also Chalmers & Chaves, 2012). These high degrees of vagueness often derive, Beck continues, from the habit of EU negotiators to couch provisions that are politically sensitive in nebulous, imprecise terms. This, so as to facilitate political agreement by creating room for manoeuvre at the implementation stages, or in order to camouflage potentially unresolved political differences. Of particular importance for present purposes, Beck's work further connects the thus created "gaps" in EU law to the CJEU's creation of precedents. In order to contain and counter the legal uncertainty deriving from these legislative voids, he asserts, the Court is required to "fill them in", over time and within the parameters set by the terms of the questions referred to it, with "judge-made rules", or rules that it derives from its previous interpretations (Ibid.; see also Barceló, 1997; Conway, 2012).

However, legal uncertainty inevitably resurfaces in these precedents since within judge-made rules, like in legislative ones, there are very few words "that do not contain some element of doubt" (Beck, 2012, pp. 266–276: see also Jacob, 2014, p. 108). The Court enjoys a margin of discretion in this regard too though, and one that exceeds the leeway it enjoys in relation to legislative provisions, as it can itself decide on the level of generality, or conversely, detail with which it describes its own dicta (Ibid.). A number of authors have in this context, similarly, called attention to the Court's ability to either equivocate, employing very broad terms; or, the other way around, confine the holdings of its rulings by delineating newly created judicial principles with a high level of precision (see besides Beck, also Conway, 2012; Jacob, 2014; Tridimas, 2012).

In this manner, the Court can essentially manipulate the likelihood of relitigation through follow-up claims, as well as the extent to which domestic courts will be in need of further clarification and, hence, are likely to send in new questions to that effect. As Beck writes: "A key factor determining the precedent weight is the level of generality or of abstraction used by the court to describe a decision. Characterising it in narrow terms allows the court to reduce the scope of its application, while a broader description potentially widens the impact of a judgment. The formulation and adaptation of the level of generality (…) is a major source of judicial discretion" (Ibid., p. 269). Jacob similarly notes: "Quite how precedents are introduced in a judgment is not just a vain technicality (…) (T)he precision employed when invoking precedents is relevant both in terms of what can be done with an earlier decision and how this is received by the parties and the broader audience" (Jacob, 2014, pp. 94–95). In short, the degree of generality or otherwise of a legal act, first, is likely to be proportional to an either greater or smaller degree of judicial discretion through precedent-based dynamics. Second, within such precedent-based dynamics, the Court enjoys an additional strategic advantage to provide incentives or disincentives for re-litigation and/or re-referral by constructing its dicta with either greater or lesser degrees of precision. In that manner, the Court can also manipulate the extent to which it will be likely to have continued opportunities to further develop or emphasize certain precedents rather than others.

In relation to Stone Sweet's second expectation, precedent-based interactions can be expected to develop especially strongly around those legal acts that enjoy a high hierarchical ranking. Within the EU legal framework, this relates typically to primary, Treaty law provisions. As a first observation, this expectation feeds in with the foregoing considerations in that highest-order legal norms are often described at particularly high levels of generality. That is, as such norms are designed to set out broad guidelines that emphasize ethical or other fundamental values which are to prevail over additionally enacted legislation, they are often couched in general formulations so that their application to a broad set of circumstances can be secured (see also Chalmers & Chaves, 2012 on "thickly evaluative norms" in EU law). In addition, to the extent that highest-order, Treaty norms are implicated in the questions brought before the Court, and insofar as the CJEU is required or chooses to emphasize them within its decisions, this is likely to strengthen positive feedback effects or cue-taking practices taking place between the Court and private litigators. As for instance outlined in Cichowski's monograph on societal interest litigation, litigators are often particularly predisposed to find opportunities for furthering their interests in Treaty-based rights or in general principles of EU law. This because, as Cichowski asserts, they are aware that "the ECJ can utilize these rights to justify a broad and purposeful interpretation" (Cichowski, 2007, p. 36). In addition, private litigants can also be expected to be especially likely to take strategic cues from Court dicta around highest-order Treaty norms as this offers opportunities to infuse their own rights claims with the highest-order, normative weight attaching to these provisions.

To the extent that feedback, cue-taking effects of litigators and/or national courts materialize, they generate important legitimacy-enhancing benefits for the Court. To begin with, whenever the Court's argumentation in a ruling is taken up on by either litigators or national courts as a model on which they base their own submissions, this entails, even if only implicitly, a reinforcement of this argumentation by those actors (McCown, 2003; Schmidt, 2012). In addition, each new claim or question that arises before the CJEU in follow-up to one of its earlier decisions also provides the Court, anew, with an opportunity to construct or further clarify its earlier holdings. In the new case, the Court can again make tactical choices with regard to which lines of reasoning to emphasize over others, as such providing new cues that litigators and national courts can use for modulating their own legal strategies, and overall, in that way, reinitiating the cycle. Over time, on the basis of such cyclic, sequential interactions that are sustained by precedents, self-reinforcing discursive dynamics start to continuously reproduce themselves within the adjudication processes as they evolve (Stone Sweet, 2004).

With use, as the precedents that underpin these self-reinforcing dynamics accumulate, they tend to grow ever more articulate and dense. As time passes, "snowballing ensues" and they come to create entire sequences of arguments and standards that should be adhered to in the court room

(Shapiro & Stone Sweet, 2002, p. 115; McCown, 2003). In this manner, as they accrete, precedents also come to limit the range of arguments and choices that are available to legal actors. In that sense, they increasingly, and incrementally, come to "channel" and condition both how actors will defend for their interests, and on what premises new cases will be adjudicated (McCown, 2003, p. 980; Stone Sweet, 2004, p. 34). Overall, through the vagaries of sequencing, they progressively move the case law along pathways that become ever more embedded within the discursive constructs adhered to in the court room and, on that basis, increasingly resistant to rollback (Ibid.; Shapiro & Stone Sweet, 2002).

As each of the political science works attest to, in the long run, through constant reinforcement, "lock-ins" emerge as some of the standards or arguments that are built up through precedent evolve into a taken-for-granted state of affairs (Stone Sweet, 2004; Schmidt, 2012). They are then referred to less and less in the court room, as this no longer serves a purpose. Or, with time, precedents become convention. Within legal scholarship Jacob similarly observes: "(T)here are certain points of EU law that have been repeated so many times over the course of innumerable decisions and continually gone unchallenged by the Member States that precedent citation seems almost superfluous. (…) They are such an entrenched part of the *acquis communautaire* that any precedent citation appears ornamental, since they are practically immune to being overturned" (Jacob, 2014, p. 212). Instead, such locked-in precedents mutate into the building blocks that come to dictate the premises of new discursive interactions (Stone Sweet, 2004).

It is precisely in these cumulative effects, and a core observation of all the political science writings, that precedents' longitudinal, legitimizing influence resides most importantly. As new judicial interactions become predicated on, not only the immediately preceding Court decisions, but also on precedents that emerged even earlier downstream but that through lock-in dynamics no longer require explicit citation, precedent-based patterns come to hold a radiating sway on the broader, normative evolution of the case law. Accordingly, and in parallel, by strategically cultivating its precedents, the Court holds a powerful tool to incrementally shape not only the disputative settings of the litigation that is likely to come before it in the near future, but also—more widely—the overarching discursive framework in which this litigation is embedded and through which the wider EU legal interpretative community receives and appraises its decisions.

3.3 Precedents and Non-judicial Interlocutors (Member States)

The above observations immediately connect to how adherence to precedent also holds a strategic value in the political realm, most notably, vis-à-vis Member States. In brief, to the extent that precedent-based practices help to recruit the support of litigant parties, and inasmuch as they aid in oiling the institutional loyalty of domestic courts, they also strengthen the Court's legitimacy vis-à-vis non-judicial, political actors.

Such perspectives hold a long lineage in both political science and legal scholarship on the CJEU. As outlined in the preceding chapter, already in the early contextualist legal scholarship authors highlighted how the Court's authority to further integration processes is, since the establishment of the principles of direct effect and supremacy, intimately tied up with the support it receives from both individual litigant parties who file follow-up claims, as well as from domestic courts who transfer these claims to the EU bench and administer compliance with the CJEU's rulings on the ground (see most prominently, Weiler, 1991). Such claims were, next, also very much engaged with in the political science works that 'discovered' the CJEU on the basis of this contextualist legal scholarship. They featured strongly, for instance, in Mattli and Burley/Slaughter's works and were, from there, transferred to the work of Alter on CJEU-national court interactions (Alter, 1996, 1998, 2008) and the writings of Conant (2002) and Cichowski (2007) on social interest litigation, from where they have continued informing recent enquiries (e.g., Kelemen, 2011; Stone Sweet & Stranz, 2012).

In addition, a further long-standing scholarly insight holds that the legitimacy judges enjoy in the extrajudicial sphere rests, to an important extent, on the perception that their activities reside within the neutral, technical judicial sphere exclusively (see e.g., Burley & Mattli, 1993; Alter, 2008). It stands to reason that the perception of CJEU activities as being non-political and taking place outside of the realm of partisan politics is vital, as it is to courts generally speaking, to the authority that it holds to act as an impartial adjudicator. In that light, to the extent that reasoning by precedent aids the Court, as outlined above, to strengthen the perception of coherence, consistency, and overall neutrality of its decisions, this also holds a value with regard to how these decisions are received by political actors. Considerations along these lines have, from the very beginning, cropped up in political science writings about the Court (as well as in legal scholarship, see e.g., Weiler, 1994). They in fact cut across the theoretical fault lines that divide this literature (*cf.* Chap. 2) as one of the single points on which the perspectives of different authors eventually converged.

Burley and Mattli (1993) "law as a mask" thesis, for instance, was essentially spun around the premise that the perceived neutrality and technical nature of legal dictates was fundamental to the Court's autonomy vis-à-vis the Member States in that it allowed the CJEU to conceal, "mask", the political implications that inhered in its rulings. They outlined this as follows: "(L)aw functions both as mask and shield. It hides and protects the promotion of one particular set of political objectives against contending objectives in the purely political sphere. In specifying this dual relationship between law and politics, we also uncover a striking paradox. Law can only perform this dual political function to the extent it is accepted as law". A "legal" decision that is transparently "political" in the sense that it departs too far from the principles and methods of the law, will invite direct political attack. It will thus fail both as mask and shield. (…) In short, a court's political legitimacy, and hence its ability to advance its own political agenda, rests on its legal legitimacy (Ibid., pp. 72–73). This reasoning also strongly informed their 1995 critical response to Garrett's intergovernmental account: "Garrett suggests that the court takes into account the interests of individual states before it in a particular case. Such particularistic interest balancing contravenes the most basic precepts of the rule of law. Age-old precepts of legal reasoning require the court to apply a principle developed in the context of one case consistently across similarly situated actors in an entire category of cases. (…) (I)f the court followed Garrett's model it would quickly get a reputation for arbitrary and capricious "political" decisions, thereby undermining its legitimacy" (Mattli & Slaughter, 1995, p. 186).

This perspective is one of the essential understandings on the Court's role that neofunctionalist and intergovernmentalist theorists would come to share. Where Garrett had indeed originally posited that "ECJ behavior will likely be conditioned by its expectations about the likely responses of member governments", the later contribution, co-authored with Kelemen and Schulz, attested to the importance of the Court conveying its decisions in a legalistic, neutral language that imparted respect for precedent (Garrett, 1995, p. 178; Garrett et al., 1998). With explicit reference to the remarks of Mattli and Burly, they noted: "Legal precedent greatly concerns the ECJ. (…) If a court's jurisprudence were to change frequently from case to case in response to pressure from the actors involved, the court would surely lose legitimacy. This is because a court's claim to power ultimately rests on its image as an impartial advocate for the law" (Garret et al., 1998, p. 157).

Observations around the political authority that is generated through the appraisal of Court decisions as decidedly non-political also re-appeared, next, in the works of the political scientists that followed up on the claims of Mattli, Burley and Garrett et al. They were for instance, and perhaps most prominently, elaborated on in Alter's trusteeship argument (*cf.* Chap. 2). 'Trustees', like the CJEU, Alter asserted, are delegated authority by their principals (*in casu*, the Member States) precisely because they personally, or their profession in general, carry their own source of expert or moral legitimacy (Alter, 2008). Accordingly, the Court's authority to act as a trustee is intimately tied in with, and dependent on, the extent to which it is perceived as "a disinterested actor applying pre-existing rules in a like fashion across a body of cases, thereby imparting a perception of procedural justice and neutral fairness" (Ibid., p. 39).

Beyond these considerations of a more general nature, the literature has also identified a number of further, more specific mechanisms through which reverence for precedent comes to bolster the Court's autonomy vis-à-vis the Member States. First, an often described dynamic relates to the manner in which precedent-based reasoning allows the Court to be "experimental" in constructing its jurisprudence. That is, to the extent that precedent-based practices enable the Court to build up its case law incrementally, on a step-by-step basis, they hold a strategic advantage in that they enable the Court to 'get a feel' of the reactions to its decisions. This then permits it to better anticipate them and, possibly, adjust its earlier holdings over the course of later proceedings, either expanding their scope or, the other way around, restricting their remit by introducing exceptions or limiting conditions when antagonism appears widespread.

References to such dynamics are commonplace in both legal works on the subject, as in political science writings. Within legal theory, to begin with, the notion that judges' engagement with precedent is not only retrospective in character, but possesses a prospective aspect as well, anticipating future litigation, is settled wisdom. MacCormick and Summers for instance spell this out as follows: "The recognition of authoritative precedent has (…) a certain backward-looking effect, to the extent that the present must be guided by what was decided in the past. But there is a forward-looking aspect to this as well; for the very existence of a practice of ascribing authority to past decisions means that one who engages in deciding a novel case does so knowing that the decision reached will itself be taken as a guide in later cases" (MacCormick & Summers, 1997, p. 2; see also Schauer, 1987). Such reflections have also been adduced in studies on the CJEU's legal reasoning (Conway, 2012; Komarek, 2013; Jacob, 2014).

From there, a number of authors have further highlighted that the CJEU often does not make the true implications of its rulings immediately apparent, but only reveals them over time once these rulings start working as precedents. Tridimas writes in this regard for instance: "(E)nsuing litigation inevitably requires revisiting the initial judgment, assessing its implications, refining its reasoning and articulating adaptations or exceptions (…). This often leads to corrective readjustments of the original principle" (Tridimas, 2012, p. 316; see also Barceló, 1997 or Beck, 2012).

In connection, an often observed method of the Court in this context is to first introduce what are to later become important new legal principles, as 'side-issues' to a decision, so as to only in subsequent cases clarify their scope and ramifications. Bengoetxea et al.'s description of the holdings of the *Martinez Sala* (C-85/96) ruling is revealing in this regard: "*Martinez Sala* is a judgment that raises fundamental questions on citizenship of the European Union, and yet it has almost passed unnoticed largely because it has always been seen and categorized as a case concerning social security (…) The judgment only discusses the citizenship issue in the final question and *obiter dictum*. Reading only the dispositif would provide no clue about the crucial issue being decided, i.e. that the status of citizenship of the Union confers in itself, once the residence rights have been acquired, a right not to be discriminated against on the basis of nationality, no other Treaty connection or Community element being necessary. This case will only attain its true significance when it starts working as a precedent, or when it is distinguished in subsequent judgments" (Bengoetxea et al., 2001, p. 52; see for similar observations for instance also Arnull, 1993; or Tridimas, 2012).

Jacob (2014) and Dawson (2014), whilst still writing from a legal perspective, have connected such observations on the Court's method of deferring the precise implications of its rulings to considerations of an expressly political nature. Jacob, in describing the discretion the Court enjoys in choosing the level of generality (or otherwise) with which it describes its past decisions (*cf.* above), remarks that—overall—the CJEU is "very fond of referring to past jurisprudence in a general manner" (Jacob, 2014, p. 126). The attraction of such "nebulous invocations", he writes, lies in the flexibility that they afford to, where necessary, "smoothen rough edges" and "mask sub-optimal translations" over the course of new judgments. This is done with a view to boost "acceptance and compliance" (Ibid., p. 98; pp. 190–191; see also Beck, 2012, pp. 269–270). As he asserts: "Precedents are very important in pre-empting potential responses to its work" (Ibid., p. 126). Dawson (2014) adds as a further line of argumentation that the CJEU's reasoning is often characterized by what he terms "repeat games". As he writes: "(i)n the context of a repeat game, a Court may set down an integrationist or other principle but do so slowly, or else limit its temporal or material impact in order to embed that principle in the long term. (…) Repeat games allow Courts to be experimental in the doctrines they develop, setting down ambitious principles, but reserving the ability to fine tune, rescind or even expand them" (Ibid., p. 428). The decision to do so depends, amongst others, Dawson asserts, on the "attitudes and levels of 'resistance' emerging from governments". Amongst others, the historical *Costa v. ENEL* judgment was framed in this light as a decision in which the Italian government won the case and in relation to which, hence, political resistance was limited. However, "at the same time, the Court was able to build on this doctrine in future cases—an integrationist principle was established, but its political impact was deferred." (Ibid., p. 429).

These considerations sit comfortably with observations that have similarly been made within political science works. For instance, using a wording very similar to that of Dawson, Mattli and Slaughter, in their last contribution to the debate, called attention to the "particular interest" of "the way in which a repeat-play strategy on the part of a particular litigant dovetails with the Court's preferred method of expanding the reach of Community law: an incremental approach implemented over a series of cases, in which national governments typically win the battle and lose the war" (Mattli & Slaughter, 1998, p. 190). They continued: "(t)he Court's standard move is to enunciate a principle of great long-term significance but to find some procedural or factual reason not to apply it to the case at hand" (Ibid.; see also Conant, 2002, p. 40). In much the same way, Garrett et al. observed that "(t)he Court may construct precedent strategically. For example, the ECJ may try to embed decisions with potentially important long-term consequences for EU jurisprudence in relatively uncontroversial cases" (Garrett et al., 1998, p. 158). As they noted, the Court at times "floated a series of trial balloons—in the form of open-ended decisions—designed to test the resolve of governments" (Ibid.,

p. 168). More recent examples of references to the Court's 'deferring' precedent strategies can be found in the writings of Blauberger or Schmidt who both make mention of processes of "fine-tuning" whereby the Court "curtails the demands" of its rulings (Schmidt, 2014, p. 773) when it becomes "sensitized to domestic concerns" (Blauberger, 2014, p. 123).

The authorship that has most forcefully engaged with these premises, however, is that of Alter. In "Masters of the Treaty", she connects observations on the Court's practices of postponing the political implications of its rulings to historical institutionalist perspectives on the different time horizons held by courts and politicians. Following a well-known judicial technique, she writes, the Court expanded its jurisdictional authority "by establishing legal principles but not applying the principles to the case at hand" (Alter, 1998, pp. 130–131). Although often bold in doctrinal rhetoric, the Court made sure that the political impact of its decisions was minimal in terms of both financial consequences and political implications. In this manner, and key to explaining the effectiveness of this method, the Court was able to play off the inherently shorter time horizons of politicians. Drawing on Pierson (1996), politicians, she held, care greatly, or even principally, about staying in office and, hence, about delivering goods to their electorate. Because the decisions of voters, which determine political success, are taken in the short run, politicians—in parallel—tend to prioritize the immediate material impact of legal decisions over the potential long-term effects of Court rulings. This also explains why they often fail to act decisively when doctrine that is counter to their long-term interests is first established. What were marginal decisions from a political perspective, however, were "revolutionary decisions from a legal perspective" (Ibid., p. 133). By limiting the immediate material consequences of its decisions, the Court was able to take advantage of the political fixation on short-run impacts and could build up its power progressively without provoking political responses.

As Alter emphasizes, however, this reasoning did not imply that Member States were fooled by the apparently technical, apolitical nature of the law (Ibid., p. 143). They understood that the legal precedents established might create political costs in the future. As she noted: "The Court's *Van Gend* and *Costa* decisions were filled with rhetoric to make politicians uneasy, and lawyers from member states had argued strongly against the interpretations the ECJ eventually endorsed" (Ibid., p. 132). What her argument entailed is that "until the ECJ began applying the doctrine in unacceptable ways, politicians lacked a compelling interest in mobilizing an attack on the Court's authority" (Ibid.). Similarly, Mattli and Burley noted in their "law as mask" argumentation that the acceptance of legal decisions was aided by the their purportedly technical, non-political nature, but that that was not to deny that the political impact of judicial decisions would not ultimately be felt (Burley & Mattli, 1993, p. 69).

However, as Mattli and Burley further pointed out, the key to understanding the way in which law gradually interpenetrates the political arena, and legal integration leads to political integration, is that a legal decision, even if has acquired political significance, is not the same as a "purely" political decision and cannot be attacked as such. "It retains an independent "nonpolitical" rationale, which must be met by a counterargument on its own terms". Accordingly, Member States cannot attack such decisions but by a "battle of proxy", and "the chances of their victory are affected by the strength of that proxy measured by independent nonpolitical criteria" (Ibid., p. 72). This is how law functioned, not only as a "mask", but also as a "shield". Alter similarly stressed the "important difference between the legal and political rules of the game" to further explain why, once "unacceptable applications" of previous CJEU doctrines transpired, national governments' ability to counter respond was limited, amongst others, by the fact that such responses would need to be framed and justified in terms that could persuade a legal audience (Alter, 1998, p. 143, 133).

These lines of reasoning have been set out in further detail by McCown (2003) who has expressly connected them to the workings of precedent. Her enquiry starts off from what has often been described in the literature as a routine, but paradoxical habit of Member States when interacting with the CJEU. That is, in submitting their written observations to the Court, Member States can often be found to adopt premises that stem from CJEU decisions to which they had originally been strongly opposed or within which they were, at the time, even the losing party (Ibid., p. 982). Burley and Mattli (1993) have for instance traced such observations back to Rasmussen's (1986) seminal contextualist legal study on the constitutionalization of EU law (*cf.*, Chap. 2). Referring to a process that "court watchers" had identified, they cited Rasmussen's study for having demonstrated that "even governments overtly hostile to the Court's authority do not seek to ask the Court to overturn a previous ruling but rather accept that ruling as a statement of the law and use it as a point of departure for making arguments in subsequent cases" (Ibid., pp. 67–68).

They continued: "After reviewing an extensive sample of briefs submitted to the Court by member governments, Rasmussen was unable to find even one instance in which a member state suggested that a prior precedent be overruled. This finding is particularly striking given that states do often strongly object to a proposed interpretation or application (…) *prior* to a particular decision." (Ibid.; original emphasis).

What underlies such puzzling behaviour, McCown asserts, is that in each new legal dispute Member States tend to find that the short-term benefits to be gained from winning the individual case at hand are more important to them than the slim chances of "scoring a moral point" by openly challenging previously created Court rules (McCown, 2003, p. 981, 989).[3] In order to promote their chances of winning the dispute, Member States will seek to advance the most effective legal arguments and this usually implies making submissions "in a language and style recognized by the Court" or "rooted in the Court's past argumentations" (Ibid., p. 981). In a study specifically geared to reviewing national governments' litigation strategies before the Luxembourg bench, Granger has similarly pointed out that: "if governments want to be "heard" by the Court, they need to speak its language, which means that they must use EU legal reasoning (*i.e.* reliance on EU precedent and interpretative methods), (…) and speak EU legalese" (Granger, 2004, pp. 6–7; see for similar observations also Weiler, 1994 or Beck, 2012). Accordingly, instead of ignoring or refuting a disliked precedent, Member States will engage with it, seeking, rather, to advance "qualifying arguments" in which they argue for a narrow interpretation or try to distinguish the settings of the new dispute from the disliked, earlier judgment explaining how it should be decided differently (McCown, 2003, p. 981, 985).

However, in two ways Member States' tactical adaptations to the 'legal rules of the game' end up strengthening the Court's autonomy, rather than Member States' ability to call the tune. First, within the legal discursive arena the Court inherently enjoys a power position. In the context of her trusteeship argument, Alter for instance pointed out that in "courtroom politics", "judges have a privileged position because they get to ask the questions, decide what is and is not relevant, and determine the

[3] In expounding this reasoning, McCown's contentions strongly mirror Alter's time horizons argument. The authorship of Alter is not engaged with, however, nor referred to. Alter, *vice versa*, has not connected her observations explicitly to the insights of studies that engage with the workings of precedent.

outcome" (Alter, 2008, p. 47). Similarly, McCown has indicated that, in comparison to litigant parties, judges have a great deal of freedom with regard to whether, how and when they engage with previous case law in the context of new disputes (McCown, 2003, pp. 978–980). In addition, it can also be pointed out that inasmuch as Member States' court room claims are, for tactical reasons, modulated along prior CJEU holdings, this strengthens the extent to which the premises of the disputes arising before the Luxembourg bench, generally, are predicated on prior Court dicta. This then further contributes to the above described leeway of the CJEU to continue engaging with its prior holdings, emphasizing certain elements rather than others, so as to, on that basis, steer the likelihood that certain of these elements, rather than others, will reappear before its bench.

Second, and at the core of McCown's argumentation, by modulating their submissions around the paradigms of earlier CJEU discourses, the Court's rules begin to shape their own arguments and Member States are left implicitly acceding to these rules (Ibid., p. 980, 985). In that manner, over time, adherence to precedent comes to foster self-reinforcing discursive dynamics that essentially run parallel to those identified above in the context of CJEU-judicial actors' interactions. As, with time, the grounds on which later disputes are adjudicated increasingly become based on "at least marginal acceptance of previous judgments", Member States come, in small, incremental steps, to accept and internalize ever more precedents and, with use, "adapt their behaviour in both implicit and explicit acknowledgments of them" (Ibid., p. 990). In the long-run, like in the context of CJEU-judicial actors' relations, precedents tend to grow increasingly resistant to rollback as reversing disliked decisions is much harder in the context of later disputes than it would have been when the issues first arose. As McCown puts it: "The key to precedents' influence is not the influence they exert over individual decision outcomes, but how they regulate how actors will defend for their interests and how they gradually shift the premises of cases" (Ibid., p. 980).

3.4 Conclusion

Through a number of distinct, but ultimately interconnected processes of gradual discursive socialization, reasoning by precedent enables the Court to advance its judicial autonomy. As the first set of premises advanced, precedent-based reasoning is expected to strengthen the legitimacy and persuasiveness of the Court's decisions in the eyes of its judicial interlocutors, that is, national courts and litigant parties. Furthermore, a conscious engagement with preceding case law provides the Court with the ability to give cues on which arguments it finds most important in the context of its interpretations rather than others. Judicial interlocutors are expected to be keen to take cues from such signals in order to strengthen the effectiveness of their own claims and submissions. Each new claim or question that arises before Luxembourg in follow-up to one of the Court's earlier decisions then provides the EU judiciary, anew, with an opportunity to further construct or clarify its holdings.

Over time, and through the build-up of such cue-giving and cue-taking processes, self-reinforcing discursive dynamics are expected to continuously reproduce themselves within the jurisprudence as it evolves. With use, as the precedents that underpin these self-reinforcing dynamics accumulate, they are expected to grow ever more articulate and dense. In that manner, they will also increasingly start limiting the range of arguments and choices available in the court room and, on that basis, progressively move the jurisprudence as a whole along pathways that become, through continuous reinforcement, increasingly resistant to rollback. In the long run, 'lock-in dynamics' will emerge as some of the standards or arguments built up evolve into a taken-for-granted state of affairs. Such locked-in precedents will require ever less citation as more time passes. Instead, they will mutate into the building blocks that come to dictate the premises of new interactions. In short, on the basis of long-term, cumulative effects, reasoning by precedent is expected to enable the Court to increasingly shape, not only the disputative settings of the litigation that is likely to come before it in the near future, but also—more widely—the larger discursive frameworks in which this litigation is embedded and through which its decisions are received and appraised.

Member States, second, are expected to similarly adopt premises from prior CJEU decisions, potentially even from decisions to which they were originally opposed. Amongst others, and as has been documented in prior studies, when intervening before the Court, national governments tend to prioritise the short-term benefits to be gained from winning the legal dispute at hand over the smaller chances of scoring a moral point by openly challenging prior Court statements. Accordingly, and similar to the interactions between the Court and judicial interlocutors, Member States will seek to advance the most effective legal strategies available in order to promote their chances of winning the dispute at hand. This will imply making submissions that are anchored in arguments considered important in previous judgments and generally demonstrating a thorough understanding of EU law and its correct prior interpretation. In the long run, however, such tactical adaptations to the legal rules of the game end up strengthening the Court's autonomy rather than Member States' ability to call the tune. As, with time, the grounds on which later disputes are adjudicated increasingly become based on at least marginal acceptance of prior dicta, Member States come in small but incremental steps to internalize ever more precedents.

In addition, reasoning by precedent also embeds several additional autonomy-strengthening effects for the Court in the context of its interactions with Member States. Amongst others, by consciously constructing its jurisprudence by means of step-by-step developments, the Court can be experimental in setting out the implications attaching to its rulings. For instance, by setting out new conclusions in a general, open-ended manner, rather than on the basis of strictly defined terms, the Court can strengthen the likelihood that follow-up claims will arise before its bench. At the same time, the use of such a general, open-ended language also affords flexibility to, in the context of follow-up litigation, either expand on the earlier dicta or, conversely, limit their contours depending on the levels of political resistance registered. As a connected technique, incremental, precedent-based reasoning also provides the Court with a strategic advantage to set out the potentially sensitive implications attaching to its rulings in similarly slow, incremental ways. In that manner, the exposure of these implications can be deferred to later stages when it is possible to present them as derivations of pre-existing rules.

The two sets of discursive dynamics are connected in that they mutually reinforce each other's workings. First, to the extent that the repetitive cue-taking dynamics taking place in the context of the Court's interactions with national courts and litigants strengthen well-functioning, smooth relations with these legal actors, this reinforces the perception of the Court's activities taking place within a technical, judicial environment exclusively and, by implication, of its decisions flowing from legal, neutral rules solely. This then alleviates the potential for political actors to claim that decisions were motivated by non-legal considerations and strengthens the likelihood that Member States will feel compelled to adapt to the legal rules of the game in the context of their own interventions before Luxembourg. The other way around, inasmuch as Member States' court room claims are modulated along prior CJEU dicta, the Court enjoys a strengthened leeway to continue engaging with these dicta, emphasizing certain elements rather than others, so as to steer the likelihood that certain of these elements, rather than others, will reappear before its bench.

References

Primary Sources

CJEU Case Law

Case C-26/62 *NV Algemene Transport- en Expeditie Onderneming van Gend & Loos v Netherlands Inland Revenue Administration* [1963] ECR 13.
Case C-6/64 *Flaminio Costa v E.N.E.L.* [1964] ECR 585.
Case C-85/96 *María Martínez Sala v Freistaat Bayern* [1998] ECR I-2691.

Other Documents

Court of Justice of the European Union. (2017). Annual Report 2016. The Year in Review. Retrieved from https://curia.europa.eu/jcms/upload/docs/application/pdf/2017-04/ragp-2016_final_en_web.pdf

Literature

Alter, K. (1996). The European Court's Political Power. *West European Politics, 19*(3), 458–487.
Alter, K. (1998). Who are the Masters of the Treaty? European Governments and the European Court of Justice. *International Organization, 25*(1), 125–152.
Alter, K. (2008). Agents or Trustees? International Courts in their Political Context. *European Journal of International Relations, 14*(1), 33–63.
Arnull, A. (1993). Owning up to Fallibility: Precedent and the Court of Justice. *Common Market Law Review, 30*(2), 247–266.
Bankowski, Z., MacCormick, N., Morawski, L., & Ruiz Miguel, A. (1997). Rationales for Precedent. In N. MacCormick & R. Summers (Eds.), *Interpreting Precedents: A Comparative Study* (pp. 481–503). Aldershot: Ashgate Publishing.
Barceló, J. (1997). Precedent in European Community Law. In N. MacCormick & R. Summers (Eds.), *Interpreting Precedents: A Comparative Study* (pp. 407–436). Aldershot: Ashgate Publishing.
Beck, G. (2012). *The Legal Reasoning of the Court of Justice of the EU*. Oxford: Hart Publishing.

Bengoetxea, J. (1993). *The Legal Reasoning of the European Court of Justice*. Oxford: Claredon Press.
Bengoetxea, J., MacCormick, N., & Moral Soriano, L. (2001). Integration and Integrity in the Legal Reasoning of the European Court of Justice. In G. de Búrca & J. Weiler (Eds.), *The European Court of Justice* (pp. 43–85). Oxford: Oxford University Press.
Blauberger, M. (2012). With Luxembourg in Mind...The Remaking of National Policies in the Face of ECJ Jurisprudence. *Journal of European Public Policy, 19*(1), 109–126.
Blauberger, M. (2014). National Responses to European Court Jurisprudence. *West European Politics, 37*(3), 457–474.
Bobek, M. (2013). Of Feasibility and Silent Elephants: The Legitimacy of the Court of Justice through the Eyes of National Courts. In M. Adams, H. de Waele, J. Meeusen, & G. Straetmans (Eds.), *Judging Europe's Judges—The Legitimacy of the Case Law of the European Court of Justice* (pp. 197–234). Oxford: Hart Publishing.
Burley, A.-M., & Mattli, W. (1993). Europe before the Court: A Political Theory of Legal Integration. *International Organization, 47*(1), 41–76.
Chalmers, D., & Chaves, M. (2012). The Reference Points of EU Judicial Politics. *Journal of European Public Policy, 19*(1), 25–42.
Cichowski, R. (2004). Women's Rights, the European Court, and Supranational Constitutionalism. *Law & Society Review, 38*(3), 489–512.
Cichowski, R. (2007). *The European Court and Civil Society: Litigation, Mobilization and Governance*. Cambridge: Cambridge University Press.
Conant, L. (2002). *Justice Contained: Law and Politics in the European Union*. Ithaca, NY: Cornell University Press.
Conway, G. (2012). *The Limits of Legal Reasoning and the European Court of Justice*. Cambridge: Cambridge University Press.
Dawson, M. (2014). How Does the European Court of Justice Reason? A Review Essay on the Legal Reasoning of the European Court of Justice. *European Law Journal, 20*(3), 423–435.
De Búrca, G. (2001). Introduction. In G. de Búrca & J. Weiler (Eds.), *The European Court of Justice* (pp. 1–8). Oxford: Oxford University Press.
Garrett, G. (1995). The Politics of Legal Integration in the European Union. *International Organization, 49*(1), 171–181.
Garrett, G., Kelemen, R. D., & Schulz, H. (1998). The European Court of Justice, National Governments, and Legal Integration in the European Union. *International Organization, 52*(1), 149–176.
Golding, M. (1984). *Legal Reasoning*. New York: Knopf.
Granger, M.-P. (2004). When Governments Go to Luxembourg...: The Influence of Governments on the Court of Justice. *European Law Review, 29*(1), 3–31.
Hart, H. L. A. (1994). *The Concept of Law*. Oxford: Clarendon Press.

Itzcovich, G. (2009). The Interpretation of Community Law by the European Court of Justice. *German Law Journal, 10*(5), 537–560.
Jacob, M. (2014). *Precedents and Case-based Reasoning in the European Court of Justice: Unfinished Business.* New York: Cambridge University Press.
Kelemen, D. (2011). *Eurolegalism: The Transformation of Law and Regulation in the European Union.* Cambridge, MA: Harvard University Press.
Komarek, J. (2009). Precedent and Judicial Lawmaking in Supreme Courts: The Court of Justice Compared to the US Supreme Court and the French Cour de Cassation. In C. Barnard & O. Odudu (Eds.), *Cambridge Yearbook of European Legal Studies* (Vol. 11, pp. 399–434). Oxford: Hart Publishing.
Komarek, J. (2013). Reasoning with Previous Decisions: Beyond the Doctrine of Precedent. *American Journal of Comparative Law, 61*(1), 149–171.
Lasser, M. D. S.-O.-L.'. E. (2009). *Judicial Deliberations: A Comparative Analysis of Judicial Transparency and Legitimacy.* Oxford: Oxford University Press.
Lenaerts, K. (2015). EU Citizenship and the European Court of Justice's 'Stone-by-Stone' Approach. *International Comparative Jurisprudence, 1*, 1–10.
Lupu, Y., & Voeten, E. (2012). Precedent in International Courts: A Network Analysis of Case Citations by the European Court of Human Rights. *British Journal of Political Science, 42*(2), 413–439.
MacCormick, N., & Summers, R. (1997). *Interpreting Precedents: A Comparative Study.* Aldershot: Ashgate Publishing.
Maduro, M. P. (2007). Interpreting European Law: Judicial Adjudication in a Context of Constitutional Pluralism. *European Journal of Legal Studies, 1*(2), 1–21.
Mattli, W., & Slaughter, A.-M. (1995). Law and Politics in the European Union: A Reply to Garrett. *International Organization, 49*(1), 183–190.
Mattli, W., & Slaughter, A.-M. (1998). Revisiting the European Court of Justice. *International Organization, 52*(1), 177–209.
McCown, M. (2003). The European Parliament before the Bench: ECJ Precedent and EP Litigation Strategies. *Journal of European Public Policy, 10*(6), 974–995.
Pelc, K. (2014). The Politics of Precedent in International Law: A Social Network Application. *American Political Science Review, 108*(3), 547–564.
Pierson, P. (1996). The Path to European Integration: A Historical Institutionalist Perspective. *Comparative Political Studies, 29*(2), 123–163.
Pierson, P. (2000). Increasing Returns, Path Dependence, and the Study of Politics. *American Political Science Review, 94*(02), 251–267.
Rasmussen, H. (1986). *On Law and Policy in the European Court of Justice: A Comparative Study in Judicial Policymaking.* Dordrecht: Martinus Nijhoff Publishers.
Shapiro, M., & Stone Sweet, A. (2002). *On Law, Politics, and Judicialization.* Oxford: Oxford University Press.
Schauer, F. (1987). Precedent. *Stanford Law Review, 39*, 571–605.

Schepel, H., & Wesseling, R. (1997). The Legal Community: Judges, Lawyers, Officials and Clerks in the Writing of Europe. *European Law Journal, 3*(2), 165–188.

Schimmelfennig, F. (2006). Competition and Community: Constitutional Courts, Rhetorical Action, and the Institutionalization of Human Rights in the European Union. *Journal of European Public Policy, 16*(8), 1247–1264.

Schmidt, S. (2012). Who Cares about Nationality? The Path-dependent Case Law of the ECJ from Goods to Citizens. *Journal of European Public Policy, 19*(1), 8–24.

Schmidt, S. (2014). Judicial Europeanisation: The Case of Zambrano in Ireland. *West European Politics, 37*(4), 769–785.

Stone Sweet, A. (2004). *The Judicial Construction of Europe*. Oxford: Oxford University Press.

Stone Sweet, A., & Stranz, K. (2012). Rights Adjudication and Constitutional Pluralism in Germany and Europe. *Journal of European Public Policy, 19*(1), 92–108.

Tridimas, T. (2012). Precedent and the Court of Justice: A Jurisprudence of Doubt? In J. Dickson & P. Eleftheriadis (Eds.), *Philosophical Foundations of European Union Law* (pp. 307–330). Oxford: Oxford University Press.

Weiler, J. (1991). The Transformation of Europe. *Yale Law Journal, 100*, 2403–2483.

Weiler, J. (1994). A Quiet Revolution. The European Court of Justice and Its Interlocutors. *Comparative Political Studies, 26*(4), 510–534.

CHAPTER 4

Case Selection and Data

4.1 Family Reunification Immigration: A Least-Likely Case

In order to evaluate whether and how precedent-based practices come, as hypothesized, to strengthen the Court's autonomy, a 'least-likely' case for observing a strong or increased judicial autonomy was selected. For these purposes, the CJEU's case law on family reunification immigration, as it developed from 1976 onwards, was singled out. In what follows, this section briefly reviews the rationale for adopting a least-likely case design. It then elaborates on how EU family reunification jurisprudence can be considered a least-likely case for the purposes of the present enquiry and why it was selected over other issue areas with similar traits.

To begin with, a least-likely case is, following Gerring, one that is "on all dimensions *except* the dimension of theoretical interest, (…) predicted not to achieve a certain outcome, and yet does so" (Gerring, 2007, p. 115; original emphasis). It is a case that provides the "most difficult" or "toughest" test for confirming a certain theory (Ibid.: George & Bennett, 2005, p. 121). To the extent that the analysis of such a case provides support for a theoretically expected outcome when it would have, on all other dimensions, been least likely to develop this outcome, this offers weighty evidence (Gerring, 2007). Accordingly, in the context of a single case set-up, least-likely cases bear a strong, if not the "strongest possible" inferential

M. De Somer, *Precedents and Judicial Politics in EU Immigration Law*, European Administrative Governance,
https://doi.org/10.1007/978-3-319-93982-7_4

leverage (Ibid., p. 115; Levy, 2008). In addition, as also emphasized in the literature, least-likely cases carry a strong external validity; i.e., they offer a strong basis for generalizing from the study's results to a larger universe. This logic is often posited with reference to the 'Sinatra inference': "if I can make it there, I can make it anywhere" (Levy, 2008, p. 12). If a theoretical expectation holds even when this is against the odds, it is likely to also hold in settings where conditions are more favourable.

For the purposes of the present study, observing a strong or increased Court autonomy is considered to be 'least likely' in the context of issue areas that are particularly politically sensitive. Following the perspectives of the political science works that emphasize the politically constrained nature of the Court's activities, CJEU judges can be considered least likely to be able to develop their decisions autonomously, that is, independent of political actors' preferences, when dealing with matters that touch on strongly held political interests (see Garrett, 1992; Garrett, Kelemen, & Schulz, 1998; or more recently, Carruba, 2005; Carruba, Gabel, & Hankla, 2012). Instead, in politically sensitive areas, the Court should be especially inclined to defer to governments' preferences. In line with the studies that emphasize the influence of Member States' interests over the Court's decisions, in those areas where antagonistic political capital is easy to mobilize, Member States' threats of noncompliance or of executing court-sanctioning measures (legislative override, competence revisions or strengthened control over appointment procedures) should be most credible. As follows from these premises, in politically sensitive areas the CJEU should be particularly prone to exercise self-restraint and accommodate Member States' interests. In that light, strongly politicised areas should also be 'most-likely' cases for observing, conversely, politically constrained Court decisions (see Levy, 2008 or George & Bennett, 2005 on the inferential optimization achieved when least-likely cases can be conceptualized in reverse as most-likely scenarios for competing theoretical claims).

EU family reunification immigration law was selected as a least-likely scope for observing a strengthened Court autonomy on account of its strong political sensitivity. To begin with, in general terms, the regulation of immigration at supra-state, EU level is, by its very nature, politically sensitive. This derives from the fact that immigration affairs touch on the governance of who enters and exits a state's territory, and possibly at later points in time, who holds legitimate claims to membership in a state's community. In these two ways, and as is well-established in immigration studies' works on the topic, the governance of immigration touches on the core of a nation's sovereign statehood (see from a large literature e.g., Joppke, 1998a, 1999). Additionally, as issues relating to the entry of non-nationals can be, as is similarly well-established, strong catalysts for the mobilisation of public opinion, policy-making on these matters also represents strong opportunities, or conversely risks, from a political actor's perspective in terms of electoral proliferation (Messina, 2007; Fetzer, 2012; Freeman, Hansen, & Leal, 2013).

These considerations are particularly pronounced in the context of family reunification immigration on account of the strong numerical importance of these migration flows. Both historically as at present, immigration for the purposes of family reunion makes up the largest migratory influx into Europe. As Western European governments brought an end to the post-WWII guest-worker programmes in the aftermath of the 1970s oil crises, immigration for the purposes of family reunion continued, and even expanded to eventually replace the earlier labour immigration programmes as the numerically most important legal immigration channel (Geddes, 2003; Messina, 2007). It has by and large retained this status. Up until 2015, as reported by Eurostat, immigration for reasons of family reunion amounted to 30% of all first residence permits issued across the EU. It therewith outnumbered all other reasons cited for the granting of residence permits (Eurostat, 2015). Figures changed following the large influx of asylum-seekers in 2015 and the following years, but remained high at 23% (Eurostat, 2017). It is not unlikely that the near future will see a shift towards a renewed numerically leading status for family reunion immigration as those individuals granted international protection from 2015 onwards may in turn make use of their rights to family reunification.

In light of this numerical importance, EU-level developments that touch on the regulation of this particular type of immigration hold strong implications for national immigration control competences more generally. Put differently, as immigration for the purposes of family reunion amounts to a very large share of foreigners gaining entry into Europe, any EU developments on the regulation of this particular type of immigration are likely to have significant consequences for governments' capacity to regulate the entry or exit of non-nationals generally speaking. Accordingly, such developments hold a high political magnitude and can be expected to be closely watched.

Family reunification was chosen over other, potentially similarly politicised areas of law on account of the particularly long-term track record of

EU legislation on these matters and, in parallel, CJEU decisions in this field. Whereas, for instance, EU provisions on asylum, low-skilled labour migration or EU citizenship are also highly sovereignty-sensitive, the development of EU legislation in these areas is much more recent and, accordingly, the track record of CJEU jurisprudence on these matters comprises a shorter timespan. More specifically, EU provisions on these subjects can be traced back to, at best, the early 1990s and, with regard to EU immigration law, the Court's jurisdiction was previously, either excluded (until the 1999 Amsterdam Treaty) or limited in regard of preliminary references to questions from last instance tribunals (until the 2007 Lisbon Treaty). EU provisions on family reunification, however, as will be set out in detail in the next section, are grounded not only in EU immigration law as it incrementally developed from the early 2000s onwards, but also in EU free movement law as adopted since the early 1960s. The first CJEU ruling of relevance identified dates back to the 1976 *Kermaschek* decision (C-40/76) in which the Court confirmed that EU free movement law also applied to the family members of moving EU workers "even if" these family members "were not nationals of a Member State". From there, and as documented in the below, the Court has, over the forty years that have followed since, issued a growing number of decisions that bear on Member States' competences to regulate the immigration of third-country nationals seeking entry for the purposes of family reunion. This particularly long-term track record, spanning over four decades, is of prime analytical importance in light of the above hypothesized long-term, sequential nature of both the causal mechanisms expected to underpin the workings of precedents, as well as the autonomy-enhancing effects expected to, over time, transpire therefrom.

4.2 Data Collection: EU Family Reunification Law, Case Law and Self-Citation Activity

In what follows, the study's data on (i) family reunification immigration law, (ii) case law and (iii) 'self-citation practices', used as proxies for precedents, are presented. As a first, general remark, the study conceptualises EU family reunification law broadly as relating to all legal provisions dealing with the rights of entry and residence for third-country national family members, as well as any conditions placed on the enjoyment of any of these rights (see similarly Peers, 2011). This broad conceptualization is needed to cover the plethora of EU legal instruments that contain provisos of this kind, and that together comprise what has been described as an increasingly complex and stratified, or "patchwork" area of EU law (Staver, 2013; see also Schweitzer, 2015; Block, 2015).

Two levels of EU law can be distinguished and will be addressed in turn in what follows. First, attention goes out to family reunion provisions in the framework of secondary legislation, more precisely, within the context of EU immigration law and EU free movement law. Second, provisions within primary, Treaty law relating, more specifically, to EU citizenship and fundamental rights, are reviewed. The section then considers the Court's judgments rendered on the basis of the identified provisions. In a third part, data on self-citation practices within the collected Court rulings, used as proxies for precedents, are presented.

4.2.1 EU Family Reunification Law

4.2.1.1 Secondary Legislation

EU Free Movement Law

Chronologically the first EU provisions on family reunification were incorporated in legislation on the free movement of workers. From their earliest conception, these legal instruments inscribed provisions that granted moving workers the right to be joined by their family members (e.g., Regulation 15/61/EEC; Regulation 38/64/EEC, Regulation 1612/68/EEC). In the spirit of the primarily economic logics underlying free movement law at the time, these rights were conferred with the aim of securing the effectiveness or 'effet utile' of the provided free movement rights and ensuring that "all obstacles to the mobility of workers" were duly eliminated (see e.g., the recital of Regulation 1612/68/EEC). On the condition that the worker had suitable housing available, joining family members were granted rights of entry and residence parallel to those of the moving worker and enjoyed access to employment and education.

From the very outset, these free movement instruments held the potential to intersect with immigration policies in that they imposed no requirements regarding the nationality of the accompanying family members. To the contrary, some of these earliest instruments even expressly stipulated that the family reunion provisions were also to apply to family members even "if these are not nationals of any Member State" (e.g., articles 10 and

11 of Regulation 1612/68/EEC). As referred to above, this reading was also confirmed in the very first case with questions to that effect to arise before the Luxembourg bench (*Kermaschek*, C-40/76).

As over the course of the following decades the scope of EU free movement law widened to start including community nationals providing or receiving services, pensioners, students, and others, the scope of ancillary rights granted to joining family members widened in parallel. This, as each widening step brought along the simultaneous creation of new categories of rights-holding family members (Barrett, 2003; Tomkin, 2009). At present, the Citizenship Directive (2004/38/EC) has grouped together and consolidated all previous free movement instruments (see for a recent discussion Guild, Peers, & Tomkin, 2014). The notion that the rights granted to accompanying family members hold irrespective of the nationality of the accompanying family members was repeatedly emphasized during the negotiations on the Directive (see e.g., COM (2001) 257; COM (2003) 199), and has also found its translation in the final text (see Articles 3, 12, 17, 23). In a number of clauses, special attention even goes out to the potentially more difficult conditions that accompanying family members 'who are not nationals of a Member State' may face (Articles 5, 6, 9, 10).

EU Immigration Law

Second, family reunification provisions have also been provided for in the framework of EU immigration law. The main instrument in this regard is the 2003 Family Reunification Directive which sets out common standards on the family reunification rights of legally resident third-country nationals (2003/86/EC).[1] In drafting the proposal for the Family Reunification Directive, the Commission based itself considerably on the provisions already in place in the context of free movement law (Strik, 2011). As a result, the rules laid down in the Family Reunification Directive overlap to a significant extent with the family reunion clauses of the EU Citizenship Directive. In parallel to moving EU citizens, the Directive grants third-country nationals that are lawfully resident within the EU territory the right to be joined by their spouse and minor children. Joining family members enjoy a right to access education and employment or self-employment. When reviewed in detail, however, a less favourable treatment

[1] In line with the opt-out rules available to them, the UK, Ireland and Denmark do not participate in the Directive.

of individuals covered by the Family Reunification Directive in comparison to those covered by EU free movement law, can be identified. As will be set out in detail in Chap. 5, this less favourable regime can largely be ascribed to the restrictive urges of national governments during the negotiations on the former Directive.

Aside from the Family Reunification Directive, EU immigration law contains a number of further 'special regimes' on family reunion for certain categories of third-country nationals. These concern, to begin with, refugees, who are granted more favourable conditions within a separate chapter of the Family Reunification Directive (Chapter V). The separate provisions provide, for instance, that refugees seeking to be reunited with their family members do not need to fulfil general income, housing or health insurance requirements. In addition, within EU legislation on asylum and temporary protection, a number of instruments contain clauses that specifically pay attention to the status of family members of those benefitting from a claim to international protection (Qualification Directive, 2011/95/EU; Directive on Temporary Protection, 2001/55/EC; Reception Conditions Directive, 2013/33/EU; Dublin III Regulation, EU 604/2013). Similar stipulations can also be found in the Returns Directive (2008/115/EC) on the procedures and standards applying to the return of third-country nationals.

In addition, highly skilled workers falling under the scope of the Blue Card Directive (2009/50/EC) are exempted from a number of the more restrictive requirements that apply to third-country nationals generally speaking. Member States may for instance not set any waiting periods on the access of family members of Blue Card holders to their labour markets. In addition, where the Blue Card holder moves between Member States, family members that were already living with him/her in the first Member State are permitted to join. Similarly, the Long-Term Residents Directive (2003/109/EC) grants family members of long-term residents with parallel rights to free movement within the Union.

As an end note, it bears highlighting that the study does not take account of family reunification clauses provided for in the context of EU Association Agreements. Doing so would require accounting for this legislation's position in the sphere and logics of EU external relations which fall outside of the scope of the present case selection (see for a recent review, however, Eisele, 2014).

4.2.1.2 *Primary Law*

EU Citizenship Provisions

Questions on family reunification under EU law also touch on primary, Treaty provisions including, to begin with, provisions on EU citizenship. Since Maastricht, the Treaties provide that: "Every person holding the nationality of a Member State shall be a citizen of the Union" (currently, Article 20 TFEU). The invocation of these provisions typically occurs in situations when rights-claimants have difficulties establishing a sufficient link with the scope of secondary EU law (for instance, when there has not been a clear exercise of free movement rights). As described above, family reunification provisions in secondary EU law only cover third-country nationals (under EU immigration law) or moving EU nationals (under free movement law). So-called 'static' EU nationals, who have not exercised free movement rights, cannot lay claim to such EU family reunion rights.

This state of affairs connects closely to the much-discussed phenomenon of 'reverse discrimination'. 'Reverse discrimination' refers to instances of differential treatment of 'own' (static) Member State nationals who are governed by domestic legislation, in comparison to EU nationals from another Member State, or third-country nationals, who reside in that same Member State but who, by virtue of falling within the scope of EU law, can benefit from more advantageous EU rules. Whereas instances of reverse discrimination can arise in all areas relating to the Union's four freedoms (i.e., besides the free movement of persons, also goods, services and capital) and whereas it has been contested both politically and legally within all these free movement spheres, its contestation has been particularly poignant in the context of family reunification provisions where it touches, amongst others, on fundamental rights' standards (see e.g., Tryfonidou, 2009; Walter, 2008; Van Elsuwege & Kochenov, 2011).

From a judicial perspective, the CJEU considered early on that situations of reverse discrimination did not necessarily pose a problem for EU law as they were to be seen as falling entirely within the remit of domestic law (*Morson & Jhanjan*, C-35/82 & C-36/82; discussed in detail below). Nevertheless, Union citizenship provisions have, in later rulings (starting with the seminal 1998 *Martinez Sala* decision), increasingly informed CJEU decisions in certain types of 'hard cases' where the possible denial of EU Treaty rights is at stake but where no secondary EU legal instruments can avail. In tandem, claimants often invoke this status in the context of free movement proceedings, usually when they have difficulties establishing their free movement 'credentials' (Spaventa, 2008). Union Citizenship then serves, as Shaw has succinctly put it, as a "backstop" legal status (Shaw, 2011, p. 34).

Fundamental Rights

Aside from EU citizenship provisions, questions on family reunification also have a strong bearing on fundamental rights' safeguards as provided for, centrally, under Article 6 TEU (see also Article 2 TEU). The connection between family reunion contexts and fundamental rights relates first, and most notably, to the fundamental right to family life. In addition, and as discussed next, connections can also be made with children's rights.

The fundamental right to family life, first, is generally recognized as embedding a right to protection of the family unit. However, neither at national level, nor in international human rights' documents has the right to family life, and the implied right to family unity, been construed as embedding an absolute right to family reunification in the event of the separation of family members across state borders (Lahav, 1997; Cholewinski, 2002). Nevertheless, "constitutional commitments" to this particular fundamental right are known to have "morally constrained" state responses towards immigration for purposes of family reunion. Whether governments "acknowledged" it themselves, or were "pressed by court rulings", the fundamental right to family life provided a moral hindrance to declining a right to entry to family members of those already resident within their territories (be they citizens or noncitizen residents) (Carens, 2003, Joppke, 1998b).

At EU level, the fundamental right to family life is enshrined, first, in Article 7 of the EU Charter which reads that "everyone has the right to respect for his or her private and family life". This is a close replication of the parallel right found in the ECHR under Article 8 that historically, and as per Article 6.3. TEU, also functions as a general principle of EU law. As noted by Peers, within the EU legal context, Article 8 ECHR is in fact, the "best known and most influential source of human rights principles forming part of the general principles of EU law" (Peers, 2011, p. 398). Furthermore, reference may also be made to Article 9 CFREU which, in analogy to Article 12 ECHR enshrines a right to marry and found a family and Article 33.1 CFREU which reads that "the family shall enjoy legal, economic, and social protection" (although questions may be raised on the justiciability of this provision, see Costello, 2014).

In addition, family reunification contexts can also touch on the protection of children's rights, more in particular, on a child's best interest to pursue a relationship with his/her parents. Again, although children's rights are usually not construed as embedding an absolute right to family reunification in the event of a separation of a child from his parents, such rights nevertheless constrain a state's ability to, in certain situations, deny the entry into or (continued) residence of parents or primary carers of minors resident within their territories; or, the other way around, of children whose parents or primary carers are residing in that state (see e.g., Stalford, 2012). At EU level, the protection of children's rights has been translated in a number of Charter articles, of which Article 24 reads, most notably, that "in all actions relating to children (…), the child's best interests must be a primary consideration" (Article 24.2) and that "every child shall have the right to maintain on a regular basis a personal relationship and direct contact with both his or her parents, unless that is contrary to his or her interests" (Article 24.3). Additionally, relevant ECHR provisions on children's rights, as well as the 1989 UN Convention on the Rights of the Child (CRC) may also be considered in this regard as they form part of the general principles of EU law (see Stalford, 2015).

4.2.2 EU Family Reunification Case Law

At a further level of analysis, all CJEU decisions rendered on the basis of the above identified EU law provisions were collected. In order to ensure a connection with immigration policy contexts, only those cases involving at least one third-country national were singled out for the purposes of the analysis. Whereas all proceedings on the basis of immigration law met this criterion as these legal provisions deal exclusively with the status of third-country nationals, the criterion was important in the context of proceedings on free movement law.[2]

[2] In line with the longitudinal set-up of the dataset, this selection criterion was in some cases applied to persons that were at the time of the proceedings non-EU nationals, but that would currently no longer qualify as such as a result of the Union's successive enlargement waves. This was the case in *Deak* (C-94/84) involving a Hungarian national, *Gül* (C-131/85) on the rights of a Cypriot national and *Ruhr* (C-189/00) which concerned a Polish national. See on the sometimes ambivalent effects of EU accession rounds from the perspective of distinguishing between EU and third-country nationals Groenendijk (2009) and Guild (2009).

The overview incorporates not only proceedings arriving before the Luxembourg bench on the basis of preliminary references sent in by national judges (Article 267 TFEU), but also those cases that arose through infringement actions initiated by the Commission (Article 258 TFEU), and through annulment actions brought by either a Member State, the Commission, the European Parliament or the Council of Ministers (Article 263 TFEU).[3] No relevant cases could be identified on the basis of Article 259 TFEU (which enables Member States to bring one another before the CJEU). On the basis of these criteria, a total of 68 cases were identified. They are set out chronologically, and with details on their respective legal bases in Table A1 in the annex.

Of the 68 cases, only 18 concerned proceedings brought before the Court on the basis of EU immigration law. In line with the moment in time when relevant immigration provisions were introduced in EU law, these cases all arose after 2003. Though relatively small in size in comparison to the overall volume of identified case law, proceedings on the basis of EU immigration law are making up an ever growing share of the CJEU's overall body of jurisprudence on family reunification. Nevertheless, the largest bulk of relevant Court decisions continues, to date, to relate to cases arising in the context of free movement law, 53 in total. Of the 53 cases on the basis of free movement legislation, 17 contained additional references to Treaty provisions on EU Citizenship. Additionally, three cases combined all three different legal bases (free movement, EU citizenship and immigration law). They were counted in each respective category. The dataset includes 58 proceedings that arose before the Luxembourg bench on the basis of the preliminary reference procedure. Eight cases were brought to the Court in the context of infringement actions, and one case concerned an action for annulment.

For the remainder of the analyses, a cut-off date of judgements rendered up until 1 June 2014 was adopted. On that basis, of the 67 cases identified, 53 were further reviewed to track the incidence and effects of precedent-based discourses. This cut-off date enabled safeguarding the analysis from repeated modifications to the quantitative structuring,

[3] With regard to the case law arising on the basis of infringement actions, the second selection criterion (involving at least one third-country national) was applied by including only those infringement proceedings that dealt either with the provisions of the Family Reunification Directive (of which the scope is restricted to third-country nationals), or related specifically to the incorrect application of free movement law provisions in situations involving third-country nationals.

elaborated on in Chap. 6, every time a new judgment was rendered. More importantly, in light of the theoretical expectation that the autonomy-enhancing value of precedents resides, principally, in its long-term, cumulative effects, definitive observations on the most recent precedent-based developments are hard to substantiate as long-term implications are yet to mature and settle in jurisprudence to come.

4.2.3 *Self-Citation Activity*

At a third and final level of analysis, information on self-citation practices within the collected case law was gathered. 'Self-citation practices' refer to instances where the Court cites its own prior rulings. Observations of such practices are used as indicators for the incidence of precedent-based reasoning. They are not, however, taken to correspond to the concept of precedents as such. That is, as will be emphasized in Chap. 6, the mere observation of self-citation does not give any information on the extent to which such a citation contributed to the Court's decision-making or of the discursive weight that it held. Observations of self-citation are therefore necessary but insufficient indicators of precedent-based reasoning. The actual precedent value of citations is taken to reside, not in their numerical incidence, but in the substance of the arguments that were being reinforced and the weight these arguments held in new proceedings (see similarly on the difference between citations and precedents, Stone Sweet, 2004; Jacob, 2014).

Information on self-citation practices can be obtained from within the CJEU's judgments. Although the Court has been reported to in the past sometimes make use of precedents by simply restating verbatim passages from earlier decisions without acknowledging their source—"as if by some remarkable coincidence a group of judges chose to express a proposition in exactly the same words" (Arnull, 1993, p. 252)—such practices of non-attribution are documented to have grown ever less prevalent over the years. At current, CJEU judges carefully refer to the earlier rulings that inform their decisions (Jacob, 2014). As a result, the analyst can retrieve the relevant citations from a judgement as he/she is reading through the text. Furthermore, the case information page on the Court's website (www.curia.eu) additionally, and conveniently, lists all references to prior rulings made for each judgment. The present study only takes account of self-citations to prior family reunification-related cases. In this manner the study's focus on precedent-based reasoning within family reunion immigration case law is preserved.

In order to control for the possibility that, in some of its earlier decisions on family reunification, the Court may have built on prior case law without referencing sources, additional efforts were made to cross-check observations for the rulings rendered during the time period 1974–2000 with content analyses of the judgments' texts. This did not result in additional observations of (non-attributed) self-citation. In all, for the 53 selected cases, 108 observations of self-citation to other cases within the record were identified. Chapters 6 and 7 engage further with the data collected on such self-citation practices and the analytical observations that can be derived on their basis.

References

Primary Sources

EU Law

Council Directive 2001/55/EC on Minimum Standards for giving Temporary Protection in the Event of a Mass Influx of Displaced Persons and on Measures promoting a Balance of Efforts between Member States in receiving such Persons and bearing the Consequences thereof [2001] O.J. L 212/12.

Council Directive 2003/86/EC on the Right to Family Reunification [2003] O.J. L 251/12.

Council Directive 2003/109/EC Concerning the Status of Third-Country Nationals Who are Long-term Residents [2003] O.J. L 16/44.

Council Directive 2009/50/EC the Conditions of Entry and Residence of Third-country Nationals for the Purposes of Highly Qualified Employment [2009] O.J. L 155/17.

Directive 2004/38/EC of the European Parliament and of the Council on the Right of Citizens of the Union and their Family Members to Move and Reside Freely Within the Territory of the Member States [2004] O.J. L 158/77.

Directive 2008/115/EC of the European Parliament and of the Council on Common Standards and Procedures in Member States for Returning Illegally Staying Third-Country Nationals [2008] O.J. L 348/98.

Directive 2011/95/EU of the European Parliament and of the Council on Standards for the Qualification of Third-country Nationals or Stateless Persons as Beneficiaries of International Protection, for a Uniform Status for Refugees or for Persons Eligible for Subsidiary Protection, and for the Content of the Protection Granted [2011] O.J. L 337/9.

Directive 2013/33/EU of the European Parliament and of the Council Laying Down Standards for the Reception of Applicants for International Protection [2013] O.J. L 180/96.
Regulation (EEC) No 15/61 of the Council on Initial Measures to Bring About Free Movement of Workers within the Community [1961] O.J. 57/1073.
Regulation (EEC) No 38/64 of the Council on the Freedom of Movement for Workers within the Community [1964] O.J. 64/965.
Regulation (EEC) No 1612/68 of the Council on Freedom of Movement for Workers within the Community [1968] O.J. 257.
Regulation (EU) No 604/2013 of the European Parliament and of the Council Establishing the Criteria and Mechanisms for Determining the Member State Responsible for Examining an Application for International Protection Lodged in one of the Member States by a Third-country National or a Stateless Person [2013] O.J. L 180/31.

EU Documents

Commission Proposal for a European Parliament and Council Directive on the right of citizens of the Union and their family members to move and reside freely within the territory of the Member States, COM (2001) 257 (final).
Commission Amended Proposal for a European Parliament and Council Directive on the right of citizens of the union and their family members to move and reside freely within the territory of the Member States, COM (2003) 199 (final).

CJEU Case Law

Case C-40/76 *Slavica Kermaschek v Bundesanstalt für Arbeit* [1976] ECR 1669.
Case C-35/82 *Elestina Esselina Christina Morson v State of the Netherlands and Head of the Plaatselijke Politie within the Meaning of the Vreemdelingenwet; Sweradjie Jhanjan v State of the Netherlands* [1982] ECR 3723.
Case C-94/84 *Office national de l'emploi v Joszef Deak* [1985] ECR 1873.
Case C-131/85 *Emir Gül v Regierungspräsident Düsseldorf* [1986] ECR 1573.
Case C-85/96 *María Martínez Sala v Freistaat Bayern* [1998] ECR I-2691.
Case C-189/00 *Urszula Ruhr v Bundesanstalt für Arbeit* [2001] ECR I-8225.

Other Sources

Eurostat. (2015). *Residence Permit Statistics.* Retrieved November 13, 2015, from http://ec.europa.eu/eurostat/statistics-explained/index.php/Residence_permits_statistics
Eurostat. (2017). *Residence Permit Statistics.* Retrieved December 28, 2017, from http://ec.europa.eu/eurostat/statistics-explained/index.php/Residence_permits_statistics

Literature

Arnull, A. (1993). Owning up to Fallibility: Precedent and the Court of Justice. *Common Market Law Review, 30*(2), 247–266.

Barrett, G. (2003). Family Matters: European Community Law and Third-Country Family Members. *Common Market Law Review, 40*(2), 369–421.

Block, L. (2015). Regulating Membership: Explaining Restriction and Stratification of Family Migration in Europe. *Journal of Family Issues, 36*(11), 1433–1452.

Carens, J. (2003). Who Should Get in? The Ethics of Immigration Admissions. *Ethics & International Affairs, 17*(1), 95–110.

Carruba, C. (2005). Courts and Compliance in International Regulatory Regimes. *The Journal of Politics, 67*(3), 669–689.

Carruba, J., Gabel, M., & Hankla, C. (2012). Understanding the Role of the European Court of Justice in European Integration. *American Political Science Review, 106*(1), 214–223.

Cholewinski, R. (2002). Family Reunification and Conditions Placed on Family Members: Dismantling a Fundamental Human Right. *European Journal of Migration and Law, 4*(3), 271–290.

Costello, C. (2014). Article 33—Family and Professional Life. In S. Peers, T. Hervey, J. Kenner, & A. Ward (Eds.), *The EU Charter of Fundamental Rights: A Commentary* (pp. 891–925). Oxford: Hart Publishing.

Eisele, K. (2014). *The External Dimension of the EU's Migration Policy. Different Legal Positions of Third-Country Nationals in the EU: A Comparative Perspective.* Leiden: Martinus Nijhoff Publishers.

Fetzer, J. (2012). Public Opinion and Populism. In M. Rosenblum & D. Tichenor (Eds.), *The Oxford Handbook of the Politics of International Migration* (pp. 301–323). Oxford: Oxford University Press.

Freeman, P., Hansen, R., & Leal, D. (2013). *Immigration and Public Opinion in Liberal Democracies.* New York: Routledge.

Garrett, G. (1992). International Cooperation and Institutional Choice: The European Community's Internal Market. *International Organization, 46*(2), 533–560.

Garrett, G., Kelemen, R. D., & Schulz, H. (1998). The European Court of Justice, National Governments, and Legal Integration in the European Union. *International Organization, 52*(1), 149–176.

Geddes, A. (2003). *The Politics of Migration and Immigration in Europe.* London: SAGE Publications.

George, A., & Bennett, A. (2005). *Case Studies and Theory Development in the Social Sciences.* Cambridge, MA: MIT Press.

Gerring, J. (2007). *Case Study Research: Principles and Practices.* Cambridge: Cambridge University Press.

Groenendijk, K. (2009). Forty Years of Free Movement of Workers: Has It Been A Success and Why? In P. Minderhoud & N. Trimikliniotis (Eds.), *Rethinking the Free Movement of Workers: The European Challenges Ahead* (pp. 11–23). Nijmegen: Wolf Legal Publishers.

Guild, E. (2009). Free Movement of Workers: From Third Country National to Citizen of the Union. In P. Minderhoud & N. Trimikliniotis (Eds.), *Rethinking the Free Movement of Workers: The European Challenges Ahead* (pp. 25–38). Nijmegen: Wolf Legal Publishers.

Guild, E., Peers, S., & Tomkin, J. (2014). *The EU Citizenship Directive: A Commentary*. Oxford: Oxford University Press.

Jacob, M. (2014). *Precedents and Case-based Reasoning in the European Court of Justice: Unfinished Business*. New York: Cambridge University Press.

Joppke, C. (1998a). Immigration Challenges the Nation-State. In C. Joppke (Ed.), *Challenge to the Nation-State: Immigration in Western Europe and the United States* (pp. 5–48). New York: Oxford University Press.

Joppke, C. (1998b). Why Liberal States Accept Unwanted Immigration. *World Politics, 50*(2), 266–293.

Joppke, C. (1999). *Immigration and the Nation-State. The United States, Germany and Great Britain*. Oxford: Oxford University Press.

Lahav, G. (1997). International Versus National Constraints in Family-Reunification Migration Policy. *Global Governance, 3*(3), 349–372.

Levy, J. (2008). Case Studies: Types, Designs and Logics of Inference. *Conflict Management and Peace Science, 25*(1), 1–18.

Messina, A. (2007). *The Logics and Politics of Post-WWII Immigration to Western Europe*. Cambridge: Cambridge University Press.

Peers, S. (2011). *EU Justice and Home Affairs Law*. Oxford: Oxford University Press.

Schweitzer, R. (2015). A Stratified Right to Family Life? On the Logic (s) and Legitimacy of Granting Differential Access to Family Reunification for Third-Country Nationals Living within the EU. *Journal of Ethnic and Migration Studies, 41*(13), 2130–2148.

Shaw, J. (2011). Concluding Thoughts—Rottmann in Context. In J. Shaw (Ed.), *Has the European Court of Justice Challenged Member State Sovereignty in Nationality Law?* EUI Working Paper, RSCAS, 2011/62. Florence: European University Institute.

Spaventa, E. (2008). Seeing the Wood Despite the Trees? On the Scope of Union Citizenship and its Constitutional Effects. *Common Market Law Review, 45*, 13–45.

Stalford, H. (2012). *Children and the European Union: Rights, Welfare and Accountability*. London: Hart Publishing.

Stalford, H. (2015). The CRC in Litigation Under EU Law. In T. Liefaard & J. Doek (Eds.), *Litigating the Rights of the Child: The UN Convention on the Rights of the Child in Domestic and International Jurisprudence* (pp. 211–230). Dordrecht: Springer.

Staver, A. (2013). Free Movement and the Fragmentation of Family Reunification Rights. *European Journal of Migration and Law, 15*, 69–89.

Stone Sweet, A. (2004). *The Judicial Construction of Europe*. Oxford: Oxford University Press.

Strik, T. (2011). *Besluitvorming over asiel- en migratierichtlijnen. De wisselwerking tussen nationaal en Europees niveau*. Den Haag: Boom Juridische uitgevers.

Tomkin, J. (2009). The Worker, The Citizen, Their Families and the Court of Justice: Tales of Free Movement from Luxembourg. In P. Minderhoud & N. Trimikliniotis (Eds.), *Rethinking the Free Movement of Workers: The European Challenges Ahead* (pp. 39–59). Nijmegen: Wolf Legal Publishers.

Tryfonidou, A. (2009). Family Reunification Rights of (Migrant) Union Citizens: Towards a More Liberal Approach. *European Law Journal, 15*(5), 634–653.

Van Elsuwege, P., & Kochenov, D. (2011). On the Limits of Judicial Intervention: EU Citizenship and Family Reunification Rights. *European Journal of Migration and Law, 13*(4), 443–466.

Walter, A. (2008). *Reverse Discrimination and Family Reunification*. Nijmegen: Wolf Legal Publishers.

CHAPTER 5

Identifying Member States' Interests

5.1 Identifying Member States' Interests: A Benchmark for Judicial Autonomy

This first analytical chapter sets out to review Member States' interests in the area of EU family reunification law. For this purpose, the drafting of the relevant EU legal instruments is scrutinized with the aim of mapping the preferences and interest-led demands voiced by different Member States. The findings in this regard serve as an *ex ante* benchmark against which the workings and effects of precedent-based reasoning are examined in the two subsequent analytical sections (Chaps. 6 and 7). More specifically, by charting Member States' preference articulation during the drafting of the provisions which, at a later stage, emerged before the CJEU, the chapter's findings serve as a yardstick against which to assess whether precedent-based reasoning strengthened the CJEU's ability to develop its jurisprudence independent of the identified political preferences. In other words, whether precedent-based reasoning strengthened the Court's judicial autonomy in this area.

Without such a prior, *ex ante* benchmark, observations of what at first sight could appear to be autonomous, Member State-sanctioning judgments would not be able to control for the problem of observational equivalence registered in earlier judicial politics studies (*cf.* Chap. 2). To recap, the problem of observational equivalence relates to the difficulty of

M. De Somer, *Precedents and Judicial Politics in EU Immigration Law*, European Administrative Governance,
https://doi.org/10.1007/978-3-319-93982-7_5

empirically distinguishing scenarios in which the Court acts autonomously from those in which, conversely, it is constrained by the preferences of Member States but rationally adapts its behaviour beforehand so that no political antagonism or retaliation measures will appear. Following these anticipation logics, the Court may pronounce adverse rulings but it will only do so when it expects that these rulings will not provoke too strong a political backlash, for instance, because the rulings are actually in line with Member States' broader policy preferences (*e.g.*, having a functioning common market) or because they steer clear from touching on issues central to Member States' political concerns (see Garrett, 1992; Garrett & Weingast, 1993; or, later, Carruba, 2005; Carruba, Gabel, & Hankla, 2008). Consequently, following the invocation of such anticipation logics, observations of CJEU rulings that sanction Member States cannot discriminate between opposing perspectives as they could be consistent with scenarios of both Court autonomy as well as Member State control, albeit for different reasons.

The method that is most commonly used to gain leverage on this observational equivalence problem consists of evaluating Member States interests as articulated in written observations that governments submit to Luxembourg prior to the rulings. The positions recorded in such written observations can then, at a later stage, be compared with the Court's final disposition of the case so as to evaluate whether the Court stayed close to the articulated preferences or, instead, developed its decisions independent from these preferences. Since Stein's (1981) first operationalisation of this method, a number of authors have followed suit (Cichowski, 1998, 2004, 2007; Carruba et al., 2008; Carruba, Gabel, & Hankla, 2012; Stone Sweet & Brunell, 2012; see Chap. 2). Such benchmarking on the basis of written observations is not without problems however. A number of difficulties can be highlighted.

First, and most importantly, written observations submitted to Luxembourg are usually too low in number (ranging from one or two, to maximum a dozen) as well as too unevenly spread across Member States to be considered a representative sample of the interests held by national governments across the Union (see for figures, Granger, 2004). In addition, interest measures based on written observations also have difficulties controlling for differences in the political weight held by different Member States within the Union's decision-making processes (so as to assess the level of control through political threats of, for instance, legislative override, that different Member States can exert). Earlier attempts at weighting

Member States' observations according to national vote shares in the Council have been the source of academic controversies as different authors advanced different strategies on how to most accurately provide for such weighting, or held different views on the added value of weighting written observations in the first place (Carruba et al., 2008, 2012; Stone Sweet & Brunell, 2012). As a third problem, it is difficult to join the perspective that written observations provide an accurate representation of Member States' interests with the study's theoretical expectation—built on the works of Burley and Mattli (1993) and McCown (2003)—that when submitting their written observations, Member States care first and foremost about presenting their arguments in a manner that maximizes their chances of winning the dispute at hand. To that purpose, and as also registered in earlier studies, Member States are expected to take strategic argumentative cues from earlier Court decisions, even from decisions to which they were opposed, if this strengthens the effectiveness of their claims in the new case at hand (*cf.* Chap. 3).

In light of the above, the present study's alternative, negotiations-based benchmark offers a number of advantages. To begin with, and starting with the third problem identified, as Member States are not operating in the context of Court proceedings, the negotiations-based strategy does not suffer from the problem that the preferences articulated by governments may be tied to short-term strategic incentives that are specific to the proceedings at hand. Second, to the extent that drafting processes taking place within the Council provide, by definition, for a context within which Member States operate collectively, debating with one another or building strategic coalitions to get their preferences across (including through log-rolling processes), the negotiations-based benchmarking method inherently controls for the fact that some governments may bring a stronger political weight to the (Council) table compared to others. Third, and in connection to the preceding point, to the extent that the stock-taking of Member States' interests is inherently reflective of a collective enterprise, the negotiations-based method also alleviates concerns connected to the representativeness of the written observations benchmark, or the ability of written observations to speak for the interests held by governments as a whole.

In order to map Member States' interests as voiced during negotiations, the below analysis draws principally on primary documents from the EU's legislative institutions: the Commission, Council and European Parliament (EP). The relevant primary documents were retrieved online through the Council register, the eur-lex database, and the European Parliament Legislative Observatory. In instances where documents were not available online, requests for access were lodged and granted through the channels indicated on the respective websites. In addition, further indications were taken from relevant secondary literature (particularly, Goedings, 2006; Peers & Rogers, 2006; Strik, 2011). Taking cues from these and other works, specific attention went out to charting the debates that surrounded the delineation of the legislation's 'personal scope', that is, the debates on the provisions governing which categories of persons would be covered by the new rules. As observed in the literature, this is where generally the largest bones of political contention, and hence, the strongest interest articulations are located.

The analysis first reviews the drafting processes in the framework of EU free movement law and then considers the negotiations in the context of EU immigration law. Specific attention has gone out to examining the negotiations leading up to the two main instruments in each of these two legal frameworks. That is, for free movement law, the Citizenship Directive (2004/38/EC) and for immigration law, the Family Reunification Directive (2003/86/EC). The discussion on each of these instruments is preceded by a review of prior law-making developments. In this manner, the analysis is able to trace the long-term development of dominant preferences. On account of the generally more contested nature of the Commission's proposal for a Family Reunification Directive, negotiations proved to be more difficult and were, for that reason, also more time consuming. Whereas the discussion of the Citizenship Directive is subdivided into four distinct drafting stages, the analyses on the Family Reunification Directive take up six subsections. The chapter concludes by retracing the findings and mapping the dominant trends in Member States' preference articulation. These findings provide the benchmarking background against which the judicial review processes on this legislation are assessed in the analytical sections that follow.

5.2 Drafting Family Reunion Rights under Free Movement Law

5.2.1 *The Early Instruments*

From the very beginning, questions on family reunion rights granted to moving Community nationals were amongst the "most hotly debated provisions" of the first free movement instruments established in the early 1960s (Regulation 15/61/EEC; Goedings, 2006, pp. 162–164). As documented by Goedings, although not originally foreseen within the Community's founding treaties, broad consensus existed around the rationale that in the absence of clauses allowing for workers' family unity to be preserved, the enjoyment of free movement rights would be seriously obstructed. Nevertheless, Germany, France and the three Benelux countries (together, a large majority of the six Member States represented at the negotiation table at the time) were careful to strictly delineate which relatives would be considered as workers' family members so as to "avoid an unwanted expansion (…) to a large circle of family members" (Ibid.). Accordingly, whereas the original Commission proposal had left the categorization of family members undefined, objections thereto by the five labour-receiving states resulted in a restriction of the personal scope of the family reunion provisos to cover spouses and children underage only.

Similar scope-restricting dynamics also characterized the drafting stages of the subsequent free movement instruments. Where, in the context of drafting Regulation 38/64/EEC, the Commission sought to extend the family circle permitted to join the moving worker to all family members economically dependent on him or her, opposition stemming from national capitals led to a watering down of this provision to the dependent family members in the first degree only (i.e., spouse, children, parents) (Ibid., p. 220). An additional Commission suggestion to abolish the conditions on the possession of suitable housing, as inserted in the first 1961 regulation, was deemed "unacceptable". Delegations particularly voiced fears around the possibility that, in the absence of such a conditional requirement, slum dwellings could develop as moving workers would accept any kind of lodgings to bring their families in (Ibid., pp. 245–246).

During the drafting stages of the third and final regulation in the context of these early instruments (Regulation 1612/68/EEC), the Commission, backed by the, at the time, immigration-sending Italian state, made another attempt at removing the lodging requirements. Again, however, similarly strong opposition was voiced by the labour-receiving Northern European states and the option was eventually shelved. In response to the political abandonment of this possibility, Italy proposed to insert a definition of 'suitable lodgings' as it feared that in the absence of such a definition this requirement could create "ample opportunities for national authorities to restrict family migration". However, when the other parties, in reply, put forward a number of strong demands in relation to 'suitability', Italy dropped its request and the matter was abandoned. The other states in any case "desired to leave all authority in these matters in the hands of national administrations" (Ibid., pp. 244–247).

These earliest instruments, and in particular the final 1968 Regulation, firmly established the ground rules of family reunion clauses in free movement law to come, including the personal scope delineations thereof. In essence, save for some modifications in the context of supplementary instruments adopted over time to cover additional types of cross-border movements,[1] the structure provided by Regulation 1612/68 was to remain consistent and provide the basis for the drafting of the Citizenship Directive more than three decades later (Guild, Peers, & Tomkin, 2014). With this new instrument, the Union's legislature sought to consolidate and streamline what had over the years grown into a hotchpotch of different, but essentially parallel-running legal regimes on different types of free movement situations.

5.2.2 *The Citizenship Directive*

Much like the drafting stages of the 1960s legislation, one of the key targets of polemics that marked this consolidation exercise related to the delineation of which individuals could lay claim to the family reunion rights to be established. Across the board, the Commission, backed by the European Parliament, aimed to address what was increasingly perceived as an overly rigid and outdated demarcation of family relations. In general terms, where Regulation 1612/68's scope designation—which covered

[1] Regulation 1251/70/EEC on the right of workers to remain in the territory of a Member State after having been employed in that State, Directive 73/148/EEC on the free movement rights of self-employed persons and persons providing or receiving services, Directive 75/34/EEC on the right to remain after having pursued a self-employed activity, Directive 90/364/EEC on free movement rights for self-sufficient persons, Directive 90/365/EEC on free movement rights for pensioners, and Directive 93/96/EEC on free movement rights for students.

only spouses and minor children—had possibly been reflective of the social realities of the 1960s when families were commonly made up of a male breadwinner, a wife in charge of the household and several children, such a scope delineation was perceived as no longer representative of modern family life realities. Most centrally, the earlier framing was viewed as unable to capture the changed and more dynamic patterns of present-day family relations marked by growing divorce rates, increased labour market participation by women, same-sex relations, unmarried couples, etc. (Ibid., p. 16). However, as observed by Guild and others, "an inevitable tension" reined between "the degree of recognition to afford to newer forms of family relationships" and, from the perspective of Member States, "the impact of the Directive on the control of immigration" (Ibid.). During the negotiations, national delegations represented in the Council, provided a strong and persistent counterweight to the Commission's legislative attempts at establishing broader and more flexible personal scope designations.

5.2.2.1 *The First Commission Proposal*

In its first proposal, the Commission envisaged "broadening the definition of family member" (COM (2001) 257). This aim was presented as flowing from the observation that the "family group has been recently undergoing rapid change and more and more people, often with children are forming de facto couples", and that "Community law cannot ignore this development" (Ibid., pp. 4–5). The 'broadening' was provided for, first, by setting out that unmarried partners were to be treated as equivalent to spouses for the purposes of falling within the Directive's scope. In addition, the Directive's personal scope would also include the descendants of spouses or partners, "even if they are not minors or dependent", as well as the parents of spouses or partners, "whether or not they are dependent" (Ibid., p. 8). Moreover, "any other family members" who were not covered by the definitions but who "in the country from which they have come, are dependents or members of the household of the Union citizen" were to have their entry and residence "facilitated". The relevant provisions in these regards were laid down in Article 2.2 (for core family members) and Article 3.2 (for additional family members whose entry was to be facilitated). These provisions were to apply "across the board" so as to do away with earlier distinctions in regard of, most notably, moving students whose family reunion rights had previously been subject to more restrictive rules. Furthermore, the Commission also provided, in Articles

12 and 13, for family members to retain a right of residence in the host state in the event of a marriage breakdown, or upon the death of the sponsoring Union citizen. This right to remain was made subject to conditions of financial self-sufficiency (through either employment or personal means).

5.2.2.2 European Parliament Opinion and Second Commission Proposal

The Commission's scope-broadening efforts received strong support in the European Parliament. In its first reading of the Commission's proposal (pursuant to the co-decision procedure), the EP even took them a step further. As set out in the explanatory memorandum accompanying this first reading, the EP's rapporteur, whilst wholeheartedly endorsing the Commission's approach, nevertheless deemed it necessary to table a number of amendments aimed at making some passages more consistent and "comprehensive". Among the "main policy issues" targeted by these considerations were the definitions of family members, considered a "crucial aspect" as it conditioned the Directive's scope (European Parliament, A5-0009/2003, pp. 53–54). The Parliament suggested, to begin with, to specifically set out that spouses or partners would be able to join the moving EU citizen "irrespective of sex", so as to expressly cover same-sex relationships. In this manner, the EP stated, the proposed legislation would more adequately "reflect and respect the diversity of family relationships in today's society" (Amendments 14 to 16, A5-0009/2003). Furthermore, in relation to additional family members whose entry was to be 'facilitated' (Article 3.2), the EP suggested to relax the dependency requirement in cases "where there are serious health or humanitarian grounds for doing so" (Ibid., Amendment 20). Finally, in regard of Articles 12 and 13, setting out family members' right to remain in the event of death or relationship breakdown, the EP deleted some of the more specific provisions so as to allow for an overall broader scope delineation. It also sought to relax the requirements accompanying this right. For example, in the event of relationship cessation, the EP proposed that the requirement for the relationship to have existed at least five years, including one in the host Member State, was reduced to a two-year timeframe (Ibid., Amendments 42 to 54).

In turn, in its second revised proposal, the Commission accepted the EP's references to "humanitarian or health grounds" in Article 3.2, and maintained a number of the amendments to Articles 12 and 13 (including the reduction from a five to a two years previous relationship for the purposes of retaining residence rights). The Commission however objected to the addition that spouses and partners could join "irrespective of sex". This, the Commission felt, would result in an "imposition on certain Member States of amendments to family law legislation" which fell outside of the Community's legislative jurisdiction (COM (2003) 199, p. 3; pp. 10–11). It had in the meantime also become clear from parallel-running Council discussions that the introduction of such a clause would meet with strong political objections.

5.2.2.3 Council Readings

Contrary to the proposal's positive reception within the EP, in the Council circles the Commission's propositions met with a highly unfavourable, even hostile political climate. In general terms, the scope-broadening ambitions of the Commission (and the EP) collided with Member States' protectionist urges in respect of their immigration control competences. Throughout the different Council discussions questions on the definitions of 'family members' were consistently framed as "key", "important", "major", or "sensitive" (see e.g., Council Documents 8675/03; 12585/03; 12218/03). They triggered considerable polemics and generated extensive debates at the different Council levels. National delegations especially found common rallying points in those suggestions that aimed to delineate such definitions more strictly.

To begin with, the Council refused to extend the Directive's personal scope to cover children or ascending relatives without age or dependency requirements. Instead, and referring to a desire to retain the "existing acquis" on core family members, Member States agreed, by unanimous vote, to restore the condition that joining children were to be 'below the age of 21' or 'dependant', and similarly added the adjective 'dependent' to the definition of accompanying relatives in the ascending line (Council Common Position (EC) No 6/2004; European Commission, SEC/2003/1293). Already during the very first stages of the Council readings, these provisions on the definition of joining children and parents had triggered considerable anxiety amongst national delegations (Council Document 10572/02). In total, no less than 14 out of the, at the time, 15 Member State delegations voiced reservations on the broadening of the legislation's scope in regard of such first-degree relatives, referring, amongst others, to the "financial consequences which could result for the host MS" (Ibid., p. 12). Denmark, which held the Council Presidency in the second half of 2002, together with 'some other delegations', even suggested to move beyond simply restoring the existing status quo by attaching new, supplementary requirements to the definitions of family members. To that effect, Member States' representatives were urged to examine whether "the age limit for descendants and the dependency condition for descendants and relatives in the ascending line be maintained as in the present acquis", or whether instead "the possibilities of raising the age limit and of broadening the concept of dependency" should be explored (Council Document, 13298/02, p. 5; Council Document, 13942/02). Eventually however, the Danish delegation did not manage to secure sufficient support for such a retrograde step amongst its counterparts (Council Document 8675/03; Council Document, 13263/03).

Similar contention also surrounded the EP's proposition to expressly include same-sex relations in the legislation's scope. As the Commission dropped this provision in its second, 2003 proposal however (COM (2003) 199), Council debates on this matter were, in parallel, discontinued from that point in time. Additionally, Council debates also resulted in the abandonment of the obligation to admit partners with whom the moving citizen had an 'attested durable relationship'. Instead, the provisions on the partner with whom the Union citizen has a durable relationship, "duly attested", were lifted out of the definitions on core family members (Article 2.2.) to instead become governed by the provisions on additional family members whose entry and residence was merely to be 'facilitated' (Article 3.2.).

Generally speaking, these provisions on core relatives, after having passed through the machinery of the different Council bodies, came out bearing a closer resemblance to the original framing of the 1960s rather than to the updated version presented by the Commission and endorsed by the EP. In essence, the relevant definitions were effectively re-reduced to cover only: (i) direct descendants under the age of 21 or dependant on the citizen, (ii) dependent direct relatives in the ascending line, (iii) spouses, and, as the single new category (iv) "registered partners". This latter category however was only covered to the extent that the legislation of the host Member State treated registered partnerships "as equivalent to married couples" (Council, (EC) No 6/2004).

Aside from the definitions of core relatives, Council discussions also targeted the provisions governing 'additional family members' whose entry and residence Member States were to 'facilitate' (Article 3.2.). Besides adding the category of partners with whom the Union citizen was in an attested durable relation to these provisions (as a result of the objections to treating such partners as core family members), Member States also tabled a number of requests to modify the precise wording of the relevant clauses. More precisely, Denmark, as well as Spain, Austria and Ireland, wanted to see the phrasing "Member States shall" replaced by the more permissive formulation "Member States may". This, with a view to making the already flexible 'facilitation' of the admission of such additional family members optional instead of mandatory and, accordingly, maximize the room for national policy manoeuvre that would be retained in respect of such family members (Council Document 12585/03, p. 15). In addition, the EP's introduction of a further clause obliging Member States to also facilitate the entry of extended family members when there are serious "health" or "humanitarian grounds" for doing so, was narrowed down to covering health concerns only (Council (EC) No 6/2004). The reference to humanitarian considerations had been considered "too broad a concept" and, on those grounds, "open to abuse" (Commission, SEC/2003/1293). Furthermore, a new recital was added to the Directive's preamble which aimed at "clarifying the notion of facilitation" so as to contain its effects (Council (EC) No 6/2004, statement of reasons). This new recital specified that the situations of extended family members who are not included in the Directive's definition and "who therefore do not enjoy an automatic right of entry and residence in the host Member State", "should be examined by the host Member State on the basis of its own national legislation, in order to decide whether entry and residence could be granted to such persons" (Recital 6, Council (EC) No 6/2004). The recital had specifically been added to address concerns around an overly lenient scope delineation in respect of extended family members that had been voiced by Greece, Spain, Denmark, the Netherlands and Austria (Council Document 6147/03; Council Document, 12585/03). In addition, in search of still further semantic precision, the UK delegation suggested to add two further requirements to the grounds governing qualification to the status of "additional family members". First, the UK proposed to introduce a condition of having lived together for at least one year in the last country of origin before family members would enjoy a right of 'facilitated' entry. Second, it wanted to further, and more clearly spell out that these provisions only applied in relation to those family units of which the sponsoring Union citizen was the "head of household" (Council Document, 6147/03, p. 12). These additional requirements did not find their way into the final, common Council position however. Likely, the Council members took account of the forewarning of a Commission representative who pointed out during the discussions that the UK's proposals would imply a "backwards step compared with existing law" (Ibid.).

A third focus of political concern related to family members' right to remain in the event of a family breakdown (Articles 12 and 13). During the discussions, Member States worked hard to introduce further requirements in relation to, specifically, family members with a third-country nationality. To begin with, in order to retain a right of residence in the event of death or departure of the sponsoring Union citizen (Article 12), such family members (but not family members with the nationality of a Member State) were required to have been resident for at least one year in the host Member State prior to the Union citizen's passing. This additional stipulation was added with the stated purpose of giving substance to "the justified concerns of delegations to prevent abuse" (Council (EC) No 6/2004). In addition, the grounds for retaining a right of residence in the event of a separation between the Union citizen and his/her partner were also modified so as to re-extend the required timeframe during which the relationship had lasted to three years (instead of two as the EP had suggested). Again, this modification had been introduced with the stated purpose of 'limiting abuses' (Council (EC) No 6/2004).

Finally, following a proposal that had been tabled by the German delegation, the Council also quashed the Commission's goal of providing for a personal scope definition that would apply "across the board" by restricting the family reunion rights granted to moving students. Referring, again, to a wish to retain the 'existing *acquis*', the family members covered in respect of students were limited to the student's spouse or registered partner and dependent children (excluding, hence, family reunification possibilities with ascending relatives) (Ibid.; Council Document, 12538/03).

5.2.2.4 *The Final Text*

In response, the Commission accepted the personal scope circumscriptions that were introduced or restored by the Council. In its communication on this decision it observed that these amendments rendered the proposed text "less ambitious". Nevertheless, as it indicated, it considered the Council position to strike a fair balance between, on the one hand, its own efforts at making "steps forward in terms of freedom of movement" and on the other, "the imposition of changes to the national law"

(Commission, SEC/2003/1293). Specifically in relation to the Council's decision to reintroduce age and dependency requirements for joining children and parents, the Commission brought into focus that these amendments had received unanimous support from all delegations. This, whereas Council decision-making on the proposal otherwise was governed by qualified majority voting (QMV). This unanimous vote will likely have been considered a strong signal that there was little political will from the part of Member States to compromise on this point, and accordingly little legislative room for manoeuvre left at the Commission's disposal. The EP, in turn, followed the Commission's lead in its second reading (European Parliament, P5_TA(2004) 0160). Accordingly, in that manner Member States' restrictionist, scope-limiting urges found their way into the Citizenship Directive's final text as adopted on 29 April 2004. As an end note it can be pointed out that a strong sense of political urgency surrounded these final stages as the following Monday (1 May 2004) 10 new Member States were to accede to the Union (including to its decision-making bodies) and EP elections were scheduled to be held one month later (June 2004).

5.3 Drafting Family Reunion Rights under EU Immigration Law

5.3.1 *Preceding Legislative Efforts*

The very first attempts at communitarising family reunion immigration policies can be traced back to the early 1990s. In 1993 governments adopted a soft-law "Resolution on the harmonization of national policies on family reunification" (SN 2828/1/93). This very first instrument had however been adopted on a purely intergovernmental basis and contained, in contrast to what its title suggested, no true harmonisation efforts (Peers, 1998; Guild & Niessen, 1996, chap. 9). Common rules had been set out only in regard of those measures that already constituted shared ground across the different Member States. By contrast, in regard of the more sensitive policy questions on which governments' positions diverged—notably, the precise definition of children being granted a right to join and rights for extended family members—Member States were left with a large margin of regulatory discretion. More precisely, in respect of such family members, the Resolution only provided for options as opposed to legal obligations (typically indicated through 'may' instead of 'shall' clauses). As a result, the instrument's personal scope remained, overall, highly circumscribed (Hedemann-Robinson, 1996).

Four years later, in 1997, a second effort was made as the Commission put forward a proposal for a single, umbrella instrument that would cover all policies related to the "admission of third-country nationals" (COM (97) 387). This comprehensive instrument would take on the format of a non-binding Convention. As was acknowledged at the outset however, the non-binding legal status would only be temporary. The Commission's medium-term goal was to change the instrument into a Community law version once the Amsterdam Treaty (already agreed on at the time), would enter into force and, with it, decision-making on immigration would be lifted out of the third intergovernmental pillar into the first, Community pillar (Ibid.; Hedemann-Robinson, 1998). The draft Convention, hence, served mostly as a familiarization exercise designed to test the political water. Amongst its key provisions, the Convention featured a wide-ranging set of common rules on family reunion immigration. As soon became clear however, this ambitious all-in-one approach proved to be politically unfeasible (see e.g., Council documents 6488/98 add. 1 and 6488/98 add. 2). After a year of intensive discussions in the Council, the then Austrian presidency observed that Member States had not reached agreement 'on any of the draft Convention's provisions' (Peers, 1998). As a result, the proposal, and with it, the Commission's aspiration to bring all immigration rules under one legal umbrella, was abandoned.

5.3.2 *The Family Reunification Directive*

In spite of their limited legal scope and effects, these two legislative texts (the 1993 Resolution and the draft Convention) were nonetheless to provide core orientation points for the Commission's first proposal for a Directive on Family Reunification as presented in December 1999. Additional impetus was provided by the conclusions of the Tampere European Council Summit held in October 1999 which called for "an approximation" of the "legal status of third country nationals to that of Member States' nationals" (Tampere European Council, Presidency Conclusions). In connection to this call, inspiration was also taken from the family reunion rights already in place in the context of preceding free movement law instruments. As indicated in the explanatory memorandum to the first proposal, these three materials together (the preceding legislative attempts, the Tampere Council conclusions, and existing free movement law) formed the backdrop to the Commission's efforts at framing, separately this time, a set of common EU rules on family reunification.

5.3.2.1 The First Commission Proposal

The first Commission proposal, pursuant to its first article, set out to establish "a right to family reunification". This right was to accrue both to "third-country nationals residing lawfully in the territory of the Member States", as well as to "citizens of the Union who do not exercise their right to free movement", in other words, to 'static' EU nationals (COM (1999) 638). As outlined in the proposal's preamble, the proposed family reunion rights were to be adopted "in conformity with the obligation to protect the family and respect family life" as laid down in "a variety of international legal instruments" (Ibid., recital 2). Furthermore, these rights were proclaimed as necessary for "making family life possible", as well as needed in order to "ensure protection of the family and the preservation or formation of family life" (Ibid., recitals 6 and 7).

In terms of the more detailed substantive rights, pursuant to the proposal's Article 4, the family reunification rights of Union citizens not exercising their right to free movement, i.e., static EU citizens, were to be governed by the rules set out in the context of free movement law. At the time, that is, prior to the adoption of the Citizenship Directive, this related most notably to Regulation18925189 1612/68 which the proposal also explicitly referred to. Lawfully resident third-country nationals, on the other hand, were provided with a distinct set of rights to family reunion that differed to greater or lesser extents from those in place in free movement law. The listing of these rights and conditions for third-country nationals took up the main part of the proposal's text.

First, in terms of the categories of third-country nationals who could qualify as 'sponsors' for the purposes of family reunion, the proposal referred to any third-country national "residing lawfully in a Member State and holding a residence permit issued by that Member State for a period of at least one year". As clarified in the accompanying explanatory memorandum, 'residence permits' had purposefully been set out in "broad terms" so that the new legislation would "include all categories of applicant (…) irrespective of the reasons for their residence" (Ibid., p. 12). In addition, the proposal also explicitly applied to the situations of refugees and persons granted a subsidiary protection status with the additional specification that the first category was excluded from the minimum one-year residence right requirement (Ibid., Article 3).

Family members, included, first, the applicant's spouse, or his/her 'unmarried partner' where the legislation of the host Member State treated the situation of unmarried couples equivalent to that of married couples (Article 5). As specified in the explanatory memorandum, unmarried partners could be "of the same sex" as the sponsor (Ibid., p. 14). In addition, the proposal's Article 5 also listed: the minor, unmarried children of the applicant or his spouse or unmarried partner, dependent relatives in the ascending line of either the applicant or his/her spouse or partner, and adult children unable to satisfy their own needs on account of health reasons. Additionally, the proposal's Article 2 established that "family reunification" referred to "the entry into, and residence in a Member State by family members (…) in order to *form* or *preserve* the family unit, whether the family relationship arose *before* or *after* the resident's entry" (Ibid., emphasis added). In other words, the draft Directive also applied to situations of family 'formation', that is, it also allowed reunion with family members with whom family relationships were established only after the sponsor's entry.

As conditional requirements, Member States could ask the applicant-sponsor for proof that he/she possessed: (i) adequate accommodation, (ii) sickness insurance for himself and his/her family members, and (iii) stable and sufficient financial resources (Article 9). In regard of this last criterion, further specifications established that Member States could not set the bar of such 'sufficient resources' higher than the amount considered as the minimum income for the purposes of receiving social assistance (or in the absence of such provisions in national law, the minimum retirement pension). As explained in the accompanying memorandum, the Commission had paid special attention to defining the above criteria "strictly" so as to avoid overly broad interpretations of these conditions that would "render the right to family reunification nugatory" (Ibid., p. 18). In addition, the proposal also provided Member States with a possibility to set a waiting period before granting family members leave to enter. This waiting period could not exceed one year however (Article 10). Finally, as indicated in each of the relevant provisos, persons with a refugee or subsidiary protection status were exempt from having to fulfil the conditional requirements and no waiting periods could be imposed in their respect.

The proposal further established that family members were to be granted a residence permit of the same duration as that held by the sponsor. In addition, at the latest after four years of residence, core family members were to be granted such a permit on a personal, autonomous basis. Such core relatives were also to be provided with access to national labour markets and to vocational training schemes. In addition, all admitted family members (core relatives as well as extended family members) were to enjoy a right to access states' education systems in the same way as Union citizens (Articles 11, 12 and 13).

In its penultimate chapter (Chapter VI), the proposal set out the grounds on which penalties could be imposed (e.g., fraudulent applications, sham marriages), the limitations applying to such penalties (e.g., respect for the principle of proportionality), as well as the judicial redress procedures to be provided for. Article 15 inserted an additional horizontal requirement which obliged Member States to carry out a 'balancing' review in each individual case when considering to reject or withdraw a right to family reunion. The elements to be taken into account in such balancing reviews were listed as relating to 'the nature and solidity of the person's family relationships', 'the duration of his residence in the Member State' and 'the existence of family, cultural and social ties with his country of origin'. This list of elements, and more generally, the requirement to carry out individual, 'balancing' assessments in each case were reproduced from ECtHR case law on Article 8 ECHR. In connection, and as a final proviso that bears highlighting, the proposal's Article 7(5) set down that Member States, "when examining an application", were to have "due regard to the best interests of minor children".

5.3.2.2 *European Parliament Opinion and Second Commission Proposal*

Similar to the dynamics characterizing the drafting processes on the Citizenship Directive described above, the Commission's proposal generally found much support in the European Parliament. After a first, more conservative report had failed to secure sufficient backing in the Parliament's chambers, and pursuant to the consultation procedure (then Article 67 EC), the EP presented a broadly liberal opinion in the format of the "Watson Report" (after its rapporteur, Graham Watson) (A5-0201/2000). The 16 amendments put forward in this report sought, predominantly, to raise the protection standards embedded in the Commission's text.

The Commission, in turn, accepted a number, but not all of the EP's amendments in a second revised text (COM (2000) 624). With the aim of safeguarding the "political feasibility" of its proposal (see Strik, 2011, p. 67), it for instance rejected the EP's suggestion to broaden the concept of 'dependency' for the purposes of family reunion with ascending relatives. It also did not follow the Parliament's suggestion of introducing a general 'standstill', or 'non-regression' clause which would prohibit Member States from backtracking on any potentially more favourable standards provided for in domestic law once the Directive would be adopted. According to the memorandum accompanying the revised text, such a standstill clause would not be "compatible with the objective of aligning national legislation" (COM (2000) 624, p. 4). The Commission did accept, on the other hand, the one scope-narrowing suggestion made by the EP, that is, to exclude persons with a subsidiary protection status from the Directive's remit. This, on the grounds that a 'harmonised concept of subsidiary protection' was still absent from Community law (Ibid., p. 2).

5.3.2.3 *First Council Readings*

Similarly in line with the dynamics that characterized the drafting of the Citizenship Directive, the Commission proposal met with strong resistance in the Council. The level of political contestation provoked by the proposal arguably even surpassed the degree registered in the context of the Citizenship Directive. This can be seen, for one, in the sheer volume of Council discussions that were held on the Commission's propositions. Overall, these discussions would come to span seven Council presidencies and form the subject of numerous meetings at working group level, in SCIFA (the Strategic Committee on Immigration, Frontiers and Asylum manned by senior national officials), and at COREPER level; in addition to being discussed in four Justice and Home Affairs Councils and three European Council meetings (see also Strik, 2011, pp. 123–124).

Again, particularly those clauses outlining the proposed instrument's personal scope proved to be especially controversial. In fact, little to none of the Commission's initial stipulations on the categories of persons that would be governed by the Directive survived the Council discussions without contestation and without—consequently—adjustments. In addition, Council discussions also particularly targeted the legal provisions that enabled Member States to make the access to the instrument's remit conditional on meeting certain requirements. Deriving from the same ambition of limiting, as much as possible, the categories of individuals able to benefit from the Directive's rights, and—hence—the number of potential immigrants that would be able to lay claim to EU law protection, national delegations sought to either expand on the conditional requirements already foreseen within the Commission's proposal, or to introduce all together new ones.

The first stages of the Council discussions took off in 2000 under the Presidencies of first Portugal, and then France. These two presidencies headed a number of meetings at working party level and in the SCIFA which, above all, made clear that contention in fact surrounded "most of the proposed Articles" (Peers & Rogers, 2006, p. 581). To begin with, in respect of third-country national sponsors, the French Presidency reported early on that Council Members were not satisfied with 'a one-year residence permit' as the single criterion governing eligibility to the status of 'sponsor'. A number of Member States requested that, additionally, the "nature of" and "reason for" a third-country national's stay would be taken into account (Council Document 9738/00). To that purpose, and following a German suggestion, discussions were held with a view to adding a criterion which would require of third-country nationals that they had "a reasonable prospect of obtaining a long-term right of residence" (Council Document 11122/00; Council Document 11524/00, p. 5). The Commission representative attending these discussions immediately pointed out that such a criterion would be based on "a vague concept", "whose introduction could lead to a restriction on the scope of the Directive" (Ibid., p. 10). Nevertheless, the requirement found its way into the compromise lines that were adopted by the end of the French presidency. Other political bones of contention related to the definitions of joining family members, the framing of conditional requirements, and the one-year limit that the Commission had attached to the waiting period provision. Some issues were even so charged that they were put on hold as they "continued to divide delegations". They were projected to future meetings so that space was afforded to proceed, for the time being, on other matters. Amongst these especially contentious matters were, first, the application of the Directive to refugees and persons with a subsidiary protection status, and second, its application to citizens of the Union not exercising their right to free movement, i.e., 'static' EU citizens (Ibid., pp. 1–2).

Council readings continued in the first half of 2001 under the auspices of the Swedish Presidency. The contentious atmosphere that had marked the first discussions did not wane, and the changes introduced around this time also continued to follow the scope-limiting pattern that had defined the parameters of the earlier discussions. Amongst others, Member States proposed to water down provisions relating to, inter alia: the definition of unmarried partners, family reunification with ascending family members and adult children, and the rules governing the examination of the applications. Furthermore, they sought to introduce an additional requirement stating that sponsors were to meet the material conditions outlined in the proposal (i.e., adequate accommodation, sickness insurance and stable resources) for a period of at least two years (Council Document 7145/01).

Contestation also continued to surround the waiting periods that could be applied at national level before granting family members a right to enter and, more in particular, the maximum length that could be attached to such waiting periods. In the Commission proposal this maximum length had been set at one year. Particularly Austria campaigned strongly for an extension of this maximum period. As expressly acknowledged, by pressing for such an extension Austria wanted to create legal room for manoeuvre that would enable it to preserve its national quota system (Council Document 8491/01; Menz, 2011). At certain points in the discussions, the Austrian delegation even upheld a "general reservation on the Directive as a whole" on account of the concerns it held in respect of this national quota system (Council Documents 7144/01; 8491/01). More precisely, at national level, Austria applied numerical ceilings, or quota, to the yearly inflow of immigrants admitted for the purposes of family reunion. All requests for family reunion lodged beyond this yearly numerical cap were backlogged for potentially several years to come. By extending the waiting period, Austria wanted to make sure that it could continue these backlogging practices.

The Austrian delegation received strong support for its quest from Germany, which itself operated a five-year waiting period in its domestic family reunification law. Across the board, Germany would in fact show itself to be the most persistent, and most ardent opponent of the Commission's broad personal scope provisos (see for similar assessments Strik, 2011; Menz, 2011). This strong opposition stemmed at least in part from the German perception that the Commission's proposal as it stood would result in a significant increase of the numbers of family-reunion immigrants arriving in Germany (Strik, 2011, p. 72). Aside from lending its support to the Austrian request for a more permissive waiting period clause, the German delegation was also behind, inter alia: the above mentioned demand for taking account of the nature and reason of third-country nationals' stays, attempts at restricting family reunion rights in relation to extended family members, suggestions to make situations of family 'formation' subject to more stringent requirements and, most strongly, a series of requests to cap the age limit for children eligible to join at 16 years instead of the age of majority as foreseen by the Commission (Ibid., pp. 83–129). In respect of this last point, it even adopted a veto position mid-2001 with which, in the context of Council unanimity voting (as per the applicable procedure), it effectively blocked any suggestion for reaching consensus that would be premised on different parameters.

A third main player of the Council debates that deserves mention is the Dutch delegation. Like Germany and Austria, the Netherlands was to make a name for its adamant protectionist standpoints vis-à-vis the Commission's propositions (Ibid., Bonjour & Vink, 2013). Aside from lending its support to the restrictionist lines advanced by the German and Austrian delegations, the Dutch representation suggested early on to amend the proposal's provisions in such a way that only those children could join which "really formed part of the family" (Council Document 6504/00, p. 5). It also pressed for a more strict delineation of the condition of 'stable resources', amongst others, by suggesting to introduce a further requirement that would demand of sponsors that they could meet this condition for at least a whole year (Council Document, 11524/00). Overall, these three restriction-minded governments are documented to have intensively cooperated by providing reciprocal support for each other's protectionist proposals. In that way, they formed a highly effective "Dutch-German-Austrian alliance" that on various occasions during the drafting stages successfully secured a weakening of the Commission's text (Menz, 2011, p. 447).

In spite of the significantly watered down text that eventually emerged out of these first discussions, the JHA Council meeting of May 2001 failed to come to an agreement. The next move was in the hands of Belgium which took over the Council presidency in the second half of 2001. In a new attempt to broker a consensus amongst the Council members it presented a series of new proposals for compromise. When this effort floundered again however, Belgium threw in the towel (Peers & Rogers, 2006). Subsequently, at their December 2001 European Council Summit in Laeken, the EU's heads of state formally appealed to the Commission to present a renewed proposal (Laeken European Council, Conclusions of the Presidency).

5.3.2.4 The Third Commission Proposal

The third Commission proposal, presented in May 2002, marked the start of a new phase in the negotiations (COM (2002) 225). In a number of ways, as Peers and Rogers (2006) point out, the Commission's new text leaned in closely to the much weakened standards that had circulated in the preceding Council discussions. Remarkably, on several points, the Commission's new provisions even went below these earlier Council standards (Ibid.). Commenting on this surprising turn towards a limited harmonisation, a Commission official pointed out that the EU's executive had felt cornered by the Laeken Council conclusions. The Laeken mandate was perceived in Commission circles as a 'trick' played by the Council bodies who, after failing to reach agreement themselves, had resorted to passing the buck back to the Commission. In turn, and in view of the strong contestation that had marked the preceding Council debates, the Commission felt it had no option but to take account of those lines of compromise that had already been reached amongst Member States (Strik, 2011, p. 62; see also the proposal's explanatory memorandum). In this light, and in keeping with what had proven to be the site of strongest political concern, the new Commission proposal particularly provided for a strongly limited personal scope delineation.

To begin with, a first and remarkable scope-limitation was effected by removing all mention of 'EU nationals who had not made use of their free movement rights'. As had expressly been stated in the first proposal, such 'static' EU citizens had initially been included with a view to remedying the much-debated phenomenon of 'reverse discrimination'. By extending the remit of EU law to the situations of static EU nationals, the Commission had sought to remedy instances of less favourable treatment of home nationals who resided in their own State in comparison to Union nationals from other Member States who, by reason of their move, could lay claim to more beneficial EU rights (*cf.* also Sect. 4.2.1). The Commission had also expressly related its efforts to do away with such instances of reverse discrimination to the concept of Union citizenship which, it stated, was to be understood as 'indivisible'. More precisely, the first proposal held that: "The family reunification of Union citizens who do not exercise their right to free movement of persons has hitherto been subject solely to national rules. This situation generates an unwarranted difference in treatment (…) National law in some circumstances regulates the family reunification of its own nationals more restrictively than Community law. As Union citizenship is indivisible, the gap must be filled." (COM (1999) 638, p. 14).

These efforts at bringing static EU citizens within the protective scope of EU law in fact followed on from earlier attempts that were made in the context of the above discussed 1997 draft Convention on immigration (COM (97) 387, Article 25). In that setting, the Commission had explicitly referred to an existing "lacuna" in EU law "as regards family reunification" of persons who had not exercised free movement rights, and to the impropriety thereof in light of "Union citizenship" as a "single citizenship" (Ibid., p. 18). Already at the time however, the proposed provisions had set off strong alarms amongst Member States. Three sets of interrelated concerns were voiced early on. First, governments feared the considerable increase in the "number of third-country nationals admitted to Member States" that a scope-extension to static home nationals would bring about. Second, they also voiced concerns around the "severe changes to national law" which would be required in addition to, as a third source of anxiety, the significant extension of Community competences that would result from such a scope expansion (Council Document 6488/98). In the subsequent Family Reunification Directive's negotiations, these provisions equally met with considerable political disquiet. As noted above, by the end of the 2000s this disquiet had grown so large that the French presidency of the time thought it best to put the discussions on all provisions dealing with EU rights for home nationals on hold. Negotiations on the Directive then continued for a while with the text segments on static EU nationals placed in between brackets (Council Document 11524/00).

The politically contested nature of the Commission's overtures towards static EU nationals is linked, to begin with, and as also reflected in the first of the three-fold set of concerns, to the numerically large group of individuals (and hence, family reunification situations) that the protection of EU law would then be extended to. That is, from a purely quantitative perspective, an inclusion of home, static nationals into the Directive's personal scope would provide for EU competences over the group of persons that is generally responsible for the largest share of all applications for family reunion with third-country nationals made. As reported by Walter (2008), in Germany, for instance, 50% of family reunion requests originate from 'static' German nationals, and in Belgium and the Netherlands these figures even amount to 80 and 90 percent respectively. In addition, as observed in academic commentaries on the reverse discrimination phenomenon, there is a further "ugly" side to this differential treatment. The group of persons behind these numbers are often non-white naturalised citizens, or native-born second or third generation nationals with a migration background whose family reunification claims, particularly in the event of spousal reunion with partners from the countries with which they have an immigration link, are politically unpopular (Van Elsuwege & Kochenov, 2011; Guild et al., 2014).

Second, and as also reflected in Member States' early remonstrations, the strong political contestation around the inclusion of static nationals also stems from the significant EU competence expansion that such a legislative step would entail. In all free movement areas (that is, aside from persons, also goods, capital and services), the dividing line between EU and national law is traditionally governed by a distinction between 'internal situations' pertaining to the exclusive preserve of national law, and situations which involve a free movement or 'cross-border' element and fall, on that basis, within the scope of EU law. In that light, resulting instances of reverse discrimination can be seen, and have been legitimized as, inevitable corollaries or "necessary evils" (Tryfonidou, 2008, p. 44) of the, in itself legitimate, division of competences between national and EU spheres of law (see e.g., Hanf, 2011). The other way around, and by inference, to remedy reverse discrimination is to touch on the division of competences that organises the EU's functioning, and that on a more fundamental level also grounds its authentication (Barnard & Odudu, 2009). Third, especially when such a competence expansion is built around Union citizenship and the indivisible nature that can be attributed thereto, as in the Commission's argumentation, the potential of a revolutionary scope expansion looms large. This both in actual effect (as all Member State nationals are automatically, by virtue of Article 20 TFEU, also EU citizens), as well as in relation to the more normative dimension of Union citizenship (what other situations of differential treatment, aside from family reunification, would then fail to meet the protection standards provided by the status of EU citizen?) (see e.g., Shuibhne, 2010).

In short, as often observed in academic commentaries and as reflected in Member States' strong reactions, there is usually "more than meets the eye" in legal discussions around the phenomenon of reverse discrimination and—correspondingly—in attempts at addressing it (Bernard, 1996, p. 82). The Commission, recognizing that its legislative ambitions in this area would not find political acceptance, indicated in the new, third proposal that it would instead propose measures on "the alignment of the rights of all Union citizens to family reunification" at a later stage (COM (2002) 225, p. 3). To date however, no such proposals have been made.

Aside from the notable retreat from its quest to provide EU family reunion rights to static citizens, the Commission's new proposal also accommodated for the protectionist urges voiced in the Council in a host of other ways. Amongst others, the new proposal changed the legal framing of those clauses governing reunification with extended family members. Whereas the situations of dependent ascending relatives and adult children with health issues had originally been covered alongside, and on the same basis as the provisions governing reunion with core family members, the new proposal now placed family reunion rights with these two sets of family members into two separate legal structures. The text still obliged governments to grant family reunion with spouses and minor children (i.e., core family members) by stipulating "Member States *shall* authorise" the entry and residence of such relatives (Article 4.1.). Using a non-compulsory "Member States *may*" phrasing however, a new Article 4.2. now made the conferral of a right to reunification with extended family members optional. In addition, the definitions governing which relatives qualified as extended family members for the purposes of reunion were also narrowed down. Relatives in the ascending line were for instance limited to only those related in the first-degree (i.e., parents but not grandparents).

The replacement of the mandatory 'shall' with the optional 'may' was in fact taken from a suggestion that had originally been made by the French and Greek delegations during the Council discussions of spring 2001. At the time, this was done with the aim of finding a basis for compromise on what proved to be a site of strong political commotion (see Council Document, 7612/01). Whereas some Member States, notably Belgium and Sweden, had supported the Commission's initial provisions on extended family members, fierce opposition had been launched by Germany and Austria. These latter two governments felt that the Directive should leave Member States free to allow reunion with extended family members "on a discretionary basis" only (Council Document 11524/00, p. 9). To that aim, they had in fact proposed to delete the instrument's clauses on non-core relatives all together, and replace them with a single, broadly-worded proviso which would stipulate that "Member States remain free to grant family reunification in other situations if they deem this necessary pursuant to Article 8 of the ECHR" (Ibid.). Such a proviso, they believed, would specify more clearly that Member States were to retain a "large measure of discretion" in relation to the admission of non-core family members (Ibid.; see also Council Documents 7144/01; 7612/01; 8491/01).

Similarly, the Commission's new proposal also governed reunification with 'unmarried partners' by means of a permissive 'may'-wording within a separate Article 4.3. Member States had strongly objected to the establishment of hard legal obligations in respect of such family members too. National concerns had related, amongst others, to stated difficulties to verify the durability of such relations or stemmed from more principled reservations, raised especially by the Southern Member States, regarding the equal treatment of heterosexual and same-sex couples (Council Documents 6504/00, 13053/02 and 13968/02).

Another modification that was introduced to cater to national delegations' restrictionist sentiments was the now separate treatment of family reunion rights granted to refugees. Previously, the clauses on refugees' rights had been attached to the various relevant provisions to which they related. In the new proposal, they were lifted out of these earlier articles and bundled together within a separate chapter (Chapter V). This was in keeping with the structure of the texts that had circulated in the preceding Council meetings. As had been foreseen in the first proposal, refugees still enjoyed a more favourable treatment in that they were exempt from the requirements relating to suitable accommodation, sickness insurance and financial resources, and insofar as no waiting periods could be imposed on the admission of their family members. However, in the new proposal the scope of these refugee provisions was significantly narrowed down to cover only situations of family 'reunification' strictly speaking, that is, reunification with those relatives with whom family ties already existed prior to the recognition of refugee status. This, in contrast to the instrument's overall scope which, as outlined above, also applies to situations of family 'formation' (Article 2).

Furthermore, Member States' concerns also found expression in the extension of the maximum waiting period allowed. This maximum length was now set at two years (instead of, previously, one year). In addition, "by way of derogation", if national legislation in force prior to the Directive's adoption provided for a longer period, so as to reflect a state's national "reception capacity", this maximum length could be extended to three years. The provision, and especially the additional derogation clause, had specifically been tailored to meet Austria's demands for legal flexibility that would enable it to uphold its domestic quota system. The reference to Member States' national "reception capacity" was in fact a verbatim reproduction of arguments that the Austrian delegation had raised earlier on in that context.

In addition, in examining applications, Member States were to provide a response within maximum 12 months' time (as different from the earlier 9 months threshold), and were only obliged to consider those applications made in relation to family members residing outside of their territories. The consideration of 'in-country applications' was now made optional by means of another 'may'-clause. As outlined in the accompanying memorandum, these amendments were also "inspired by points agreed in the Council" (COM (2002) 255, p. 7). Member States were also offered a possibility to re-check whether the sponsor still satisfied the requirements in relation to accommodation, health insurance and financial resources at the moment when the residence permits of admitted family members were renewed for the first time. This new option had been introduced to respond to Member States' demands for stricter controls on these conditions, and for legal options that would enable them to repeat such controls also once leave for family reunification had been granted.

As a final noteworthy personal scope reduction, the new proposal introduced a derogation clause to the definitions of core family members that allowed Member States, if they already had legislation in place to this effect at national level, to verify whether children over the age of 12 met a 'condition for integration'. Pointing out that the "age limit up to which children may join their parents" had been "one of the key questions" of the negotiations, the Commission sought, by means of this derogation clause, to provide Member States with "some room for manoeuvre" (COM (2002) 225, p. 6). Especially Germany had strongly opposed the first proposal's provisions on joining children. The age limit defined by the Commission as "below the age of majority" amounted, for most Member States, to an age limit set at 18 years. The German family reunion rules of the time however capped the age for joining children at 16 years. Refusing to modify its more restrictive domestic provisions, the German delegation had, mid-2001, even voiced a veto position on this point. The new derogation clause, hence, was specifically designed to get around this German resistance (Menz, 2011; Strik, 2011).

In spite of the many accommodations that were made to meet Member States' concerns, the Commission also strategically infused the new text with a number of counterbalancing provisions. Or, provisions that were specifically aimed at offsetting, or curtailing, the more restrictionist outcomes that could be expected from the modifications introduced in the new proposal. Some of these counterbalancing provisos were inserted as 'stand-alone', generic clauses, others were specifically coupled to distinct stipulations.

To begin with, where the Commission had previously rejected the EP's suggestion of introducing a general 'standstill', or 'non-regression' clause, a centrally placed provision now spelled out that Member States were prohibited from retroactively introducing less favourable provisions in the core areas covered by the Directive once it was adopted (Article 3.6, COM (2002) 225). This standstill clause specifically referred to (i) the definitions of sponsors and family members, (ii) the option to re-check the availability of stable resources, health insurance and suitable housing and (iii) third, the now extended waiting period. As expressly stated in the accompanying memorandum, the standstill clause had purposefully been introduced with the aim of limiting Member States' use "of the flexibility or exceptions introduced in certain provisions of the proposal" (Ibid., p. 6). Furthermore, this general standstill clause was supplemented with two extra 'redlining' stipulations linked to two specific, new provisions so as to especially prevent these provisions from acquiring a generalized working. First, a redlining provision was coupled to the derogation clause allowing Member States to verify whether joining children above the age of 12 met an integration condition. Second, such a stipulation was also added to the derogation clause granting Member States the option to extend the waiting period to three years, instead of the standard two years' maximum duration. Commenting on this third proposal, a Commission official later elucidated that these supplementary redlining stipulations were specifically introduced as additional safety valves to these two problematic provisos in case the general standstill clause would not be endorsed by Member States (Strik, 2011, pp. 92–93).

Additionally, in drafting the new proposal the Commission was careful to provide for governments' protectionist leanings chiefly within the framework of 'derogation' clauses. These derogation clauses were worded in very precise terms, so as to leave little space for additional flexibility, and were clearly set apart from the core clauses to which they related and which, conversely, were ascribed a generalized working (COM (2002) 225; Strik, 2011).

As a final point, the third Commission proposal also retained the numerous references to the general principles of EU law that had featured in the first draft text. Amongst these, most notably, reference was made to the principles of proportionality, effectiveness, and access to effective legal remedies (see e.g., recital 14 or Article 18). This, in addition to the references to fundamental rights standards in both the preamble (e.g., numbers 3, 8 and 9) and the main text. Amongst others, Article 5(5) reminded Member States, with reference to the UN Convention on the Rights of the Child, that they were to have 'due regard to the best interests of minor children'. Furthermore, as set out above, Article 17 enshrined a horizontal requirement, taken over from ECtHR jurisprudence, to carry out individual examinations of each claim to family reunification in which elements such as the 'nature and the solidity of a person's family relationships', the 'duration of residence', etc. were to be taken into account. On account of its horizontal nature, this last clause would also apply when Member States consider rejecting a claim for family reunion on grounds of failing to meet any of the conditional requirements, including, for instance, the condition for integration in respect of children joining after they reach the age of 12. In addition, the Commission also retained the explicit rights-based formulation of 'family reunification' that had featured in its first proposal. More specifically, although slightly modified, the new proposal's first article still outlined that the Directive's purpose related to the exercise of the 'right to family reunification'.

5.3.2.5 Renewed Council Debates

Council discussions restarted on the basis of the new proposal in the summer of 2002. In spite of the significantly lowered harmonisation standards that were now on the table, the first readings of the new text at working party level already revealed that the Commission's less ambitious propositions would still not be sufficient to allay Member States' concerns (see e.g., Council Document 10857/02). Once more, the German, Austrian and Dutch delegations took the lead in raising a number of objections to the new set of provisions. Similar to the above dynamics, these objections especially targeted the instrument's personal scope, or the clauses regulating the categories of persons to which the new EU-level rights would accrue. As Council discussions continued, the already weakened standards that the Commission had presented in this respect were lowered even further.

The first provision to wither in the new round of discussions was the Commission's generic standstill clause. This clause had been introduced to prevent Member States from retroactively lowering their protection standards in respect of, specifically: the definitions of family members or sponsors, the possibility of re-checking whether conditional requirements were met, and the waiting periods allowed. Early on, a host of Member States (Germany, Spain, Greece, Austria and Italy) had entered scrutiny reservations on this clause. Amongst others, they expressed concerns over the fact that this clause could "limit the discretion of the Member States" (Ibid., p. 6). Austria was moreover particularly distressed about the standstill clause's connection to the waiting period proviso (Ibid.; see also Council Document 11787/02).

Contention also surrounded, as before, the definitions of family members. Greece for instance even upheld scrutiny reservations on holding hard legal obligations in relation to a sponsor's spouse and minor children (Council Document 10857/02, p. 6). In addition, together with Spain and Portugal, it voiced concerns regarding the admittance of unmarried partners (possibly of the same sex as the applicant), even though the relevant provisions in this respect had now been made optional by means of a 'may' clause (Ibid., p. 8). The weakened, and now separate chapter on family reunion rights for refugees also continued to generate anxieties amongst the Council members. This, again, mostly in respect of the provisions outlining which relatives could join the sponsor-refugee (Ibid., pp. 14–16).

Other politically important rallying points concerned the age limits established. To begin with, in relation to spouses, where their minimum age had previously been defined in broad terms as at least 'the age of legal majority' (amounting, in light of standard European practices to, *de facto* 18 years of age), the Netherlands now pressed for a more precise stipulation outlining that Member States could also set this limit at 21 years (Ibid., p. 9). This new Dutch request stemmed from a change in the Netherlands' government composition which from mid-2002 came to encompass a stronger right-wing component (Bonjour & Vink, 2013). Whereas the Dutch proposal initially enjoyed limited support amongst the Council members, it nevertheless found its way into the final agreement reached due to last-minute backing from Belgium and Denmark which, although not bound by the Directive on account of its opt-out position, had an interest in securing EU rules that would be closely aligned to its own domestic legislation (which set an age limit of 24 years) (Strik, 2011; Council Document 6585/03). In order to promote this proposal for a tightened age limit amongst its counterparts, the Dutch delegation had coupled it to a stated goal of combatting forced marriages. This was the policy rationale that would become stressed most frequently thereafter, and that would eventually also find its way into the Directive's final text

(Article 4.5). However, as a member of the Dutch delegation later admitted, the forced marriages reasoning had been no more than a political pretext. It had not been the Netherlands' main purpose behind the request for a stricter age limit, 'but it didn't hurt either' (Strik, 2011, p. 104).

In addition, apart from the age limits established for spousal reunion, governmental concerns also still enveloped the age caps set in respect of joining children. In the fall of 2002 Austria re-opened debates on these provisions by requesting that applications for joining minors be submitted before they reach the age of 15. This, so as to better fit with the provisions in place in its domestic law for reunification with children (Council Document 14272/02). This Austrian proposal could originally count with only limited support. However, through Austrian insistence, and the support that it lent, in trade off, to the requests of other Member States (most notably the Dutch 21 year age limit for spousal reunion), the suggested amendment was not cast off the table either (Strik, 2011). Eventually it found its way into the Council's agreement text through a compromise suggestion brokered by the then Greek presidency. A possibility was provided for Member States to request that applications of joining children were submitted before the age of fifteen. However, and as part of the compromise, if such requests were submitted after the age of fifteen, Member States would still be obliged to authorise the entry of such minors but could do so on "grounds other than family reunification". The new provision was also phrased as a 'derogation' clause, and supplemented with a standstill stipulation (Council Document, 6912/03).

In addition, the Austrian delegation also launched a plea for a conditional requirement of "appropriate language abilities" to be added to the list of conditions (health insurance, housing and stable resources) set out in Article 7 (Council Document 10857/02). It found support for this amendment, once more, with its German and Dutch counterparts who both also sought to provide for additional integration-related requirements. Whereas a number of governments initially objected to the introduction of extra conditions, under the stewardship of the Danish presidency a clause was nevertheless inserted which would permit Member States to require of third-country nationals that they "comply with integration measures" (Council Document 14272/02, p. 13; Council Document 13053/03, p. 12; see Groenendijk, 2011 on the ambiguity surrounding this specific clause).

5.3.2.6 *The Final Text*

Eventually, by the beginning of 2003 most of the remaining divisive issues were cleared out, and in late February Member States finally reached a political agreement (Council Documents 6906/03 and 6912/03). The discussions had spanned more than three years. Aside from deleting the general standstill provision and adding further age limits and integration requirements, the final political agreement also embedded a number of additional measures that, on the whole, had the effect of further restricting the Directive's protective reach.

Amongst others, where prior to Member States' renewed discussions, the Directive would have required national administrations to provide a decision on family reunion applications within 9 months, or in "exceptional circumstances" maximum 12 months, the new text now read that in "exceptional circumstances" the period could be "extended" without any further qualifications. Scope restricting measures were also introduced to the chapter on refugees and to the provisions governing the grant of an autonomous residence permit to family members. Furthermore, where the material conditions (health insurance, housing and stable resources) listed in Article 7.1 had previously been accompanied by a 'non-discrimination clause' which prohibited Member States from applying these requirements in ways that would amount to discriminatory treatment between third-country nationals and their own citizens, the text of the political agreement was silent on any such safeguards.

Member States' qualms about the conditional requirements also led to a more flexible phrasing of the relevant stipulations. Particularly the two strongest points of governmental concern in that respect, that is, (i) the definition of what these requirements entailed and (ii) the extent to which sponsors were required to continue meeting them once family members were admitted, were re-moulded into new, open-textured phrasings. These new, more general formulations had been necessary for breaking up outstanding national reservations by opening up space for multiple interpretations and, hence, adaptability to suit different domestic preferences or practices. To begin with, the second concern (on the extent to which the conditional requirements could be re-checked), was addressed by adding a new ground for rejection which enabled Member States to decline or withdraw family members' residence permits "where the conditions laid down by this Directive are not or no longer satisfied" (Article 16.1(c)). Linguistic modifications had also been made in regard of what these requirements entailed so as to address the first set of concerns. For instance, where the Commission proposal had defined 'stable resources' to be of an amount not higher than the sum considered for the granting of social assistance (COM (2002) 225), the text around which Member States reached agreement now read that stable resources referred to a sum "sufficient to maintain himself/herself and the members of his/her family without recourse to the social assistance system" (Council Document 6912/03, p. 11).

In March 2003, one month after Member States reached their agreement, the European Parliament re-issued an opinion on the Commission's third proposal (A5-0086/2003). This second EP opinion proposed amendments to almost all of the instrument's articles. In the main, these amendments all advocated a return to the first, 1999 Commission proposal, and in some stipulations the EP even envisaged a treatment above the level provided for in the 1999 version. Amongst others, the EP suggested to delete the option of providing a waiting period all together. It also proposed to introduce a general standstill provision that would address all of the instrument's articles, along with a similarly horizontal non-discrimination clause. In the explanatory memorandum that accompanied the new opinion, the EP showed itself highly critical of the Commission proposal, faulting it, amongst others, for having "harmonised downwards", with the aim of arriving at the "lowest common denominator for the current laws governing this area in the various Member States" (Ibid., p. 45). However, by having tabled its proposals only after Member States had finally reached their political agreement, the EP *de facto* side-lined itself (Strik, 2011, pp. 131–132). On the other hand, it can also be questioned whether, had the opinion arrived at a more timely moment, the EP would have been able to exercise any influence. As registered by Strik, the Parliament's points of view were generally perceived in Council circles as 'unrealistic' and 'too far removed from what was politically feasible' (Ibid.).

On the whole, as some commentators contend, the Commission's realpolitik strategy of limiting the instrument's scope to allay the concerns of Member States (in its third proposal), turned out to be "a tactical error" (Peers & Rogers, 2006, pp. 589–590). As became clear throughout the developments that followed, the new proposal was not greeted in the Council as a task accomplished. Instead, national delegations used the new proposal as a next lever from which to press for further scope-limiting adjustments. Provisions deemed too constraining were deleted and, conversely, new clauses were introduced in the text where a need for more exclusion grounds was felt. As another drafting technique, governments' representatives also modified the phrasing of a number of, originally, mandatory requirements so that their obligating character was made undone (e.g., changing 'shall' into 'may' phrases). Efforts were also made to adapt the degree of precision with which the grounds for qualification to the Directive were spelled out, or, conversely, with which the grounds for exclusion were described. In regard of the grounds for qualification, Member States strived for a high degree of linguistic detail so that little space for ambiguity would be left, and—hence—little malleability would be provided to cover more situations within the remit of EU law than those politically envisaged. Conversely, although stemming from the same objective, in respect of the grounds governing exclusion from the Directive, a broad, generalizable language was favoured so as to maximize legal flexibility, and—hence—adaptability to suit restrictive national policy preferences. The text that finally came out of these different drafting efforts, however, has been criticized by legal commentators for lacking in clarity and moving beyond permissible degrees of legal ambivalence. Peers, for instance, has accused the Directive's final shape, and particularly the personal scope delineation thereof, of "violating principles of clear and precise drafting" (Peers, 2011, p. 472; see also Labayle & De Bruycker, 2012).

Member States, from their part, are reported to have been highly complacent about the result that was finally attained and the legal manoeuvrability that it afforded. The Dutch delegation for instance stated that it was very satisfied with the negotiations' final outcome. It was a result that they could 'confidently bring home' as it would hardly require them to make changes to their existing domestic system (Strik, 2011, p. 130). Additionally, speaking at a Brussels conference, a former Council official described the atmosphere in the press room at the Directive's official presentation as very "festive". Behind the scenes, champagne bottles were popped to celebrate the adoption of the first Directive that "does not need transposition" (former Council official, 2014).

5.4 Conclusion: A Contested Personal Scope

On the whole, and as emerges from quotes such as the one above, Member States worked hard during negotiations on EU family reunion provisions to retain a maximum degree of legal discretion in regard of especially those clauses setting out the legislation's personal scope. In other words,

Member States were especially watchful over those clauses regulating the categories, and hence, numbers, of individuals that would be able to lay claim to the new EU-level rights. The more inclusive the legislation's personal scope, the more family reunification situations and, hence, entry claims of foreigners that would be lifted out of the sphere of exclusive domestic immigration control to instead become governed by EU law. Conversely, the more narrow the latter, the fewer the categories of persons, and hence numbers of family reunification situations that would henceforth fall to be treated by EU-level rules. As already emerged in the very earliest drafting stages on the first, 1960s free movement instruments, a well-defined delineation of which persons could enjoy EU family reunion rights was perceived as necessary in order to avoid an 'unwanted expansion' of EU provisions to individuals and immigration situations beyond those politically envisaged. At later stages, in the context of the Citizenship Directive, Member States for instance also referred to the potentially high financial consequences that could result from an overly lenient personal scope definition, or more generally the 'imposition of changes to national law' that a broad personal scope delineation could bring about. Similarly, in the context of the Family Reunification Directive, Member States voiced concerns around the fact that the high level of rights-standards initially attached to the personal scope definitions would 'limit' their discretion, or requested derogations from the general rules outlining the Directive's personal scope so that they could adopt national rules that would enable them to take account of their national 'reception capacity' in respect of immigration. Overall, similar sets of concerns and preferences around the legislation's personal scope consistently marked Member States' discussions from the very earliest instruments as drafted during the 1960s up to the most recent law-making processes in the context of the Citizenship Directive and the Family Reunification Directive.

More specifically, this particular personal scope sensitivity translated in high degrees of contestation around, first, the clauses and provisions governing which categories of persons could qualify either as 'sponsor' or as 'joining family member'. Second, much debate also surrounded the clauses laying down the conditions or requirements which Member States could set to the eligibility to these statuses or the grounds on which Member States could justify individuals' exclusion from the remit of the EU legal instruments to be adopted. These two sets of interrelated personal scope sensitivities are summarized in turn.

To begin with, in respect of the first observation, Member States sought to provide for a narrow reach of the definitions of 'sponsor' or 'family member' by first, and most straightforwardly, excluding certain categories of individuals from the definitions' premises. For instance, and most notably, national delegations systematically and vehemently opposed the Commission's attempts at extending the definitions of 'sponsors' in such a way as to also cover the family reunification situations of 'static' EU nationals. Amongst others, concerns were voiced around the considerable increase in numbers of 'third-country nationals admitted' which such a personal scope extension to static EU nationals would bring about and, in connection, the large expansion of EU competences that this would entail. In addition, much attention went out to making sure that the respective definitions were described with high levels of detail so that minimum flexibility would attach to them and they would not allow for reading more categories of persons in them than those specifically provided for. To that purpose, national delegations for instance made efforts to ensure that the concepts of joining 'spouse' or 'registered partner' were clearly delineated, and that the provisions on joining children specified that such children had to be underage or dependent on the sponsor and, in any event, not married. Furthermore, much debate also surrounded which categories of relatives would be considered as 'core' family members (in respect of which the instruments provided for more stringent legal obligations) and which family members would, instead, be covered under the label of 'extended' family members (in respect of which the obligations for Member States were more lenient). For instance, whereas the Commission's original proposals had included ascending relatives within the clauses on core family members, over the course of the different Council debates this category of family members was moved into the clauses governing family reunion with extended relatives in relation to which Member States were merely to 'facilitate' entry (in the context of free movement law), or the admission of which 'could be' (instead of, 'had to' be) authorised (in the context of the Family Reunification Directive).

In respect of the second site of personal scope concerns, i.e., the conditional requirements which could be set on the qualification to the status of 'sponsor' or 'family member', Member States resorted to opposing drafting techniques. That is, where the definitions governing eligibility to the instruments' scope were set out with much attention to linguistic detail, the provisions governing the conditions that could be set to such eligibility were instead drafted in an ambivalent, generalizable language. The policy preferences underpinning this contrasting drafting technique were the same however. By phrasing the conditional requirements (most centrally, housing, health insurance and 'sufficient' or 'stable' resources conditions) in ambiguous, multi-interpretable terms, Member States sought to widen the grounds on which access to the new EU rights could be refused, and hence by means of which the numbers of individuals able to lay claim to the new rights could be reduced. In addition, in the context of the Family Reunification Directive, further barriers to such rights were erected in the format of supplementary integration requirements and through options to apply extended waiting periods before granting entry rights to family members.

Overall, the analysis shows that Member States invested considerable energy during the drafting stages to ensure that the EU-level rights granted would not accrue to more categories of individuals than those politically envisaged and, accordingly, that the reach of EU law would not come to embed more immigration situations than those specifically provided for. These findings on Member States' dominant political interests and concerns provide a benchmark against which, in the next sections, the judicial review processes on EU family reunification law, and the extent to which the Court developed its jurisprudence autonomously, are examined.

References

Primary Sources

EU Law

Council Directive 73/148/EEC on the Abolition of Restrictions on Movement and Residence within the Community for Nationals of Member States with regard to Establishment and the Provision of Services [1973] O.J. L 172/14.

Council Directive 75/34/EEC Concerning the Right of Nationals of a Member State to Remain in the Territory of Another Member State after having pursued therein an Activity in a Self-Employed Capacity [1975] O.J. L 14/10.

Council Directive 90/364/EEC on the Right of Residence [1990] O.J. L 180/26.

Council Directive 90/365/EEC on the Right of Residence for Employees and Self-Employed Persons who have ceased their Occupational Activity [1990] O.J. L 180/28.

Council Directive 93/96/EEC on the Right of Residence for Students [1993] O.J. L 317/59.
Council Directive 2003/86/EC on the Right to Family Reunification [2003] O.J. L 251/12.
Regulation (EEC) No 15/61 of the Council on Initial Measures to Bring About Free Movement of Workers within the Community [1961] O.J. 57/1073.
Regulation (EEC) No 38/64 of the Council on the Freedom of Movement for Workers within the Community [1964] O.J. 64/965.
Regulation (EEC) No 1612/68 of the Council on Freedom of Movement for Workers within the Community [1968] O.J. 257.
Regulation (EEC) No 1251/70 of the Commission on the Right of Workers to Remain in the Territory of a Member State after Having Been Employed in that State [1970] O.J. L 142/24.

EU Documents

Commission Proposal for a Council Act establishing the Convention on rules for the admission of third-country nationals to the Member States, COM (97) 387 (final).
Commission Proposal for a Council Directive on the right to family reunification immigration, COM (1999) 638 (final).
Commission Amended Proposal for a Council Directive on the right to family reunification immigration, COM (2000), 624 (final).
Commission Proposal for a European Parliament and Council Directive on the right of citizens of the Union and their family members to move and reside freely within the territory of the Member States, COM (2001) 257 (final).
Commission Amended Proposal for a Council Directive on the right to family reunification immigration, COM (2002) 225 (final).
Commission Amended Proposal for a European Parliament and Council Directive on the right of citizens of the Union and their family members to move and reside freely within the territory of the Member States, COM (2003) 199 (final).
Common Position (EC) No 6/2004 adopted by the Council on 5 December 2003 with a view to adopting Directive 2004/.../EC of the European Parliament and of the Council of ... on the right of citizens of the Union and their family members to move and reside freely within the territory of the Member States, O.J. C 54/E12.
Communication from the Commission to the European Parliament and the Council on guidance for application of Directive 2003/86/EC on the right to family reunification, COM (2014) 210 (final).
Communication from the Commission to the European Parliament pursuant to the second subparagraph of Article 251 (2) of the EC Treaty concerning the

common position of the Council on the adoption of a European Parliament and Council Directive on the right of citizens of the Union and their family members to move and reside freely within the territory of the Member States, SEC/2003/1293 (final).

Council of the European Union Outcome of Proceedings on the Commission proposal for a Convention on rules for the admission of third-country nationals, 6488/98 ADD 1.

Council of the European Union Outcome of Proceedings on the Commission proposal for a Convention on rules for the admission of third-country nationals, 6488/98 ADD 2.

Council of the European Union Outcome of Proceedings on the Proposal for a Council Directive on the right to Family Reunification, 6504/00.

Council of the European Union Note on the Proposal for a Council Directive on Family Reunification, 9738/00.

Council of the European Union Outcome of Proceedings on the Proposal for a Council Directive on Family Reunification, 11122/00.

Council of the European Union Outcome of Proceedings on the Proposal for a Council Directive on Family Reunification, 11524/00.

Council of the European Union Outcome of Proceedings on the Amended Proposal for a Council Directive on the right to Family Reunification, 7144/01.

Council of the European Union Note from the Presidency on the Proposal for a Council Directive on the right to Family Reunification, 7145/01.

Council of the European Union Outcome of Proceedings on the Proposal for a Council Directive on the right to Family Reunification, 7612/01.

Council of the European Union Introductory Note from the Council Secretariat on the Amended Proposal for a Council Directive on the right to Family Reunification, 8491/01.

Council of the European Union Outcome of Proceedings on the Proposal for a European Parliament and Council Directive on the right of citizens of the Union and their family members to move and reside freely within the territory of the Member States, 1057/02.

Council of the European Union Outcome of Proceedings on the Amended Proposal for a Council Directive on the right to family reunification, 10857/02.

Council of the European Union Outcome of Proceedings on the Amended Proposal for a Council Directive on the right to family reunification, 11787/02.

Council of the European Union Outcome of Proceedings on the Amended Proposal for a Council Directive on the right to family reunification, 13053/02.

Council of the European Union Outcome of Proceedings on the Amended Proposal for a Council Directive on the right to family reunification, 13968/02.

Council of the European Union Note from the Presidency on the Examination of Key Issues of the Proposal for a European Parliament and Council Directive on the right of citizens of the Union and their family members to move and reside freely within the territory of the Member States, 13298/02.

Council of the European Union Progress Report on the Proposal for a European Parliament and Council Directive on the right of citizens of the Union and their family members to move and reside freely within the territory of the Member States, 13942/02.

Council of the European Union Outcome of Proceedings on the Amended Proposal for a Council Directive on the right to family reunification, 14272/02.

Council of the European Union Outcome of Proceedings on the Proposal for a European Parliament and Council Directive on the right of citizens of the Union and their family members to move and reside freely within the territory of the Member States, 6147/03.

Council of the European Union Note from the Presidency on the Amended Proposal for a Council Directive on the right to family reunification, 6585/03.

Council of the European Union Draft Minutes of the 2489th meeting of the Council of the European Union Justice, Home Affairs and Civil Protection held in Brussels on 27/28 February 2003, 6906/03.

Council of the European Union Note from the General Secretariat of the Council on the Council Directive on the right to family reunification, 6912/03.

Council of the European Union Progress Report on the Proposal for a European Parliament and Council Directive on the right of citizens of the Union and their family members to move and reside freely within the territory of the Member States, 8675/03.

Council of the European Union Note from the Presidency on the Political Agreement on the Amended Proposal for a European Parliament and Council Directive on the right of citizens of the Union and their family members to move and reside freely within the territory of the Member States, 12218/03.

Council of the European Union Note from the Presidency on Political Agreement on the Amended Proposal for a European Parliament and Council Directive on the right of citizens of the Union and their family members to move and reside freely within the territory of the Member States, 12585/03.

Council of the European Union Draft Statement of the Council's Reasons on the Common Position adopted by the Council with a view to the adoption of a Directive of the European Parliament and of the Council on the right of citizens of the Union and their family members to move and reside freely within the territory of the Member States, 13263/03.

Council of the European Union Press Release 1962nd Council meeting Justice and Home Affairs, Brussels 21 September 2009, 13467/09.

European Parliament Legislative Resolution on the proposal for a Council Directive on the right to family reunification immigration, A5-0201/2000.

European Parliament Report on the Proposal for a European Parliament and Council Directive on the right of citizens of the Union and their family members to move and reside freely within the territory of the Member States, A5-0009/2003.

European Parliament Report on the amended proposal for a Council Directive on the right to family reunification immigration, A5-0086/2003.
European Parliament Legislative Resolution on the Council Common Position with a View to the Adoption of a Directive of the European Parliament and of the Council on the right of citizens of the Union and their family members to move and reside freely within the territory of the Member States, P5_TA(2004)0160.
Green Paper on the right to family reunification of third-country nationals living in the European Union (Directive 2003/86/EC), COM (2011) 735 (final).
Laeken European Council, Conclusions of the Presidency [2001] EU Bulletin 17.12.2001.
Report from the Commission to the European Parliament and the Council on the application of Directive 2004/38/EC on the right of citizens of the Union and their family members to move and reside freely within the territory of the Member States, COM (2008) 840 final.
Tampere European Council, Conclusions of the Presidency [1999] EU Bulletin No. 10/1999.

LITERATURE

Barnard, C., & Odudu, O. (2009). *The Outer Limits of European Union Law*. Portland, OR: Hart Publishing.
Bernard, N. (1996). Discrimination and Free Movement in EC Law. *International and Comparative Law Quarterly, 45*(1), 82–108.
Bonjour, S., & Vink, M. (2013). When Europeanization Backfires: The Normalization of European Migration Politics. *Acta Politica, 48*(4), 389–407.
Burley, A.-M., & Mattli, W. (1993). Europe before the Court: A Political Theory of Legal Integration. *International Organization, 47*(1), 41–76.
Carruba, C. (2005). Courts and Compliance in International Regulatory Regimes. *The Journal of Politics, 67*(3), 669–689.
Carruba, C., Gabel, M., & Hankla, C. (2008). Judicial Behavior under Political Constraints: Evidence from the European Court of Justice. *American Political Science Review, 102*(4), 435–452.
Carruba, J., Gabel, M., & Hankla, C. (2012). Understanding the Role of the European Court of Justice in European Integration. *American Political Science Review, 106*(1), 214–223.
Cichowski, R. (1998). Integrating the Environment. *Journal of European Public Policy, 5*(3), 387–405.
Cichowski, R. (2004). Women's Rights, the European Court, and Supranational Constitutionalism. *Law & Society Review, 38*(3), 489–512.
Cichowski, R. (2007). *The European Court and Civil Society: Litigation, Mobilization and Governance*. Cambridge: Cambridge University Press.

Garrett, G. (1992). International Cooperation and Institutional Choice: The European Community's Internal Market. *International Organization, 46*(2), 533–560.

Garrett, G., & Weingast, B. (1993). Ideas, Interests and Institutions: Constructing the European Community's Internal Market. In J. Goldstein & R. Keohane (Eds.), *Ideas and Foreign Policy: Beliefs, Institutions, and Political Change* (pp. 173–206). Ithaca, NY: Cornell University Press.

Goedings, S. (2006). *Labor Migration in an Integrating Europe. National Migration Policies and the Free Movement of Workers, 1950–1968.* Den Haag: Sdu Uitgevers.

Granger, M.-P. (2004). When Governments Go to Luxembourg...: The Influence of Governments on the Court of Justice. *European Law Review, 29*(1), 3–31.

Groenendijk, K. (2011). Pre-departure Integration Strategies in the European Union: Integration or Immigration Policy? *European Journal of Migration and Law, 13*, 1–30.

Guild, E., & Niessen, J. (1996). *The Developing Immigration and Asylum Policies of the European Union. Adopted Conventions, Resolutions, Recommendations, Decisions and Conclusions.* The Hague: Kluwer Law International.

Guild, E., Peers, S., & Tomkin, J. (2014). *The EU Citizenship Directive: A Commentary.* Oxford: Oxford University Press.

Hanf, D. (2011). 'Reverse Discrimination' in EU Law: Constitutional Aberration, Constitutional Necessity, or Judicial Choice? *Maastricht Journal of European and Comparative Law, 18*, 29–61.

Hedemann-Robinson, M. (1996). Third-Country Nationals, European Union Citizenship and Free Movement of Persons: A Time for Bridges Rather than Divisions. *Yearbook of European Law, 16*(1), 321–362.

Hedemann-Robinson, M. (1998). From Object to Subject?: Non-EC Nationals and the Draft Proposal of the Commission for a Council Act Establishing the Rules for the Admission of Third Country Nationals to the Member States. *Yearbook of European Law, 18*(1), 289–335.

Labayle, H., & De Bruycker, P. (2012). Impact de la jurisprudence de la CEJ et la CEDH en matière d'asile et d'immigration. *Étude Parlement Européen, DG des Politiques Internes.*

McCown, M. (2003). The European Parliament before the Bench: ECJ Precedent and EP Litigation Strategies. *Journal of European Public Policy, 10*(6), 974–995.

Menz, G. (2011). Stopping, Shaping and Moulding Europe: Two-Level Games, Non-State Actors and the Europeanization of Migration Policies. *Journal of Common Market Studies, 49*(2), 437–462.

Peers, S. (1998). Building Fortress Europe: The Development of EU Migration Law. *Common Market Law Review, 35*, 1235–1272.

Peers, S. (2011). *EU Justice and Home Affairs Law.* Oxford: Oxford University Press.

Peers, S., & Rogers, N. (2006). *EU Immigration and Asylum Law: Text and Commentary*. Leiden: Martinus Nijhoff Publishers.
Shuibhne, N. (2010). The Resilience of EU Market Citizenship. *Common Market Law Review, 47*(6), 1597–1628.
Stein, E. (1981). Lawyers, Judges, and the Making of a Transnational Constitution. *American Journal of International Law, 75*(1), 1–27.
Stone Sweet, A., & Brunell, T. (2012). The European Court of Justice, State Noncompliance, and the Politics of Override. *American Political Science Review., 106*(1), 204–213.
Strik, T. (2011). *Besluitvorming over asiel- en migratierichtlijnen. De wisselwerking tussen nationaal en Europees niveau*. Den Haag: Boom Juridische uitgevers.
Tryfonidou, A. (2008). Reverse Discrimination in Purely Internal Situations: An Incongruity in a Citizens' Europe. *Legal Issues of Economic Integration, 35*(1), 43–67.
Van Elsuwege, P., & Kochenov, D. (2011). On the Limits of Judicial Intervention: EU Citizenship and Family Reunification Rights. *European Journal of Migration and Law, 13*(4), 443–466.
Walter, A. (2008). *Reverse Discrimination and Family Reunification*. Nijmegen: Wolf Legal Publishers.

CHAPTER 6

Quantitatively Structuring Precedents

6.1 Introduction

In what follows, the analysis proceeds by charting whether and how recourse to precedent-based reasoning reinforces the Court's judicial autonomy. Or, whether and how precedent-based reasoning enables the Court to develop its jurisprudence independent of the preferences of political actors, as identified in the preceding chapter.

First, and the object of the present chapter, the analysis proceeds with a quantitative structuring of observations of CJEU self-citations within the collected case law record. These observations are used as proxies for precedents. In a next and final analytical chapter (Chap. 7), this quantitative structuring is used as a blueprint that guides further qualitative, contextualized evaluations of the precedent-based structures that, from a numerical perspective, appeared most prominent for the case law's development as a whole.

The need for a quantitative review, preceding the qualitative one, stems from the requirement to adopt a longitudinal outlook to the study of precedent-based processes and their effects. More precisely, as was emphasized in Chap. 3, the manner by which precedents are expected to strengthen the Court's autonomy resides, not necessarily in the influence held by one singular case on a next one, but rather, is expected to emerge from the manner by which sequences of precedents progressively, and cumulatively, build on one another as the case law develops. In order to

M. De Somer, *Precedents and Judicial Politics in EU Immigration Law*, European Administrative Governance,
https://doi.org/10.1007/978-3-319-93982-7_6

capture these long-term processes and effects, a longitudinal and, by consequence, voluminous case law record is needed (see above, Sect. 4.2).

The first, quantitative exercise serves to facilitate and systematize the analytical engagement with this sizeable dataset. More in particular, by evaluating and comparing the numerical self-citation trends and patterns within the record, the quantitative review indicates where the most important precedent-based developments are most likely to be found. In that way, the model serves as a numerical roadmap that can direct the focus of enquiry of further qualitative analyses. In addition, by parsing the data on the basis of objective, numerical criteria, the model also guards such further qualitative engagement from problems related to selective case sampling on the dependent variable; in the context of this study: autonomous Court behaviour. As documented in Chap. 2, such selective sampling on the dependent variable has in the past hindered judicial politics analyses of the Court's role.

The quantitative model is inextricably connected to the further qualitative reviews that follow. In the qualitative analyses, each of the citation structures numerically highlighted is subjected to in-depth examinations geared, more specifically, at uncovering the discourses and arguments that underpinned them. The need for further qualitative analyses derives, first, from the expectation that what lends precedents an autonomy-strengthening value is not necessarily the number of times a case is cited in follow-up rulings, but more importantly, the substance of the arguments that were being reinforced through such citations. Accordingly, self-citation is not taken to correspond to the concept of precedent-based reasoning as such, as the mere observation of self-citation, in and of itself, does not give any information on the discursive weight the citation held in the context of new proceedings. In other words, observations of self-citation are considered as only the beginning of an enquiry into precedent. They are necessary but insufficient indicators of precedent-based reasoning (see similarly on the difference between citations and precedents, Stone Sweet, 2004; Jacob, 2014). Second, and in connection, the follow-up qualitative review also serves to capture the fine-grained, causal mechanisms, of mostly a discursive nature, that are theoretically expected to underpin the autonomy-strengthening effects of precedents. Following the two-fold structure of the study's theoretical arguments (*cf.* Chap. 3), and as will be detailed further in the next chapter, the qualitative analyses particularly review the precedent-based discursive interactions taking place between the Court and its judicial interlocutors (national courts and litigant parties) and, second, between the Court and the Member States. These qualitative reviews, to the extent that they enable collecting the contextualized evidence necessary for corroborating similarly context-dependent causal mechanisms, also shield the study from reproducing 'grand theory' constructs of the Court's role which, although largely abandoned by contemporary qualitative scholarship, are still employed—for easy operationalisation purposes—in the context of quantitative analyses. In sum, by combining both quantitative and qualitative orientations, and in line with the traditional argument for conducting mixed methods' research (Creswell & Clark, 2010), the analysis as a whole seeks to combine the strengths of each approach whilst offsetting their respective weaknesses.

In what follows, the three steps that together comprise the quantitative model are presented in their respective consecutive order.[1] They are first outlined in abstract, objective terms so that the model's external reliability is provided for. In the next subsection the three different steps are applied to the dataset. In a final section, the numerical observations that can be derived from this application are outlined. These observations provide the structure that guides the focus of the qualitative, in-depth analysis carried out in the next chapter.

6.2 A Self-Citation Sequencing Model

6.2.1 Step 1: Citation Scores

The quantitative structuring operates on the basis of observations of self-citation; or, when courts cite their own rulings. As detailed in the data collection section (4.2.3), for CJEU rulings such observations can be retrieved with ease either from the texts of the judgments themselves, or from the 'case information page' on the CJEU's website.

Observations of self-citation allow for arriving at two measures relevant for the study of precedent-based reasoning. First, and straightforwardly, they provide information on how many rulings judges have used to ground their new decisions in. Put differently, they reveal how embedded that ruling is in earlier case law. Second, when working with a 'closed dataset', that is, when all relevant cases in the domain have been identified and assembled, figures on self-citation also allow for obtaining insights into

[1] Parts of this model were previously published in De Somer and Vink (2015).

how many times each judgment was cited subsequently in follow-up proceedings within the dataset. That is, by mapping all citations to prior rulings in the case law record, it becomes possible to, next, register how many times each judgment was cited in sequence in that record by tracking how often the judgment in question appears within the assembled figures on prior citations.

As its first step, the model starts off by collecting the absolute counts on both types of measures. Within social network analyses (see e.g., Fowler & Jeon, 2008; Derlén & Lindholm, 2014), such counts have been defined, respectively, as *outward* and *inward* citation scores.[2] The first, *outward* scores refer to the number of citations used to embed a new decision; or, expressed more graphically, the citation counts that come *from within* judgments. Such scores are revealing in that they allow to tap information on the extent to which judges used an either larger or smaller amount of references to earlier judgments to ground the decision at hand (see similarly on ECtHR outward citation scores, Lupu & Voeten, 2012). The second, *inward* citation scores or degrees indicate, instead, the number of times that a certain case was cited in follow-up proceedings; or, in other words, citations *to* a case. These scores are revealing in that they allow to evaluate which judgments are likely to have provided important argumentative materials for the further development of the case law in that, with the benefit of hindsight, they were comparatively often rehearsed over the course of new lines of case law.

6.2.2 *Step 2: Relative Citation Scores*

Both types of citation scores, however, are sensitive to the effects of time. Two interrelated and interacting sets of time-dependent susceptibilities are highlighted in turn in what follows. As will be outlined, each of these two temporal susceptibilities needs to be controlled for when computing

[2] Whilst borrowing elements from social network analyses, the study adopts a different quantitative strategy that is less labour-intensive and that allows for a better access to the 'moving target' nature that is expected to characterize precedent-based developments. As will be detailed throughout the chapter, the different steps that together comprise the quantitative exercise are set up in such way as to display the value which certain self-citation scores held vis-à-vis others during certain episodes of the case law's long-term development. Accordingly, the numerical findings deriving from the model's application are also well-attuned for directing the focus of the subsequent qualitative reviews towards the progressively moving nature of precedents.

the inward and outward citation scores of a case if these scores are to accurately reflect the phenomena they are meant to indicate.

To begin with, and as the first time-dependent susceptibility, whilst outward citations can be expected to increase with the volume of jurisprudential material available to choose from, inward citations, inversely, are likely to be lower for those cases that were decided most recently as recent cases invariably had fewer opportunities for reinforcement in follow-up rulings (see also Jacob, 2014; Lupu & Voeten, 2012; Pelc, 2014). More in particular, with regard to outward citation scores, first, the earlier a judgment was decided, the fewer preceding case law was available to ground the decision in. Accordingly, in that light and all else equal, an equal number of citations to prior rulings in a given judgment x rendered a decade ago, is likely to carry more weight than that same amount of citations within a judgment y that was decided only a few years ago. After all, in the context of the newer judgment y, much more jurisprudential material was available to choose from. With regard to inward citation counts, all else equal, the same number of references to a given judgment x rendered a decade ago is likely to, inversely, carry *less* weight than that same amount of citations to a judgment y that was decided recently. After all, the earlier decision had much more opportunities for reinforcement in comparison to the newer one. This first set of temporal sensitivities can be controlled for by weighing both the (i) outward and (ii) inward citation counts of each judgment against, respectively, (i) the number of cases that preceded it for the outward scores and, (ii) for the inward scores, the number of cases that followed on from it. In this manner, it is possible to retrieve, for each judgment in the dataset, their respective 'relative' outward and inward citation scores or degrees.

To illustrate, computing the relative inward citation scores of the above hypothetical judgment x that was rendered a decade ago would amount to weighing the absolute inward scores of x, or the number of times it was cited in follow-up proceedings, against the number of cases that followed since x was rendered. If, for instance, x was cited 5 times out of the 50 judgements that were rendered since, it will hold a relative inward citation score of 5 out of 50, or 10%. The same amount of subsequent citations, 5, to the more recent judgment y will become weighed against the, invariably, lesser amount of cases that have followed since y was rendered. If, for instance, since judgment y was rendered a further 25 cases have been decided, y's relative inward citation score will amount to 5/25, or, 20%. Whilst in absolute terms, the two judgments hold equal inward citation scores, their relative scores reflect the different value of such absolute counts depending on the difference in opportunities these cases have had for reinforcement in follow-up rulings. The same holds by analogy, but taking account of the preceding rulings, for the computing of cases' relative outward citation scores. Figure 6.1 below provides a first graphic illustration of the inward and outward scores of the hypothesized cases x and y in relation to the number of rulings that preceded them or that followed since their rendering.

A second time-dependent susceptibility needs to be accounted for however. That is, in line with the theoretical hypotheses, it is expected that as time passes 'lock-in effects' will come to characterize the precedent-based discourses that operate within the case law. More precisely, as outlined in Chap. 3, through repeated interactions and discursive reinforcements, precedent-based arguments or standards are expected to become so well-known and established that they acquire a 'taken-for-granted' status within the judicial interpretative environment. They will then be referred to less and less in the court room, as their explicit rehearsal will no longer serve a purpose.

In that light, it can be remarked that not the entire volume of jurisprudence that precedes a certain case is likely to be of relevance to judges when presenting their new decision. With regard to outward scores, or references to preceding case law, judges can be expected to not reconsider all of the decisions that predate a new legal claim when presenting their deliberations as citations to commonly accepted points of law will appear ornamental or eccentric (Jacob, 2014, p. 12). In parallel, and on account of the same time-related dynamics, inward citation scores of cases (citations in follow-up rulings), can be expected to decrease as more time passes and a case's argumentative premises become ever more embedded within the judicial environment.

In light of these considerations, when comparing, first, different outward citation counts across a case law record, it is still likely that an equal number of references to an earlier case x holds more value in comparison to that same amount of references in a later judgment y. In the context of the later judgment y, judges had more jurisprudential material available to ground their decision in. However, in view of the lock-in effects expected to underpin the workings of precedent, it would be injudicious to consider each and every ruling that predated the judgment y in the framework of such a comparison. Some of the predating rulings are likely to no longer hold an added value in the court room, as they will have evolved into a

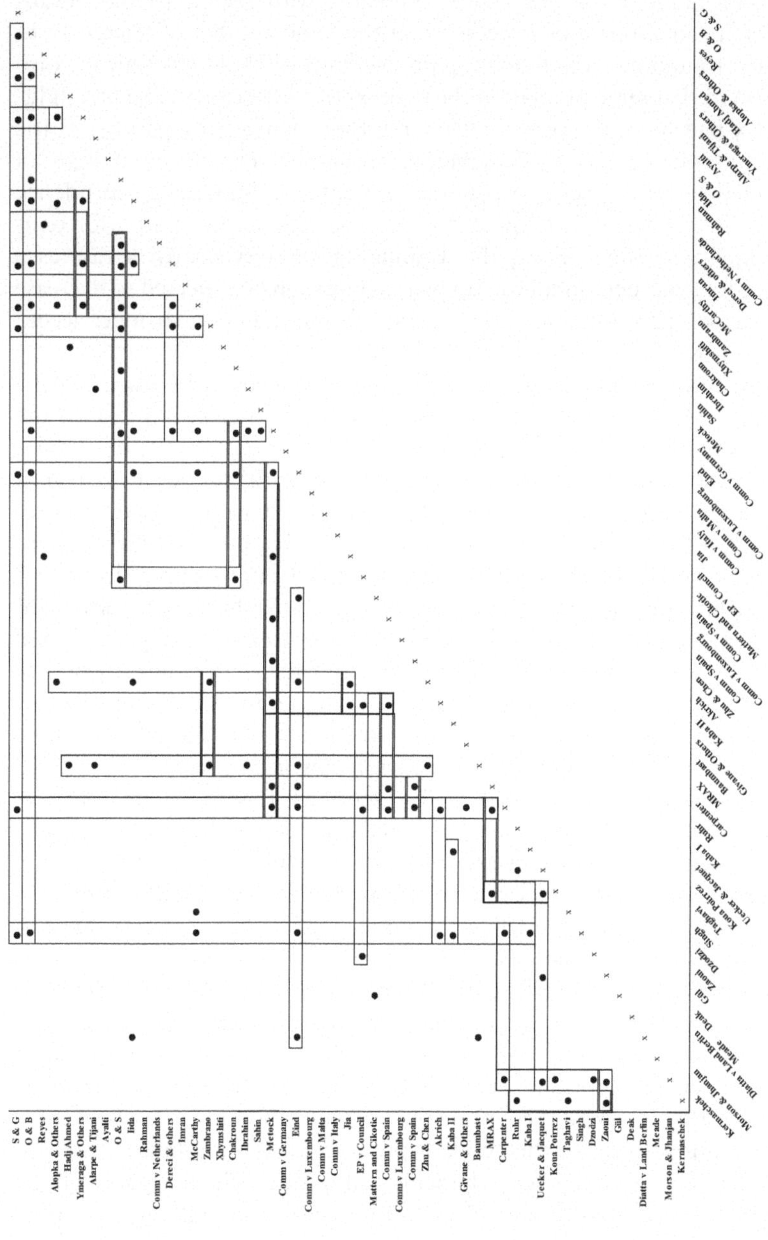

Fig. 6.1 Dominant self-citation structures

taken-for-granted state of affairs. Similarly, with regard to the inward scores, it can also still be expected that the same number of references to an earlier judgment x in follow-up proceedings will hold *less* value in comparison to that same number in the context of a later case y. The first judgment x had more opportunities for reinforcement in comparison to the later judgment y. Again however, it would be misguided, in light of expected lock-in effects, to consider the entire volume of jurisprudence that followed on from judgment x as reasonable opportunities for reinforcement. As time passes, the argumentative relevance of a case as a source for precedent in follow-up proceedings can be expected to decrease as the case's premises come to progressively enjoy an ever stronger acceptance within the court room.

This second temporal susceptibility, is controlled for by weighing the absolute (i) outward and (ii) inward scores of each case, not against the entire volume of cases that preceded or followed on from it, but rather, against the number of cases that (i) preceded or (ii) followed on from it during the time periods in which the case is likely to have held an argumentative added value in the court room. To that purpose, the outward scores of each case are weighed, not against all cases that preceded it, but only against the number of cases that preceded it within timeframes delineated by the first judgment the ruling refers to as the starting point, and the last citation it makes as the end point. In parallel, the inward scores of every judgment are weighed, not against the entire volume of case law following on from it, but only against the cases that succeeded within a time period delineated by the first decision in which the case was cited and the last follow-up citation that can be identified. Cases that cite only one, or no preceding rulings, or are only cited once or never in follow-up proceedings (i.e., cases with inward or outward citation counts of '0' or '1'), are excluded from the model's further assessments. It would not be possible, for such cases, to define temporal borders between first and last inward or outward citations. The exclusion of the scores of these cases does not affect the overall research findings however, as an incidence of only one prior or follow-up reference, or none at all, excludes such scores from having been significantly grounded within earlier decisions, or from having been an important source for precedent in follow-up proceedings.

To further illustrate these principles, when computing the relative outward citation scores of the above hypothesized earlier ruling x, that ruling's 5 references to earlier judgments will not be weighed against all the judgments that were rendered previously (50), but only against those rendered between the first case it refers to and the last case it cites. If the number of cases within the timeframe bordered by these first and last references is, for instance, 25, x's relative outward citation score will amount to 5 out of 25, or 20%. Similarly, in relation to the hypothetical more recent judgment y, the equal amount of 5 references to preceding rulings will not be weighed against all the judgments that were rendered previously (75), but only against those rendered between the first and last judgment it refers to. If this number is, for instance, 20, y will hold a relative outward citation score of 5/20, or 25%. Should these temporal borders not be applied to the computing of cases' relative outward citation scores, such scores would inevitably decrease the further down the line judgments are rendered. This, because the number of rulings referred to would invariably become weighed against an ever growing volume of preceding jurisprudence as ever more decisions are rendered. Such findings would then suggest, incorrectly, that judgments are invariably less significantly embedded in preceding case law as more time passes. Or, inversely, that only the rulings rendered early on were significantly grounded in preceding Court decisions.

Second, illustrating these principles in respect of inward scores, in analogy to the above, a supposed number of 5 follow-up citations to the hypothesized earlier judgment x will be weighed, not against all cases that have followed since x, but only against the number of cases that were rendered in between a time period defined by the case with the first subsequent citation as the start point and the last identified follow-up citation as the end point. If the number of cases rendered in this timeframe is again, for instance, 25, judgment x's relative inward citation score will amount to 5/25, or 25%. The same example can also be conjectured for the more recent decision y. In addition, and similar to the above reflections on relative outward scores, should temporal limits not be applied to the computing of relative inward scores, the model would inevitably record decreasing trends in such scores for the earlier rulings, as the absolute inward citation counts (i.e., the number of times the case was cited in follow-up rulings) of such earlier cases would become weighed against an ever growing volume of jurisprudence. This would then suggest that the earlier a ruling was decided, the less significance it held as a precedent for the future development of the case law. Or, inversely, that the more recent rulings are invariably more important from a precedent-based perspective.

6.2.3 *Step 3: Dominant Scores—Citation Structures*

As the model's third and final step, the results of each judgment's relative outward and inward citation scores are gathered in order to compare the scores that, across the board, appeared most important or dominant from a numerical perspective. To that effect, a benchmark is adopted that allows for a selection of the inward and outward scores which hold, comparatively, a strong value within the jurisprudence record overall. For instance, and as will be further illustrated in the below, in the context of the present analysis a 20% benchmark, or threshold was applied. This 20% threshold allowed for singling out, by and large, one third of the numerically most important, or dominant scores within the record. Depending on the dataset and research goals that guide a study, other benchmarks can be set at higher or lower threshold values so as to select either smaller or larger shares of dominant scores for further review.

The dominant inward and outward citation structures, selected on the basis of the comparative assessments, signpost what are likely to have been the most important precedent-based discursive developments within the case law's evolution at large. As can be observed, on account of the temporal limits applied, what these final measures provide are, deliberately, not fixed-in-time scores that pin down those judgments that hold the strongest inward or outward citation values within the dataset. Instead, the measures are intentionally limited to indicating, rather, the comparatively most important outward or inward scores held by certain judgments within certain, delimited timeframes or episodes of the case law's overall development. Accordingly, when taken together, the measures constitute a roadmap or blueprint that charts the chronological sequencing of dominant self-citation patterns as they progressively emerge, take hold and eventually move on to provide the basis for new patterns to appear. In that way, the numerical measures are also well-attuned to guide the focus of enquiry of the further qualitative review towards the 'moving target' nature that is expected to characterize precedent-based discourses as they sequentially follow up on one another.

6.3 Self-Citation Structures in CJEU Case Law on Family Reunification Immigration

6.3.1 Quantitative Structuring

In what follows, the different steps are applied to the collected dataset. As outlined in the data collection section (3.2), a total of 67 cases on family reunion have appeared before the Luxembourg bench since the first, 1976 *Kermaschek* case. As also outlined in that section, of these 67, only the judgements rendered up until June 2014, a total of 53, were considered for the purposes of the analysis. Within these 53 rulings, 108 observations of self-citation were identified.

For the purposes of applying the numerical model, the Court's decisions were ordered chronologically by date of judgment. Following the model's first step, all absolute citation counts on the outward and inward scores were assembled for each judgment. The outward scores (cases referred to) were assembled first, which subsequently allowed for retrieving the inward scores (subsequent references). That is, by tracking how many times a case appeared in the collected data on outward citations, that case's inward citations were identified. The collecting exercise was facilitated by means of an excel point chart in which all judgments were positioned in their respective chronological order on both the horizontal, as well as the vertical axes (see below, Fig. 6.1). Each observation of a 'self-citation' was marked by a point. A diagonal line was put in place to indicate where a case meets itself on the other axis. In this manner, the outward and inward scores of each case could easily be registered. By tracing, first, within the figure all the points allotted to a judgment along the horizontal axis, each judgment's respective outward citation counts could easily be recorded. By inference, by tracing for each judgment all points allotted to it on the vertical axis, the judgment's inward citation counts could be retrieved.

Next, following the model's second step, the relative outward inward citation scores were computed for each judgment by weighing the absolute outward citation counts against the number of cases that preceded it within timeframes bordered by the first ruling referred to as the start point, and the last citation made as the end point. The same was done, in analogy but taking account of follow-up references, for the inward citation counts so as to retrieve, for each judgment, its relative inward citation scores. Table 6.1 provides an overview of the scores for each case.

Table 6.1 Relative citation scores/case

			Outward citations	*Preceding cases*	*Relative outward scores*	*Inward citations*	*Succeeding cases*	*Relative inward scores*
1	*Kermaschek*	C-40/76	0	–	–	3	8	***38%***
2	*Morson & Jhanjan*	C-35/82	0	–	–	5	9	***56%***
3	*Meade*	C-238/83	0	–	–	0	–	–
4	*Diatta v land Berlin*	C-267/83	0	–	–	3	28	*11%*
5	*Deak*	C-94/84	0	–	–	0	–	–
6	*Gül*	C-131/85	0	–	–	1	–	–
7	*Zaoui*	C-147/87	2	2	***100%***	1	–	–
8	*Dzodzi*	C-297/88 & 197/89	1	–	–	1	–	–
9	*Singh*	C-370/90	0	–	–	8	41	*20%*
10	*Taghavi*	C-243/91	1	–	–	1	–	–
11	*Koua Poirrez*	C-206/91	1	–	–	2	5	***40%***
12	*Uecker & Jacquet*	C-64/96	3	10	***30%***	1	–	–
13	*Kaba I*	C-356/98	1	–	–	1	–	–
14	*Ruhr*	C-189/00	2	12	*17%*	0	–	–
15	*Carpenter*	C-60/00	2	8	***25%***	9	38	***24%***
16	*MRAX*	C-459/99	2	5	***40%***	4	12	***33%***
17	*Baumbast & R*	C-413/99	1	–	–	6	29	***21%***
18	*Givane & others*	C-257/00	1	–	–	0	–	–
19	*Kaba II*	C-466/00	2	5	***40%***	0	–	–
20	*Akrich*	C-109/01	2	7	***29%***	4	10	***40%***
21	*Zhu & Chen*	C-200/02	1	–	–	5	24	***21%***
22	*Comm v Spain*	C-157/03	2	2	***100%***	1	–	–

			Outward citations	Preceding cases	Relative outward scores	Inward citations	Succeeding cases	Relative inward scores
23	*Comm v Luxembourg*	C-165/05	0	–	–	0	–	–
24	*Comm v Spain*	C-503/03	3	6	*50%*	1	–	–
25	*Mattern and Cikotic*	C-10/05	1	–	–	1	–	–
26	*EP v Council*	C-540/03	3	13	*23%*	2	10	*20%*
27	*Jia*	C-1/05	2	2	*100%*	2	19	*11%*
28	*Comm v Italy*	C-91/07	0	–	–	0	–	–
29	*Comm v Malta*	C-87/07	0	–	–	0	–	–
30	*Comm v Luxembourg*	C-57/07	0	–	–	0	–	–
31	*Eind*	C-291/05	7	22	*32%*	6	21	*29%*
32	*Comm v Germany*	C-192/07	0	–	–	0	–	–
33	*Metock & others*	C-127/08	7	17	*41%*	8	19	*42%*
34	*Sahin*	C-551/07	1	–	–	0	–	–
35	*Ibrahim*	C-310/08	2	17	*12%*	1	–	–
36	*Chakroun*	C-578/08	3	8	*38%*	1	–	–
37	*Xhymshiti*	C-247/09	0	–	–	1	–	–
38	*Zambrano*	C-34/09	2	5	*40%*	4	15	*27%*
39	*McCarthy*	C-434/09	5	30	*17%*	7	13	*54%*
40	*Imran*	C-155/11	0	–	–	0	–	–
41	*Dereci & others*	C-256/11	3	7	*43%*	5	10	*50%*
42	*Comm v Netherlands*	C-508/10	0	–	–	1	–	–

(*continued*)

Table 6.1 (continued)

			Outward citations	*Preceding cases*	*Relative outward scores*	*Inward citations*	*Succeeding cases*	*Relative inward scores*
43	*Rahman*	C-83/11	0	–	–	1	–	–
44	*Iida*	C-40/11	6	38	*16%*	4	6	***67%***
45	*O & S*	C-356/11 & C-357/11	7	17	***41%***	1	–	–
46	*Ayalti*	C-513/12	0	–	–	0	–	–
47	*Alarpe & Tijani*	C-529/11	2	19	*11%*	1	–	–
48	*Ymeraga & others*	C-87/12	3	6	***50%***	3	4	***75%***
49	*Hadj Ahmed*	C-45/12	2	21	*10%*	0	–	–
50	*Alopka & others*	C-86/12	4	28	*14%*	2	2	***100%***
51	*Reyes*	C-423/12	2	17	*12%*	0	–	–
52	*O & B*	C-456/12	9	42	***21%***	1	–	–
53	*S & G*	C-457/12	10	44	***23%***	0	–	–

On the basis of these results, and following the model's third and final step, the scores that held comparatively high outward or inward citation values were selected for further qualitative review. For this purpose, a threshold benchmark value was set at 'above 20%'. In other words, those outward and inward scores displaying an average self-citation activity of at least one out of every five preceding or succeeding decisions were singled out. On this basis, 19 relative outward citation scores, out of the total 53, were highlighted as holding a comparatively strong or 'dominant' value. These dominant outward scores are expected to indicate the decisions for which CJEU made comparatively strong efforts to ground its reasoning in prior dicta. In parallel, on the basis of the 20% threshold, 18 out of the total 53 relative inward scores were singled out as likely to have held a comparatively strong precedent relevance for subsequent proceedings for certain episodes of the case law's overall development. In all, as can be noted, the 20% benchmark resulted in a selection of, by and large, one third of the total number of citation scores.

The selected scores or structures are underlined within the above table. In addition, they are also marked in the below point chart (Fig. 6.1) by means of frames put in place around the respective scores. The dominant outward citation structures are framed along the vertical axis and the dominant inward citation structures are framed along the horizontal axis. These frames depict the episodes in the case law's overall development to which the dominant scores relate, as well as the length or duration of each. Furthermore, as intended and of particular importance in light of the study's theoretical expectations, they also chart the sequencing of such structures as precedent-based discursive patterns progressively emerge, take hold and follow up on one another as the case law evolves.

6.3.2 Numerical Observations

A number of observations can be derived from the model's findings as presented in the figure above. In what follows a set of general traits and trends are highlighted. Next, these trends are reviewed in more detail following the chronological order of the case law as it evolved over time. These more detailed observations provide a structure that will guide the focus of the subsequent qualitative analyses.

6.3.2.1 *General Trends*

As a first general observation, most dominant citation structures, both outward and inward, remain close to the moment in time when the judgment to which they relate was rendered. More precisely, the dominant outward citation structures show a tendency to refer back to rulings that are not very far removed from the moment in time when the case was rendered and, in parallel, cases tend to have strong follow-up citation scores especially during the periods immediately following on from their delivery. As also follows from this observation, as cases follow up on one another, the dominant patterns gradually travel along and move upward on the horizontal axis or outward on the vertical axis. Some exceptions to this trend catch the eye. First, in terms of dominant inward scores, along the horizontal axis, the scores registered for *Singh, Carpenter, Baumbast, Zhu & Chen, Eind* and *Metock* indicate long-lasting follow-up citation structures suggesting that these judgments continued to hold a precedent relevance for a long line of cases that followed afterwards. In respect of dominant outward scores, along the vertical axis, particularly the lengthy periods covered by *Eind*, *Metock* and, more recently, *O&B* and *S&G* attract the attention.

In addition, the model's findings also render the 'density' or intensity of self-citation within these intervals visible. In that respect, and as a second observation, especially the dominant structures identified in the most recent period of the case law's development, more precisely, the period following on from the *Zambrano* ruling, is characterized by a high density of self-citation activity, suggesting an important role for precedent-based developments in these more recent rulings.

6.3.2.2 *Trends and Patterns over Time: Structuring the Qualitative Analysis*

In the next analytical chapter, each of the identified dominant inward and outward citation structures, as depicted in Fig. 6.1, will be subject to qualitative, contextualized reviews of the discourses that underpinned them. This qualitative discourse analysis will follow the chronological order of the jurisprudence's argumentative development, tracing the patterns set out by the numerically identified structures as they sequentially travel through the case law record.

Starting at the outset, the two very first rulings rendered by the CJEU on family reunification immigration questions, the 1976 *Kermaschek* decision and the 1982 *Morson & Jhanjan* case, also mark the first two dominant inward citation scores registered in the record. This suggests that these first two rulings immediately provided doctrinal principles that would come to hold a significant precedent relevance for the case law that followed in sequence. Accordingly, in a first phase, the qualitative analysis starts by examining the discourses and arguments advanced in *Kermaschek* and *Morson & Jhanjan* and reviewing how the weight of these discourses in later case law. On that basis, the analysis also immediately sheds light on the dominant outward scores, or references to preceding case law, registered for *Zaoui*, *Koua Poirrez* and *Uecker & Jacquet* in which reference is made to *Kermaschek* and *Morson & Jhanjan*.

As the case law further evolved, a higher incidence of self-citation observations and, accordingly, also more dominant patterns can be registered within the numerical findings. Three dominant inward scores particularly catch the eye on account of their long-term nature in the period following on from the very first developments. That is, the follow-up citation scores linked to the 1992 *Singh* ruling and those connected to the later, 2002 *Carpenter* and *Baumbast* decisions. The long-lasting patterns registered for these cases suggest that all three of them held a precedent relevance for a long line of cases that followed afterwards. Particularly the inward scores of *Singh* and *Carpenter* stretch almost the entire evolution of the case law. Additionally, and entrenched by these three long structures, the inward scores linked to the *MRAX* ruling also display comparatively dominant values, albeit of a less long-lived nature. These four cases, and the discourses that underpinned their precedent-based relevance for the case law that followed are the subject of a further set of qualitative, in-depth reviews. The discursive, in-depth reviews of these dominant inward scores also shed further light, in analogy to the above, on the dominant outward scores registered for *Kaba II*, *Commission v Spain* (C-157/03) and *Commission v Spain* (C-503/03).

In a next phase, the qualitative review traces the dominant inward citation scores registered for the 2003 *Akrich* ruling, followed by the dominant outward scores registered for the *Jia* case which relate closely to the outcome of *Akrich*. Next, the analysis turns to a review of, in sequence, the dominant inward citation scores relating to the *Zhu & Chen*, *Eind* and *Metock* decisions. Each of these three judgments display a long-lasting dominant inward citation structure, suggesting, again, that each of them introduced discursive elements that would come to hold an argumentative precedent value for a long line of cases to follow. In addition, besides the long timeframe that the *Metock* inward scores cover, they also display a strong 'density', or intensity of self-citation, suggesting that this ruling held an important value as a precedent, not only for a long time period to come but also for a large amount of cases rendered within that (long) period. Moreover, *Metock* as well as *Eind* (rendered in 2007) display, besides their dominant inward scores, also far-stretching dominant outward scores, suggesting that these two judgments were at the same time important for future case law as well as significantly grounded in earlier jurisprudential developments. A final set of dominant structures reviewed for this episode of the Court's case law relates to the dominant outward and inward scores of the 2006 *EPvCouncil* decision and the dominant outward scores of the related 2010 *Chakroun* ruling. The dominant outward scores for both rulings suggest that both of them were significantly embedded within the Court's preceding decisions. This is in itself noteworthy as these two rulings relate to the first proceedings that arose before Luxembourg on family reunion provisos within the framework of EU immigration law (instead of, until then, free movement law).

The most recent phase of the case law's development, that is the phase following on from the 2011 *Zambrano* decision, is marked by a further increased incidence and density of self-citation observations. This suggests an augmented importance of precedent-based developments from *Zambrano* onwards. The dominant inward citation structures identified for this recent period relate to those of, first, the *Zambrano* case and thereafter those of *McCarthy*, *Dereci*, *Iida*, *Ymeraga* and *Alopka*. Each of these cases followed on to one another within a timeframe that does not cover more than three years (from 2011 to 2014). In addition, and simultaneously, the qualitative reviews of this most recent phase also shed light on the dominant outward scores registered for the *O&S* case as well as those connected to *Zambrano*, *Dereci* and *Ymeraga*. These latter three cases, like *Metock* and *Eind*, display dominant scores both in respect of their outward references as in regard of their inward citations which suggests that they were at the same time significantly embedded within earlier jurisprudential developments whilst holding an important precedent relevance for case law to come.

A final phase of the case law record is defined by the dominant outward scores registered for the 2014 *O&B* and *S&G* decisions. The outward scores linked to *O&B* and *S&G* in fact define the longest-stretching outward scores registered for the case law overall, stretching back to the 1992 *Singh* ruling. This suggest that both decisions built on argumentative elements deriving from, by and large, the case law's entire prior evolution.

6.4 Conclusion

The above numerical findings provide a systematization of observations of self-citations within the CJEU's family reunification jurisprudence. The need for such a quantitative systematization is connected, first, to the study's explicitly longitudinal outlook which calls for a dataset of Court rulings that spans a sufficiently long time period and is, by consequence, voluminous. On the basis of the above numerical exercise, the data were parsed so as to display the relative numerical importance held by different self-citation scores. A threshold value was adopted which allowed for identifying the most important scores within the record as a whole. These findings, and as the model's prime aim, provide a blueprint that guides the further qualitative reviews into the discourses underpinning the identified patterns. In addition, to the extent that the model allows for selecting the data for further qualitative review by means of objective, numerical criteria, it also guards the analysis as a whole from problems related to selective sampling on the dependent variable (*in casu*, autonomous Court behaviour).

The next chapter proceeds with in-depth and contextualized analyses of the discourses and arguments that underpinned the numerically identified self-citation structures. In line with the presentation of the numerical findings above, these qualitative analyses follow the chronological order of the case law record as it evolved.

References

Primary Sources

CJEU Case Law

Case C-40/76 *Slavica Kermaschek v Bundesanstalt für Arbeit* [1976] ECR 1669.

Case C-35/82 *Elestina Esselina Christina Morson v State of the Netherlands and Head of the Plaatselijke Politie within the meaning of the Vreemdelingenwet; Sweradjie Jhanjan v State of the Netherlands* [1982] ECR 3723.

Case C-238/83 *Caisse d'Allocations Familiales de la Région Parisienne v Mr and Mrs Richard Meade* [1984] ECR 2631.

Case C-267/83 *Aissatou Diatta v Land Berlin* [1985] ECR 567.

Case C-94/84 *Office national de l'emploi v Joszef Deak* [1985] ECR 1873.

Case C-131/85 *Emir Gül v Regierungspräsident Düsseldorf* [1986] ECR 1573.

Case C-147/87 *Saada Zaoui v Caisse régionale d'assurance maladie de l'Ile-de-France (CRAMIF)* [1987] ECR 5511.
Cases C-297/88 & C-197/89 *Massam Dzodzi v Belgian State* [1990] ECR I-3763.
Case C-370/90 *The Queen v Immigration Appeal Tribunal and Surinder Singh, ex parte Secretary of State for Home Department* [1992] ECR I-4265.
Case C-206/91 *Ettien Koua Poirrez v Caisse d'allocations familiales de la région parisienne, substituée par la Caisse d'allocations familiales de la Seine-Saint-Denis* [1992] ECR I-6685.
Case C-243/91 *Belgian State v Noushin Taghavi* [1992] ECR I-4401.
Case C-64/96 *Land Nordrhein-Westfalen v Kari Uecker and Vera Jacquet v Land Nordrhein-Westfalen* [1992] ECR I-3171.
Case C-356/98 *Arben Kaba v Secretary of State for the Home Department* [2000] ECR I-2623.
Case C-413/99 *Baumbast and R v Secretary of State for the Home Department* [2002] ECR I-7091.
Case C-60/00 *Mary Carpenter v Secretary of State for the Home Department* [2002] ECR I-6279.
Case C-459/99 *Mouvement contre le racisme, l'antisémitisme et la xénophobie ASBL (MRAX) v Belgian State* [2002] ECR I-6591.
Case C-189/00 *Urszula Ruhr v Bundesanstalt für Arbeit* [2001] ECR I-8225.
Case C-257/00 *Nani Givane and Others v Secretary of State for the Home Department* [2003] ECR I-345.
Case C-466/00 *Arben Kaba v Secretary of State for the Home Department* [2003] ECR I-2219.
Case C-109/01 *Secretary of State for the Home Department v Hacene Akrich* [2003] ECR I-9607.
Case C-200/02 *Kunqian Catherine Zhu and Man Lavette Chen v Secretary of State for the Home Department* [2004] ECR I-9925.
Case C-157/03 *Commission of the European Communities v Kingdom of Spain* [2005] ECR I-2911.
Case C-503/03 *Commission of the European Communities v Kingdom of Spain* [2006] ECR I-1097.
Case C-540/03 *European Parliament v Council of the European Union* [2006] ECR I-5769.
Case C-1/05 *Yunying Jia v Migrationsverket* [2006] ECR I-00001.
Case C-10/05 *Cynthia Mattern and Hajrudin Cikotic v Ministre du Travail et de l'Emploi* [2006] ECR I-3145.
Case C-165/05 *Commission of the European Communities v Grand Duchy of Luxemburg* [2005] not yet reported.
Case C-291/05 *Minister voor Vreemdelingenzaken en Integratie v R. N. G. Eind* [2007] ECR I-10719.

Case C-57/07 *Commission of the European Communities v Grand Duchy of Luxemburg* [2007] ECR I-183.
Case C-87/07 *Commission v Malta* [2007] OJ C 82.
Case C-91/07 *Commission v Italy* [2007] OJ C 82.
Case C-192/07 *Commission v Germany* [2007] OJ C 117.
Case C-551/07 *Deniz Sahin v Bundesminister für Inneres* [2008] ECR I-10453.
Case C-127/08 *Blaise Baheten Metock and Others v Minister for Justice, Equality and Law Reform* [2008] ECR I-6241.
Case C-310/08 *London Borough of Harrow v Nimco Hassan Ibrahim and Secretary of State for the Home Department* [2010] ECR I-1065.
Case C-578/08 *Rhimou Chakroun v Minister van Buitenlandse Zaken* [2010] ECR I-1893.
Case C-34/09 *Gerardo Ruiz Zambrano v Office national de l'emploi (ONEM)* [2011] ECR I-1177.
Case C-247/09 *Alketa Xhymshiti v Bundesagentur für Arbeit—Familienkasse Lörrach* [2010] ECR I-11845.
Case C-434/09 *Shirley McCarthy v Secretary of State for the Home Department* [2011] ECR I-3375.
Case C-508/10 *European Commission v Kingdom of the Netherlands* [2012] OJ C174/7.
Case C-256/11 *Murat Dereci and Others v Bundesministerium für Inneres* [2011] ECR I-11315.
Case C-40/11 *Yoshikazu Iida v Stadt Ulm* [2013] OJ C 9/10.
Case C-83/11 *Secretary of State for the Home Department v Muhammad Sazzadur Rahman and Others* [2013] OJ C 331/6.
Case C-155/11 *Bibi Mohammad Imran v Minister van Buitenlandse Zaken* [2011] ECR I-0595.
Case C-356/11 & C-357/11 *O and S v Maahanmuuttovirasto and Maahanmuuttovirasto v L* [2013] OJ C 26/19.
Case C-529/11 *Olaitan Ajoke Alarape and Olukayode Azeez Tijani v Secretary of State for the Home Department* [2013] OJ C 225/20.
Case C-45/12 *Office national d'allocations familiales pour travailleurs salariés (ONAFTS) v Radia Hadj Ahmed* [2013] OJ C 225/40.
Case C-86/12 *Adzo Domenyo Alokpa and Others v Ministre du Travail, de l'Emploi et de l'Immigration* [2013] OJ C 344/21.
Case C-87/12 *Kreshnik Ymeraga and Others v Ministre du Travail, de l'Emploi et de l'Immigration* [2013] OJ C 225/44.
Case C-423/12 *Flora May Reyes v Migrationsverket* [2014].
Case C-456/12 *O. v Minister voor Immigratie, Integratie en Asiel and Minister voor Immigratie, Integratie en Asiel v B. Reference for a preliminary ruling: Raad van State—Netherlands* [2014] OJ C135/5.

Literature

Creswell, J., & Clark, V. (2010). *Designing and Conducting Mixed Methods Research*. Thousand Oaks, CA: SAGE Publications.

Derlén, M., & Lindholm, J. (2014). Goodbye *van Gend en Loos*, Hello *Bosman*? Using Network Analysis to Measure the Importance of Individual CJEU Judgments. *European Law Journal, 20*(5), 667–687.

De Somer, M., & Vink, M. (2015). 'Precedent' and Fundamental Rights in the CJEU's Case Law on Family Reunification Immigration. *European Integration Online Papers, 19*, 1–33.

Fowler, J., & Jeon, S. (2008). The Authority of Supreme Court Precedent. *Social Networks, 30*, 16–30.

Jacob, M. (2014). *Precedents and Case-based Reasoning in the European Court of Justice: Unfinished Business*. New York: Cambridge University Press.

Lupu, Y., & Voeten, E. (2012). Precedent in International Courts: A Network Analysis of Case Citations by the European Court of Human Rights. *British Journal of Political Science, 42*(2), 413–439.

Pelc, K. (2014). The Politics of Precedent in International Law: A Social Network Application. *American Political Science Review, 108*(3), 547–564.

Stone Sweet, A. (2004). *The Judicial Construction of Europe*. Oxford: Oxford University Press.

CHAPTER 7

Qualitatively Charting Precedents

7.1 Introduction

This chapter starts off from the numerical observations presented in the preceding quantitative analysis. It proceeds, more precisely, with in-depth and contextualized analyses of the discursive elements and patterns that underpinned the dominant self-citation structures identified within the case law's long-term evolution. The need for such further qualitative analyses derives, as observed above, from the expectation that what lends precedents an autonomy-enhancing value is not necessarily the numerical frequency with which a case is cited, but more importantly, the substance of the arguments that were being reinforced through such citations and the discursive weight they held in the context of new proceedings. Second, and in connection, the below qualitative review also serves to capture the causal mechanisms, of mostly a discursive nature, that are theoretically expected to underpin the autonomy-strengthening effects of reasoning by precedent. On that basis, to the extent that it enables collecting the contextualized empirical evidence necessary to corroborate similarly context-dependent hypotheses, the qualitative analyses also guard the analysis as a whole from reproducing binary, metatheoretical frameworks which are still employed in quantitative analyses where they hinder opportunities at generating consensual understandings (*cf.* Chap. 2). Following the two-fold structure of the study's theoretical framework (Chap. 3), attention particularly goes out to examining the discursive interactions taking place

M. De Somer, *Precedents and Judicial Politics in EU Immigration Law*, European Administrative Governance,
https://doi.org/10.1007/978-3-319-93982-7_7

between, first, the Court and its judicial interlocutors, that is national courts and litigant parties and, second, the Court and Member States.

The analysis draws, first and foremost, on the texts of the judgments which embed the Court's presentation of its reasoning and, to greater or lesser extents, also provide information on the discourses advanced by private litigants, domestic courts and/or national governments. In addition, further information derives from the 'Reports of the Hearing' which were retrieved for all the cases for which such a report was available (that is, all cases that had an oral hearing). These reports are prepared by the Judge-Rapporteur and contain a description of the factual and legal settings of the case, along with the questions referred and summaries of the written observations submitted by national governments. These reports were useful for gaining additional insights into the arguments and discourses put forward by the Court's interlocutors.[1]

The analysis follows the chronological order of the case law record as it developed from the first, 1976 *Kermaschek* ruling onwards and trails, more precisely, the sequences of dominant self-citation structures identified in the preceding chapter. The case law's long-term development was subdivided into five episodes which are reviewed in their respective order. A first episode and concurrent subsection reviews the very earliest developments, from the *Kermaschek* ruling up to the case law of the early 1990s (Sect. 7.2). In a next stage, the analysis moves on to consider the jurisprudential developments as they further evolved from the 1992 *Singh* judgment onwards, reviewing the dominant inward citation patterns registered for the latter ruling, as well as those relating to *Carpenter, MRAX* and *Baumbast* (Sect. 7.3). A third section reviews the jurisprudential developments of the early 2000s up to the late 2000s, analysing the patterns connected to *Akrich, Jia, Zhu & Chen, Eind, Metock, EPvCouncil* and *Chakroun* (Sect. 7.4). Next, the analysis considers the developments that have followed on from the 2011 *Zambrano* decision, examining the discourses underpinning the citation patterns related to, besides *Zambrano, McCarthy, Dereci, Iida, O&S, Ymeraga* and *Alopka* (Sect. 7.5). The final

[1] Since 1994 such reports are no longer published within the European Court Reports. Instead, for Reports of the Hearing from 1994 onwards, individual requests on the cases of interest have to be made with the Court's press and information unit. On the basis of such requests, Reports of the Hearing were obtained for more or less two thirds of the cases selected for qualitative review. They are on file with the author.

subsection looks at the most recent case law developments reviewed, that is, those connected to *O&B* and *S&G* (Sect. 7.6).

The qualitative reviews presented in the below analysis provide the third and final set of observations of the study's three-fold empirical strategy. On the basis of these final observations, the next and final chapter retraces ***whether*** and if so, ***how***, reasoning by precedent leverages the Court's judicial autonomy in the area of family reunification by comparing the findings on Member States' interests presented in Chap. 5 with those on precedent-based discursive interactions traced in Chap. 6 and qualitatively reviewed in what follows below. Accordingly, whereas the present chapter traces the chronological order of the case law's long-term evolution, the analytical focus is shifted in the next chapter which joins together the different sets of discursive dynamics observed across the case law's evolution, independent of their chronological ordering, and reviews their cumulative effects.

7.2 The Mid 1970s—Early 1990s: Derived Rights and the Internal Rule

The first two dominant self-citation patterns identified in the case law record relate to the inward scores of the first *Kermaschek* judgment rendered in 1976, and its successor, rendered several years later, *Morson & Jhanjan*. The ***Kermaschek*** case, first, dealt with the social security rights granted to family members of moving workers under EU free movement legislation. More specifically, in proceedings over a conflict between the Yugoslav spouse (Mrs Kermaschek) of a German national (Mr Kermaschek) and the German social security administration, a German social law court wanted to know whether the relevant free movement rules applied to the situation at hand and, more precisely, if this was the case even "if the spouse is not a national of a Member State" (*Kermaschek*, p. 1671). The Court stated, first, and in very precise terms, that the nationality of the members of the family "does not matter for this purpose", and hence that third-country national family members were not excluded from the legislation's personal scope. However, the Court added that it followed from a literal interpretation of the legislation that direct rights were provided to moving workers only. Family members, on the other hand, could only claim "derived rights" (Ibid., p. 1676). In the Court's view, the provisions at stake referred to two clearly distinct categories of persons, that is, "workers on the one hand, and the members of their family and their survivors on the other". Accordingly, as the Court continued, "whereas the persons belonging to the first category can claim the rights to benefits covered by the regulation as rights of their own, the persons belonging to the second category can only claim derived rights, acquired through their status as a member of the family or a survivor of a worker" (Ibid., pp. 1676–1677). Following from this 'derived rights' reasoning, Mrs. Kermaschek was found not to enjoy any rights under the legislation in question. The rights referred to were provided to the worker, that is, to Mr. Kermaschek, and his situation was not such as to fall within the protective scope of EU free movement law.

The *Kermaschek* decision foreclosed, from that moment in time, any further questions on whether family members with a third-country nationality were covered by the scope of free movement law. The derived rights rule, on the other hand, which the Court had set out in more general terms, was to become the subject of a host of further requests for clarification. In fact, all subsequent references to *Kermaschek*, which define the judgment's dominant inward citation scores, relate to questions on the correct application and precise implications of the derived rights formula. In that manner as well, these questions would come to provide the CJEU with opportunities to further flesh out this rule over the course of cases to follow.

To begin with, in *Zaoui* which also concerned questions on the entitlement to social security rights of the non-EU national spouse (Mr Zaoui) of a French citizen, the Court re-confirmed, with reference to *Kermaschek*, that the members of the family of a worker can only claim derived rights, that is to say, "rights acquired through their status as members of a worker's family" (*Zaoui*, paragraph 11). On that basis it then considered that the social security rights' claims at stake referred to a type of rights which individuals received in capacities other than that of being a member of a worker's family and that, hence, such rights did not constitute derived rights. Moreover, the situation of Mr. Zaoui's French spouse was also not such as to fall within the scope of EU law.

The derived rights rule also featured in the Court's *Taghavi* decision. With reference to *Kermaschek*, the Court repeated that the members of a worker's family can only claim "derived rights, that is to say, rights acquired through their status as members of a worker's family" (*Taghavi*, paragraph 7). On that basis, the Court ruled again that the third-country national spouse of a Member State citizen could not lay claim, under EU law, to rights provided for as personal rights. In the *Ruhr* case which embeds the third and final inward citation of *Kermaschek*, the plaintiff, Mrs. Ruhr, challenged the application of the derived rights rule in situations where, as she pleaded, such an application could affect the freedom of movement of a Member State national (*Ruhr*, paragraphs 8–9). More precisely, Mrs. Ruhr, who was the third-country national spouse of a German citizen, stated that in her situation, the failure of Germany to grant her the unemployment benefits to which she was entitled in Luxembourg where she had previously resided and worked would force her to move back to Luxembourg instead of continuing to reside in Germany with her husband. In such a situation, she continued, Mr. Ruhr would be obliged to move there too. Following this reasoning, should the derived rights rule be applied to her case, her husband Mr. Ruhr, a community national, would be faced with an obligation to transfer his residence to Luxembourg which would affect his freedom of movement. The Court answered, however, that the "interpretation given (…) in *Kermaschek* continues to hold good" (Ibid., paragraph 24). None of the claims that had been made nor any of the "observations lodged" could undermine that conclusion (Ibid., paragraph 22). On the basis of these firm holdings, no further follow-up questions, and accordingly, citations arose.

The second pattern of numerically dominant inward or subsequent citation scores identified in the model is the pattern linked to the Court's 1982 ***Morson & Jhanjan*** ruling. Similar to the dominant scores of *Kermaschek* above, an in-depth review of these subsequent citations reveals that they were not connected, or not in the first place, to possible factual similarities between the proceedings in *Morson & Jhanjan* and those in the cases that followed thereafter. Rather, like the scores for *Kermaschek*, they related to the establishment and subsequent refinement of a new judicial principle. More specifically, the *Morson & Jhanjan* decision would lay the doctrinal groundwork for the "internal rule" which was to become a fundamental guiding principle for subsequent case law.

The *Morson & Jhanjan* case concerned the situations of two Suriname nationals, Mrs. Morson and Mrs. Jhanjan, who wished to establish themselves in the Netherlands with, respectively, their Dutch daughter and Dutch son. The two Dutch nationals, the daughter of Mrs. Morson and the son of Mrs. Jhanjan, had always lived and worked within the Netherlands without ever having used their free movement rights. In other words, they were 'static' EU nationals. Although their situations would not ordinarily fall within the scope of EU free movement law, the applicant parties raised questions on the incidence of 'reverse discrimination' in respect of their treatment under domestic Dutch law compared to the more favourable treatment which moving Union citizens could receive in the Netherlands under EU law. More precisely, they claimed that a refusal to grant them residence permits, such as the permits provided to family members falling within the scope of EU free movement provisions, amounted to an infringement of these provisions when read together with the 'prohibition on discrimination' enshrined in primary Treaty law (*Morson & Jhanjan*, p. 3726). The Court held, however, that, as the situation of the two Dutch nationals did not come "within the area to which Community law applies" to begin with, the primary provisions on non-discrimination could not be invoked in their respect. As it further added, such a conclusion did not only emerge from the wording of the relevant provisions, but also accorded with "their purpose, which is to assist in the abolition of all obstacles to the establishment of a common market in which the nationals of the Member States may move freely within the territory of those states in order to pursue their economic activities" (Ibid., paragraph 15). It then added, in more general terms, that "the Treaty provisions on freedom of movement for workers and the rules adopted to implement them cannot be applied to cases which have no factor linking them with any of the situations governed by Community law" (Ibid., paragraph 16). This holding would become known thereafter as the purely or wholly internal rule.

The rule featured centrally in the cases that followed on from *Morson & Jhanjan*. In fact, all subsequent citations registered for *Morson & Jhanjan*, which define the case's dominant inward scores, relate to the judgment's holdings on the internal rule. To begin with, these holdings were repeated verbatim in both the *Zaoui* (paragraph 15) and *Dzodzi* (paragraph 23) cases which arose out of questions sent to the EU judiciary by French and Belgian tribunals respectively. Both times, the 'internal rule' was cited to support the conclusion that the situations of the family members of 'static' EU nationals at hand did not fall within the scope of application of EU law. When some years later, in the context of the *Koua Poirrez* case, a French court again questioned (after the plaintiff had submitted arguments along such lines) whether the non-discrimination principle enshrined in EU Treaty law precluded situations of reverse discrimination, the Court firmly re-endorsed its earlier holdings. With reference to *Morson & Jhanjan*, it emphasized that it had "consistently held" that "Articles 7 and 48 of the Treaty", embedding the non-discrimination clause and guaranteeing workers' right to free movement respectively, "may be invoked only where the case in question comes within the area to which Community law applies". The regulations adopted to implement these Treaty provisions could, "similarly", not be "applied to cases which have no factor linking them with any of the situations governed by Community law and all elements of which are purely internal to a single Member State" and, consequently, "Community legislation regarding freedom of movement for workers cannot be applied to the situation of workers who have never exercised the right to freedom of movement within the Community" (*Koua Poirrez*, paragraphs 10–12).

In 1993 as the Maastricht Treaty's entry into force introduced the concept of Union Citizenship, the 'internal rule' judicial state of affairs was challenged again. More specifically, in the case of ***Uecker & Jacquet***, a German higher court requested clarification on whether the new "fundamental principles of a Community moving towards European Union" continued to permit Member States to apply rules of national law "incompatible with the principle of non-discrimination" against their own nationals who, following Maastricht, were now also Union nationals (*Uecker & Jacquet*, paragraph 12). *Uecker & Jacquet* concerned, more specifically, the situations of Mrs. Uecker and Mrs. Jacquet who were two third-country national spouses of 'static' German citizens. Mrs. Uecker and Mrs. Jacquet resided with their husbands in Germany and sought to lay claim to the employment rights provided to family members of Union citizens under free movement legislation. Under German domestic family reunification law, their employment rights were contested.

The Court repeated in respect of these situations that, as it had "consistently held", the "Treaty rules governing freedom of movement and regulations adopted to implement them cannot be applied to cases which have no factor linking them with any of the situations governed by Community law and all elements of which are purely internal to a single Member State" (Ibid., paragraph 16). To that effect, it summoned the support of its prior *Morson & Jhanjan* decision, as well as the reinforcement thereof in the later *Zaoui* and *Koua Poirrez* rulings. Consequently, and as in *Koua Poirrez*, the Court posited that "Community legislation regarding freedom of movement for workers cannot be applied to the situations of workers who have never exercised the right to freedom of movement within the Community" (Ibid., paragraph 17). With these holdings reiterated, it reviewed their continued relevance in light of, as the German court had asked, "the fundamental principles of a Community moving towards European Union" (Ibid., paragraph 22). In that regard, it first noted that "citizenship of the Union" was "not intended to extend the scope *ratione materiae* of the Treaty also to internal situations which have no link with Community law". On that basis, and rehearsing the reasoning adduced in *Morson & Jhanjan*, "(a)ny discrimination which nationals of a Member State may suffer under the law of that State" remained "within the scope of that law" and therefore needed to be dealt with "within the framework of the internal legal system of that State" (Ibid., paragraph 23).

The internal rule holdings of *Morson & Jhanjan* reappeared one last time within the collected case law in the context of the *Carpenter* case of the early 2000s which is discussed in the next subsection. As will further emerge in the below, both this internal rule as well as the preceding 'derived rights rule', established and further refined on the basis of these earliest precedent-based developments, would come to strongly condition the premises on which the subsequent litigation in this area was articulated, debated and decided.

7.3 The 1990s: The Internal Rule, 'Effet Utile', Fundamental Rights and EU Citizenship

As time progressed, the case law record became marked by a higher incidence of self-citation observations and, accordingly, more dominant patterns. Three dominant inward scores catch the eye in the period immediately following on from the earliest developments on account of their longitudinal nature. That is, particularly the inward scores linked to the *Singh*, *Carpenter* and *Baumbast* rulings display a long-lasting dominant pattern suggesting that these cases held a precedent relevance for a long line of cases that followed afterwards. Especially the dominant inward scores of *Singh* and *Carpenter* span almost the entire development of the case law record. Additionally, and entrenched by these three long structures, the inward citation scores linked to the *MRAX* ruling also display comparatively dominant values, albeit of a less long-lived nature. These four cases, *Singh, Carpenter, Baumbast* and *MRAX* and their follow-up citations are discussed in what follows.

To begin with, the 1992 ***Singh*** case concerned the situation of Mr. Singh, an Indian national married to Mrs. Singh, a British national. Previously, Mr. and Mrs. Singh had resided in Germany for two years where Mrs. Singh had been employed in exercise of her free movement rights. The couple had been back in the UK for five years. During this period, they had separated and at a later time their marriage was formally dissolved which resulted in the revocation of Mr. Singh's right to remain under British domestic immigration law. Proceedings were lodged against this deportation order and the case was eventually referred to Luxembourg as the UK judiciary was uncertain whether, upon return from having exercised free movement rights in another Member State, EU free movement law continued to apply and whether its provisions could, hence, be invoked by Union nationals against their own state. Not the Treaties, nor any secondary legislation, were considered to provide stipulations that could guide the answer to such questions.

As registered in the decision's report for the hearing, the UK government vehemently argued for a negative answer to the questions raised in the written observation that it submitted. To that purpose, it advanced a series of different arguments and rationales. To begin with, it referred to the Court's earlier *Morson & Jhanjan* ruling to contend that Community law "does not apply to circumstances 'wholly internal' to a Member State". More in particular, as it continued, "a national of a Member State or the spouse of such a person cannot rely on Community law to avoid the application to him or her of national legislation relating to immigration" (Report for the hearing *Singh* case, p. 4270). In that respect it also pointed out that Mrs. Singh's right to return to the UK was conferred on her by British law. If, on the other hand, Community rules would be applied to her situation, the UK government stated, the British authorities would have been able "to refuse Mrs Singh the right of entry and residence on grounds of public policy, public security or public health" or "to deport her" even though as a British citizen she could not be deported under UK law (Ibid., p. 4271). In addition, the UK government asserted that "every Member State has a legitimate interest in preventing its own nationals and their spouses from relying on Community law in order to circumvent conditions imposed by national immigration law". More specifically, it pointed out that the "British rules on immigration have in particular as their legitimate object to prevent foreigners from obtaining a right of residence in the United Kingdom by way of fictitious marriages". In all, it believed that "the granting of a right of residence to the spouse, children under the age of 21 or other dependent relatives of a British citizen who are not nationals of a Member State would create a real risk of abuse because that citizen would merely have to travel to another Member State for the purpose of there pursuing an economic activity in order for nationals of non-member countries to be allowed to enter and reside in the United Kingdom following his or her return" (Ibid.). Adding thereto, the UK government contended that if EU free movement legislation would also apply to return movements, "the rights of Member States with regard to immigration would be undermined". As a final argument, in its view, such an application of EU law would also lead to the "peculiar consequence" that, "whereas the national rules governing the residence of non-nationals is designed to ensure for them a permanent status", by applying Community law such a right of residence "could be granted only so long as the Community national was exercising an activity covered by the Treaty". It would then be "at least paradoxical if the right of residence of a spouse of a national of a Member State should depend, not on matrimonial ties, but rather on the continuing exercise by that national of an economic activity" (Ibid., pp. 4272–4273).

Countering arguments of this kind, and as registered in the case's report for the hearing, Mr. Singh asserted that "if a Community national were free to establish herself with her spouse only in Member States other than her own, the objective of free movement of persons between Member States could not be attained since that freedom would apply only as between some of them" (Ibid., p. 4273). Adding thereto, he stated that a failure to recognise the exercise of free movement rights in the "Member State of which the employed person is a national", could "distort patterns of employment in Member States and migration between such States" which would be contrary to the objects formulated in the EEC Treaty. Furthermore, he also supported his arguments with references to previous CJEU case law on the freedom of movement. In that respect he cited, amongst others, *Morson & Jhanjan* to emphasize that, as the Court had held in articulating the internal rule principle, Community law provisions "may be invoked only where the case in question comes within the area to which Community law applies" (Ibid., p. 4274). Arguing that, in the case at hand, Mrs. Singh's situation came "within the area to which Community law applies", and adopting an *a contrario* reasoning, it followed from the above CJEU dictum that it was open to her to invoke such Community law provisions, also "against her own Member State" (Ibid., p. 4275).

In spite of the contentious nature of the questions raised, the Court's reasoning on the *Singh* case was rather succinct. It centred, above all, on purpose-oriented arguments around the '*effet utile*' or 'useful effectiveness' of the legislation at issue. Such *effet utile* reasoning had also featured, albeit more on the side, in *Morson & Jhanjan*. In *Singh*, the Court pointed out, with references to other free movement decisions (not involving family reunification questions), that "the activities of the Community shall include the abolition, as between Member States, of obstacles to freedom of movement for persons" (*Singh*, paragraph 15). Similarly, it held that "the provisions of the Treaty relating to the free movement of persons are intended to facilitate the pursuit by Community citizens of occupational activities of all kinds throughout the Community, and preclude measures which might place Community citizens at a disadvantage when they wish to pursue an economic activity" (Ibid., paragraph 16). From there, and engaging with the questions put forward, it reasoned that "a national of a Member State might be deterred from leaving his country of origin in order to pursue an activity as an employed or self-employed person as envisaged by the Treaty in the territory of another Member State if, on returning to the Member State of which he is a national in order to pursue an activity there as an employed or self-employed person, the conditions of his entry and residence were not at least equivalent to those which he would enjoy under the Treaty or secondary law in the territory of another Member State" (Ibid., paragraph 19). The Court continued: "(h)e would in particular be deterred from so doing if his spouse and children were not also permitted to enter and reside in the territory of his Member State of origin under conditions at least equivalent to those granted them by Community law in the territory of another Member State" (Ibid., paragraph 20). Consequently, and as its final dictum, it followed that Community law required a Member State "to grant leave to enter and reside in its territory to the spouse, of whatever nationality, of a national of that State who has gone, with that spouse to another Member State in order to work there as an employed person (…) and returns to establish himself or herself (…) in the territory of the State of which he or she is a national" (Ibid., paragraph 25). In such contexts, "(t)he spouse must enjoy at least the same rights as would be granted to him or her under Community law if his or her spouse entered and resided in the territory of another Member State" (Ibid.).

The Court also engaged with some, but not all, of the arguments that had been advanced by the British government. To begin with, in respect of the logic that under Community law Mrs. Singh could be deported, whereas if UK law were applied to her situation she would, as a British citizen, be protected from such measures, the Court referred to Article 3 of the fourth protocol to the ECHR to highlight that, in any event, "a State may not expel one of its own nationals or deny him entry into its territory" (Ibid., paragraph 22). Furthermore, it also emphasized that "as regards the risk of fraud referred to by the United Kingdom", "the facilities created by the Treaty cannot have the effect of allowing the persons who benefit from them to evade the application of national legislation and of prohibiting Member States from taking the measures necessary to prevent such abuse" (Ibid., paragraph 24).

Overall, whilst clarifying the specific situation of Mr. and Mrs. Singh under EU law, the judgment remained silent on the more far-reaching implications that could flow from the continued application of EU law to the situations of 'returnees'. Depending on the exact ramifications, the outcome of *Singh* potentially opened up the door for a large range of new 'return-style' situations, and hence categories of persons (and their family members) to be brought within the aegis of EU law. As also expressed in the UK's written observations, EU free movement law could in that way start making strong inroads into—or, in the UK's phrasing, "undermine"—Member States' domestic immigration competences. For instance, and as raised by the British government, would the judgment's holdings also apply if the 'free movement' move 'to' and 'from' another Member State had been designed with the sole purpose of evading the application of more restrictive domestic immigration law? In addition, how long exactly would the protection of EU free movement law continue to apply? Only so long as the returning national was engaged in gainful employment or also beyond? Furthermore, how long exactly would an EU national be required to have resided or have been employed in another Member State before being able to lay claim to the continued protection of EU law upon his/her return? Would a couple of weeks or months suffice, or was a more significant period required? In addition, did the judgment's family reunion implications relate only to spouses, as per its dispositif, or also to other family members such as children as mentioned in passing in the text's operative part? Also, what if the family relationships did not yet exist prior to the first move, but were only established in the second, other Member State? In broader terms when the Court held that rights needed to be granted to returning EU nationals so as to eliminate any 'obstacles' or 'deterrent effects' to free movement rights, did it refer to the first movement, that of the EU national to the other Member State, or was the move back to the home State also a form of 'free movement' protected by EU law? In addition, by stating that Member States were not prohibited from taking measures to prevent abuse, but not applying these statements to the settings at hand, the Court also left the exact leeway granted through this dictum uncertain (see on these, and more questions opened up by *Singh* e.g., Watson, 1993; Barrett, 2003; Tryfonidou, 2009; Peers, 2009).

As could be expected, these questions created a strong demand for further clarification. In addition, by relaxing the requirements in regard of situations that could be regarded as not (or no longer) 'wholly internal' to Member States (in the case at hand, 'return situations'), the *Singh* judgment also opened up opportunities for private litigants to advance new rights claims with the aim of extending the favourable EU law application of *Singh* to their own situations. As will emerge in what follows, a self-reinforcing process was set in motion as the Court, in turn, continued setting out its decisions on the claims and questions following from *Singh* in ambiguous, multi-interpretable phrasings which, then again, triggered further litigation and related questions from domestic tribunals. In that manner, and on the basis of such 'increasing returns' logics, the Court was able to continue constructing its dicta on these politically sensitive questions in slow, step-by-step ways, unveiling their exact ramifications only over the course of time as new proceedings were brought before its bench. With the exception of the *Kaba I* and *Kaba II* cases, all subsequent references to *Singh* relate to questions on the precise remit of the judgment's scope. As the case law progressed, the questions left unaddressed by *Singh* would intertwine with further questions that arose in new factual settings. In so doing, they would come to cut across the jurisprudence's entire argumentative development. This is what defines the identified numerically important inward citation scores of *Singh* and, more in particular, the especially long-stretched nature of these scores. The most recent decisions on questions stemming from this 1992 judgment were rendered in March 2014 (*O&B* and *S&G*). In the discussions that follow below, the precise contours of *Singh* as put into question in the context of, in sequence, *Carpenter*, *Akrich*, *Eind*, *McCarthy*, *O&B* and *S&G* will receive further treatment as each of these cases is addressed in the context of the case law's episodes to which they relate.

The first in this list, *Carpenter*, is addressed immediately below, as this judgment also relates to the next dominant inward citation pattern identified after *Singh*. Like *Singh*, the dominant subsequent references to *Carpenter* would also come to span almost the entire development of the case law, marking a structure that similarly reaches up to the *S&G* case of 2014. In addition, the subsequent inward scores to *Carpenter* display a strong 'density', or intensity of self-citation activity and one that exceeds the level registered for *Singh*. Especially during the first couple of years that followed on from *Carpenter*'s delivery, almost every other subsequent judgment contained a reference to the latter judgment.

Carpenter concerned the situation of the third-country national (Filipino) spouse, Mrs. Carpenter, of a UK national, Mr. Carpenter. Mr. Carpenter sold advertising space in journals within the UK, but also in other Member States which required him to occasionally travel to the continent for short periods of time. When he was abroad, Mrs. Carpenter cared for the children of Mr. Carpenter's first marriage. Mrs. Carpenter had originally entered the UK on the basis of a temporary visa which she had overstayed. Whilst unlawfully resident in the UK, she had met and married Mr. Carpenter. Her subsequent application for a leave to remain as the spouse of a British national had been denied under UK immigration law and she was facing a deportation order. In the proceedings that were lodged against that deportation order, Mrs. Carpenter relied on Community law provisions arguing that, under these provisions, and as the spouse of a Community national, she was to be granted a leave to remain. More specifically, and taking cues from the Court's derived rights rule, Mrs. Carpenter 'admitted' to not enjoy a right of her own to reside in any Member State but nevertheless claimed "that her rights derive from those enjoyed by Mr Carpenter to provide services and to travel within the European Union" (*Carpenter*, paragraph 21). Additionally, and reproducing prior *effet utile* arguments, she held that by taking care of Mr. Carpenter's children she facilitated his right to provide services across the Union. Accordingly, should she be deported, her husband's right to provide services would be restricted (Ibid., paragraph 17). On top of that, should she be deported, Mr. Carpenter would in fact be required to go live with her in the Philippines, or would have to separate the members of his family unit. In both cases, his business would be affected (Ibid., paragraph 21).

The UK government argued strongly against the claims put forward by Mrs. Carpenter. To that purpose, it took cues from the preceding *Singh* case to which it had in fact been the losing party only a few years earlier. More precisely, it cited *Singh* to argue that Mr. Carpenter's situation (and, accordingly, that of Mrs. Carpenter), when in the UK, was not covered by EU law as his right to reside in the United Kingdom was granted to him, as a British citizen, under domestic UK law as "the Court had confirmed (…) in *Singh*" (Ibid., paragraph 22). In any event, since Mr. Carpenter had not exercised his right to freedom of movement to begin with, in the

UK's view, his spouse could also not rely on the premises of the preceding *Singh* case (Ibid., paragraph 24).

In presenting its considerations, the Court first challenged the perspective that Mr. Carpenter's situation was 'wholly internal' to the UK and therefore not covered by the scope of EU law. As it established, to the extent that a "significant proportion of Mr Carpenter's business consists of providing services, for remuneration to advertisers established in other Member States" and "in so far as the provider travels for that purposes to the Member State of the recipient" such services, and hence, Mr. Carpenter's situation, came "within the meaning of services" provided for in primary, Treaty law (Ibid., paragraph 29). The Court then moved on to consider EU secondary legislation on the freedom to provide services adopting both literal, as well as purpose-oriented ('effet utile') interpretation techniques. The final conclusion it derived in this respect, however, was that this secondary legislation "does not govern the right of residence of members of the family of a provider of services in his Member State of origin", such family reunion rights were only foreseen in instances where the provider of services moves to another Member State (Ibid., paragraph 36). Therefore, the answer to the questions raised depended on "whether, in circumstances such as those in the main proceedings, a right of residence in favour of the spouse may be inferred from the principles or other rules of Community law" (Ibid.). In what followed, two such principles were reviewed.

To begin with, and as the first of these two principles, the Court examined the application of fundamental rights considerations to the situation at hand. It pointed out in that respect that it had to be "remembered that the Community legislature has recognised the importance of ensuring the protection of the family life of nationals of the Member States in order to eliminate obstacles to the exercise of the fundamental freedoms guaranteed by the Treaty" (Ibid., paragraph 38). Next, the Court further elaborated on this connection between, on the one hand, fundamental rights considerations, and on the other, 'the exercise of the fundamental freedoms guaranteed by the Treaty'. In so doing, it tied a fundamental rights-based language to the preceding *effet utile*-oriented argumentation structures. More precisely, the Court argued that "(i)t is clear that the separation of Mr and Mrs Carpenter would be detrimental to their family life and, therefore, to the conditions under which Mr Carpenter exercises a fundamental freedom". As it continued in the same paragraph, that freedom "could not be fully effective if Mr Carpenter were to be deterred from exercising it by obstacles raised in his country of origin to the entry and residence of his spouse" (Ibid., paragraph 39). To that effect, the Court also summoned the support of its preceding *Singh* holdings were it had stated, independent of fundamental rights considerations, that the freedom of movement and establishment granted to a Community national could not be "fully effective if such a person may be deterred from exercising them by obstacles raised in his or her country of origin to the entry and residence of his or her spouse" (*Singh*, paragraph 23). The Court further expanded on these arguments by referring to Article 8 ECHR. It pointed out in this respect, first, that "(t)he decision to deport Mrs Carpenter constitutes an interference with the exercise by Mr Carpenter of his right to respect for his family life within the meaning of Article 8" which, as it pointed out, was "among the fundamental rights which according to the Court's settled case-law (…) are protected in Community law" (*Carpenter*, paragraph 41). Even though "no right of an alien to enter or to reside in a particular country is as such guaranteed by the Convention", the removal of a person from a country where close members of his family are living "may amount to an infringement of the right to respect for family life" as guaranteed by said Article 8 (Ibid., paragraph 42). With reference to ECtHR case law, the Court further highlighted that "(s)uch an inference will infringe the Convention if it does not meet the requirements of paragraph 2 of that article, that is unless it is (…) in particular, proportionate to the legitimate aim pursued" (Ibid.).

This provided the argumentative connection to, as the second principle, a review of the situation in light of the principle of proportionality. In that respect the Court noted, first, that whilst "Mr Carpenter's spouse had infringed the immigration laws of the United Kingdom by not leaving the country prior to the expiry of her leave to remain as a visitor", her conduct had nevertheless "since her arrival in the United kingdom in September 1994, (…) not been the subject of any other complaint that could give cause to fear that she might in the future constitute a danger to public order or public safety" (Ibid., paragraph 44). In that light, "(a) decision to deport Mrs. Carpenter, taken in circumstances such as those in the main proceedings" would not strike "a fair balance between the competing interests, that is, on the one hand, the right of Mr Carpenter to respect for his family life, and, on the other hand, the maintenance of public order and public safety" (Ibid., paragraph 43). In other words, it would constitute "an infringement which is not proportionate to the aim pursued" (Ibid., paragraph 45). As its final dictum, the Court concluded that the

Treaty provisions on the freedom to provide services, "read in the light of the fundamental right to respect for family life" precluded the refusal of a right to reside to Mrs. Carpenter (Ibid., paragraph 46).

On the whole, and as with *Singh*, whilst the Court's *Carpenter* ruling clarified the specific position of Mr. and Mrs. Carpenter under EU law, it left the further implications that could be derived from its dicta unaddressed. Some of the questions on the precise ramifications of *Carpenter* followed on from those that had been opened up by *Singh*, others were all together new and added to the uncertainties that had been triggered by the latter.

To begin with, the *Carpenter* ruling did not provide any clarification on the categories of family members in relation to which 'returnee' EU nationals could claim family reunion rights. Could, besides spouses, for instance also children be covered by EU law in return situations, or could right claims also be made in respect of other family members such as ascending relatives? Also, as after *Singh*, what if the family relationships did not yet exist prior to the first move, but were only established in the second, other Member State? Would such new relatives acquire derived rights under EU law even if they did not originally hold such rights in the home state prior to the move? In addition, how long exactly would the protection of EU law continue to accrue upon an EU national after his/her return to his/her home state? Would it entail life-long rights, or would the protection only apply so long as the returning national was engaged in a gainful employment activity? Furthermore, how much time exactly would an EU national have to spent in another Member State before being able to lay claim to EU rights in his/her home State upon returning? *Carpenter* seemed to suggest that also very short periods of time would suffice to trigger the continued application of EU law, but again, no precise stipulations were provided.

Besides not addressing a number of uncertainties that were triggered by *Singh*, *Carpenter* also gave rise to a further set of questions in and of itself. These were added to, and became intertwined with, the uncertainties post *Singh*. For instance, and in respect of the categories of family members to which the new returnee rights applied, what if no children had been involved in the *Carpenter* case and, accordingly, Mrs. Carpenter would not have been 'facilitating' the exercise of Mr. Carpenter's EU rights by providing childcare? In other words, what exact weight was to be attached to the Court's 'effet utile' considerations? As a follow-up question, was a direct link between the family member's activities and the Union Citizen's exercise of his/her EU rights required (e.g., as in *Carpenter*, freeing the Union citizen from childcare), or did the mere presence of a family member already constitute a 'facilitating' element in that, on that basis, the Union citizen's right to family life was safeguarded? If the latter interpretation was correct, again, what other sets of family reunion rights could accrue on the basis of claims relating to the protection of the fundamental right to family life?

This leads on to a further and more general series of questions opened up by *Carpenter*. By having constructed its dicta in broad, Treaty-based provisions, the Court's *Carpenter* decision also gave rise to a host of uncertainties in respect of the precise application and implications of such primary clauses. As mentioned, questions could be raised on the precise ramifications of the fundamental right to family life as a general principle of EU law. Similar queries could also be made, however, in respect of the precise contours of the proportionality review conducted in *Carpenter*. Moreover, by using Treaty provisions on the freedom of services to circumvent the fact that the situation of Mrs. Carpenter was not covered by secondary law, questions could also be advanced on the exact rights, or limitations to such rights, that could henceforth be derived directly from the EU Treaties. For instance, staying in the *Carpenter* context, once Mrs. Carpenter was granted a right to reside on the basis of Treaty law, could she also lay claim to further rights, e.g. to access to the labour market, as is possible for family members covered by the scope of secondary legislation? Conversely, in respect of limits, would Member States be able to restrict residence rights granted to family members directly on the basis of Treaty law on grounds of public policy, public security or public health as provided for in secondary legislation (see on these and other questions post *Carpenter*, e.g., Acierno, 2003; Barrett, 2003)?

On account of these various questions, and—similar to *Singh*—because *Carpenter* loosened the requirements for (return) situations to fall within the scope of EU law, the decision provided strong incentives for private individuals to test the case's ramifications in the context of their own family reunification claims. In addition, and more so than *Singh*, by anchoring its *Carpenter* decision in broad, highest-order primary law provisions, the Court further increased the likelihood that 'increasing returns' or 'positive feedback' litigation would follow which, next, would provide continued opportunities to further construct or refine its holdings. As outlined in Chap. 3, two reasons account for the strengthened likelihood of follow-up legal claims in the context of cases built around broad, Treaty norms.

First, as such highest-order norms are, by their very design, intended to cover a wide range of circumstances and are, accordingly, described at high levels of generality, individuals in a wide range of situations can find a point of connection to them. In addition, to the extent that these provisions embed, also by their very design, 'highest-order' norms which are to prevail over all additionally enacted legislation, private individuals are also incentivized to appeal to these norms in order to boost the normative strength of their own legal claims.

In light of these observations, and as could be expected, *Carpenter* became cited in a large number of follow-up proceedings. As registered in its numerically dominant inward scores, the 'density' of these citations, especially in the first five years following on from its rendering, was very high. In this first period, *Carpenter* was in fact cited in almost every other ruling that followed. In addition, and as also numerically recorded, whilst this high level of density would gradually decrease as time passed, overall, the inward citation scores of *Carpenter* nevertheless display a longevity that spans almost the entire case law's development which suggests that the judgment continued to hold a precedent relevance up onto the most recent period. As can also be seen from the numerical observations presented in Fig. 6.1 in Chap. 6, some of these follow-up citations—that is, those in *Akrich, Eind* and most recently, *S&G*—run parallel to the inward citations of *Singh*. As will be detailed in the below, these citations were made in relation to questions on the precise scope of application of EU law in returnee situations. In addition, an even larger number of inward citations following from *Carpenter* relates to the Treaty provisions that featured in the judgment. These follow-up citations to Treaty clauses arose both in judicial contexts related to 'returnee situations', but also appeared in contexts materially unrelated to the specific facts of *Carpenter* (e.g., the subsequent citations in *MRAX, Commission v Spain, C-157/03; Commission v Spain*, C-5043/03 and *EPvCouncil*). As will be documented in what follows, of these Treaty law invocations, especially the fundamental rights-based arguments of *Carpenter* would come to hold a strong precedent relevance for the lines of case law to follow.

This was for instance the case for the first follow-up citations to *Carpenter* made in the context of the ***MRAX*** proceedings. *MRAX* concerned a series of challenges that had been raised by a Belgian anti-discrimination NGO, MRAX ('Mouvement contre le racisme, l'antisémitisme et la xénophobie'), against a number of administrative and border control practices by the Belgian State in relation to third-country national spouses of Community nationals. Amongst others, the Belgian authorities were challenged for having refused residence permits to third-country national spouses of Community nationals who had entered the Belgian territory unlawfully, or whose visa had expired. In addition, third-country national spouses had also been sent back at the Belgian border on grounds of not possessing the requisite visa or identity documents. Furthermore, challenges were also raised in respect of the judicial remedies available to such spouses whose entry or residence had been denied. In the context of these challenges, the Belgian Conseil d'État had referred questions to the EU judiciary requesting a review of the compatibility of the contested Belgian practices with secondary EU free movement law as well as with such general principles of EU law as proportionality, non-discrimination as well as the fundamental right to family life.

The Belgian State, in its written observations on the case, defended its practices as stemming from the need of being able to conduct effective border control and other checks on foreigners entering its territory (see *MRAX*, paragraphs 43–45; paragraph 67). The Austrian government, which also intervened in the case, supported these Belgian contentions (Ibid., paragraph 68; paragraph 83). In spite of the immigration control concerns raised, however, the Court came to hold that the rights guarantees provided to the family members of moving EU nationals under EU law precluded control measures such as those applied by the Belgian state.

In presenting these conclusions, which came to significantly bootstrap Belgium's (and, by implication, other Member States') room for policy manoeuvre in respect of the admission and residence of such family members, the holdings of the preceding *Carpenter* ruling received much weight. This, mostly, to signpost and reinforce the status of fundamental rights principles in the context of applying EU family reunion provisions and, more specifically, the importance of such fundamental rights for ensuring the 'effet utile' of the latter provisions. The Court in fact started its reasoning on the *MRAX* case by rehearsing, with reference to *Carpenter*, "the importance of ensuring protection for the family life of nationals of the Member States in order to eliminate obstacles to the exercise of fundamental freedoms guaranteed by the Treaty" (*MRAX*, paragraph 53). At a further point in its considerations, the Court also revisited this fundamental rights/effet utile connection in the context of its examination of the case in relation to the principle of proportionality. In this regard it held that "to send back a third country national married to a national of a Member State where he is able to prove his identity and conjugal ties" was, "in view of the importance which the Community legislature has attached to the protection of family life", "disproportionate and, therefore, prohibited" (Ibid., paragraph 61).

The fundamental rights/effet utile argumentative link established in *Carpenter*, and reinforced in *MRAX*, subsequently re-appeared in the context of ***Commission v Spain*** (C-156/03) and ***Commission v Spain*** (C-503/03). Like *MRAX* the settings of these two cases showed little to no connection to the settings that had been at the basis of the *Carpenter* holdings which they would come to reinforce. The cases had been lodged by the Commission against Spain's restrictive entry and visa policies vis-à-vis third-country national family members of moving Union nationals. In at least one of these two proceedings, the Commission explicitly acknowledged that the Court's decision in *MRAX* constituted the background to the complaints that it had filed against the Spanish practices (*Commission v. Spain*, C-157/03, paragraph 21).

In both infringement cases, the Court showed itself keen to use the follow-up claims as an opportunity to further reinforce the discursive link between fundamental rights considerations and 'effet utile' arguments. In fact, in the two cases, the Court started its reasoning by drawing attention, "as a preliminary point", to "the importance of ensuring protection for the family life of nationals of the Member States in order to eliminate obstacles to the exercise of the fundamental freedoms guaranteed by the Treaty" (*Commission v. Spain*, C-157/03, paragraph 26; and similarly, *Commission v. Spain*, C-503/03; paragraph 41; paragraph 47). Both times as well, it cited, to that effect, the holdings of *Carpenter* as well as their reinforcement in *MRAX*. On that basis, and again for the two sets of proceedings, the Court also held that the leeway which the Spanish government had counted on having, breached the rights afforded to family members of moving Union nationals under EU law.

MRAX would thereafter become cited again in *Eind* and *Metock* which are discussed in Sect. 7.4. As can be noted, and is also clear from the numerical findings registered in Fig. 6.1 in Chap. 6, in that way the four follow-up citations to *MRAX*, which define the case's dominant inward scores, run parallel to the inward citation scores of *Carpenter*. This, in spite of the fact that the two cases show little to no connections in respect of their material settings. Instead, the parallel trend is linked to the fact that the precedent value of *MRAX* relates most significantly, and as in the above *Commission v Spain* proceedings, to the case's reinforcement of the connection between fundamental rights arguments and 'effet utile' considerations as first articulated in *Carpenter*.

A fourth, dominant inward citation structure identified in the Court's case law in this second phase of its development relates to the 2002 ***Baumbast*** decision. Similar to *Singh* and *Carpenter*, the *Baumbast* ruling would incite many and long-lasting follow-up references, which suggests that this case too held a long-lasting precedent relevance for future case law.

Baumbast concerned the situations of two families, the Baumbast family and the family of Mrs. R. Both families had moved to the UK following the exercise of free movement activities by, for the Baumbast family, Mr. Baumbast, a German national, and for the R family, Mrs. R's husband, a French national. Both Mrs. Baumbast and Mrs. R held a third-country nationality (Colombian and US respectively). Both families also had children. In the R family, these children held dual French-US citizenship, in the Baumbast family one daughter held dual German-Colombian citizenship whilst another daughter, who was the natural child of Mrs. Baumbast only, held Colombian citizenship. The children of both families had been enrolled in the British education system following their families' move to the UK.

The situations of the two families were also similar in that, after some time, their link with EU free movement law had become tenuous and, on that basis, the EU-derived residence rights of Mrs. Baumbast and Mrs. R were put at stake. First, the situation of Mrs. R had changed following her divorce from her EU national husband which, pursuant to the then applicable free movement rules (prior to the Citizenship Directive), caused her to lose her status as spouse of a moving Community national. Mrs. R had been granted custody over her children but they also retained regular contact with their father who still resided and worked in the UK. In the case of the Baumbast family, their residence rights under free movement law were disputed following a career change by Mr. Baumbast which led him to end his employment activities in the UK and instead take up employment in non-EU countries. The situations raised a number of questions on the (continued) application of EU law following changes to workers' or family members' statuses which none of the then applicable secondary free movement instruments provided stipulations on. Against that background, the British Immigration Appeal Tribunal referred the families' cases to Luxembourg together with an extensive series of questions on how these situations had to be interpreted in light of EU law.

To begin with, the British tribunal put forward a set of questions on the position and rights of the children involved. It requested, more precisely, clarification on whether the Baumbast children could continue the education they had started in the UK as family members of an EU national exercising free movement rights where, first, the children's parents were divorced, or where, second, the EU national parent had ceased to be a worker for the purposes of EU law, or where, third, the children were themselves not citizens of the Union. In follow up to this first set of questions, the referring court also wanted to know whether, if the children concerned could indeed continue to enjoy a right to education (*i.e.*, in case the first set of questions was answered in the affirmative), these children's primary carers, 'whether or not citizens of the Union', were in parallel entitled to a right of residence so that the continued right of education of the children would be 'encouraged' or 'facilitated'. Third, in regard of the specific situation of Mr. Baumbast, the UK tribunal asked whether, upon ceasing to be a worker for the purposes of secondary EU free movement law, he could nevertheless derive residence rights directly on the basis of Treaty law on EU citizenship pursuant to Article 18 EC (now Article 21 TFEU). If such was the case, the referring court also asked whether, next, and "consequently", his wife and children could enjoy derivative "residence, employment and other rights" on the basis of these Treaty provisions too (*Baumbast*, paragraph 28).

The Court addressed each set of questions in turn. First, in respect of the children's situations, it came to hold that a right to education continued to accrue to them independent of the three elements raised by the UK tribunal. That is, independent of the fact that the Union citizen parents with which they had come had ceased to be migrant workers, independent of the fact that the parents had meanwhile divorced, and irrespective of the children's nationality. In short, the right to education granted to accompanying minors of moving Union nationals was interpreted as continuing to have effect also beyond the exercise of the free movement rights from which it was derived. In presenting this conclusion the Court drew, as above, strongly on 'effet utile' or purpose-oriented arguments. Amongst others, it argued that "(i)n circumstances such as those in the Baumbast case, to prevent a child of a citizen of the Union from continuing his education in the host Member State by refusing him permission to remain might dissuade that citizen from exercising the rights to freedom of movement" which would "create an obstacle to the effective exercise of the freedom (…) guaranteed by the EC Treaty" (Ibid., paragraph 52).

On the basis of this first set of answers, the Court then considered the second, follow-up question referred. That is, whether in order for children to continue enjoying their sustained right to education, such children's primary carers were to be granted a parallel right to reside with them in the host state. In respect of this second question, the applicant parties, Mrs. R and the Baumbast family, had both appealed to 'effet utile' arguments, as well as to the fundamental right to family life to support their claims. Amongst others, as registered in the judgment's text, they had submitted that the "provisions of Community law must be interpreted broadly so that the rights granted are effective, particularly where a right as fundamental as the right to family life is concerned". In addition, they stated that "in the case of minor children who have spent all their life living with their mother and continue to do so, the refusal to afford her a right of residence during the continuation of the children's education is an interference with their rights which impairs the exercise of those rights". Finally, such a refusal would be "a disproportionate inference with family life" and on those grounds "contrary to Article 8 *ECHR*" (Ibid., paragraph 65). Conversely, the German and UK governments which submitted written observations, argued that residence rights for primary carers could not be deduced from free movement provisions governing the right to education for children of moving workers as these provisions regulated only the situations of persons who enjoyed the status of 'child of a migrant worker' (Ibid., paragraph 66; paragraph 74).

The Court nevertheless followed the effet utile/fundamental rights-based arguments advanced by Mrs. R and the Baumbast family. Amongst others, it stated that a refusal to grant parents a "right to remain in the host Member State during the period of their children's education (…) might deprive those children of a right which is granted to them by the Community legislature" (Ibid., paragraph 71). In addition, and joining this argument to fundamental rights premises, it posited that the provisions at stake had to be "interpreted in the light of the requirement of respect for family life laid down in Article 8 *ECHR*" (Ibid., paragraph 72). Accordingly, the right that EU law conferred on children of migrant workers to pursue their education "under the best possible conditions" necessarily implied that that child "has the right to be accompanied by the person who is his primary carer and, accordingly, that that person is able to reside with him in that Member Stated during his studies". To refuse to grant permission to remain "to a parent who is the primary carer of the child exercising his right to pursue his studies in the host Member State infringes that right" (Ibid., paragraph 73).

The Court then considered the third question that had been raised in regard of Mr. Baumbast, *i.e.*, whether, after no longer qualifying as a worker under secondary free movement law, he could derive residence rights in the UK directly on the basis of his status as an EU citizen. Again, the Court answered affirmatively. In so doing, it also, once more, went against the interpretations that had been advanced by the intervening British and German governments. Both had argued that a right of residence could not be derived directly from Article 18 EC as "the limitations and conditions referred to in that paragraph show that it is not intended to be a free-standing provision" (Ibid., paragraph 78).

The Court countered this by holding, first, and with reference to preceding case law (*Grzelczyk*, C-148/99), that "Union citizenship is destined to be the fundamental status of nationals of the Member States" (Ibid., paragraph 82). In addition, it posited that the Treaty did not "require that citizens of the Union pursue a professional or trade activity, whether as an employed or self-employed person, in order to enjoy the rights provided (…) on citizenship of the Union". Moreover, there was "nothing in the text of that Treaty to permit the conclusion that citizens of the Union who have established themselves in another Member State in order to carry on an activity as an employed person there are deprived, where that activity comes to an end, of the rights which are conferred on them by the EC Treaty by virtue of that citizenship" (Ibid., paragraph 83). Next, the Court acknowledged, in direct connection to the observations of the UK and Germany, that "admittedly", the "right for citizens of the Union to reside within the territory of another Member State is conferred subject to the limitations and conditions laid down by the EC Treaty and by the measures adopted to give it effect" (Ibid., paragraph 85). Such limitations and conditions were, as it conceded, "based on the idea that the exercise of the right of residence of citizens of the Union can be subordinated to the legitimate interest of the Member States. In that regard, (…) beneficiaries of the right of residence must not become an 'unreasonable' burden on the public finances of the host Member State" (Ibid., paragraph 90; original emphasis). Nevertheless, as the Court continued, "those limitations and conditions" had to be applied "in compliance with the limits imposed by Community law and in accordance with the general principles of that law, in particular the principle of proportionality". That meant, more precisely, that "national measures adopted on that subject must be necessary and appropriate to attain the objective pursued" (Ibid., paragraph 91). The Court then pointed out, in respect of the proportionality principle, that Mr. Baumbast had sufficient resources, that neither he nor any of the members of his family had needed social assistance and that they possessed comprehensive sickness insurance in Germany (Ibid., paragraph 92). In that light, a refusal "to allow Mr Baumbast to exercise the right of residence which is conferred on him by Article 18 (1) EC" would amount to a "disproportionate interference with the exercise of that right" (Ibid., paragraph 93). Accordingly, the Court ruled that "(a) citizen of the European Union who no longer enjoys a right of residence as a migrant worker in the host Member State can, as a citizen of the Union, enjoy there a right of residence by direct application of Article 18(1) EC. The exercise of that right is subject to the limitations and conditions referred to in that provision, but the competent authorities and, where necessary, the national courts must ensure that those limitations and conditions are applied in compliance with the general principles of Community law and, in particular, the principle of proportionality" (Ibid., paragraph 94).

In case of an affirmative answer of this kind, the UK tribunal had also asked whether, in sequence, Mr. Baumbast's wife and children could enjoy derivative "residence, employment and other rights" on the basis of the Treaty provisions on Union citizenship too. However, "in the light of the answer given to the first two questions" (which granted a right to education and residence to the Baumbast children and, on that basis, a derived right of residence to Mrs. Baumbast), the Court considered that it was not necessary to answer this follow-up question (Ibid., paragraph 96).

Like *Singh* and *Carpenter*, the Court's *Baumbast* decision further relaxed the requirements governing the categories of persons covered by the scope of EU law. That is, this scope was extended to apply, first, to the situations of children exercising a right to education even beyond the free movement from which this right was initially derived, and second, on that basis, residence rights were also afforded to such children's primary carers. As pointed out by Barrett (2003, p. 389), in so doing, the Court granted EU-based residence rights to persons who were in fact "two steps removed from the person enjoying the original right to free movement". Such rights were now conferred, not on the worker, nor on the child of the worker, but rather on the primary carer of the child of the worker. In addition, on the basis of Treaty provisions on Union citizenship, the *Baumbast* ruling also conferred rights on EU nationals who were not, or no longer, covered by the scope of secondary free movement law provisions.

Also in line with *Singh* and *Carpenter* however, the precise implications of these scope expansions, beyond the immediate situations of the Baumbast and R families, were left unaddressed. First, in respect of the continued education rights for children, questions could be raised on how long exactly such rights would continue to accrue. Would such rights continue to hold effect also past the age of majority? Did the premises of *Baumbast* only apply to courses already embarked on during the exercise of the parent's initial free movement activities, or could new courses also fall within the scope of the granted rights? Could the Court's decision perhaps be interpreted as giving rise to a lifelong right to education in the host state (see, e.g., Van der Mei, 2003)?

Second, much uncertainty also surrounded the extension of rights to 'primary carers'. To begin with, the above questions on the length or conditions governing the (continued) right to education also applied to the situations of primary carers in so far as their residence rights were derived from and, on that basis, arguably connected to these education rights. In addition, the judicial creation of this new category of persons that could lay claim to EU law protection also raised a number of queries in and of itself. The Court had provided little to no precise indications in respect of the exact definition of 'primary carer' and hence, *Baumbast* also gave rise to much ambiguity around which persons could be seen as covered by the new status. For instance, were family ties needed in order to qualify as a child's primary carer? If so, to what degree? Could grandparents be viewed as primary carers, and sisters, brothers or uncles and aunts too? Or, was the status exclusive to parents? If so, could stepparents or adoptive parents be covered as well? Moreover, could a child have more than one primary carer? And if so, what would the maximum number be? In addition, and similar to the questions raised in the aftermath of *Carpenter*, could primary carers, beyond residence rights, also lay claim to a right to first admission or, thereafter, a right to work? In this light as well, bringing the *Baumbast* ruling together with the holdings of *Singh*, it could be questioned whether the protective reach of EU law would also extend to the situations of primary carers in 'returnee contexts' (see on these and more questions in regard of the 'primary carer' concept post *Baumbast* e.g., Cambien, 2012).

Third, and on a more general level, the Court's dicta around the residence rights that could be derived directly on the basis of primary EU citizenship provisions also raised a host of questions. As all Member State nationals are also EU nationals, the answers to these questions potentially affected the situations and rights claims of a vast number of individuals (see also Chap. 5). Amongst others, the *Baumbast* ruling raised questions (as *Carpenter* had done) on the precise conditions that Member States could attach to rights granted directly on the basis of primary law. In *Baumbast* the Court listed, in the context of its proportionality review, the possession of sufficient resources and health insurance so as to avoid that the persons involved would become an 'unreasonable' burden on the public finances of the host Member State. However, no mention was made of public policy, security or health considerations which could justify a refusal or withdrawal of EU rights in the framework of secondary law. In addition, the Court did not specify whether the residence rights provided on the basis of EU citizenship provisions could, in turn, give rise to a further rights, such as, a right to family reunification. This in spite of the fact that the referring UK Tribunal had explicitly asked for guidance in this respect.

Overall, and again similar to the above observations on *Singh* and *Carpenter*, by extending the protective scope of EU law to new situations but refraining from outlining the precise contours of this extension, *Baumbast* opened the door for a large set of follow-up claims to follow. In this manner as well, the decision's premises also increased the likelihood that the Court would be provided with further opportunities to continue setting out its holdings. In addition, as in the context of the *Carpenter* case, to the extent that the *Baumbast* premises were, at least in part, grounded in broad, Treaty norms that could be applied to many situations and that held a high normative appeal, the likelihood that follow-up legal claims would follow was further strengthened. As registered in the quantitative findings, *Baumbast* was to indeed acquire numerically significant, long-lasting inward citation scores. More precisely, and as documented in what follows, *Baumbast* would provide key argumentative materials to such further landmark judgments as *Zhu & Chen*, *Eind* and *Zambrano*.

7.4 The 2000s: Further Refinements

The need for further clarification that flowed from the Court's ambiguous dicta in *Singh*, *Carpenter*, *MRAX* and *Baumbast* came to strongly define the next stage of the Court's case law. More precisely, the questions opened up by these preceding judgments, either separately or in combination, strongly conditioned the claims and questions that arose before the Luxembourg bench in the following decade. As the new legal claims, premised on these preceding decisions would, in turn, lay the groundworks for yet further jurisprudential developments to follow, the original holdings of *Singh, Carpenter, MRAX* and *Baumbast* became ever more refined and embedded in—simultaneously—ever more dense and articulate argumentative structures and standards.

In what follows, the analysis traces, first, the dominant outward and inward scores related to the *Akrich* ruling, followed by the shorter dominant outward scores of the *Jia* case which relate to the outcomes of *Akrich*. Next, the section reviews, in sequence, the dominant citation structures linked to *Zhu & Chen, Eind* and *Metock*. Each of these three judgments displays long-lasting dominant inward citation scores, suggesting that each of them introduced elements that would come to hold an important precedent value for a long line of cases to follow. The inward scores of the 2008 *Metock* ruling display, besides their long-lasting character, a strong density, or 'intensity' of self-citation, suggesting that the ruling held an important value as a precedent, not only for a long time period to come but also for a large amount of cases rendered within that period. Moreover, *Metock* as well as *Eind* have, besides their dominant inward scores, far-stretching dominant outward scores suggesting that these two judgments were at the same time also significantly grounded in earlier judgments. The last citation structures reviewed in this subsection relate to the dominant outward and inward scores registered for *EPvCouncil* and the dominant outward scores related to *Chakroun*. These two rulings, and their citation scores, are interconnected in that they mark the Court's first dicta on family reunion provisions in the context of EU immigration law rather than free movement law.

7.4.1 The Akrich *and* Jia *Cases*

In ***Akrich***, the Court was asked to give "further guidance" on the precise application and ramifications of *Singh* (*Akrich*, paragraph 44). More precisely, questions were referred on whether these principles continued to hold good also when the exercise of free movement rights had deliberately been "manufactured" with the sole purpose of evading the application of domestic immigration law. The proceedings at hand concerned the situation of Mr. Akrich, a Moroccan national who had on several occasions infringed UK immigration law, amongst others, by re-entering UK territory clandestinely after having been deported and by making use of stolen or false identity cards. During one of his stays, Mr. Akrich had married a UK national. He thereafter applied for leave to remain on the basis of his status as a spouse of a UK national. This application was refused however. Subsequently, in order to generate a right of residence for Mr. Akrich, his UK national spouse, Mrs. Akrich, moved from the UK to Ireland where she took up a short-term employment. She intended to return to the UK to then lay claim to the more favourable family reunion provisions provided for in EU law as a '*Singh*-style' returnee. In fact, upon being questioned by a British official in Dublin, Mrs. Akrich made it perfectly clear that she had moved "because we had heard about EU rights, staying six months and then going back to the UK" (Ibid., paragraph 36).

However, upon Mrs. Akrich's return, Mr. Akrich's application for a right to remain, this time on the basis of EU law, was refused again. The British Secretary of State had considered that Mrs. Akrich's move to Ireland had been "no more than a temporary absence deliberately designed (…) to evade the provisions of the United Kingdom's national legislation" and that, hence, "Mrs Akrich had not been genuinely exercising rights under the EC Treaty" (Ibid., paragraph 37). In the context of the appeal proceedings that were subsequently lodged, the UK Immigration Appeal Tribunal called on the EU judiciary to clarify the precise implications of *Singh* for situations such as those at issue. In presenting its request for further clarity, the UK tribunal took direct cues from the CJEU's dicta in *Singh*. It rehearsed, amongst others, a section of that judgment in which the CJEU had held that "the facilities created by the Treaty cannot have the effect of allowing persons who benefit from them to evade the application of national legislation and of prohibiting Member States from taking measures necessary to prevent such abuse" (Ibid., paragraph 41). Considering, next, that this proviso did not "clearly resolve" whether family reunion rights such as those granted in the context of *Singh* could also accrue in situations where free movement rights had been exercised "precisely to avoid the ordinary operation of United Kingdom immigration law", it referred two questions to Luxembourg (Ibid., paragraphs 43–44). First, it questioned whether, a Member State is "entitled to regard the intention of the couple, when moving to the other Member State, to claim the benefit of Community law rights when returning to the Member State of nationality, notwithstanding the non-national spouse's lack of qualification under national legislation" as, rehearsing *Singh* again, "a reliance on Community law in order to evade the application of national legislation". In follow up, and second, the referring tribunal asked whether, "if so", the Member State of nationality would then be entitled to refuse a right of entry into its territory to the non-national spouse (Ibid., paragraph 45).

As explicitly acknowledged by the Court, with these questions, it was "essentially" called on to "ascertain the scope of the judgment in *Singh*" (Ibid., paragraph 46). It used the opportunity thus presented to, first, re-articulate that in the context of return movements, a spouse of a Member State national must enjoy, in the Member State national's home state, "at least the same rights as would be granted to him or her under Community law if his or her spouse entered and remained in another Member State" (Ibid., paragraph 47). With this basic premise reconfirmed, however, and deviating somewhat from the terms of the questions posed, the Court moved on to hold that the free movement legislation to which the above interpretation related in fact only covered "freedom of movement within the Community". It was "silent as to the rights of a national of a non-Member State, (…) to access the territory of the Community" (Ibid., paragraph 49). On that basis, the Court posited that in order to benefit from the rights provided under EU free movement law, "the national of a non-Member State, who is the spouse of a citizen of the Union, must be lawfully resident in a Member State when he moves to another Member State to which the citizen of the Union is migrating or has migrated" (Ibid. paragraph 50). This holding would become known thereafter as the 'prior lawful residence requirement'. The Court further elaborated on this requirement by pointing out that, where a right to remain did not exist in favour of a third-country national spouse of an EU national in the first place, the failure to grant such a right upon an EU national's move to another Member State could not constitute a "less favourable treatment" than that which the EU national enjoyed before he/she made use of the opportunities afforded by the Treaty (Ibid., paragraph 53). Or, if the citizen's spouse "does not already have a valid right to remain in another Member State", the absence of any such right cannot have "a dissuasive effect" (Ibid., paragraph 54).

After establishing this 'prior lawful residence requirement', the Court moved on to engage with the UK Tribunal's question on whether the exercise of free movement rights with the sole purpose of evading the application of national law could be considered an 'abuse' of such free movement rights. In that respect, the Court set out, in no unclear terms, that "the motives which may have prompted a worker of a Member State to seek employment in another Member State are of no account as regards his right to enter and reside" (Ibid., paragraph 55). It further added: "Nor are such motives relevant in assessing the legal situation of the couple at the time of their return to the Member State of which the worker is a national. Such conduct cannot constitute an abuse within the meaning of paragraph 24 of the *Singh* judgment" (Ibid., paragraph 56).

In addition, and as a further set of considerations to be attached to the newly established 'prior lawful residence' requirement, the judgment's final section engaged with fundamental rights principles. More specifically, the Court held that in contexts where the prior lawful residence requirement was not met, and hence the situation fell outside the scope of EU law, Member States were to nevertheless have regard to "respect for family life under Article 8 *ECHR*" (Ibid., paragraph 58). As it further articulated, "(e)ven though the Convention does not as such guarantee the right of an alien to enter or to reside in a particular country, the removal of a person from a country where close members of his family are living may amount to an infringement of the right to respect for family life as guaranteed by Article 8(1) of the Convention". Thereafter, and with reference to its preceding *Carpenter* ruling, the Court emphasized that "(s) uch an interference will infringe the Convention if it does not meet the requirements of paragraph 2 of that article, that is unless it is (…) in particular, proportionate to the legitimate aim pursued" (Ibid., paragraph 59). How exactly these fundamental rights principles were to be applied to the specific situation of Mr. Akrich was not elaborated on however.

In all, and at face value, *Akrich* could, and generally was at the time of its rendering, considered a "rationalising judgment" (Tryfonidou, 2009, p. 637). The new 'prior lawful residence' requirement considerably curtailed the reach of the preceding *Singh* holdings. In that respect, *Akrich* also offered a comfort blanket to Member States and to the UK government in particular which had, arguably, won the case at hand as Mr. Akrich could not derive a right of residence on the basis of EU law. Instead, his situation, and the situations of others like him, remained within the exclusive sphere of Member States' national immigration control competences and the EU rights granted to 'returnees' following from *Singh* could, at least, not be used to 'rectify' previously unlawful residences.

However, and as some contemporaneous academic commentaries were quick to point out, the more liberal elements that had been coupled to this new prior lawful residence condition in the judgment's final section carried potentially significant, long-term legal consequences (see e.g., Schiltz, 2005; Spaventa, 2005). As Spaventa for instance phrased it: "The ruling in *Akrich*, despite appearances, represents only a very limited concession to the Member States' regulatory competences in the field of migration. What it gives with one hand, it almost entirely takes away with the other."

(Spaventa, 2005, p. 238). First, by stating that the 'abuse of rights' stipulation of *Singh* could not be construed in such a way as to have regard to the "motives which may have prompted a worker" to move to another Member State, *i.e.*, it could not be used to penalise situations in which a worker moved precisely with the aim of evading the application of EU law, the Court seemed to strongly restrict the leeway that could have originally been read in this dictum in *Singh*. In addition, the fundamental rights dicta in *Akrich*, and the Court's silence on their precise application, were also singled out as potentially embedding significant, long-term consequences (Ibid.; Schiltz, 2005).

Furthermore, the precise scope and contours of the new prior lawful residence requirement were also left unaddressed and, accordingly, raised questions in and of themselves. Amongst others, it was difficult to wed this new condition with the Court's previous holdings in such judgments as *Carpenter* or *MRAX*. For instance, in light of the fact that in the *Carpenter* case, Mrs. Carpenter had been unlawfully resident in the UK, it could be questioned whether, if her situation would have been judged in light of *Akrich*, she would still have been able to derive a right of residence on the basis of EU law. On that basis, it was also unclear whether, more generally, *Akrich* provided a delimitation of the *Carpenter* holdings. Contrary interpretations could also be adduced however. For instance, as the *Carpenter* ruling was in fact premised on Treaty law provisions on free movement, whereas in *Akrich*, the Court had considered the situation only in light of secondary law, it could be questioned whether Mr. Akrich would have been able to derive a right of residence if his situation had been judged in light of primary law provisions (Ibid.; Peers, 2009). Similarly, the Court also failed to outline how this new 'prior lawful residence requirement' weighed up to the *MRAX* judgment in which it had held that a refusal to grant residence permits to third-country national spouses of moving EU citizens on the ground that the spouses had entered unlawfully, constituted a 'disproportionate' interference with EU free movement rights (Spaventa, 2005). Additionally, and independent of previous rulings, the prior lawful residence requirement was, in and of itself, not clearly defined. For instance, how far back in time could Member States go to investigate the possible lack of a prior lawful residence? In connection, but taking account of future developments, what if Mr. Akrich had in the meantime been granted a right of residence in Ireland (White, 2004)? Moreover, it was not clear from the Court's reasoning whether the new requirement related to situations of prior 'unlawful' residence only, or whether the situations of third-country national family members seeking reunification from outside the Union's territory were also excluded from the scope of EU law. Phrased differently, whether the 'prior lawful residence' condition targeted only those situations where there had been a prior 'unlawful' residence or whether the requirement had to be construed as also relating to situations where there had 'not yet been any residence' at all (Spaventa, 2005; Peers, 2009).

This last question would set the stakes of the *Jia* proceedings that were presented two years after *Akrich*. In that manner, in *Jia*, discussed immediately below, the Court was presented with a further opportunity to clarify the precise contours of the prior lawful residence requirement that had itself arisen out of an effort to clarify the holdings of *Singh*. Three years after *Jia* (and accordingly, five years after *Akrich*), the Court would yet again be presented with questions on the precise application of the prior lawful residence requirement in the context of the *Metock* case which is discussed further below. In addition, and further adding to *Akrich*'s dominant inward citation scores, the ruling's holdings were also invoked in the context of *Commission v Spain* (C-503/03) and in *EPvCouncil*. In these two latter cases, *Akrich*, in spite of its *prima facie* rationalising outcome, was invoked to reinforce the more liberal, fundamental rights holdings which had also been advanced in the judgment and which, themselves, represented a reinforcement of the fundamental rights premises of *Carpenter*. In both *Commission v Spain* and *EPvCouncil*, the fundamental rights-based holdings of *Akrich* were used to support rights-strengthening conclusions. That is, in *Commission v Spain*, discussed above, the Court summoned the support of its earlier *Akrich* dicta, as well as those of *Carpenter*, to emphasize the need for a strict interpretation of the concept of public policy in order to protect the fundamental right to family life (*Commission v Spain*, C-503/03, paragraph 47). In *EPvCouncil* which will receive further treatment below, the legal claims that were referred by the European Parliament were premised in part on the fundamental rights arguments that the Court had advanced in *Akrich* and earlier, in *Carpenter* (*EPvCouncil*, paragraph 31).

The ***Jia*** case, first, related to the situation of Mrs. Jia, the retired Chinese mother of a Chinese national who was living in Sweden with his spouse, a German national (Mrs Schallehn). The German national spouse, Mrs. Schallehn, was exercising her free movement rights under EU law as a self-employed person. Mrs. Jia had been granted a temporary traveller's visa to visit the couple in Sweden. Upon arrival however, she applied for a permanent leave to remain on the basis of her status as the dependent ascending relative of (the spouse of) a Community national exercising free movement rights. This application was rejected, however, on the grounds that there was insufficient proof of Mrs. Jia's financial dependence on her son.

In the proceedings that were subsequently lodged against this rejection, the Swedish Alien Appeals Board decided to refer a set of questions to the EU judiciary. To begin with, it requested clarification on the precise meaning and scope of the concept of 'dependence' within EU free movement law and what means of proof State authorities could demand of applicants to prove such dependence. In addition, it raised a number of questions on how to assess the situation presented "(i)n the light of the judgment in (...) *Akrich*" (*Jia*, paragraph 24). More specifically, it wanted to know whether it followed from the prior lawful residence requirement established in *Akrich* that the family reunion provisions in EU law had to be interpreted "as meaning that a national of a non-Member State related to a worker (...) must be lawfully within the Community in order to have the right to permanently reside with the worker". It also asked whether, if this was the case, such a lawful residence requirement then implied that the relative held at the time of application a residence permit "valid for or intended to lead to permanent residence in one of the Member States" or whether a "residence permit on other grounds for a shorter or longer stay", for instance, as in the case pending before it, "a valid visa" would be sufficient. Furthermore, and specifically engaging with the anomalies between the Court's holdings in *Akrich* versus those of *Carpenter*, the referring tribunal asked whether, if a right of residence was denied to a third-country national family member of a Union citizen because he or she was not lawfully resident in the Community, this could—with reference to the *Carpenter* dicta—"restrict the right of the citizen of the Union to freedom of establishment" as provided for under primary Treaty law (Ibid.).

The Court started by joining and rephrasing the *Akrich*-related questions as asking "essentially" whether Community law required Member States to make the grant of a residence permit to a third-country national family member "subject to the condition that that family member has previously been lawfully resident in another Member State" (Ibid., paragraph 25). As it continued, the referring tribunal wished to know "more precisely whether the condition of previous lawful residence (...) also applies to Ms Jia's situation" (Ibid., paragraph 27). From there, the

Court proceeded by distinguishing the facts giving rise to the *Akrich* judgment from the settings at hand in *Jia*. That is, in *Jia*, and different from the *Akrich* case, it was "not alleged that the family member in question was residing unlawfully in a Member State or that she was seeking to evade national immigration legislation illicitly". On the contrary, "Ms Jia was lawfully in Sweden when she submitted her application" (Ibid., paragraph 31). As the Court then held, rather concisely, it followed "that the condition of previous lawful residence in another Member State, as formulated in the judgment in *Akrich*, cannot be transposed to the present case and thus cannot apply to such a situation" (Ibid., paragraph 32). On that basis, the answer to the questions raised was therefore that "Community law does not require of Member States to make the grant of a residence permit to nationals of a non-Member State, who are members of the family of a Community national (…) subject to the condition that those family members have previously been residing lawfully in another Member State" (Ibid., paragraph 33).

With these statements, the Court, arguably, did not clarify the holdings of *Akrich* much beyond their application to the specific facts of *Jia*. By joining together the different *Akrich*-related questions of the Swedish tribunal, the Court created the opportunity for itself to provide only a minimum level of clarification. In that way, it also avoided the specific question on how to read *Akrich* in light of the different, and arguably incongruent, premises of *Carpenter*. In addition, *Jia* also gave rise to new uncertainties in and of itself. For instance, at a first glance the Court's new dicta seemed to provide support for the interpretation that the 'prior lawful residence requirement' related only to situations where there had been a prior 'unlawful' residence instead of, more broadly, to all situations where there had not been 'any residence' in the EU before. On the other hand however, the Court had thought it important to point out that Mrs. Jia was lawfully resident in Sweden when she submitted her application. This could be taken to mean that the door was still open for the second interpretation too (see Tryfonidou, 2007; Olivier & Reestman, 2007; Peers, 2009).

In addition to its *Akrich*-related questions, the Swedish tribunal had also raised queries on the dependency requirement enshrined in EU family reunion provisions. More precisely, it had asked whether 'dependence' of the family member had to be interpreted as meaning that the family member was dependent on the Union citizen to attain "the lowest acceptable standard of living in his country of origin or country where he is normally resident" (Ibid., paragraph 24). Furthermore, it had asked for clarification on whether the relevant EU provisions allowed Member States to request documentary evidence as proof of a situation of dependence. As the referring tribunal highlighted, the EU law was ambiguous in respect of these two questions and preceding CJEU case law had not sufficiently clarified matters either (Ibid.; paragraphs 22 & 23). The Court answered, in relation to the first question, that the phrasing 'dependent on them', as provided for in the legislation, was to be interpreted as meaning that family members "need the material support of that Community national or his or her spouse in order to meet their essential needs in the State of origin". In respect of the second question it stated that applicants were to be able to adduce proof of such need for material support "by any appropriate means" but that "a mere undertaking from the Community national or his or her spouse to support the family members concerned need not be regarded as establishing the existence of the family members' situation of real dependence" (Ibid., paragraph 43). In constructing this open-ended formulation, the Court invoked its preceding *Zhu & Chen* decision that had been rendered a few years earlier and in which, amongst others, similar dependency-related questions had been raised.

7.4.2 Zhu & Chen, Eind *and* Metock

Zhu & Chen related to the situation of a Chinese family resident in the UK whose eight-month-old daughter, Catherine Zhu, had acquired Irish citizenship on account of *ius soli* Irish citizenship rules applicable in Belfast where she was born. As stated in the judgment's discussion of the facts, it was "common ground" that Mrs. Chen, Catherine's Chinese mother, had taken up residence in the island of Ireland precisely "in order to enable the child she was expecting to acquire Irish nationality and, consequently, to enable her to acquire the right to reside (...) with her child in the United Kingdom" (*Zhu &* Chen; paragraph 11). However, the application for permanent residence permits in the UK by Mrs. Chen for herself and for her daughter, on the basis of her daughter's rights under EU free movement law, had been denied by the British authorities. Amongst others, the British Secretary of State had considered that a child of eight months could not be exercising EU free movement rights (Ibid., paragraph 14). In the proceedings that were subsequently lodged against this refusal a host of further uncertainties on the application of EU free movement law to the circumstances at hand were identified by the UK Immigration

Appellate Authority before which they appeared. The latter tribunal subsequently sent no less than seven questions, including a number of subquestions, to Luxembourg.

First, and in line with the Secretary of State's objections, the referring tribunal asked whether a minor could in fact be found to exercise free movement rights. No provision in secondary free movement legislation provided for unequivocal answers in either the affirmative or negative sense. Next, if the EU judiciary found that this was possible, the referring tribunal wanted to know whether, in turn, the minor could act as a sponsor for family reunification with family members such as, in the case at hand, her "mother and primary carer" (Ibid., paragraph 15). If so, the tribunal also wanted to know on what legal basis this could be the case. Should the mother-primary carer be considered a "dependent relative"? Or would the mother-primary carer have to be granted a right to reside with the minor EU national because she lived with that national in her country of origin? Or, as a third option, would such a right have to be granted on another "special basis"? Furthermore, the UK court also asked whether the "receipt of child care" could be construed as constituting services for the purpose of secondary EU legislation on the freedom to provide and receive services. In addition, it also sought clarification on whether the condition of possessing 'sufficient resources' could be regarded as satisfied when these resources were not possessed by the EU national in her own capacity, but rather when these resources were provided by the EU national's "third country national parent who accompanies her". In a further set of questions, the UK tribunal also asked for a review of the situation in light of primary Treaty law. In that respect it asked, to begin with, whether, in case baby Catherine was found to not qualify for residence in the host State under any other provision of EU law, she could nevertheless derive such a right directly on the basis of primary Treaty provisions on Union citizenship, more precisely, on the basis of Article 18 EC (now Article 21 TFEU). In follow up the referring tribunal also asked, as above, whether, if so, baby Catherine could, on the basis of such primary Treaty provisions, in turn act as a sponsor for family reunification with her mother. With these questions, the referring tribunal, arguably, asked for guidance on the principles that the EU judiciary had established in *Baumbast* in respect of the rights that could be derived directly from Treaty provisions on EU citizenship. More precisely, these questions raised the issue of whether the *Baumbast* premises could be transposed to cover the situations of minor EU citizens as well, and whether these premises could also be found to apply to situations in which there had possibly not yet been a previous exercise of free movement rights (as had been the case in *Baumbast*). Moreover, the follow-up question on whether EU citizenship provisions could be found to give rise to further derived rights to family reunification (in case, with Catherine's mother), explicitly re-opened the question that had previously been raised to that effect in respect of Mr. Baumbast's family members but which the CJEU had, at the time, not addressed. As the final question referred, the UK tribunal asked, arguably also taking cues from preceding CJEU dicta, what the effect was of "the principle of respect for fundamental human rights under Community law". In particular, as it singled out, it wanted clarification on the extent to which the applicant parties could rely on Article 8 ECHR and the respect for family life enshrined therein, also taking into account that baby Catherine, on account of her Irish citizenship, could no longer acquire Chinese citizenship and, accordingly, could not take up permanent residence in China under the applicable Chinese rules (Ibid., paragraphs 13–15).

As the referring court indicated, this final, fundamental-rights related question also derived from the claims that the plaintiffs had advanced. As emerges from *Zhu & Chen*'s report for the hearing, the plaintiffs' claims had in fact centrally revolved around the argumentation that, in cases where EU law did not provide clear stipulations, the legal lacunae had to be "fulfilled", as they phrased it, with regard to fundamental rights principles and, particularly, with regard to children's best interests (Report for the hearing *Zhu & Chen*, paragraph 93). Amongst others, they put forward that, as the Treaty did "not state that citizenship of the Union does not extend to minors", to exclude minors from its scope would be an overly restrictive interpretation which would not accord with the spirit of such instruments as, inter alia, the ICCPR (International Covenant on Civil and Political Rights), the EU Charter of Fundamental Rights and the UN Convention on the Rights of the Child (CRC) (Ibid., paragraphs 25–29). Following a similar line of reasoning, the appellants also held that, if Catherine enjoyed a right of residence, her mother, as her primary carer, had to be bestowed with a parallel right to remain in the UK. Again, although no specific provision for such a right could be found in EU law, the EU judiciary was to "fulfil that lacuna by reference to Article 8 ECHR and to the CRC". In connection, and invoking 'effet utile' arguments, they stated that "if Catherine is to enjoy her Community rights as a minor (…) then it is imperative that she is able to exercise such rights with the assistance of her primary carer, since otherwise her rights are illusory" (Ibid., paragraph 48). At various points in their submissions, the appellants also invoked the Advocate General (AG)'s Opinion on the *Baumbast* case. They especially took cues from those lines of reasoning in which the AG had argued for a favourable outcome for Mr. Baumbast or his family members and contended that these lines of reasoning extended to their situation too (Ibid., paragraphs 49; 79). Considering that the Court's judgment in *Baumbast* was delivered in September 2002 whilst the order for reference in *Zhu & Chen* arrived in Luxembourg in May 2002, the applicants will not have had access to the reasoning adopted by the Court in *Baumbast* yet and were, instead, limited to taking cues from the AG's Opinion, which was available as from July 2001.

The UK and Irish governments, which intervened, objected strongly to the interpretations suggested by the appellants. To begin with, they argued that given that baby Catherine had in fact never moved from one Member State to another Member State (Belfast being a part of the UK), her claims based on the exercise of free movement rights had to be rejected at the outset (Report for the hearing, paragraph 19). Instead the situation presented was to be regarded as 'purely internal' to the UK and, hence, Community law could not be found to apply (Ibid., paragraph 18). This general observation was supplemented with a range of further contentions that targeted the specific questions raised before the EU judiciary and the arguments advanced by the appellants. To that purpose, both governments also resorted to taking strategic cues from preceding Court dicta in order to support a restrictive interpretation of EU law in the situation at hand.

Amongst others, Ireland referred to the Court's preceding *Carpenter* judgment to argue that secondary legislation on the freedom to provide and receive services could in any case not apply to Catherine while she was in her 'country of birth' as, similarly, Mr. Carpenter had not been able to derive a right on the basis of such secondary legislation in his country of origin either (instead rights had been derived directly from Treaty law) (Ibid., paragraphs 21–22; see paragraphs 33–35 for similar British contentions). In addition, both governments also made strategic reference to *Baumbast*. The UK government, which had been the losing party to that case, for instance used *Baumbast* as a point of departure from which it argued that, unlike the Court's findings in respect of the *Baumbast* children, baby Catherine would not be "liable to be deterred from exercising freedom of movement" if her mother would not be a granted a right to remain in the UK (Ibid., paragraph 37). The Irish government drew on *Baumbast* to point out that, although the Court had recognised in that judgment that "Article 18 EC does indeed enshrine the right of residence", it had also posited that that right was "only conferred subject to limitations and conditions laid down by the Treaty and by the measures adopted for its implementation". Accordingly, there was "no authority for the proposition that Article 18 EC confers an independent right to move and reside freely in the Union" or that that right would be "unconditional". To hold otherwise, the Irish government continued, would in fact be to render the Union's secondary free movement legislation, which outlined the limits and conditions for the exercise of that right, "redundant" (Ibid., paragraph 58). In addition, Ireland also submitted that the facts that had given rise to the *Baumbast* ruling were to be distinguished from those at hand in *Zhu & Chen*. It highlighted in that regard that, unlike Mr. Baumbast, Catherine Zhu "has not moved from another Member State, she has never chosen in her own right to exercise her Treaty rights in the United Kingdom, she has never been employed or self-employed in that State and she is completely dependent on Mrs Chen" (Ibid., paragraph 86).

That last observation, Catherine's dependence on her mother, was also used by both governments to further contend that it would be impossible to hold that Catherine's mother could be granted a right to reside with her daughter on the ground that she was a 'dependent relative' of her daughter. In fact, such would be a "reversal of reality" as it was clear from the case file that Catherine was financially dependent on Mrs. Chen and her husband, not *vice versa* (Ibid., paragraphs 36; 54–59). In that light as well, Ireland pointed out that the Union legislators had deliberately drawn a distinction between first, "members of a worker's family who have the right to install themselves in the host state with the worker" and second, "those for whom the Member States must merely facilitate the admission". In respect of ascending relatives, only those "dependent on the worker" could fall within the first category. To "reverse reality" and hold that Mrs. Chen could be considered as dependent on her daughter for the purpose of falling within the first category would in fact mean that there had been no reason for the Union's legislators to draw a distinction between different categories of family members in the first place (Ibid., paragraph 59). Furthermore, and as emerges from the text of the *Zhu & Chen* judgment, both governments also contested that Catherine could satisfy the 'sufficient resources' condition, laid down in secondary law, on the basis of the resources that her mother possessed. This condition was to be interpreted, they submitted, as meaning that the person concerned held those resources personally. The resources of accompanying family members could not be taken into account for the purpose of satisfying that condition (*Zhu & Chen*, paragraph 29). As a final set of objections, both governments also contested the appellants' claims to fundamental rights protection standards. The UK government, whilst acknowledging—in verbatim replication of CJEU dicta—that "it is well established that fundamental rights form an integral part of the general principles of law whose observance the Court ensures", stated that it was "equally clear that those rights cannot in themselves have the effect of extending the scope of the Treaty" (Report for the hearing, paragraph 101). In addition, both governments also extensively engaged with ECtHR case law on Article 8 ECHR to emphasize that, in light of that case law, a decision to not grant residence rights to Mrs. Chen would not infringe the standards set by the ECHR (Ibid., paragraphs 102–110). More precisely, they cited a host of ECtHR decisions to illustrate that the Strasbourg Court "recognises that States have the right, subject to their Treaty obligations, to control the entry of non-nationals onto their territory" and that, in that light, "Article 8 does not impose a general obligation on States to accept the settlement of a non-national spouse or another family member on their territory" (Ibid., paragraphs 108–109).

The Court first considered the situation of baby Catherine. In contrast to the argument of the British and Irish governments that Catherine could not lay claim to Community rights as she had never moved across state borders, the Court held that "(t)he situation of a national of a Member State who was born in the host Member State and has not made use of the right to freedom of movement cannot, for that reason alone, be assimilated to a purely internal situation" (*Zhu & Chen*, paragraph 19). The Court then moved on to, similarly, discard the contention that a young child like Catherine could not exercise EU free movement rights. As it stated in that regard "(t)he capacity of a national of a Member State to be the holder of rights guaranteed by the Treaty and by secondary law (…) cannot be made conditional upon the attainment of a minimum age" (Ibid., paragraph 20). In support of that dictum it cited, amongst others, its earlier *Baumbast* decision and, more in particular, the sections of that decision in which it had established that the children concerned continued to hold a right to education under Community law independent of the fact that the link with the parent-migrant work had become tenuous or had ceased to exist (Ibid., paragraph 20).

With these basic premises established, Catherine's situation was further assessed in light of the invoked legal provisions. To begin with, Catherine was found to not be able to derive permanent residence rights from secondary legislation on the freedom to provide and receive services. The child-care services received were not covered by that legislation. Next, Catherine's situation was reviewed in light of Treaty provisions on Union citizenship. In that respect, the Court started off, as in *Baumbast* to which it also referred, by rehearsing the dictum that "Union citizenship is destined to be the fundamental status of nationals of the Member State (see, in particular, Baumbast, paragraph 82)" (Ibid., paragraph 25). With a further reference to *Baumbast* it moved on to state that "(a)s regards the right to reside in the territory of the Member States provided for in Article 18(1) EC, it must be observed that that right is granted directly to every citizen of the Union by a clear and precise provision of the Treaty". However, at the same time, that right was also "subject to the limitations and conditions imposed by the Treaty and by the measures adopted to give it effect" (Ibid., paragraph 26). With regard to those limitations and conditions then, secondary legislation required of Member State nationals who wished to benefit from this right of residence that they were covered by sickness insurance and that they had sufficient resources to avoid becoming a burden on the social assistance of the host state (Ibid., paragraph 27). As was clear from the order of reference, Catherine had both sickness insurance as well as sufficient resources, provided by her mother, to avoid becoming a burden on the host state's social assistance system (Ibid., paragraph 28). In regard of the objections of the Irish and UK governments that the sufficient resources condition required that the resources were possessed personally, the Court pointed out that such an interpretation would in fact add a supplementary requirement "as to the origin of those resources" to the legislative provisions as they stood (Ibid., paragraph 33). This would be unjust as "provisions laying down a fundamental principle such as that of the free movement of persons must be interpreted broadly" (Ibid., paragraph 31). In addition, such an interpretation would not be "in accordance with the principle of proportionality" as also upheld in *Baumbast* (Ibid., paragraph 32). In fact, it would amount to a "disproportionate interference with the exercise of the fundamental right to freedom of movement and of residence" (Ibid., paragraph 33). Accordingly, and in all, "in circumstances like those of the main proceedings", EU Treaty provisions on Union citizens' rights were found to "confer on a young minor who is a national of a Member State, is covered by appropriate sickness insurance and is in the care of a parent who is a third-country national having sufficient resources for that minor not to become a burden on the public finances of the host Member State, a right to reside for an indefinite period in that State" (Ibid., paragraph 41).

On that basis, the Court moved on to review Mrs. Chen's situation, and whether she could derive any residence rights on the basis of the EU rights enjoyed by her daughter. To begin with, the Court pointed out, as the UK and Irish governments had done, that Mrs. Chen could not be considered a dependent relative of her daughter. The situation was in fact "exactly the opposite" in that her daughter was dependent on her (Ibid., paragraph 44). On the other hand however, and revisiting *Baumbast* to that effect, "a refusal to allow the parent (…) who is the carer of a child to whom Article 18 EC and Directive 90/364 grant a right of residence, to reside with that child in the host Member State would deprive the child's right of residence of any useful effect" (Ibid., paragraph 45). Accordingly, "and for that reason alone", these effet utile considerations led to the conclusion that where a "young minor who is a national of another Member State" enjoys a right to reside for an indefinite period in the host Member State on the basis of EU law provisions, "those same provisions allow a parent who is that minor's primary carer to reside with the child in the host Member State" (Ibid., paragraph 46). This was the Court's final dictum on Mrs. Chen's situation. As emerged clearly from the "for that reason alone"-statement, the Court chose to not engage with any of the fundamental rights considerations that had explicitly featured in the questions referred by the UK tribunal, and that had also been amply referred to in the submissions of the appellants and the intervening Member States. It therewith also departed from the mixed 'effet utile—fundamental rights' discourses on which the *Baumbast* ruling, and earlier, the *Carpenter* decision had been built and from which both the referring tribunal, as well as the intervening parties had taken cues.

On the whole, *Zhu & Chen* was to effect a major extension of the *Baumbast* holdings which themselves had already entailed a large expansion of the scope of EU law. In this manner, *Zhu & Chen* also answered some of the questions that had been left unaddressed by *Baumbast*. For instance, and most clearly, in *Baumbast* the Court had—arguably strategically—chosen not to address the referred question on whether, in case Mr. Baumbast could derive residence rights directly on the basis of primary

Treaty law, such Treaty-based rights could, in turn, also give rise to derived rights to family reunification with his wife and children. In *Zhu & Chen* the Court now made it plain that Catherine's Treaty-based right of residence, in turn, gave rise to a derived right of residence for her primary carer-mother.

On the other hand however, and in spite of such answers, *Zhu & Chen* left even more issues opened up by *Baumbast* or even earlier, *Carpenter*, untouched. Amongst them, for instance, questions on how many 'primary carers' a child could be seen as having or needing for the purposes of ensuring the effectiveness of its EU rights. In addition, were effective family ties with the primary carer required, and if so, to what degree? Moreover, it could also be questioned whether primary carers who were granted a derived right of residence could also lay claim to further rights such as access to the labour market (see on such questions following from *Zhu & Chen* e.g., Hofstotter, 2005). In addition, by not picking up on the fundamental rights issues raised, the Court did not clarify whether a refusal to grant Mrs. Chen a right to reside would have also amounted to a breach of baby Catherine's fundamental right to family life. Or whether, in line with the Court's holdings in *Baumbast* and *Carpenter*, findings of such a fundamental rights' breach would, in and of themselves, be sufficient to support the view that the useful effectiveness of Catherine's EU rights was compromised. Possibly, by refraining from examining the situation at hand in light of fundamental rights principles the Court sought to steer clear from venturing, for the time being, into further questions on which other categories of family members could then also be found to enjoy derivative rights of residence. That is, and as could also be asked post *Baumbast*, should the fundamental right to family life be upheld as a decisive factor in the case at hand, on what grounds then could additional residence rights be denied to Catherine's other core family members (in the settings at hand, a father and brother)?

In spite of having left such further ramifications unaddressed, the *Zhu & Chen* ruling was to cause strong political reactions amongst and within Member States. As an illustration, the case was to trigger much political upheaval in Ireland where, amongst others, it fed directly into the discussions on a referendum on the continuation of Irish *ius soli* citizenship rules. This referendum, held in 2004, eventually resulted in a significant tightening of the applicable *ius soli* rules in respect of children "born to certain non-nationals" (Hofstotter, 2005, p. 11). In fact, following the referendum, situations like those at issue in *Zhu & Chen* would no longer be possible as the new stipulations inserted a requirement of prior lawful settlement of at least three years for third-country nationals before a child born to them could acquire Irish citizenship (Ibid.; see also Mancini & Finlay, 2008, p. 582).

As registered in its dominant and long-lasting inward citation scores, the *Zhu & Chen* case provoked much follow-up citations. Aside from its reference in *Akrich* reviewed above, it also featured in *Eind* which is discussed immediately below. Thereafter, *Zhu & Chen* would also provide important argumentative elements for the 2011 landmark *Zambrano* ruling. The ruling also continued to hold a precedent relevance for such more recent cases as *Iida* and *Alopka & Others* which are discussed further below.

After *Zhu & Chen*, the next ruling registered to have incited much, and long-lasting follow-up citations is *Eind*. In addition, and as indicated above, aside from its long-lasting dominant inward scores, the *Eind* ruling is also characterized by many, and far-stretching dominant outward scores. These 'double' numerical observations suggest that *Eind* was significantly embedded in prior case law as well as important, from a precedent-based perspective, for the lines of case law that followed.

Eind concerned the situation of Mr. Eind, a Dutch national who had worked and resided in the UK in exercise of his EU free movement rights, and Ms. Rachel Eind, his Surinam daughter, who had joined him in the UK directly from Surinam. After remaining in the UK for some time, Mr. Eind had moved back to the Netherlands and Ms. Rachel Eind had joined him. In the Netherlands, Mr. Eind had stopped being economically active due to ill health. Instead, he relied on social assistance. Ms. Rachel Eind applied for a permit to reside with her father in the Netherlands on the basis of her status as the family member of a returning Community national (following the principles established in *Singh*). The request was refused by the Dutch authorities however on the grounds that, since her father was no longer engaged in any economic activities, nor possessed sufficient resources to avoid becoming a burden on the state's social assistance system, his situation, and accordingly hers as well, fell outside the scope of EU law. In the proceedings that were subsequently lodged against this refusal, the District Court of The Hague set the administrative decision aside with reference to the CJEU's decision in *Singh* (*Eind*, paragraph 14). The case then reappeared before the Dutch Council of State as the Dutch Minister for immigration affairs filed an appeal. In sequence, and noting that Community law did "not give an unequivocal answer to the issues raised by the case", the Council of State referred a series of questions on the precise ramifications of *Singh* to Luxembourg (Ibid., paragraph 15).

To begin with, the Dutch Council of State asked whether the fact that Ms. Eind had not previously held a right of residence in the Netherlands under Dutch national law, had a bearing on the rights she could subsequently derive from EU law in the Netherlands. In addition, questions were also raised on whether Mr. Eind's cessation of employment activities, and his receipt of welfare benefits affected his entitlement, and that of Ms. Eind, to EU free movement rights upon his return. As a final question, the Council of State also wanted to know "what significance for the answers to the previous questions" was to be attached to the fact that the third-country national, Ms. Eind, was a member of the family of a citizen of the Union, Mr. Eind, who had exercised his right to free movement pursuant to Article 18 of the Treaty. With this final question, the referring court arguably took cues from the CJEU's preceding dicta in *Baumbast* and *Zhu & Chen* on the importance of Treaty provisions and requested clarification on whether and how these dicta could be extended to 'returnee' situations.

As appears from *Eind's* 'Report for the hearing', five Member States submitted written observations on the case (the Czech Republic, Denmark, Germany, the Netherlands and the UK). Across the board, these written observations all shared the same, broad goal of adducing arguments as to why, in the case at issue, no rights could be derived from EU law. Amongst others, all of the intervening Member States stressed the importance they attached to the requirement of sufficient resources for the purposes of applying EU law. Additionally, the Netherlands, Denmark and Germany also argued that, in order to benefit from EU family reunion provisions in return situations, a third-country national family member was to have already enjoyed a right of residence in the Member State of origin prior to the first move (Report for the hearing *Eind*, pp. 7–9). As is also reproduced in the text of the judgment, the Dutch and Danish governments additionally submitted that, if a right of residence did not already exist in favour of the third-country national family member of an EU national in that national's state of origin, a refusal to grant such a right upon the EU national's return could not have a deterrent effect on his free movement rights. More precisely, "Mr Eind could not have been deterred from exercising that freedom, through moving to the United Kingdom, by the fact that it would be impossible for his daughter to reside with him once he returned to his Member State of origin, given that at the time of the initial move Miss Eind did not have a right to reside in the Netherlands" (*Eind*, paragraph 33). As can be noted, this final line of reasoning in fact amounts to an almost verbatim reproduction of the argumentation that the Court had adduced in *Akrich* to support a limitation of the contours of *Singh*.

The Court started off its reasoning on *Eind* by considering, first, the situation of Mr. Eind. It accepted in that respect, to begin with, that the right of EU nationals to reside in the territory of another Member State "is not unconditional". With reference to, amongst others, *Zhu & Chen*, it rehearsed that this right is "recognised subject to the limitations and conditions imposed by the Treaty and by the measures adopted for its implementation" (Ibid., paragraph 28). Amongst these limitations and conditions, the Court held, was the provision that Member States could require of Union citizens to ensure that they are covered by sickness insurance and have sufficient resources to avoid becoming a burden on the social assistance system of the host Member State (Ibid., paragraph 29). On the other hand however, as the Court continued, since he was a Dutch national, Mr. Eind's right to reside in the territory of the Netherlands could not be "refused or made conditional" (Ibid., paragraph 31). As can be recalled, similar arguments had previously been adduced in *Singh*, although in the context of that ruling they had not had an immediate bearing on the case's final outcome, but rather, had featured as a side issue. As its final dictum on Mr. Eind's rights then, the Court stated that "the right of the migrant worker to return and reside in the Member State of which he is a national, after being gainfully employed in another Member State, is conferred by Community law, to the extent necessary to ensure the useful effect of the right to free movement for worker". In addition, that interpretation was also said to be supported by the introduction of the status of citizen of the Union, "which is intended to be the fundamental status of nationals of the Member States" (Ibid., paragraph 32).

On the basis of these premises, the Court then examined the situation of Ms. Rachel Eind. To begin with, the Court held that the arguments of the Dutch and Danish governments, according to which a refusal to grant ancillary residence rights to Ms. Eind would not constitute an obstacle to Mr. Eind's free movement rights, could "not be accepted" (Ibid., paragraphs 33–34). Instead, the Court held, "(a) national of a Member State could be deterred from leaving that Member State (…) if he does not have the certainty of being able to return to his Member State of origin" (Ibid., paragraph 35). Furthermore, "that deterrent effect would also derive simply from the prospect, for that same national, of not being able, on returning to his Member State of origin, to continue living together with close relatives, a way of life which may have come into being in the host Member State as a result of marriage or family reunification" (Ibid., paragraph 36). In all, and rather different from its conclusions in *Akrich*, "(b)arriers to family reunification are therefore liable to undermine the right to free movement which the nationals of the Member States have under Community law, as the right of a Community worker to return to the Member State of which he is a national cannot be considered to be a purely internal matter" (Ibid., paragraph 37). Furthermore, the Court also engaged with the related argument of the Dutch, Danish and German governments who had held that, in order to benefit from residence rights in return situations, family members of returning EU nationals were to have already enjoyed a right of residence in the state of origin prior to the first move. This argument, the Court stated, would amount to imposing an additional condition that was "not laid down, expressly or by implication, in any provision of Community law". Such an imposition of an additional condition could not be accepted. This, first, in light of the fact that, according to its "settled case-law", "secondary Community legislation on movement and residence cannot be interpreted restrictively". To this effect, the Court invoked, amongst others, its dicta in the preceding *Baumbast* case (Ibid., paragraph 43). In addition, and revisiting its earlier mixed 'fundamental rights-effet utile' reasoning, such an additional requirement would also "run counter to the objectives of the Community legislature, which has recognised the importance of ensuring protection for the family life of nationals of the Member States in order to eliminate obstacles to the exercise of the fundamental freedoms guaranteed by the Treaty". To that purpose, the Court invoked *Carpenter* and *MRAX* (Ibid., paragraph 44). In all, it followed that, "in circumstances such as those in the case before the referring court, Miss Eind has the right to install herself with her father, Mr Eind, in the Netherlands, even if the latter is not economically active" (Ibid., paragraphs 37–38). The Court further specified that a person in the situation of Ms. Eind could enjoy that right "so long as she has not reached the age of 21 years or remains a dependant of her father" (Ibid., paragraph 40). As an endnote, the Court held that, in view of the answers that it had provided, there was no need to answer the further questions referred by the national court, amongst them, most notably, the question on the possible bearing that primary

Treaty provisions on EU citizens' rights (Article 18 EC) could have on the situation at hand (Ibid., paragraph 46).

On the whole, with these premises, the Court's *Eind* ruling significantly extended the premises of *Singh*. For instance, and most clearly, *Eind* now made clear that the protection afforded by EU law in return contexts, following from *Singh*, did not end when the returning national stopped meeting the requirements governing qualification to the scope of secondary free movement law (i.e., when he/she stopped being economically active or was not, or no longer, in the possession of sufficient resources). In addition, the *Eind* decision also made plain that the family reunion rights granted in *Singh* did not only accrue to spouses but that children—as specified, up until the age of 21 or when dependent on the EU national—were covered by the *Singh* principles as well. Furthermore, by stating that a 'deterrent effect' could derive simply from the prospect, for an EU national, of not being able to continue living 'a way of life which may have come into being in the host Member State as a result of marriage or family reunification' the Court explicitly recognized that the rights granted in return contexts, following from *Singh*, also applied to situations of 'family formation'.

To the extent that *Eind* confirmed and extended the holdings of *Singh*, it simultaneously narrowed the implications of *Akrich* in which, at face value, the Court had seemed to re-shift the balance towards Member States' domestic immigration control competences. More precisely, *Eind* could be interpreted as confirming that between the two possible interpretations of the *Akrich*-established 'prior lawful residence' requirement, the narrower one was to be favoured. That is, different from *Jia* where the Court's engagement with the matter had not undone it of all ambiguity, the *Eind* decision seemed to more clearly indicate that the 'prior lawful residence requirement' could only be used to restrict EU rights in situations where there had in fact, like in *Akrich*, been a prior 'unlawful' residence, not in situations where, like in *Eind*, family members had never held a 'prior lawful residence' as they had only ever resided in third countries before (see Bierbach, 2008).

On the other hand, *Eind*—and in line with the above trends—also perpetuated other questions or gave rise to all together new uncertainties. For instance, it remained uncertain, as had also been the case after *Singh*, for how long exactly an EU national would have to reside outside of the territory of his host State, in exercising free movement rights, for such a residence to be considered sufficiently genuine to trigger the continued protection of EU law upon his/her return? Furthermore, and in line with earlier indicated techniques, stating that the answers to the first set of questions provided sufficient indications to the national court, the Court held that there was "no need" for clarification on the extent to which rights could possibly, additionally, accrue to Mr. Eind, or more generally to returning EU nationals, directly on the basis of Treaty provisions (Ibid., paragraph 46). Finally, whilst providing further indications on how to interpret the *Akrich* 'prior lawful residence requirement' it was difficult to join the outcome of *Eind* with the principles that had been articulated in *Akrich* in respect of that requirement, and that had also been reproduced by the British and Danish governments in their written observations on *Eind*. More precisely, it was difficult to see how the *Eind* outcome could be wedded with the central premise of *Akrich* that the refusal to grant a residence right to a third-country national family member of a returning EU national could not be found to have a dissuasive effect on that national's free movement rights if such a right had not already existed prior to the first move (*Akrich*, paragraphs 53–54). Accordingly, whereas *Jia* had started pulling at the comfort blanket which Member States had been given in *Akrich*, *Eind* pulled harder. Not only was the reach of the prior lawful residence requirement curtailed, the central premises on which this requirement had been built—and hence, the judgment overall—could now be called into question.

This last uncertainty was soon to be resolved as, a few years later, in the context of the *Metock* proceedings, the Court came to definitively and explicitly overrule *Akrich*. Like *Eind*, *Metock*'s numerical citation scores display dominant trends in regard of both their outward, as well as their inward trends, suggesting that the judgment was at the same time well-grounded in earlier case law, as well as important, from a precedent perspective, for the proceedings that followed.

The ***Metock*** case concerned the joined disputes of four mixed 'EU-national, third-country national' couples resident in Ireland. The third-country nationals had all, prior to their marriage to the EU national, been unable to derive a right of residence under Irish domestic immigration law. Subsequent to their marriages, they had all claimed residence rights as spouses of moving Union nationals under EU law. These residence rights claims had all been rejected, however, on the grounds that none of the third-country nationals satisfied the condition of 'prior lawful residence' that had been inscribed in Irish law following the Court's *Akrich* judgment. In sequence, the four couples brought proceedings against that rejection claiming that the imposition of such a condition was incompatible with the Citizenship Directive (2004/38/EC) which had in the meantime entered into force and in which no such 'prior lawful residence' requirement had been inscribed. Arguing that the 2004/38 Directive was to be interpreted as regulating the conditions of entry and residence for family members of moving EU citizens "exhaustively", the application of such a condition by Ireland was said to infringe EU free movement law (*Metock*, paragraph 41).

The Irish High Court, before which the proceedings eventually appeared, referred the case to Luxembourg for further clarification. It asked, first, whether Directive 2004/38/EC permitted a Member State "to have a general requirement that a non-EU national spouse of a Union citizen must have been lawfully resident in another Member State prior to coming to the host Member State". In addition, it wanted to know whether the "scope of application" of the Directive's family reunion provisions included third-country national spouses irrespective of, first, "when and where" the marriage with the moving Union national had taken place (i.e., whether it also covered situations of family 'formation') and, second, independent of "when or how" the non-EU national had entered the Member State (Ibid., paragraph 47).

The *Metock* file prompted no less than ten Member States to submit written observations. These were joined with the arguments that had been filed by the Irish Minister for Justice and, as emerges from the judgment's text, generally followed similar lines of reasoning. To begin with, the Irish Minister argued that the 'prior lawful residence requirement' was in line with the "discretion" that Union law left to Member States in respect of the situations of "nationals of non-member countries" (*Metock*, paragraph 45). This argument was supported, the Minister contended, by the CJEU's judgments in *Akrich* and *Jia*. In addition, the Irish Minister also submitted that there was a "division of competences" between the Member States and the Community, "under which the Member States have competence in relation to the admission into a Member State of nationals of non-member countries coming from outside Community territory", whilst the Community, on the other hand, "has competence to regulate the movement of Union citizens and their family members within the Union" (Ibid., paragraph 44). This argument too can be seen as a rephrasing of earlier Court dicta in *Akrich* (see *Akrich*, paragraph 49). Furthermore, the Minister, "and several of the governments that have submitted observations" contended that especially "in a context typified by strong pressure of migration", it was "necessary to control immigration at the external borders of the Community" (*Metock*, paragraph 71). An interpretation of Directive 2004/38 according to which Member States would be prohibited from instating a prior lawful residence requirement "would undermine the ability of the Member States to control immigration at their external frontiers", in addition to having "serious consequences (...) by bringing about a great increase in the number of persons able to benefit from a right of residence in the Community" (Ibid., paragraphs 72–73). Finally, Member States also argued that such an interpretation of the Directive would lead to "unjustified reverse discrimination" insofar as nationals of the host Member State who had never exercised free movement rights (i.e., 'static' EU nationals) would not have access to such more beneficial rights of entry and residence for their third-country national family members (Ibid., paragraph 76).

The Court started out its reasoning on these sensitive issues by stating that "as regards family members of a Union citizen", "no provision of Directive 2004/38 makes the application of the directive conditional on their having previously resided in a Member State" (Ibid., paragraph 49). Arguably, on the basis of this opening premise, the first question referred was essentially answered. However, and likely in view of the sensitive nature of this answer (as also emerges from the above Member States' submissions), the Court attached a long series of further considerations to this premise. In addition, it can also be pointed out that, although perhaps unequivocal at face value, the Court's opening premise was not necessarily so straightforward when considered in light of the fact that Regulation 1612/68, which preceded the Directive and on which *Akrich* had been based, had not provided for a prior lawful residence stipulation either.

The Court elaborated on this opening statement with a number of in-depth, literal interpretations of specific provisions of Directive 2004/38. More precisely, the exact wording of the Directive's articles 3(1), 2(2), 5(2), 6(2), 7(2), 9(1), 10(1) and 10(2) were subjected to detailed scrutiny. For each of these provisions, the Court then concluded that nothing in their wording suggested that they made the access to the rights conferred on their basis conditional on family members having had a 'prior lawful residence' (Ibid., paragraphs 50–54). Accordingly, as followed, "(i) n those circumstances, Directive 2004/38 must be interpreted as applying to all nationals of non-member countries who are family members of a Union citizen (...) without distinguishing according to whether or not the national of a non-member country has already resided lawfully in another Member State" (Ibid., paragraph 54).

The Court then submitted that this interpretation was also supported by its earlier case law (Ibid., paragraph 55). This statement was at least somewhat puzzling in light of the fact that it explicitly opposed the preceding *Akrich* decision. Instead, in order to support this statement a long line of cases, excluding *Akrich*, was cited with the aim of highlighting the importance that the Court attached to "ensuring the protection of the family life of nationals of the Member States in order to eliminate obstacles to the exercise of the fundamental freedoms guaranteed by the EC Treaty". To that purpose, the Court referred to each of its preceding decisions in which it had reinforced such mixed 'effet utile-fundamental rights' discourses. That is, in their respective chronological order, *Carpenter, MRAX, Commission v Spain* (C-157/03), *Commission v Spain* (C-503/03) and *Eind* (Ibid., paragraph 56).

From there, the CJEU acknowledged that it was "true that the Court held in paragraphs 50 and 51 of *Akrich*, that in order to benefit from the rights provided for in Article 10 of Regulation No 1612/68, the national of a non-member country who is the spouse of Union citizen must be lawfully resident in a Member State". That conclusion, however, had to be "reconsidered". Referring once more to *MRAX* and *Commission v Spain* (C-157/03), the Court posited that the "benefit of such rights cannot depend on the prior lawful residence of such a spouse in another Member State" (Ibid., paragraph 58).

In a next stage of its argumentation, the Court engaged, extensively, with the contentions put forward by the intervening Member States, and the Irish Minister for Justice most notably. To begin with, and replicating the discourse of the Irish Minister for Justice, the above, new interpretation was found to be consistent with the "division of competences between the Member States and the Community" (Ibid., paragraph 60). In fact, it was "common ground", the Court held, that the Community "has competence to enact the necessary measures to bring about freedom of movement for Union citizens" (Ibid., paragraph 61). With reference to the above listing of its earlier mixed 'fundamental rights-effet utile' dicta the Court then held that "(a)s already pointed out in paragraph 56 above, if Union citizens were not allowed to lead a normal family life in the host Member State, the exercise of the freedoms they are guaranteed by the Treaty would be seriously obstructed" (Ibid., paragraph 62). From there the Court argued that, "consequently", "within the competence conferred on it by (...) the Treaty, the Community legislature can regulate the conditions of entry and residence of the family members of a Union citizen in the territory of the Member States, where the fact that it is impossible for the Union citizen to be accompanied or joined by his family in the host Member State would be such as to interfere with his freedom of movement by discouraging him from exercising his rights of entry into and residence in that Member State" (Ibid., paragraph 63). In other words, "the Community legislature has competence to regulate, as it did by Directive 2004/38, the entry and residence of nationals of non-member countries who are family members of a Union citizen (...) including where the family members were not already lawfully resident in another Member State" (Ibid., paragraph 65). Accordingly, and revealing a new implication attached to its earlier mixed 'effet utile-fundamental rights' dicta, "the interpretation put forward by the Minister for Justice and by several of the governments that have submitted observations that the Member States retain exclusive competence (...) to regulate the first access to Community territory of family members of a Union citizen who are nationals of non-member countries" had to be "rejected" (Ibid., paragraph 66).

Two afterthoughts were added to the conclusion that Member States did not retain exclusive competence over third-country national family members' first entry. First, the Court stated that, to conclude otherwise would have the effect that the freedom of movement of Union Citizens "would vary from one Member State to another, according to the provisions of national law concerning immigration, with some Member States permitting entry and residence of family members of Union citizen and other Member States refusing them" (Ibid., paragraph 67). Such variations would not be compatible with the Union objective of creating "an internal market characterised by the abolition, as between Member States, of obstacles to the free movement of persons" (Ibid., paragraph 68). Second, and with reference to the Family Reunification Directive (2003/86/EC) which had then recently entered into force, the interpretation suggested by the intervening Member States would lead to the "paradoxical outcome" that Member States would be obliged, pursuant to this new immigration law instrument, to authorise the entry and residence of the family members of third-country nationals even where these family members were not already lawfully resident, whilst they would remain "free to refuse the entry and residence of the spouse of a Union citizen in the same circumstances" (Ibid., paragraph 69).

Next, the Court engaged with two further lines of reasoning that had been adduced by the intervening Member States. To begin with, the Court examined the contention that a prohibition to uphold a condition of prior lawful residence would "undermine" Member States' "ability to control immigration at their external frontiers" which would be especially problematic "in a context typified by strong pressure of migration" (Ibid., paragraph 71). It pointed out in that regard, first, that "it is not all nationals of non-member countries who derive rights of entry into and residence in a Member State from Directive 2004/38, but only those who are family members (…) of a Union citizen who has exercised his right of freedom of movement" (Ibid., paragraph 73). In addition, Member States were also invited to find consolation in the observation that pursuant to the Directive's Chapter VI they could still, "where this was justified, refuse entry and residence on grounds of public policy, public security or public health" (Ibid., paragraph 74). Moreover, they could also adopt "the necessary measures to refuse, terminate or withdraw any right conferred by that directive in the case of abuse of rights or fraud, such as marriages of convenience". This last point, however, with the understanding that any such measure had to be "proportionate and subject to the procedural safeguards provided for in the directive" (Ibid., paragraph 75).

Second, governments had also argued that a revocation of the prior lawful residence requirement would lead to "unjustified reverse discrimination" as static, home nationals would not be able to lay claim to the more beneficial EU rights (Ibid., paragraph 76). The Court revisited in that regard, first, its 'internal rule' dicta according to which "Treaty rules governing freedom of movement for persons and the measures adopted to implement them cannot be applied to activities which have no factor linking them with any of the situations governed by Community law" (Ibid., paragraph 77). Accordingly, and in line with the reasoning adopted in early 'internal rule' cases such as *Morson & Jhanjan* or *Uecker & Jacquet* (discussed in the first subsection), "(a)ny difference in treatment between those Union citizens and those who have exercised their right of freedom of movement as regards the entry and residence of their family members, does not therefore fall within the scope of Community law" (Ibid., paragraph 78). Put differently, and as Peers phrased it, the Court reminded Member States that they could not "have their cake and eat it too". Or, Member States could not, at the same time "insist upon national competence" and then "complain about the results which they have themselves created by exercise of that competence" (Peers, 2009, pp. 191–192).

This, especially, in light of the deliberate legislative choice made during the negotiations on the Family Reunification Directive not to bring static, home nationals within the scope of the new instrument as the Commission had originally proposed (Ibid., *cf.* Chap. 4). If Member States objected to the state of affairs, and because of the fact that the situation of static nationals had deliberately been left within the sphere of national competences, they were free to enact changes to their domestic immigration rules so as to bring these in line with the standards applied within EU law and, in that way, do away with instances of reverse discrimination. In addition, the Court also reminded Member States that they were all parties to the ECHR "which enshrines in Article 8 the right to respect for private and family life" (*Metock*, paragraph 79).

Having established all of the above, the Court moved on to, less elaborately, consider the follow-up questions that had been referred alongside the central question on the permissibility of a 'prior lawful residence requirement'. That is, and as the first follow-up question, whether the family reunion provisions in EU free movement law also applied to situations of family 'formation'. Furthermore, the Irish court had also asked whether EU law covered the situations of non-EU national spouses independent of "when or how" the non-EU national had entered the Member State. The Court's engagement with these follow-up questions generally followed the lines of reasoning that had been adduced in respect of the first question in that its reasoning also turned on a combination of literal interpretations and teleological, 'effet utile'-oriented reviews of relevant EU law provisions.

Amongst others, the Court posited, in respect of the first follow-up question, that the provisions of Directive 2004/38 "cannot be interpreted restrictively, and must not in any event be deprived of their effectiveness" (*Metock*, paragraph 84). To this purpose, it also referred to *Eind*. In addition, none of the Directive's provisions on joining family members were found to state anything along the lines which would support the view "that the Union citizen must already have founded a family at the time when he moves to host Member State in order for his family members who are nationals of non-member countries to be able to enjoy a right of residence there" (Ibid., paragraph 87). As it continued, "(w)here a Union citizen founds a family after becoming established in another Member State, the refusal of that Member State to authorise his family members who are nationals of non-member countries to join him there would be such as to discourage him from continuing to reside there and encourage him to leave in order to be able to lead a family life in another Member State or in a non-member country" (Ibid., paragraph 89).

In respect of the second follow-up question the Court similarly noted that it made no difference whether the entry had taken place "before or after" the third-country national became a family member of the Union citizen since, in any event, to refuse a right of residence to such a family member would "be liable to discourage that Union citizen from continuing to reside in that Member State" (Ibid., paragraph 92). This interpretation was also found to be borne out of the "necessity of not interpreting the provisions of Directive 2004/38 restrictively and not depriving them of their effectiveness" (Ibid., paragraph 93). The Court then further limited Member States' room for policy manoeuvre by outlining that "(f)rom the time when the national of a non-member country who is a family member of a Union citizen derives rights of entry and residence in the host Member State from Directive 2004/38, that State may restrict that right only in compliance with Articles 27 and 35 of that Directive" (Ibid., paragraph 95). Compliance with Article 27—which enshrines, inter alia, procedural safeguards and embeds references to the principle of proportionality—was particularly required where a "Member State wishes to penalise the national of a non-member country for entering into or residing in its territory in breach of the national rules on immigration before becoming a family member of a Union citizen" (Ibid., paragraph 96). In this context, the Court also referred back to its conclusions in *MRAX* (Ibid., paragraph 97). In all, neither the circumstances in which a third-country national family member of a Union citizen entered a host state (lawfully or not), nor where and when the family bonds had been established could detract from the rights that such a family member enjoyed under EU free movement law.

In all, where in preceding scope-extending rulings as *Singh, Carpenter, Eind* etc., the Court had left some margin of uncertainty as to the exact implications to be taken from these rulings—and hence, the exact inroads made into Member States' domestic immigration control competences—the *Metock* decision was clear. The comfort blanket originally provided in *Akrich* was now decisively taken away. Because of the *Metock* ruling, and as emerges from a 2008 Commission report on the implementation of Directive 2004/38, several Member States had to adapt the prior lawful residence requirements that they had inscribed in national law after *Akrich*.[2] In addition, the *Metock* outcomes also affected the domestic practices of seven further Member States who provided for analogous prior lawful residence conditions at administrative level (COM (2008) 840, p. 4).[3]

As is not surprising, the judgment provoked a host of political reactions at EU and national levels. At EU level, first, *Metock* became the subject of a series of Justice and Home Affairs Councils in the fall of 2008 and during the first half of 2009 (see Peers, 2009). The conclusions of one of these Council meetings for instance read that it was considered necessary and "a priority" that Member States would "closely monitor and tackle abuse and fraud of the fundamental principles of the right to free movement of persons in the coming years". In that light, Member States were also called on to "exchange information on abuse and fraud and report to the Commission on systematic trends". Should such "systematic trends" be detected, the Council was to "revert to the issue" (Council Document 13467/09, p. 10). Furthermore, at least three Member States (Ireland, Denmark and the Netherlands) indicated, in response to a reporting request of a network of academic experts, that they had campaigned for a re-opening of the Citizenship Directive amongst their counterparts after the *Metock* ruling with a view to investing the instrument with new, and more stringent requirements (Fernhout & Wever, 2011). In addition, and moving to the national level, the same reporting exercise revealed that in the aftermath of *Metock* at least seven Member States stepped up their efforts at detecting, and combatting forms of "abuse" of EU free movement rules (Ibid., pp. 16–17).[4]

Taking a bird's eye view on the political shockwaves post-*Metock*, at least one commentator asserted that this ruling could well "prove to be the straw that broke the camel's back" (Currie, 2009, p. 326). As she further observed, the "dissatisfaction and threats of rebellion expressed" may be just as much a "response to the cumulative build-up of judgements on the free movement entitlement of Union citizens (...) as it is a reaction to the specific judgment itself". Tensions were "clearly running high" and the Court was advised to "tread carefully in the future if it wishes to avoid

[2] Besides Ireland, also Finland, the UK and Denmark.

[3] The seven other Member States referred to in the Commission report are Austria, the Czech Republic, Germany, Greece, Cyprus, Malta and the Netherlands.

[4] The Member States mentioned in this respect are Denmark, France, Hungaria, Ireland, Lithuania, the Netherlands and Sweden.

the risk of further uprising" (Ibid.). As will emerge in the below, reviews of *Metock*'s large number of follow-up citations in such cases as *Chakroun, McCarthy, Dereci, Iida, O&S* and *O&B*, seem to indicate that, at least to some extent, the Court started vacillating in regard of the precise implications to be taken from the more general, programmatic principles that it had put forward in *Metock*.

7.4.3 **EPvCouncil *and* Chakroun**

The first ruling in this list of follow-up citations to *Metock* is the *Chakroun* ruling which, itself is closely related to the preceding *EPvCouncil* judgment. *Chakroun* and *EPvCouncil* connect to the last set of dominant trends highlighted at the beginning of this section. That is, the numerically dominant outward and inward scores linked to *EPvCouncil*, and the dominant outward scores connected to *Chakroun*. The dominant outward scores of both cases suggest that both rulings were significantly grounded in preceding case law. This is in and of itself noteworthy as the two rulings, and what explains their interconnection, relate to the first two cases to arrive before Luxembourg on the Family Reunification Directive (2003/86/EC). As will be detailed in what follows, in pronouncing its considerations on these first family reunification questions in the context of EU immigration law, the Court strongly built on the dicta that it had advanced earlier in its free movement case law.

The questions in ***EPvCouncil***, to begin with, arrived before the Court no more than three months after the Family Reunification Directive had entered into force (on 3 October 2003). They arose in the context of an action for annulment initiated by the European Parliament. More specifically, the EP challenged three of the Directive's derogation clauses on the grounds that they were not compatible with fundamental rights' standards as provided for in the general principles of EU law. To begin with, the EP sought the annulment of the final subparagraph of the Directive's Article 4(1) pursuant to which, "by way of derogation", children over 12 years and arriving independently from the rest of their family could be subjected to a "condition for integration". Second, the EP contested the derogation clause in the Directive's Article 4(6) which permitted Member States to request that applications for family reunion with minor children are submitted before the children concerned reach the age of 15. Third, the EP also raised fundamental rights-related objections in regard of the waiting periods of up to two (or even three) years that could be imposed before family members were admitted pursuant to the Directive's Article 8. As argued by some commentators, these EP challenges could at least to some extent be seen as offshoots of the Directive's ardent and complex negotiation history in which the Parliament had not been able to exercise much influence (see Chap. 4). Aiming to get its points across nevertheless, the EP then opted for the judicial route. In addition, the EP's legal actions are also said to have been further induced by strategic and coordinated lobbying efforts from several human rights NGOs with its MEPs (Menz, 2011, pp. 445–446; Strik, 2011, pp. 132–133).

In general terms, and as transposed in the judgment's text, the EP submitted that the three contested provisions did "not respect fundamental rights—in particular the right to family life and the right to non-discrimination—as guaranteed by the *ECHR* and as they result from the (...) general principles of Community law" (*EPvCouncil*, paragraph 30). Furthermore, the EP also invoked the Charter, in particular its Article 7 (on the right to family life), as well as the Charter's provisions on children's rights and the non-discrimination clause enshrined in Article 21(1) CFREU (Ibid., paragraph 31). Adding thereto, a long list of international human rights instruments was cited including, *inter alia*, the ICCPR and the CRC (Ibid., paragraph 33). In respect of its claims relating to the fundamental right to family life the EP took explicit cues from the Court's *Carpenter* and *Akrich* decisions which were presented as providing support for the interpretation that the fundamental 'right to respect for family life' also covered 'the right to family reunification' (Ibid., paragraph 31).

As can be recalled from Chap. 4, the three provisions that were singled out by the EP were also amongst the provisions that had proven to be most politically sensitive during the negotiation processes on the Family Reunification Directive. They had been inserted, precisely, with the aim of accommodating a number of national sovereignty concerns that had hindered Council discussions. The first of these three provisions, the derogation clauses permitting an additional 'condition for integration' in respect of family reunion requests with children above the age of 12, had been introduced with the specific aim of allaying German concerns over what had been perceived as overly liberal stipulations in regard of the age limits. These concerns had at a certain point during the negotiations even led to a veto from the German delegation. The second contested provision, permitting Member States to request that applications for family reunion with minor children were submitted before such children reached the age of 15, stemmed from similar efforts at accommodating Austrian demands for more stringent age requirements. The final provision challenged by the EP, the waiting period enshrined in the Directive's Article 8, had been inserted to put another set of Austrian concerns to rest. That is, and as a leitmotif marking the negotiations on the instrument in its different stages, Austria had continuously demanded legal possibilities that would enable it to maintain the family reunion quota system which it operated at national level.

Accordingly, it bears little surprise that the judicial challenges raised by the EP on these three specific provisions prompted strong reactions from within the Council. As emerges from the case's Report for the hearing, the Council submitted observations to the Court in which it called attention, first, to the 'difficulty' that had marked the harmonization efforts in this area of law (Report for the hearing *EPvCouncil*, paragraph 26). As it also pointed out, the derogation clauses that had been added to the instrument were based on the premise that, when applying these clauses at national level, Member States would have due regard to their fundamental rights obligations (Ibid., paragraph 27). Furthermore, the Council questioned how the Court could review the legality of the contested provisions in purely abstract terms, i.e., without information on the specific circumstances in which, and how, these clauses would be implemented in domestic law. In that respect, the Council also took cues from the *Carpenter* decision, referring, in particular, to the emphasis placed in that judgment on the importance of taking "specific circumstances" into account (Ibid., paragraph 28). At a further point in its submissions, the Council added that nothing in the Directive prejudged the outcome of "the weighing of the individual and collective interests that would present itself in each individual case", and that the Directive's articles 17 and 5(5) in any event obliged Member States to have regard to the ECHR and to the best interests of children as provided for by the CRC (Ibid., paragraph 34).

In addition to these Council submissions, Germany had also requested, and received, leave to intervene before the Court in its own name. It generally provided support for the lines of reasoning advanced in the Council's submissions, but also highlighted the importance that it attached to the derogation clause entitling Member States to ask that children above the age of 12 met a 'condition for integration'. As it pointed out, this derogation clause had been one of the central points that had allowed the Council's Members to reach a compromise and, accordingly, one of the central points that had enabled the eventual adoption of the Directive for which, as Germany stressed, a unanimity vote had been required (Ibid., paragraph 72).

The Court first reviewed the issues raised around this 'condition for integration' as provided for in the Directive's Article 4(1). It started out its reasoning by reinforcing the fundamental rights dicta that it had adduced, first, in *Carpenter*, from which both parties had taken cues, and second, in *Akrich*, which the EP had invoked. More precisely, the Court repeated, with reference to both judgments, that the "right to respect for family life within the meaning of Article 8 of the ECHR is among the fundamental rights which, according to the Court's settled case-law, are protected in Community law" (*EPvCouncil*, paragraph 52). Additionally, and again with reference to both judgments, it highlighted that although the protection provided by Article 8 ECHR "does not guarantee as a fundamental right the right of an alien to enter or to reside in a particular country, the removal of a person from a country where close members of his family are living may amount to an infringement of the right to respect for family life as guaranteed by Article 8(1) of the ECHR" (Ibid., paragraph 53). From there, the Court further unpacked the meaning and implications of these earlier dicta by embarking on a lengthy and detailed exposition of the principles to be taken into account in the context of Article 8 ECHR. To that purpose, it also extensively referred to ECtHR's case law on said Article 8. Amongst others, the Court called attention to such ECtHR principles as the need to have regard to the "fair balance that has to be struck between the competing interests of the individual and of the community as a whole" (Ibid., paragraph 54). In addition, the "importance to a child of family life" was also highlighted, and in that regard the Court cited the Charter's provisions on the right to family life and children's rights (Ibid., paragraphs 56–59).[5] Ending its observations on fundamental rights standards, the Court referred to the Directive's Article 5.5 and 17. As it highlighted, and as the Council had also submitted, these articles demanded of Member States to take due account of children's best interests (Article 5.5) and, pursuant to Article 17, to have regard, in the examination of each individual application, for such factors as the "nature and solidity of the person's family relationship", "the duration of his residence", and "the existence of family, cultural and social ties" with a person's country of origin (paragraphs 63–65). As was further set out in

[5] This reference to the EU Charter's provisions in *EPvCouncil* in fact marked the very first Charter reference made in a CJEU judgment (see Iglesias Sanchez, 2012).

respect of Article 17, it was "apparent" from the above considerations on Article 8 ECHR that the criteria spelled out in that article corresponded "to those taken into consideration by the *ECtHR* when it reviews whether a State which has refused an application for family reunification has correctly weighed the competing interests" (Ibid., paragraph 64).

In all, and against the background of these extensive fundamental rights considerations which, together, took up more than five pages in the judgment's text, the Court held that the Directive's 'condition for integration' derogation clause, could not be regarded as running counter to fundamental rights obligations "either in itself or in that it expressly or impliedly authorises the Member States to act in such a way" (Ibid., paragraph 76). More precisely, the clause could "not be regarded as running counter to the right to respect for family life" as "(i)n the context of a directive imposing precise positive obligations on the Member States", it preserved "a limited margin of appreciation for those States which is no different from that accorded to them by the *ECtHR* (…) for weighing, in each factual situation, the competing interests" (Ibid., paragraph 62).

Similar lines of reasoning were then applied, though in less elaborate terms, to the further two provisions that were challenged by the EP. To begin with, Article 4.6, entitling Member States to request that applications for family reunion with minors are submitted before they reach the age of 15, "could not be regarded as running counter to the fundamental right to family life (…) either in itself or in that it expressly or impliedly authorises the Member States to act in such a way" (Ibid. paragraph 90). Rather, whilst the clause gave "Member States the option of applying the conditions for family reunification which are prescribed by the Directive only to applications submitted before children have reached 15 years of age", it could not "be interpreted as prohibiting the Member States from taking account of an application relating to a child over 15 years of age" or even "as authorising them not do so" (Ibid., paragraph 85). Moreover, as was highlighted, the clause had to "be read in the light of the principles set out in Article 5(5) (…) which requires the Member States to have due regard to the best interests of minor children, and in Article 17, which requires them to take account of a number of factors, one of which is the person's family relationships" (Ibid., paragraph 87).

In respect of the final contested provision, the waiting period proviso inscribed in Article 8, the Court also held that it could not be "regarded as running counter to the fundamental right to respect for family life or to the obligation to have regard to the best interests of children, either in itself or in that it expressly or impliedly authorises the Member States to act in such a way" (Ibid., paragraph 103). More precisely, "(l)ike the other provisions contested in the present action", Article 8 was found "to authorise the Member States to derogate from the rules governing family reunification laid down by the Directive" (Ibid., paragraph 97). It was to be remembered, however, that "as apparent from Article 17 of the Directive, duration of residence in the Member State is only one of the factors which must be taken into account by the Member State when considering an application and that a waiting period cannot be imposed without taking into account, in specific cases, all relevant factors" (Ibid., paragraph 99). In addition, when carrying out the analysis of all such relevant factors, Member States were also to have "due regard to the best interests of minor children" (Ibid., paragraph 101).

In its final analysis, the Court stated that, while the Directive as a whole left "the Member States a margin of appreciation", this margin was "sufficiently wide to enable them to apply the Directive's rules in a manner consistent with the requirements flowing from the protection of fundamental rights" (Ibid., paragraph 104). As its closing words, the Court added that the "(i)mplementation of the Directive is subject to review by the national courts since, as provided in Article 18 thereof, the Member States shall ensure that the sponsor and the members of his/her family have the right to mount a legal challenge where an application for family reunification is rejected or a residence permit is either not renewed or is withdrawn or removal is ordered". As the Court further emphasized, "(i)f those courts encounter difficulties relating to the interpretation or validity of the Directive", it was "incumbent on them to refer a question to the Court for a preliminary ruling" (Ibid., paragraph 106).

In all, accordingly, the three contested provisions were not found to infringe fundamental rights standards "in and of themselves, either impliedly or expressly". On that basis, at least at face value, the Council was able to leave the court room victoriously. It would not take long, however, before a different set of implications of the fundamental rights considerations that had been so carefully spelled out in *EPvCouncil* would emerge. In 2008, two years after the rendering of *EPvCouncil*, the Court received the first response to its closing plea that, in case of interpretative difficulties, it was incumbent upon national courts to send in questions for a preliminary ruling. The Dutch Council of State referred two such questions in the context of the *Chakroun* case. In this way as well, the EU judiciary was presented with a renewed opportunity to further construct the holdings of *EPvCouncil* and expound their more precise ramifications when applied to actual national implementing measures (instead of, as in *EPvCouncil*, in abstract terms). As documented in what follows, the conclusion borne out of this application was very different from the originally uncontroversial one that had been reached in *EPvCouncil*.

Chakroun concerned the request for family reunification of Mr. Chakroun, a Moroccan national lawfully resident in the Netherlands, with his wife, Mrs. Chakroun, a Moroccan national resident in Morocco. Mr. Chakroun had resided in the Netherlands for 36 years when the request was made. He had married Mrs. Chakroun two years after he moved to the Netherlands and, accordingly, the couple had been married for 34 years at the time when the request for family reunion was lodged. The Dutch authorities had denied Mr. Chakroun's request on the grounds that he did not possess an income that was sufficient to meet the income requirement that the Netherlands applied to applications for family 'formation', as the couple's situation was considered to be. More specifically, Mr. Chakroun's income was, by and large, a 100 euros below that income standard. If, however, the application of Mr. Chakroun would have been considered as relating to a situation of family 'reunification' in the strict sense (i.e., reunification with family members with whom family ties were already established prior to the move to the host country), the income of Mr. Chakroun would have met the lower income standard that the Netherlands applied to such situations.

Mrs. Chakroun challenged this refusal in light of the provisions of the Family Reunification Directive. She raised two specific points. First, Mrs. Chakroun pointed out that the income requirement applied to situations of family 'formation' amounted to 120% of the Dutch minimum wage (*Chakroun*, paragraph 24). This, she contended, was incompatible with the Directive's Article 7(1)(c) which read that Member States were allowed to require of sponsors that they had stable and regular resources defined as resources "sufficient to maintain himself/herself and the members of his/her family, without recourse to the social assistance system of the Member State concerned". As Mr. Chakroun's income was above the minimum wage, he had resources that were sufficient to meet his needs, and that of his family, Mrs. Chakroun asserted, without recourse to the Dutch social assistance system. As the Dutch government explained in its written observations, however, the 120% threshold was applied in the Netherlands in order to exclude the situations of persons who, as was conceded, were not able to qualify for "general" social assistance, but who could nevertheless still lay claim to "special assistance". That is, assistance which could be granted in "exceptional circumstances" by local authorities after an examination of the specific situation said to give rise to special needs. Accordingly, by applying a 120% standard, the Dutch government had sought to use a reference amount above which an applicant was no longer entitled to any form of social benefits, either general or in the form of special assistance (Ibid., paragraphs 25–28).

As the second point of contestation, Mrs. Chakroun challenged the distinction that was drawn by the Netherlands between situations of family 'reunification' and situations of family 'formation' for the purposes of checking the applicant's resources. As Mrs. Chakroun pointed out, no such distinction was made in the Directive's provisions on the conditional requirements that Member States were able to uphold and accordingly, she contended, the Dutch practices infringed those provisions (Ibid., paragraph 29). Finally, as a third and more general point, Mrs. Chakroun added that the Dutch authorities, in failing to take account of the long duration of Mr. Chakroun's residence in the Netherlands and of the long duration of the couple's marriage, had disregarded their obligation to examine all the relevant factors in each individual situation as prescribed by the Directive's Article 17 (Ibid., paragraph 38). The Dutch government however submitted, conversely, and also with reference to Article 17, that the distinction drawn was not prohibited as it was but "one way in which account may be taken of the nature and solidity of family ties". As was added, the Dutch government also considered that it was "possible that the interests at stake will be greater in the case where the family relationship already existed before the principal person became resident in the Netherlands" and that, "as a general rule", the family relationship is "less intense" in cases of family formation (Ibid., paragraph 57). In addition, "for the sake of completeness", it also observed that "even where the family relationship arose after the arrival of the principal person in the Netherlands, and the income condition is not met, residence of the family members will nevertheless be permitted if Article 8 of the ECHR so requires" (Ibid., paragraph 58).

As can be recalled from the preceding chapter, the two contested points in *Chakroun* related, like the issues raised in *EPvCouncil*, to points that had been especially sensitive during Council discussions on the Directive. To begin with, in respect of the sufficient resources requirement, where the Commission had originally aimed to phrase this requirement in very precise terms so as to make sure that it could not be applied in a way that would 'render the right to family reunification nugatory', Member States had invested much efforts in—conversely—making sure that the condition allowed for a large degree of manoeuvrability so that it could suit different domestic policy practices. Notably the Dutch delegation had been behind a number of requests for investing this requirement with additional flexibility. Second, the question on whether the Directive would cover family formation situations as well, or whether—conversely—it would be limited to situations of family reunification strictly speaking had also been the subject of much political debate. Especially Germany had voiced a number of concerns in that respect. Eventually however, only the scope of the more favourable rules governing the family reunion requests of refugees (Chapter V) had been narrowed down to exclude situations of family 'formation'. The remainder of the instrument applied, as per Article 2(d), to the entry and residence of family members "whether the family relationship arose before or after the resident's entry".

The Court started its reasoning on the issues raised by referring back to *EPvCouncil*. As it reiterated, the Directive was to be interpreted as imposing "precise positive obligations, with corresponding individual rights on the Member States, since it requires them, in the cases determined by the Directive, to authorise family reunification of certain members of the sponsor's family" (Ibid., paragraph 41). Accordingly, since "family reunification" was "the general rule", the sufficient resources faculty that was provided had to be "interpreted strictly" (Ibid., paragraph 43). Furthermore, as the Court continued, "the margin for manoeuvre" which the Member States were recognised as having by means of that faculty, could not be used by them "in a manner which would undermine the objective of the Directive, which is to promote family reunification and the effectiveness thereof" (Ibid.; paragraphs 43–47). This last statement was especially noteworthy as none of the Directive's provisions mentions such an objective (see also Hardy, 2012). From there, the Court re-emphasized, as it had done in *EPvCouncil*, that the measures concerning family reunification had to be "adopted in conformity with the obligation to protect the family and respect family life enshrined in many instruments of international law" (Ibid., paragraph 44).

On the basis of these first, rights-based premises, the Court then proceeded with a literal interpretation of the provision subject to review. It referred in that respect amongst others to the second sentence of Article 7(1)(c) which entitles Member States to take account of the level of minimum national wages and pensions when evaluating the sponsor's resources.

On that basis, and referring back to the family reunification 'promoting' objectives, the Court came to hold that "since the extent of needs can vary greatly depending on the individuals", Article 7(1)(c) had to be "interpreted as meaning that the Member States may indicate a certain sum as a reference amount, but not as meaning that they may impose a minimum income level below which all family reunifications will be refused". Such an interpretation was also presented as supported by Article 17 of the Directive which, as the Court highlighted, and similar to *EPvCouncil*, "requires an individual examination of applications for family reunification" (Ibid., paragraphs 47–48). Accordingly, and in all, the Dutch application of the sufficient resources requirement, using a reference standard equivalent to 120% of the minimum income, was "precluded" by the Directive (Ibid., paragraphs 49–52).

The second question was then addressed on the basis of similar lines of reasoning. As the Court stated, with the exception of the Chapter on refugees, the Directive's provisions, pursuant to Article 2(d), applied both to what the Netherlands referred to as family reunification and to what they considered as family formation (Ibid., paragraphs 59–61). The Court then adduced further fundamental rights considerations to complement this interpretation. To begin with, the Court cited the Directive's sixth recital which referred to the requirement to "protect the family and establish or preserve family life" (Ibid., paragraph 62). In addition, the interpretation was also presented as "consistent with Article 8 of the ECHR and Article 7 of the Charter, which do not draw any distinction based on the circumstances in and time at which a family is constituted" (Ibid., paragraph 63). In all, having regard to the "lack of distinction, intended by the European Union legislature", and taking account of the "necessity of not interpreting the provisions of the Directive restrictively and not depriving them of their effectiveness", Member States were found to not have a "discretion to reintroduce that distinction in their national legislation transposing the Directive". In support of these holdings, the Court also referred, "by way of analogy", to its conclusions in *Metock* (Ibid., paragraph 64). Finally, in regard of the Dutch government's argument that family reunification would in any event be authorised if the standards set by Article 8 ECHR so required, the Court was short. "Suffice it to note", it held, that Mrs. Chakroun "had still not been authorised to join her husband to whom she had been married for 37 years" (Ibid., paragraph 65).

In all, *Chakroun* exposed the true implications of the fundamental rights' dicta formulated in *EPvCouncil*. As was clear now, the Council's original victory had been short-lived (if it had existed at all) and where Member States had perhaps won the battle in the earlier judgment, *Chakroun* seemed to indicate that they were losing the war. By filling in the open-textured phrases that Member States had carefully crafted during the negotiations with tightly-knit judicial rules, the Court effectively neutralised the space for manoeuvre that had been envisaged during the Council discussions. The outcome was especially painful for the Netherlands which had been amongst the most ardent campaigners for a flexible 'sufficient resources' condition in those discussions and which now found itself penalised for exercising exactly the flexibility that it had counted on having created (see on this Dutch twist of fate, Bonjour & Vink, 2013). The Netherlands' reactions to the *Chakroun* ruling were, accordingly, fierce.

At national level, to begin with, the Dutch Minister for Justice proposed changing the Dutch social security legislation in such a way as to heighten the reference amount applied for defining 'minimum incomes' and accordingly, the reference amount that—following *Chakroun*—could be used as the threshold against which to assess whether sponsors for family reunification met the 'stable and regular resources' requirement. In presenting this proposal to the Dutch Parliament, the Dutch Minister specifically linked it to the outcomes of *Chakroun* and framed it as part of the immigration policy measures that were being enacted in the aftermath of that judgment (TK 2009–2010 32175 (11)). In addition, the Dutch government also targeted the EU level in its attempts at counteracting the effects of *Chakroun*. To that purpose, a position paper was presented in March 2011, stemming, as its introduction stated, from the "concerns about the number of immigrants" arriving in the EU "without prospects", and putting "pressure on receiving societies" (Dutch position paper, p. 1). The Dutch government indicated that it believed the time had come for "a new balance to be struck between a strict asylum and immigration policy and one that is just". To that aim, a series of amendments to the existing EU legal framework were proposed with the further indication that the Dutch were "keen to enter into discussion with other EU member states and European institutions" on the basis of these proposals. Whilst the position paper also addressed such other EU immigration instruments as the Dublin Regulation and the Qualification Directive, the amendments proposed in respect of family reunification provisions were by far the most extensive and far-reaching. First, in respect of the Family Reunification Directive, the Dutch government argued for an increase of the age requirement for partners to 24 years. It also proposed to tighten the income requirement and requested that Member States could ask for the "deposit of a bond" to guarantee that any costs incurred by the government in relation to the alien or the sponsor could be recovered (Ibid., p. 5). Furthermore, the Dutch government also suggested to introduce such measures as, amongst others: a maximum of one partner per sponsor every ten years, an assessment to prove that ties with the proposed host country are stronger than those with the country of origin, a possibility to revoke temporary residence permits if holders do not fulfil civic integration conditions, and more. In addition, the paper also targeted family reunion provisions in EU free movement law, that is, in the Citizenship Directive (2004/38). In that respect, the Dutch government first "observed" that there was "a risk of family reunification migrants from third countries sidestepping national immigration regulations by invoking the right to the free movement of persons". The "generous protection afforded to EU citizens and their family members" sometimes stood in the way of "effectively maintaining public order" (Ibid., p. 7). In order to counter this "misuse of the 'Europa route'", several measures were suggested in order to re-limit the scope of EU free movement law to the situations for which "it was actually intended". Specifically targeting the *Metock* ruling, the "first admission of third-country nationals" was presented as "unrelated" to free movement and, accordingly, one of the proposals advanced aimed at excluding the regulation of such first entries from the scope of the Citizenship Directive. As was further detailed, the Netherlands also believed that "it should be possible to hold illegal residence prior to the application for a review under EU law against people" (Ibid., pp. 5–7). This Dutch position paper was to constitute the background to a series of discussions that were held at EU level on the possibility of re-opening the Family Reunification Directive in the spring of 2012. After having published a green paper on this possibility, and organising a consultation round, the Commission eventually indicated that it would not proceed with such a re-opening however (COM (2011) 735; COM (2014) 210).

7.5 The 2010s: A New Paradigm and Its Fine-Tuning

This sensitive environment post *Metock* and *Chakroun* was to mark the climate in which the Court rendered a next, and third decision in what was becoming a series of politically controversial rulings. With the *Zambrano* ruling of March 2011 the Court extended the implications of its preceding *Baumbast* and *Zhu & Chen* holdings to new and yet uncharted territories. As is the subject of this subsection, *Zambrano* and its successors were to provide the groundworks for a further, more recent series of jurisprudential developments to unfold. As highlighted in the above numerical observations, this more recent phase in the case law's development is also characterized by an increased 'density', or intensity of self-citation activity suggesting a strong and increased importance of precedent-based developments from *Zambrano* onwards.

7.5.1 **Zambrano, McCarthy *and* Dereci**

Zambrano concerned the situation of the Zambrano family, consisting of Mr. Ruiz Zambrano and his wife, both Colombian nationals, and their three minor children. The Zambranos had been resident in Belgium for several years in spite of the rejection of their asylum application and the fact that Mr. Zambrano did not have a work permit. The oldest child of the family had been born in Colombia and was a Colombian national. The two youngest children however had been born in Belgium and had, on the basis of then applicable Belgian nationality rules which provided for *ius soli* stipulations in exceptional circumstances, acquired Belgian citizenship. Legal disputes on the family's situation arose when Mr. Zambrano was denied unemployment benefits after having lost the job he had taken up in spite of not holding a work permit. The case eventually appeared before the Luxembourg bench as the questions on Mr. Zambrano's right to such unemployment benefits turned, amongst others, on the question of whether Mr. Zambrano could enjoy a right of residence in Belgium. In that latter respect, Mr. Zambrano had argued that he was to be granted such a right on the basis of the EU rights that his children enjoyed as minor Belgian, and hence, EU citizens. More specifically, in his pleadings, he had invoked the family reunion provisions enshrined in the Citizenship Directive, as well as EU primary law with reference to the CJEU's *Zhu & Chen* decision. In addition, Mr. Zambrano also alleged that the refusal to grant him a right to reside in Belgium would breach fundamental rights standards, more precisely, the right to family life as enshrined in Article 8 ECHR in combination with the prohibition to expel persons from the territory of the State of which they are nationals as provided for by Article 3(1) of the fourth Protocol to the ECHR (*Zambrano*, paragraph 31).

Against that background, the Brussels' Employment Tribunal, before which the case had arisen, referred three questions on the situation of the Zambrano family to the EU judiciary. To begin with, the referring tribunal wanted to know to what extent the Belgian Zambrano children could derive a right of residence in Belgium directly on the basis of primary law "irrespective" of whether they had previously exercised free movement rights. Taking direct cues from the CJEU's *Zhu & Chen* decision, as Mr. Zambrano had done, the tribunal also asked, in follow up, whether if the children could derive residence rights in Belgium on the basis of Treaty law (irrespective of the fact that there had not been a prior exercise of free movement rights), the need to safeguard the "useful effect" of these Treaty-based rights then demanded that the children's ascending relative upon whom they depended was granted an ancillary right of residence as well. Third, the referring court asked, with further reference to *Zhu & Chen*, whether the ascendant relative concerned had to be granted an "exemption from the requirement to hold a work permit", if "were it not for the requirement to hold a work permit under the national law of the Member State in which he resides", that ascendant relative would fulfil "the condition of sufficient resources and the possession of sickness insurance" (Ibid., paragraph 35).

Eight Member States intervened before the Court. Besides the Belgian government against which the claims were directed, written observations were also submitted by Denmark, Germany, Ireland, Greece, Austria, Poland and the Netherlands. As emerges from the case's 'Report for the hearing', these intervening Member States all argued for negative answers to the three questions raised (Report for the hearing *Zambrano*). Most of them also supported their arguments in that respect with references to the absence of any 'cross-border' element in the *Zambrano* case file which, as they contended, called for the application of the internal rule. Or, as the situation did not have a single factor linking it with any of the situations governed by Community law it was to be considered 'wholly internal' to Belgium and hence to be governed by Belgian law only. In addition, Poland and Belgium added that, because the situation was to be regarded as 'purely internal', the Court had to decline competence to pronounce itself on the matters put forward.

Furthermore, as additionally emerges from the written observation submitted by Belgium, the Belgian state also invested much efforts to distinguish the case file of *Zambrano* from the facts which had given rise to scope-extending conclusions in such cases as *Zhu & Chen*, *Baumbast*, *Carpenter* and *Singh*. Amongst others, the Belgian state pointed out that, unlike the situation of the *Zambrano* children, both the *Zhu & Chen* and *Baumbast* rulings had dealt "clearly and exclusively" with the situations of Union citizens residing in a Member State other than that of which they possessed the nationality (Written Observation of the Belgian Government, paragraph 20). In addition, the Belgian government also drew attention to the Court's repeated confirmation, from *Morson & Jhanjan* onwards, that EU law provisions could not be applied to situations which have no factor linking them with any of the situations governed by Community law (Ibid., paragraphs 21–23). Only in "exceptional cases" could the Court be found to depart from this core judicial principle, and this, only when such was needed for the purpose of eliminating obstacles to citizens' free movement rights. As examples of such exceptional cases, the Belgian government referred to *Singh* and *Carpenter* where the applicants' freedom to, respectively, move as a worker or provide services had been found to be at risk. In the *Zambrano* case on the other hand, no such risk was present. To begin with, Mr. Zambrano's children had never made use of the right to move to another Member State and, in any event, should they do so, given their young age, this could not be construed as a movement for the purposes of paid work or providing services as had been the case in *Singh* and *Carpenter* (Ibid., paragraph 24). As a final line of reasoning to distinguish *Zambrano* from earlier judicial outcomes, the Belgian state drew attention to the Court's holdings in *Zhu & Chen* according to which the rights to be derived directly on the basis of Treaty law remained, in any event, subject to the limitations and conditions imposed by the Treaty and by the measures adopted to give effect to those Treaty provisions. More specifically, in *Zhu & Chen*, the Court had established that the residence rights granted to baby Catherine on the basis of Treaty law were subject to Catherine's possession of sufficient resources. As was also clear from that latter ruling, in cases involving minor EU citizens, the sufficient resources condition could be met by resources adduced by a third party, such as the minor's parents (Ibid., paragraph 32). In such contexts, the parents could then, in turn, derive ancillary rights to reside with the minor EU citizen so as to ensure the useful effectiveness of the latter's EU rights (Ibid., paragraph 33). As was clear from these Court holdings however, the sufficient resources, possibly adduced by the minor's parents, had to exist prior to the grant of ancillary residence rights to such parents. It went without saying, the Belgian government continued, that EU law could not be construed in such a way as to demand of Member States that they granted a right of residence and a right to work to parents of minor Union citizens, in order for such parents to be able to acquire the resources necessary to satisfy the sufficient resources requirement which itself conditioned the grant of residence rights for the minor citizen and, rounding the circle, the ancillary rights of residence that those parents could lay claim to (Ibid., paragraph 34). As Mr. Zambrano, unlike the mother of baby Catherine in *Zhu & Chen*, did not possess sufficient resources independent of his right to reside in Belgium, the situation of his children and that of himself was not such as to fall within the scope of the premises articulated by the Court in that latter judgment (Ibid., paragraph 33).

The Court's engagement with the sensitive and complex questions raised by *Zambrano* was, as noted by many commentators, unusually short (Hailbronner & Thym, 2011; Lansbergen & Miller, 2011; Shuibhne, 2011; Dawson, 2014). It comprised no more than seven operative paragraphs. At least one explanation for this unusual conciseness relates to the complexity of the case which is likely to have triggered much discussion amongst the Court's judges and, accordingly, to have raised difficulties in coming to an agreement (Dawson, 2014, pp. 432–433; Hailbronner & Thym, 2011, p. 1259).[6]

The Court started by pointing out that, as had also been argued by Member States, the situation of the Zambrano children did not fall within the scope of secondary free movement legislation, notably the Citizenship Directive, as this secondary legislation only related to Union citizens' movement and/or residence in a Member State "other than that of which they are a national" (Ibid., paragraph 39). However, as it continued, by virtue of Article 20 TFEU, the Zambrano children "undeniably" enjoyed the status of EU citizens on account of their Belgian nationality (Ibid., paragraph 40). From there, the Court noted that, as it "had stated several times", "citizenship of the Union is intended to be the fundamental status

[6] As can also be noted in this regard, the *Zambrano* case was decided in Grand Chamber formation, comprising 15 judges, which is likely to have further hindered consensus building (Dawson, 2014).

of nationals of the Member States". To that effect, it invoked, amongst others, *Baumbast* and *Zhu & Chen* (Ibid., paragraph 41). This led on to the *Zambrano* ruling's most central premise. As the Court came to hold: "Article 20 TFEU precludes national measures which have the effect of depriving citizens of the Union of the genuine enjoyment of the substance of the rights conferred by virtue of their status as citizens of the Union" (Ibid., paragraph 42). A 'deprivation' of the 'genuine enjoyment' of such rights would be at stake if a third-country national with dependent minor children would be refused a right of residence and a work permit in the Member State where those children are nationals and reside (Ibid., paragraph 43). This, as the Court continued, because it could be "assumed that such a refusal would lead to a situation where those children, citizens of the Union, would have to leave the territory of the Union in order to accompany their parents". Similarly, if a work permit were not granted, such a person "would risk not having sufficient resources to provide for himself and his family, which would also result in the children, citizens of the Union, having to leave the territory of the Union" (Ibid., paragraph 44). On that basis, the Court concluded that Article 20 TFEU precluded a Member State from refusing residence and employment rights to a third-country national upon whom his minor, EU national children are dependent, "in so far as such decisions deprive those children of the genuine enjoyment of the substance of the rights attaching to the status of European Union citizen" (Ibid., paragraph 45).

As is not surprising, this conclusion "set off alarms in several European capitals" (Legomsky, 2011, pp. 830–831). Political discussions at national level stirred by *Zambrano* could be identified, for instance, in Denmark, Ireland and the Netherlands (Ibid.; Fernhout & Wever, 2011; Schmidt, 2014). As emerges from an interview with a responsible Commission official some months after the rendering of *Zambrano*, the judgment also triggered a lot of "thinking and caution" amongst Member States interacting at EU level (De Somer, 2012, p. 15). Nonetheless, and these first reactions aside, the potential for larger conflict embedded in *Zambrano* would not materialize for the time being. Although the short reasoning adduced by the Court was full of revolutionary, programmatic rhetoric that certainly gave rise to political unease, the actual implications of this rhetoric beyond the factual situation at hand in *Zambrano* remained, also on account of the short reasoning, unclear. Adding thereto, and especially for Member States with strict nationality acquisition rules, factual situations such as those at issue in *Zambrano* were unlikely to surface often. As an interview with an official at the Belgian Foreigners Office some months after *Zambrano* for instance revealed, even though the Belgian government had lost the case, concerns about the larger impact of *Zambrano* remained limited for the time being. This, because the ruling's premises were interpreted as relating exclusively to *Zambrano*-like dependent minors. As Belgium had in the meantime tightened the *ius soli* rules on the basis of which the *Zambrano* children had been able to acquire Belgian citizenship, "not a lot of new *Zambrano* situations were expected to occur" (Ibid.). Similar interpretations of *Zambrano* also marked discussions in the Netherlands. For instance, in addressing the Dutch Parliament on *Zambrano* and its implications, the Dutch Minister for Immigration stated that, because the Court's reasoning was very concise, the ruling was probably to be seen as one that had been 'tailor-made' to solace the atypical and complex situation of the Zambrano family (TK 2010–2011 19637 Nr 1408, p. 2). As the Dutch rules on nationality acquisition were much stricter than those that had been applied in respect of the Zambrano children in Belgium, incidences of *Zambrano*-like situations in the Netherlands would be 'exceptional'. Accordingly, 'at the moment', there was no need to attach consequences to the judgment beyond those related to the specific facts of *Zambrano*. As the Minister ended his address however, he would be keeping a close watch on the follow-up case law that was to be expected and the Netherlands would also be participating in meetings with Member States' immigration law experts that had been convened at EU level precisely with the aim of investigating the effects of *Zambrano* (Ibid., pp. 2–3).

In light of these, for the time being, contained reactions, a further explanation for the unusually concise nature of the Court's reasoning in *Zambrano* relates to the strategic room for manoeuvre afforded by such minimalistic, open-ended discourses to readjust or fine-tune initial holdings depending on Member State reactions. Or, such terse, elastic discourses provided the Court with opportunities to launch 'trial balloons' by means of which it could get a first feel of political responses or levels of resistance. On that basis, it could then, over next lines of case law, adjust the demands of its earlier holdings, either expanding or restricting them. As also pointed out by Hailbronner and Thym (2011, p. 1257), "(p)robable is that the open formulations of the *Ruiz Zambrano* judgment deliberately leave room for later refinement, which will also allow the Court to take on board political and academic criticism". Similarly, Lenaerts, who sat as a judge on the *Zambrano* case, explained the conciseness of the

Court's reasoning as stemming from the need of being sure "in cases such as *Ruiz Zambrano*, where the ECJ is drawing the external contours of the Treaty provisions on EU citizenship", "of the steps taken, of the direction in which it goes and the consequences of its decisions". In politically sensitive contexts such as those of *Zambrano*, "judicial prudence counsels in favour of limiting the argumentative discourse". It was "left to future cases to decide whether the ECJ would opt for a strict or broad interpretation" (Lenaerts, 2015, p. 3).

Certainly many questions required addressing after *Zambrano*. To begin with, it can be pointed out that the *Zambrano* ruling, by extending the premises of *Zhu & Chen*, or even *Baumbast* or *Carpenter*, but doing so with only minimal justifications, perpetuated a number of uncertainties that had been in the balance since these earlier judgments. For instance, whereas *Zambrano* indicated, as had remained unaddressed in *Zhu & Chen* or *Baumbast*, that family members granted a derivative right to reside on the basis of primary EU citizenship provisions could, in addition, also lay claim to employment rights, the judgment remained silent on whether any further social or economic rights (beyond such employment rights) could be attached to the first set of residence rights. *Zambrano*, like preceding rulings, also did not specify whether any temporal limits could be attached to the rights to reside (and work) deriving from Treaty provisions. Could such rights accrue to primary carer, family members for an indefinite period of time, or were such rights to be granted only until the minor EU citizens reached majority age or ceased to be dependent on the primary carer (Hailbronner & Thym, 2011)? In addition, could the rights provided accrue to more than one primary carer (Cambien, 2012)? Or, what if a minor EU citizen depended on two parents of which one enjoyed a right to reside but the other did not (Van Elsuwege & Kochenov, 2011)? In addition, what limits, if any, could be placed on the rights granted to the family members directly on the basis of EU citizens' Treaty rights? Could public policy, security or health considerations justify the refusal or revocation of such rights, as is the case for rights granted on the basis of secondary legislation? For instance, how would the *Zambrano* principles apply to the situation of primary carer-parents charged with criminal offences (Hailbronner & Thym, 2011)?

Beyond perpetuating previous questions, *Zambrano* also raised uncertainties in and of itself. Most importantly, and as came readily to the fore, the Court had not specified the precise reach or contents of the new "substance of the rights" doctrine on which the *Zambrano* outcome had turned most centrally. Accordingly, it remained unclear to what extent this new judicial principle could be used to bring other, formerly 'purely internal situations' within the aegis of EU law. *Zambrano* only established that a situation where EU citizen children "would have to leave the territory of the Union" fell within the scope of the "substance of the rights" protected "by virtue of their status as citizens of the Union". What other situations, however, could be brought under this new "substance of the rights" umbrella? Essentially, as formulated by Hailbronner and Thym (2011, p. 1253) by "projecting" EU citizenship rights onto "purely internal situations", the Court had crossed a "crucial conceptual threshold" and opened the door for a potentially infinite series of EU law extensions. However, and in line with the above observations, by refraining from defining this new category of EU citizenship rights, the Court had merely positioned itself for a "great leap forward" to then "stop half-way" (Ibid., p. 1270).

For instance, questions could be raised on the interaction between the new judicial doctrine and other Treaty rights such as those provided for in Article 21 TFEU (on EU citizens' right to freedom of movement and residence), the non-discrimination principle embedded in Article 18 TFEU or the fundamental rights standards inscribed in Article 6 TEU (Ibid.; Lansbergen & Miller, 2011; Van Elsuwege & Kochenov, 2011). If such Treaty rights would come to be included within the "substance of the rights" of which the deprivation could trigger EU law protection (independent of whether the situation presents a cross-border element), arguably, the new "substance of the rights" doctrine could be used to extend EU law to an large number of situations that would otherwise be considered 'purely internal' to a Member State. Especially the Court's silence on the interaction of this new paradigm with fundamental rights standards raised many questions in light of the fact that the *Zambrano* case file had embedded clear fundamental rights implications. Both Mr. Zambrano, as well as the referring tribunal had also grounded their submissions in fundamental rights premises. In so doing, these interlocutors had taken cues from the Court's earlier fundamental rights discourses, and the repeated reinforcement thereof over the course of preceding case law.

In light of the many questions raised by *Zambrano* and the possibly revolutionary outcomes that could transpire depending on the answers to these questions, an extensive number of follow-up claims and preliminary references arose before Luxembourg in the period that followed. As will be documented below, the increased self-citation activity registered in the numerical model for the case law since *Zambrano* can essentially be related to the numerous claims and questions prompted by the new 'substance of the rights' doctrine introduced in the latter judgment. Litigants were quick and numerous to pick up on the judgment with a view to extending the new rights doctrine to their own situations. On that basis, and in light of the uncertainties raised, domestic courts also referred a large volume of follow-up questions to the EU judiciary which then provided the latter with opportunities to further set out the precise implications of *Zambrano*. A self-reinforcing process of 'repeat games' was again set in motion as, due to the vast scope-extending potential of *Zambrano*, the answers provided through such follow-up judgments rarely addressed all potential implications that could be derived from the first ruling, or were themselves to raise new and further sets of questions.

The first case to provide further indications on the implications of *Zambrano*, however, had already been pending before Luxembourg when the latter judgment was rendered. As stated by Legomsky (2011, p. 831), the "ink on *Zambrano* was barely dry", when eight weeks later, the Court pronounced itself on the applicability of the 'substance of the rights' doctrine in the *McCarthy* case. The ***McCarthy*** proceedings had been brought before the EU judiciary in November 2009, two years prior to the *Zambrano* ruling, on the basis of claims that, also in light of this timing, were unrelated to *Zambrano*. Instead *McCarthy* concerned the rights claims of Mrs. McCarthy, a national with double UK-Irish citizenship, who sought to rely on the family reunion provisions enshrined in the Citizenship Directive to claim residence rights in the UK for her Jamaican husband, Mr. McCarthy. Mrs. McCarthy had always resided in the UK where she had never been a worker, self-employed or self-sufficient person. Instead, she relied on the receipt of state benefits. As Mrs. McCarthy had claimed, and as was subsequently referred in a question by the UK Supreme Court to Luxembourg, the situation demanded clarification on whether, on account of her double nationality, Mrs. McCarthy could lay claim to rights in secondary free movement law in that, besides being a UK citizen, she was also an Irish citizen residing in the UK. Or, whether she could, on that basis, be regarded as a Union citizen residing "in a Member State other than that of which they are a national" as per Article 3 of the Citizenship Directive (*McCarthy*, paragraph 21).

The Court started out its reasoning on these questions by articulating a series of first, "preliminary observations". Amongst these, it pointed out, with reference to *Metock*, that the Citizenship Directive "aims to facilitate the exercise of the primary and individual right to move and reside freely within the territory of the Member States that is conferred directly on Union citizens by the Treaty" (Ibid., paragraph 28). Next, the Court restated that a Member State is precluded, "as a principle of international law", from refusing its own nationals "the right to enter its territory and remain there". On that basis, a Member State was also precluded from "expelling its own nationals from its territory or refusing their right to reside in that territory or making such right conditional". To that effect, the Court invoked both *Singh* and *Eind* where similar considerations had been adduced, albeit as side issues (Ibid., paragraph 29).

With these "preliminary observations" established, the Court then moved on to consider Mrs. McCarthy's qualification to rely on the provisions of the Citizenship Directive. In that respect, it posited, first, that "while it is true" that, as it had held above with reference to *Metock*, the Directive "aims to facilitate and strengthen the exercise of the primary and individual right to move and reside freely within the territory of the Member States", the fact remained that "the subject of the directive concerns, as is apparent from Article 1(a), the conditions governing the exercise of that right" (Ibid., paragraph 33). Accordingly, and referring to the other set of preliminary observations made, the Directive's provisions could not be applied to the situation of a person residing in the Member State of which he is a national as, under a principle of international law, that person's right of residence in that Member State "cannot be made subject to conditions" (Ibid., paragraph 34). Next, the Court proceeded with a series of literal interpretations of the Citizenship Directive's provisions which, when taken together, provided support for the finding that the "residence" to which the Directive's provisions referred, was "linked to the exercise of the freedom of movement for persons" (Ibid., paragraph 35). Accordingly, "in circumstances such as those of the main proceedings, in so far as the Union citizen concerned has never exercised his right of free movement and has always resided in a Member State of which he is a national" the Directive's provisions could not be found to apply (Ibid., paragraph 39). As was added, rather succinctly, that "finding cannot be influenced by the fact that the citizen concerned is also a national of a Member State other than that where he resides" (Ibid., paragraph 40). Indeed, as the Court continued, "the fact that a Union citizen is a national of more than one Member State does not mean that he has made use of the right of freedom of movement" (Ibid., paragraph 41). As a last consideration in this respect, the Court held that because Mrs. McCarthy's situation was not covered by the Citizenship Directive, the situation of her spouse could not be covered by its provisions either. To that purpose, it revisited the 'derived rights rule' that had been construed in its early, 1990s free movement case law (*cf.* the first sub-section). As the Court re-stated, with reference to, amongst others, its 1992 *Taghavi* decision, the rights conferred on family members "are not autonomous rights of those family members, but derived rights, acquired through their status as members of the beneficiary's family" (Ibid., paragraph 42).

Next, in a second part of the judgment, the Court examined Mrs. McCarthy's situation in light of primary law and, notably, in light of the newly established "substance of the rights" doctrine. In that respect it first rehearsed, as also posited in *Zambrano*, that "citizenship of the Union is intended to be the fundamental status of nationals of the Member States" and that, in that light, "Article 20 precludes national measures which have the effect of depriving Union citizens of the genuine enjoyment of the substance of the rights conferred by virtue of that status" (Ibid., paragraph 47). However, as the Court then continued, "no element of the situation of Mrs McCarthy" indicated that the national measure at issue had the "effect of depriving her of the genuine enjoyment of the rights associated with her status as a Union citizen, or of impeding the exercise of her right to move and reside freely within the territory of the Member States, in accordance with Article 21 TFEU" (Ibid., paragraph 48). On that basis, and "by contrast with the case of *Ruiz Zambrano*", the national measure was found not to "have the effect of obliging Mrs McCarthy to leave the territory of the European Union". Indeed, and rehearsing the above 'preliminary observation' once more, "Mrs McCarthy enjoys, under a principle of international law, an unconditional right of residence in the United Kingdom since she is a national of the United Kingdom" (Ibid., paragraph 50). By way of conclusion, the Court revisited its 'internal rule' premises. On that basis, it also signalled the continued judicial relevance of this 'internal rule' post *Zambrano*. As followed from all of the above, the Court held, "the situation of a person such as Mrs McCarthy has no factor linking it with any of the situations governed by European Union law" and is hence "confined in all relevant respects within a single Member State" (Ibid., paragraph 55).

Whereas according to some commentators *McCarthy* provided "welcome clarity" on the limits of the "substance of the rights" doctrine (Hailbronner & Thym, 2011, p. 1270), others have pointed at the numerous questions that remained unanswered or that were newly created.

Amongst others, *McCarthy* has been faulted for insufficiently and unclearly distinguishing the facts of the situation of Mrs. McCarthy from those of the Zambrano family. For instance, whereas in *McCarthy* the 'principle of international law' according to which Member States cannot expel their own citizens took centre stage in the Court's reasoning, the situation of the Zambrano family was never examined in light of that principle which raised questions on whether, on the basis of such an examination, the conclusions in *Zambrano* would have been different (Van Elsuwege & Kochenov, 2011). The other way around, and as pointed out in many commentaries, whereas in *Zambrano* the deportation of the parent of the minor Union citizens was a key element in reaching the conclusion that the "substance of the rights" of these citizens was in the balance (as such a deportation would force the citizens to leave the Union territory), the presence of a similar element in the McCarthy case was not picked up on. That is, the Court did not engage with the questions that could be raised on whether the pending deportation of Mrs. McCarthy's spouse could be seen as obliging her to leave the Union territory as well (Ibid.; Legomsky, 2011; Lansbergen & Miller, 2011).

In addition, beyond the problems that could be raised in respect of *McCarthy's* dissimilar application of the 'substance of the rights' doctrine, the first part of the ruling also gave rise to a host of uncertainties. For instance, the finding that Mrs. McCarthy could not rely on her Irish nationality in the UK for the purposes of free movement law, on account of the fact that she also possessed UK citizenship, was difficult to wed with the Court's earlier findings in *Zhu & Chen*. As can be recalled, in that earlier ruling, the Court had established that an Irish national (baby Catherine) resident in the UK who, like Mrs. McCarthy, had never crossed any Member State borders could nonetheless derive rights from EU Treaty provisions for her and her family members. In that light, it could be questioned whether Mrs. McCarthy would have been able to claim similar EU law protection, and hence, have been better off if, paradoxically, she would have denounced her British nationality (Guild, Peers, & Tomkin, 2014, pp. 49–53; Legomsky, 2011; see for a different perspective on the relation between the two rulings, Lenaerts, 2011).

In any event, and in spite of these questions, on a first reading the *McCarthy* ruling seemed to provide support for the interpretation, favoured and awaited by Member State officials, that *Zambrano* had been 'tailor-made', and hence was to be seen as confined to the atypical circumstances that had given rise to that judgment. In that respect, the Court's efforts at distinguishing *McCarthy* from *Zambrano*, even if not satisfactory from the perspective of legal commentators, was successful in defusing the heightened 'state of alert' that *Zambrano* had provoked amongst Member States. As for instance emerged from the interview with the official at the Belgian Foreigners Office, although there had not been "too much concern" after *Zambrano*, there was nevertheless a sense of "relief" when the limited interpretation of that latter ruling was confirmed by *McCarthy* (De Somer, 2012, p. 15).

As was foreseeable in light of the many uncertainties raised by *Zambrano* and left unresolved (or further extended) by *McCarthy*, it would not take long for new questions on the application of the 'substance of the rights' doctrine to arrive before Luxembourg. Two weeks after the rendering of *McCarthy*, and hence, only two months and a half after *Zambrano*, the CJEU was presented with the case of ***Dereci*** which was referred by an Austrian High Court. The proceedings concerned the joined files of five third-country nationals who all had family ties to one or more Austrian nationals but who all, on the basis of Austrian immigration law, had been denied residence rights. The Austrian family members of these third-country nationals were all resident in Austria and had never made use of EU free movement rights. Aside from this first set of commonalities however, the situations of the third-country nationals differed in that some of them had unlawfully entered the Austrian territory whilst others had been legally resident prior to their (continued) residence rights being denied. In addition, the nature of the ties with their respective Austrian family members also varied. For instance, in the first case, Mr. Dereci (whose name was lent to the case), a Turkish national, was married to an Austrian national with whom he had three children, all of which were still minors and all of which held Austrian citizenship. Another third-country national, Mrs. Heiml, had married an Austrian national and had subsequently entered Austria lawfully. Her residence permit had now expired however. Mr. Maduike, a Nigerian national, had entered Austria unlawfully and had, after entry, married an Austrian national. In addition, the proceedings also included the case files of two adult third-country nationals (aged 29 and 52 years respectively) who were financially dependent on their Austrian mother and father respectively.

Prior to *Zambrano*, the cases would not have raised any questions on the application of EU law, or at least not straightforwardly, as the Austrian national family members had never moved to or resided in a state other than Austria and were, hence, 'static EU nationals' whose situations and rights claims were 'wholly internal' to Austria. In light of the unclear scope of application of *Zambrano*, however, the Austrian Court had considered that "questions arose" as to "whether the indications given by the Court in its judgment of 8 March 2011 in Ruiz Zambrano (…) may be applied to one or more of the disputes in the main proceedings" (*Dereci*, paragraph 30). More precisely, it asked, first in relation to the specific situation of Mr. Dereci whether Article 20 TFEU precluded a Member State from refusing a right of residence to a third-country national whose spouse and children were resident in that Member State and held the nationality of that Member State. In addition, a similar question was put forward with reference to a spouse only for the case of Mrs. Heiml and Mr. Maduike. Furthermore, the situations of the two adult third-country nationals, dependent on Union citizen parents, were also questioned in light of the rights deriving from Article 20 TFEU. In follow up, and in case of an affirmative response to one or more of these first questions, the Austrian court also wanted to know "(u)nder what conditions, exceptionally, does the right of residence which follows from EU law not exist" or, phrased differently, "under what conditions" could such a right of residence be "denied" (Ibid., paragraph 35).

Eight Member States submitted written observations. Generally speaking, as summarised in the text of the judgment, these eight governments all argued that the situations presented did not preclude a Member State from refusing a residence right to the third-country nationals concerned. More specifically, they contended, in line with the above observations, that "the principles laid down in Ruiz Zambrano" applied only "to very exceptional situations in which the application of a national measure would lead to the denial of the genuine enjoyment of the substance of the rights conferred by virtue of the status of citizen of the Union". In this case however, "the events which gave rise to the proceedings" differed "substantially from those which gave rise to the aforementioned judgment in so far as the Union citizens concerned were not at risk of having to leave the territory of the Union" (Ibid., paragraph 40; Report for the hearing *Dereci*, paragraphs 46–53).

The Court started out its considerations on the case by examining, first, whether the situations of the applicants were such as to fall within the scope of secondary EU law. More in particular, whether their situations could be treated either by the provisions of the Family Reunification Directive or by those of the Citizenship Directive. As could be expected, in that it had not been claimed by the applicants, nor questioned by the referring court, neither of the instruments were found to apply to the case files. Nevertheless, the Court invested much discursive efforts, especially in respect of the Citizenship Directive, to highlight the instruments' non-applicability. For instance, the Court invoked its immediately preceding *McCarthy* decision to emphasize that a "Union citizen, who has never exercised his right of free movement and has always resided in a Member State of which he is a national, is not covered by (…) Directive 2004/38" (Ibid., paragraph 54). In this light, the Court also re-invoked, as it had done in *McCarthy*, the 'derived rights rule' that stemmed from its early 1990s case law. With explicit reference to *McCarthy* it rehearsed that "in so far as a Union citizen is not covered by (…) Directive 2004/38, their family member is not covered by that concept either, given that the rights conferred by that directive on the family members of a beneficiary of that directive are not autonomous rights of those family members, but derived rights" (Ibid., paragraph 55). Adding thereto, the Court stated, with reference to *Metock*, that "(i)ndeed, not all third country nationals derive rights of entry into and residence in a Member State from Directive 2004/38, but only those who are family members (…) of a Union citizen who has exercised his right of freedom of movement" (Ibid., paragraph 56).

With these premises rehearsed, the Court then moved on to consider the applicability of Treaty provisions on EU citizenship, and more specifically, the applicability of the 'substance of the rights' doctrine established in *Zambrano*. To begin with, as it re-stated with reference to *Zambrano*, "citizenship of the Union is intended to be the fundamental status of nationals of the Member States" (Ibid., paragraph 62). Furthermore, and again with reference to *Zambrano*, the Court held that "Article 20 TFEU precludes national measures which have the effect of depriving Union citizens of the genuine enjoyment of the substance of the rights conferred by virtue of that status" (Ibid., paragraph 64). In order to analyse whether this would be the case in the settings at hand, the Court re-entered into the facts that had given rise to the judgment in *Zambrano*. As it stated, in *Zambrano*, the Court had "considered in particular" that the refusal of residence rights to a third-country national with dependent minor Union citizens "would lead to a situation where those children, who are citizens of the Union, would have to leave the territory of the Union in order to accompany their parents". In those circumstances, these children would have been "unable to exercise the substance of the rights conferred on them by virtue of their status as citizens of the Union" (Ibid., paragraph 65). From there, and without adding any further considerations, the Court held that it followed that "the criterion relating to the denial of the genuine enjoyment of the substance of the rights (…) refers to situations in which the Union citizen has, in fact, to leave not only the territory of the Member State of which he is a national but also the territory of the Union as a whole" (Ibid., paragraph 66). Adding thereto, and in line with the argumentation advanced in Member States' written observations, the Court posited that that criterion is "specific in character" (Ibid., paragraph 67). In addition, it spelled out that "the mere fact that it might appear desirable to a national of a Member State, for economic reasons or in order to keep his family together in the territory of the Union, for the members of his family (…) to be able to reside with him in the territory of the Union, is not sufficient in itself to support the view that the Union citizen will be forced to leave Union territory if such a right is not granted" (Ibid., paragraph 68). These premises led to the Court's final conclusions on the case. Before arriving there however, the Court additionally considered whether "on the basis of other criteria, inter alia, by virtue of the right to the protection of family life", a right of residence could not be refused in the proceedings at hand. This question had to be "tackled" however "in the framework of the provisions on the protection of fundamental rights which are applicable in each case" (Ibid., paragraph 69).

In what followed, the Court considered the scope of application of fundamental rights in the framework of EU law. It first reiterated that the Charter of Fundamental Rights, in line with the horizontal provisions enshrined therein, could "be addressed to the Member States only when they are implementing European Union law". The Charter could not "extend the field of application of European Union law beyond the powers of the Union" (Ibid., paragraph 71). Accordingly, if in the present case the referring court considered that the situations of the applicants were covered by the scope of EU law, it was to examine whether a refusal of residence rights would undermine the right to respect for family life as provided for in Article 7 of the Charter. On the other hand, and following a discursive strategy similar to the one used in *Akrich*, if the referring court took the view that the situations presented were not covered by EU law, it had to "undertake that examination in light of Article 8(1) of the ECHR" (Ibid., paragraph 72). All the Member States, "after all", were parties to the ECHR (Ibid., paragraph 73).

As its final dictum on the case, the Court posited that Member States were not precluded from refusing residence rights to third-country national family members of Union citizens who never exercised their right to freedom of movement, provided that such a refusal would not lead, for the Union citizens concerned, to the 'denial of the genuine enjoyment of the substance of the rights' they enjoy as EU citizens. This latter issue, however, was a "matter for the referring court to verify" (Ibid., paragraph 74). As the follow-up questions on whether any conditions could be attached to rights granted on the basis of the 'substance of the rights' doctrine were raised only in the event of affirmative answers to the first questions, the Court considered that it was not necessary to address them (Ibid., paragraph 75).

In all, by heightening the threshold for situations to satisfy the new 'substance of rights' criterion, *Dereci* followed *McCarthy* in curtailing the revolutionary potential of *Zambrano*. In that manner, the judgment also provided further comfort to Member States in respect of the domestic competences they retained after *Zambrano*. As in *McCarthy*, and in even more explicit terms, the *Zambrano* outcome was presented as one that was "specific in character" and one that Member States could, accordingly, interpret as confined to the atypical facts that had given rise to the latter judgment.

However, and in that respect also similar to *McCarthy*, whilst *Dereci* re-indicated, in general terms and on a first reading, that the ramifications of *Zambrano* remained limited, definitive answers to the further, more specific questions opened up by *Zambrano* remained unaddressed. For instance, the precise interaction between the 'substance of rights' doctrine with EU citizens' rights to free movement and residence as inscribed in Article 21 TFEU remained ambiguous (Adam & Van Elsuwege, 2012). Furthermore, and different from *Zambrano* and *McCarthy*, whilst in *Dereci* the Court explicitly engaged with fundamental rights considerations, their exact interaction with the new 'substance of the rights' doctrine continued to be unclear. By setting out a two-tier scheme of application of fundamental rights, one for situations falling within the scope of EU law (to be judged on the basis of the Charter) and another for situations falling outside this scope (to be examined on the basis of the ECHR), the Court seemed to indicate that a breach of fundamental rights in and of itself would not suffice to trigger the application of the 'substance of the rights' doctrine and, hence, bring a situation within the scope of EU law (Ibid., Lenaerts, 2015). However, the reasoning advanced by the Court in this regard, arguably, was not "very helpful" and did not provide much guidance to national courts on how precisely to apply this new two-tier fundamental rights protection scheme (Adam & Van Elsuwege, 2012). In addition, the Court's open-textured final dictum which stated that the presence or absence of a deprivation effect to the 'genuine enjoyment of the substance of the rights' attaching to Union citizenship was 'a matter for the referring court to verify', appeared to delegate this final, sensitive responsibility to the referring court. Amongst others, in so doing, this dictum then also left the door open for that domestic court to conclude that the facts presented in *Dereci* did warrant the application of Treaty law, and hence, required a review in light of the fundamental rights standards of the Charter (Ibid.).

7.5.2 **Iida, O&S, Ymeraga *and* Alopka**

As followed, more questions on the correct interpretation of the new doctrine established in *Zambrano*, and further applied in *McCarthy* and *Dereci*, appeared before the Luxembourg bench providing the latter, anew, with opportunities to continue constructing its holdings. Such opportunities were presented more precisely, and in chronological order, in the cases of *Iida*, *O&S*, *Ymeraga* and *Alopka*. Generally, the curtailing line taken in *McCarthy*, and continued in *Dereci*, was carried on—with references to both rulings—in these four follow-up cases. *Zambrano*, on the other hand, would become referred to ever less.

To begin with, in ***Iida*** the Court received a question from a German court on the situation of a third-country national father, Mr. Iida, of a minor German citizen. The minor German citizen had moved from Germany to Austria with her German mother. Mr. Iida was permanently separated from the mother of his daughter, but the couple had not officially divorced. Mr. Iida regularly travelled to Austria to visit his daughter and *vice versa*, during school holidays his daughter travelled to Germany. The referring court had sent in an extensive series of questions (five in total, but counting sub-questions the number amounted to 12) on whether, in the settings at hand, Mr. Iida could derive residence rights in Germany on the basis of EU law. The questions centred mostly around fundamental rights standards as provided for in the Charter, in the ECHR, or as general principles of EU law. In general terms, the German court wanted to know whether a refusal to grant a residence permit to Mr. Iida would infringe such fundamental rights standards. It had raised fundamental rights-related questions both in connection to the family reunion provisions of the Citizenship Directive, as well as in relation to the rights that could be derived directly on the basis of Treaty law (Article 21 TFEU). In respect of primary law, the referring court had also taken explicit cues *Zhu & Chen* (*Iida*, paragraph 32). The new 'substance of rights' doctrine was not referred to as *Iida* was, like *McCarthy*, already pending before the CJEU before *Zambrano* was rendered. The *Dereci* case, which arrived later, had leapfrogged *Iida* on account of the application of the accelerated procedure.

The Court first reviewed, as in *McCarthy* and *Dereci*, whether Mr. Iida could derive any rights from secondary free movement law. In that context, the Court pointed out, with reference to *Metock* and *Dereci*, that "not all third-country nationals derive rights of entry into and residence in a member State from Directive 2004/38, but only those who are a 'family member' (…) of a Union citizen who has exercised his right of freedom of movement" (Ibid., paragraph 51). As the Court then asserted, both Mr. Iida's daughter as well as her mother were Union citizens who had exercised their free movement rights within the meaning of the Citizenship Directive. In considering, first, whether any derivative residence rights accrued to Mr. Iida on the basis of his daughter's free movement rights the Court invoked the reasoning it had applied in *Zhu & Chen*. In spite of the overall liberalizing outcome of *Zhu & Chen*, the case was now invoked, to, rather, rehearse the rationale that in a situation where a Union citizen is dependent on a third-country national, the third-country national cannot be considered a 'dependant ascending relative' of that Union citizen (Ibid., paragraph 55). Accordingly, Mr. Iida could not be considered a dependent ascending relative of his daughter. Next, the Court examined whether Mr. Iida could derive any residence right on the basis of his relation to his daughter's German mother. As the Court held, as long as the couple's marriage had not been formally terminated, Mr. Iida continued to enjoy the status of spouse. However, as it then advanced, the Directive required that the family member of the Union citizen exercising EU free movement rights "accompanies or joins" that citizen. In other words, a family member like Mr. Iida could only derive residence rights in the Member State that hosts the moving Union citizen; in the case at hand, Austria and not Germany. To that effect, the Court referred to *Metock* and *Eind*, citing again previously liberalizing decisions to now reach a more restrictive conclusion, (Ibid., paragraphs 63–64).

Next, the Court investigated whether Mr. Iida could derive any residence rights from Treaty provisions on Union citizenship. In that respect, it started off by re-invoking the derived rights rule—which, originally, stemmed from its 1990s case law on secondary free movement law—and applying it, this time, to the examination of primary law. More precisely, it held with reference to *McCarthy* and *Dereci*, where it had similarly revisited this rule (albeit in relation to secondary law), that "(l)ike the rights conferred by Directive 2004/38 on third-country nationals who are family members of a Union citizen (…) any rights conferred on third-country nationals by the Treaty provisions on Union citizenship are not autonomous rights of those nationals but rights derived from the exercise of freedom of movement by a Union citizen" (Ibid., paragraph 67).

The Court then referred back to the conclusions reached in *Zhu & Chen*, *Eind* and *Dereci*. A separate paragraph was spent on each of these three judgments. For instance, and notably, *Dereci* was invoked to refer to the 'substance of the rights' doctrine as first introduced by *Zambrano*. *Zambrano*, however, was not referred to and would in fact not make any appearance in the Court's reasoning on *Iida*. Instead, it was on the basis of *Dereci* that the Court re-stated that there are "very specific situations" in which, "despite the fact that the secondary law on the right of residence of third-country does not apply and the Union citizen concerned has not made use of his freedom of movement, a right of residence exceptionally cannot (…) be refused to a third-country national who is a family member of his if, as a consequence of refusal, that citizen would be obliged in practice to leave the territory of the European Union altogether, thus denying him the genuine enjoyment of the substance of the rights conferred by virtue of his status" (Ibid., paragraph 71). *Zhu & Chen* was invoked, next, in order to re-state that a child's right of residence would be deprived of 'any useful effect' if that child's primary carer were not granted a right to reside with the child in the host Member State (Ibid., paragraph 69). *Eind*, third, was cited in order to re-articulate that an EU citizen worker could be discouraged from leaving the Member State of which he is a national when there is a prospect "on returning to his Member State of origin, that he will not be able to continue living together with close relatives, a way of life which may have come into being in the host Member State" (Ibid., paragraph 70). In all, and bringing together its engagement with these three preceding decisions, the Court submitted that the "common element" between the three cases resided in the fact that, although they were "governed by legislation which falls a priori within the competence of the Member States, namely legislation on the right of entry and stay of third-country nationals", they nonetheless all had an intrinsic connection with the freedom of movement of a Union citizen which prevented "the right of entry and residence from being refused to those nationals in the Member State of residence of that citizen" (Ibid., paragraph 72).

On that basis, the Court went on to note that, conversely, the absence of a residence right under EU law for Mr. Iida had clearly not discouraged his daughter, nor his spouse from exercising their free movement rights as they had already moved to Germany. Accordingly, it could not "validly be argued" that a denial of residence rights to Mr. Iida would be "liable to deny Mr Iida's spouse or daughter the genuine enjoyment of the substance of the rights associated with their status of Union citizen or to impede the exercise of their right to move and reside freely within the territory of the Member States" (Ibid., paragraph 76). In addition, the CJEU posited that this finding could not be affected by considerations around the "purely hypothetical prospect" of exercising free movement rights. The same was held to apply "to purely hypothetical prospects of that right being obstructed" (Ibid., paragraph 77). For instance, the hypothetical prospect of the daughter and spouse being compelled to move back to Germany.

To end, the Court engaged with the fundamental rights that had been "mentioned by the referring court". It repeated, with reference to *Dereci*, that the provisions of the Charter could be addressed to the Member States "only when they are implementing EU law", and that they could not be upheld to "extend the field of application of European Union law" (Ibid., paragraph 78). However, in contrast to *Dereci* where the final call in that respect had been left to the national tribunal, the Court now unequivocally stated that Mr. Iida's situation showed "no connection with European Union law" and that hence the conformity of a refusal to grant him a residence right with fundamental rights could not be examined by reference to the Charter (Ibid., paragraphs 80–81). The other leg of the two-tier fundamental rights scheme provided in *Dereci*, that is, examination in light of the ECHR, was not referred to.

It would reappear, however, in the next set of questions on the 'substance of the rights' doctrine to arrive in Luxembourg in the joined cases of ***O&S***. The cases, referred by a Finnish court, related to the situations of two third-country national women who had both been married Finnish nationals. Both times, one child had been born of the marriage, and both times the child had acquired Finnish nationality. The two marriages had in the meantime been formally dissolved and the third-country national women had been granted sole custody of their Finnish national and, hence, Union citizen child. At later stages, both women had remarried with a third-country national. Out of these two marriages another child had been born with a third-country citizenship. In the context of these multifaceted circumstances, the referring Finnish court had asked to what extent the "principles set out by the Court in (...) *Ruiz Zambrano*" precluded the Finnish state from refusing residence rights to the third-country national husbands of the women who held custody of a minor Union citizen (*O&S*, paragraphs 32–33).

As before in *Dereci*, all the Member States which submitted written observations (besides Finland, also Denmark, Germany, Italy, the Netherlands and Poland) argued that the *Zambrano* principles did not preclude such a refusal as these principles related to "altogether exceptional situations" only (Ibid., paragraphs 37–39). More specifically, the settings in *O&S* were distinguished from the 'exceptional situation' in *Zambrano* in that the third-country national spouses were not the biological fathers of the Union citizen minors from which they sought to derive a right to reside, nor had custody over them. In addition, Member States also pointed out that, as the Union citizen children's mothers in *O&S* had a permanent right to reside in Finland, these children would, different from the circumstances in *Zambrano*, not be obliged to leave the territory of the Union.

As in the preceding cases, the Court first considered the situations in light of the Citizenship Directive. In that respect it referred back to its earlier dicta in *Metock*, as also rehearsed in *Dereci*, that "not all third country nationals who are family members of a Union citizen derive rights of entry and residence from that directive, but only those who are family members of a Union citizen who has exercised his right of freedom of movement" (Ibid., paragraph 41). Next, and in application of that principle, as the Union citizen children concerned had not made use of any free movement rights, they could not claim residence rights for their family members on the basis of secondary free movement law. However, as the Court continued, since "citizenship of the Union is intended to be the fundamental status of nationals of Member States", the Finnish children concerned "as nationals of a Member State, enjoy the status of Union citizens under Article 20(1) TFEU and may therefore rely on the rights pertaining to that status, including against the Member State of which they are nationals" (Ibid., paragraph 44). In that respect, the Court invoked *McCarthy* and *Dereci*.

On this basis, the CJEU moved on to consider the 'substance of the rights' doctrine as introduced in *Zambrano*. As it rehearsed, in that latter judgment the refusal to grant a residence right to a third-country national in the Member State where his minor Union citizen children were resident, was found to have "the consequence that those children, who are citizens of the Union, would have to leave the territory of the Union in order to accompany their parents" (Ibid., paragraph 46). With reference to both *Zambrano* and *Dereci* the Court then held that the "criterion of the denial of the genuine enjoyment of the substance of the rights conferred by the status of citizen of the Union referred (…) to situations characterised by the circumstance that the Union citizen had, in fact, to leave not only the territory of the Member State of which he was a national but also that of the European Union as a whole" (Ibid., paragraph 47).

Following a discursive strategy similar to the one eventually adopted in *Dereci*, the Court then held that "whether the refusal of the applications for residence permits submitted (…) in circumstances such as those at issue in the main proceedings entails, for the Union citizens concerned, a denial of the genuine enjoyment of the substance of the rights conferred by their status" was a matter "for the referring court to establish" (Ibid., paragraph 48). Nevertheless, and different from *Dereci*, in *O&S* the Court came to attach a number of guiding principles to this reversing of charges back to the national level.

To begin with, "when making that assessment", the national court had to take into account that the mothers of the Union citizens had been granted permanent residence permits in Finland so that, "in law, there was no obligation for them, or the dependent Union citizens, to leave that Member State or the European Union as a whole" (Ibid., paragraph 50). On the other hand, however, "the fact that the children are part of reconstituted families" was also relevant. As the Court submitted, should residence permits not be granted to the third-country national husbands, and should the mothers of the Union citizen children concerned then decide to leave the territory of the Member State "in order to preserve the family unit", the effect would be such as to deprive the Union citizen children of all contact with their biological fathers. However, in case such residence permits were not granted, and the mothers would decide instead "to stay in the territory of that Member State in order to preserve the relationship (…) of the Union citizens who are minors with their biological fathers", this "would have the effect of harming the relationship of the other children, who are third-country nationals, with their biological fathers" (Ibid., paragraph 51). That said, and invoking *Dereci*, "the mere fact that it might appear desirable, for economic reasons or in order to preserve the family unit in the territory of the Union, for members of a family consisting of third-country nationals and a Union citizen who is a minor to be able to reside with that citizen in the territory of the Union in the Member State of which he is a national is not sufficient in itself to support the view that the Union citizen would be forced to leave the territory of the Union if such a right of residence were not granted" (Ibid., paragraph 52).

Overall, in carrying out its assessment, the referring court was to "examine all the circumstances" of the case in order to determine whether a refusal of residence rights for the third-country national husbands would be "liable to undermine the effectiveness of the Union citizenship enjoyed by the Union citizens concerned" (Ibid., paragraph 53). Ending its considerations on the 'substance of the rights' doctrine, the Court re-invoked the two-tier fundamental rights scheme introduced in *Dereci.* More precisely, it repeated that, should the referring court find that in the circumstances before it, a denial of the 'genuine enjoyment of the substance of the rights attaching to Union citizenship' was not at stake, such a finding would be "without prejudice to the question whether, on the basis of other criteria, inter alia by virtue of the right to the protection of family life", such a right could not be refused. Citing the relevant section of the *Dereci* ruling it concluded that "that question must be addressed in the framework of the provisions on the protection of fundamental rights which are applicable in each case" (Ibid., paragraph 59).

The *O&S* ruling did not end on these premises. Rather, the Court was to add an entire new set of considerations by continuing its examination of the case in light of the Family Reunification Directive. This, in spite of the fact that this instrument had not been mentioned in the questions referred by the Finnish court. In what followed, the holdings of *EPvCouncil*, and their subsequent application in *Chakroun*, were further extended to cover the residence rights of the third-country national husbands in the settings at hand.

As a starting point, and referring amongst others to the Directive's preamble, the Court put forward that the "European Union legislature" had conceived of the "nuclear family" broadly in the context of setting up the instrument (Ibid., paragraphs 64–65). However, it was also clear from the Directive's provisions that the instrument did not apply to the situations of family members of a Union citizen (Ibid., paragraph 66). This had also been confirmed previously in *Dereci* which was cited to that effect (Ibid., paragraph 67). On the other hand, and in contrast to the circumstances of the *Dereci* proceedings, the female spouses in *O&S* were lawfully resident third-country nationals, as were the children of these women with their second husbands (Ibid., paragraph 68). Therefore, and in view of the Directive's "purpose" which, as the Court had held in *Chakroun*, "is to promote family reunification", as well as in light of the "protection" that the Directive aimed "to give to third country nationals, in particular minors", its application could not be excluded solely because a minor Union citizen was also part of the families concerned (Ibid., paragraph 69).

Having established in this way that the families' situations were covered by the Directive's scope, the Court continued by extracting further principles from *EPvCouncil* and *Chakroun* to guide the application of the instrument to the settings at hand. First, it rehearsed the premises of *EPvCouncil* according to which the Directive was to be seen as imposing "on the Member States precise positive obligations, with corresponding clearly defined individual rights" since "it requires them, in the cases determined by that directive, to authorise the family reunification of certain members of the sponsor's family, without being left a margin of appreciation" (Ibid., paragraph 70). On that basis, the Court went on to consider the conditional requirements set out in article 7 and, more precisely, the sufficient resources requirement that had also been the subject of the *Chakroun* case. In that respect, it repeated, with reference to the latter case, that "since authorisation of family reunification is the general rule", "the faculty provided for in Article 7(1)(c) of Directive 2003/86 must be interpreted strictly". Accordingly, "(t)he margin which the Member States are recognised as having must therefore not be used by them in a manner which would undermine the objective and the effectiveness of that directive (*Chakroun*, paragraph 43)" (Ibid., paragraph 74).

Additionally, extensive attention went out to the relation between fundamental rights as protected by the Charter and the application of the Directive. To begin with, as could be seen from the Directive's preamble, the Court stated, the instrument "respects the fundamental rights and observes the principles enshrined in the Charter" (Ibid., paragraph 75). In that respect, especially Article 7 of the Charter (right to respect for private and family life) and the Charter's provisions on children's rights were highlighted, with reference, again to the considerations that had similarly been adduced in *EPvCouncil* (Ibid., paragraph 76). On that basis, the Court held that Article 7(1)c could not "be interpreted and applied in such a manner that its application would disregard the fundamental rights set out in those provisions of the Charter" (Ibid., paragraph 77). More generally, Member States had to "make sure they do not rely on an interpretation of an instrument of secondary legislation which would be in conflict with the fundamental rights protected by the legal order of the European Union" (Ibid., paragraph 78). Finally, although it was "true that Articles 7 and 24 of the Charter, while emphasising the importance for children of family life, cannot be interpreted as depriving the Member States of their margin of appreciation when examining applications for family reunification", still "in the course of such an examination and when determining in particular whether the conditions laid down in Article 7(1) of Directive 2003/86 are satisfied, the provisions of that directive must be interpreted and applied in the light of Articles 7 and 24(2) and (3) of the Charter". Such was, "moreover", also "apparent from recital 2 in the preamble and Article 5(5) of that directive" which required of "Member States to examine the applications for reunification in question in the interests of the children concerned and with a view to promoting family life" (Ibid., paragraphs 79–80).

As its final statements in respect of the Family Reunification Directive, the CJEU held, first, and unequivocally, that the requests for residence permits concerned in the proceedings were covered by that Directive. This, in spite of the fact that the instrument had not originally been invoked in the questions presented to Luxembourg and, more significantly, in spite of the fact that the situations concerned related, at least in part, to 'family members of Union citizens' which, pursuant to the Directive's Article 3, would be excluded from the instrument's personal scope. As can be recalled from Chap. 4, the application of EU immigration law to 'static' Union citizens had been strongly rejected by Member States during the Council discussions. Second, and continuing its conclusions, the Court held that the sufficient resources requirement laid down in Article 7(1)(c) granted Member States the "faculty of requiring proof that the sponsor has stable and regular resources" but that that faculty had to be exercised in the light of Charter articles "which require the Member States to examine applications for family reunification in the interests of the children concerned and also with a view to promoting family life". With these holdings, the Court essentially reinforced the sensitive conclusions that had been reached in *Chakroun* and that, themselves, were built on the rights-based discourses adduced in *EPvCouncil* (but not applied in that latter). Ending its statements however, and replicating earlier argumentative strategies, it was ultimately for the referring court to ascertain "whether the decisions refusing residence permits at issue in the main proceedings were taken in compliance with those requirements" (Ibid., paragraph 82).

Six months after *O&S*, in May 2013, the Court was to render a further follow-up judgment to the premises articulated in *Zambrano* and further set out in *McCarthy*, *Dereci*, *Iida* and *O&S*. That is, in ***Ymeraga*** the Court was presented with the situation of a naturalized adult Luxembourg national, Mr. Ymeraga, who sought family reunification with his Kosovan parents and siblings. Mr. Ymeraga had never exercised any free movement rights. The referring Luxembourg tribunal had, following from *Zambrano* and the successor judgments, asked for clarification on the extent to which a person in his situation could derive family reunification rights directly on the basis of Article 20 TFEU. Additionally, the referring tribunal had also specifically coupled this question to Charter provisions on, inter alia, non-discrimination (Article 21), equality before the law (Article 20), the protection of family life (Article 33) and children's rights (Article 24) and wanted to know how these Charter provisions interacted with Article 20 TFEU in settings such as those at issue (*Ymeraga*, paragraph 22).

In line with preceding 'substance of the rights' cases, the CJEU first examined Mr. Ymeraga's situation in light of secondary legal instruments, that is, the Family Reunification Directive and the Citizenship Directive. Again, and as had not been questioned or claimed in the case file, the situation of Mr. Ymeraga was found to not be covered by either. In light of the Citizenship Directive, specifically, the Court referred back to *Dereci* and *McCarthy* to repeat that its provisions do not apply to a "Union citizen who has never exercised his right of freedom of movement" (Ibid., paragraph 30). In that context, it also revisited the 'derived rights' rule as re-introduced by the latter two judgments. That is, as the Court repeated, "in so far as a Union citizen is not covered" by the Directive, neither are his family members as the rights conferred by the directive on family members "are not autonomous rights (…), but derived rights" (Ibid., paragraph 31).

On that basis, the Court examined Mr. Ymeraga's situation in light of Article 20 TFEU. To that purpose, it first reinforced the transposition, as established in *Iida*, of the 'derived rights rule' to such primary Citizenship provisions. That is, similar to the above, but now with reference to Article 20 TFEU, the Court submitted that "any rights conferred on third-country nationals by the Treaty provisions on Union citizenship are not autonomous rights of those nationals but rights derived from the exercise of freedom of movement by a Union citizen" (Ibid., paragraphs 34–35).

As it continued, "in this respect, (…) there are very specific situations in which, despite the fact that the secondary law on the right of residence of third-country nationals does not apply and the Union citizen concerned has not made use of his freedom of movement, a right of residence, cannot exceptionally, without undermining the effectiveness of the Union citizenship that citizen enjoys, be refused to a third-country national who is a family member of his if, as a consequence of refusal, that citizen would be obliged in practice to leave the territory of the European Union altogether" (Ibid., paragraph 36). To this purpose, the Court referred to both *Iida* and *Dereci*. In addition, the Court also repeated, with reference to *Dereci*, that "the mere fact that it might appear desirable to a national of a Member State, for economic reasons or in order to keep his family together in the territory of the Union, for the members of his family (…) to be able to reside with him, is not sufficient to support the view that the Union citizen will be forced to leave the Union territory if such a right is not granted" (Ibid., paragraph 38). On that basis, the situation of Mr. Ymeraga was found not to be such as to "support the view that a refusal to grant a right of residence may have the effect of denying *Mr Ymeraga* the genuine enjoyment of the substance of the rights conferred by virtue of his status as citizen of the Union" (Ibid., paragraph 39).

The Court ended its reasoning with considerations on the Charter provisions that had been invoked by the referring court. As the settings at hand were not covered by either the Family Reunification Directive, nor the Citizenship Directive, and as a refusal to grant residence rights to his family members would not have the effect of denying Mr. Ymeraga the genuine enjoyment of his EU citizenship rights, Mr. Ymeraga's situation was found to not be governed by EU law. Accordingly, and with reference to *Iida* and *Dereci*, the conformity of a refusal to grant residence rights to his family members with fundamental rights could not be examined in light of the Charter (Ibid., paragraphs 40–43). Nevertheless, and re-invoking the two-tier scheme that had been adduced before, this finding did not "prejudge the question whether, on the basis of (…) the *ECHR*, to which all the Member States are parties" a right of residence to the third-country national family members could not be refused (Ibid., paragraph 44).

In October 2013 the Court rendered a further follow-up judgment to the questions opened up by *Zambrano* in ***Alopka***. The case concerned the situation of Mrs. Alopka, a Togolese national who was mother to two French national baby twins who had been born in Luxembourg out of a relation between Mrs. Alopka and a French national. Mrs. Alopka had, at the time, been unlawfully resident in Luxembourg. Following the birth of the twins, she had been granted a temporary leave to remain but this leave had expired and an extension had been denied. The French national father to the twins had recognised the two children, enabling them to acquire French nationality, but had shortly thereafter left the picture. The two babies had always remained in Luxembourg, where they continued to need maternity care on account of their premature births. Mrs. Alopka had argued that it was not possible for them to move to France on account of their continued need for medical treatment in Luxembourg and due to the fact that there were no family relations with the children's biological father.

In these settings, the Luxembourg 'Cour administrative' referred questions on the extent to which Article 20 TFEU and, "if necessary", read in conjunction with the Charter, precluded the refusal of a right to reside and work to a third-country national with sole responsibility for minor Union citizens. In addition, and taking further cues from preceding Court dicta, it wanted to know if such a decision to refuse residence rights had to be regarded "as being in the nature of decisions depriving those children, in their country of residence, in which they have lived since birth, of effective enjoyment of the substance of the rights attaching to the status of citizen of the European Union also in the situation where their other direct ascendant, with whom they have never shared family life, is resident in another Member State of the European Union" (*Alopka*, paragraph 19).

In providing an answer to these questions, the Court first rehearsed the application of the 'derived rights rule' to primary citizenship provisions as established in *Iida* and reinforced in *Ymeraga*. More precisely, with reference to that latter ruling, the Court repeated that "any rights conferred on third-country nationals by the Treaty provisions on Union citizenship are not autonomous rights of those nationals but rights derived from the exercise of freedom of movement by a Union citizen" (Ibid., paragraph 22). Next, the CJEU observed, as it had done in *Zhu & Chen*, that given the fact that Mrs. Alopka's two sons were dependent on her, Mrs. Alopka could not possibly be considered a dependent ascending relative of her sons for the purpose of falling within the scope of the family reunion provisions of the Citizenship Directive. However, and with reference to the main holdings of *Zhu & Chen*, the Court asserted that in situations in which the 'sufficient resources' condition is satisfied, the Citizenship Directive, as well as Article 21 TFEU, grant residence rights to a parent who is the primary carer of a minor child as otherwise the residence rights which the minor enjoys under these two provisions would be deprived of their useful effect (Ibid., paragraphs 28–29). In that respect, the Court also further reinforced the holdings of *Zhu & Chen* in which it had held that, when assessing whether the sufficient resources condition is met, it suffices that the resources are available to the Union citizens. In other words, that there is no requirement as to the origin of those resources (Ibid., paragraph 27). Ultimately, and as before, in the settings at hand it was "for the referring court to ascertain" whether Mrs. Alopka's children had "on their own, or through their mother" sufficient resources and comprehensive sickness insurance and whether they could, on that basis, enjoy a right of residence in the host Member State which, by implication, would also require the grant of a residence permit to Mrs. Alopka (Ibid., paragraphs 30). In case these conditions were not satisfied, neither the Citizenship Directive, nor Article 21 TFEU could be interpreted as precluding the refusal of a residence right to Mrs. Alopka (Ibid., paragraph 31).

On that basis, the Court then examined Mrs. Alopka's situation in light of the 'substance of the rights' doctrine connected to Article 20 TFEU. In that respect, the Court first rehearsed the accumulated sequences of arguments and standards that had been attached to this doctrine over the course of the preceding rulings. That is, as it had "held before": "there are very specific situations in which, despite the fact that the secondary law on the right of residence of third-country nationals does not apply and the Union citizen concerned has not made use of his freedom of movement, a right of residence cannot, exceptionally, without undermining the effectiveness of the Union citizenship that citizen enjoys, be refused to a third-country national who is a family member of his if, as a consequence of refusal, that citizen would be obliged in practice to leave the territory of the European Union altogether, thus denying him the genuine enjoyment of the substance of the rights conferred by virtue of the status of citizen of the European Union" (Ibid., paragraph 32). Again however, and as above, the final responsibility in making the assessment as to whether a denial of 'the genuine enjoyment of the rights' was at stake was delegated to the national level. Or, as the Court concluded, it was "for the referring court to determine whether, in the light of all the facts of the main proceedings" a denial of residence rights to Mrs. Alopka would oblige her Union citizen children to "leave the territory of the Union altogether" (Ibid., paragraphs 33–35). The Charter-based, fundamental rights questions which had also been advanced by the referring tribunal were not addressed. These final dicta do not, arguably, and as will be addressed in the conclusion, provide the final words on the 'substance of the rights' doctrine and its precise ramifications.

7.6 Recent Developments: *O&B* and *S&G*

The most recent dominant numerical structures considered relate to the outward scores of *O&B* and *S&G* rendered in March 2014. Both cases were referred by the Dutch Council of State and both raised questions on the application of EU free movement law in the context of 'return movements'. As emerges from the especially long time period which their outward scores span, such questions have continued marking the case law as from the 1992 *Singh* judgment onwards. As also testified to by *O&B* and *S&G*, the emergence of a new paradigm since *Zambrano* has not done away with the need for guidance on preceding judicial developments. Rather, these questions have remained in the balance and, as documented in the below, have mixed and mingled with the questions opened up by the Court's case law on the 'substance of the rights' doctrine.

To begin with, in ***O&B***, questions were raised, first, on the continued applicability of the Court's holdings on 'returnee situations' after the EU judiciary had held, from the *McCarthy* ruling onwards, that the scope of application of the Citizenship Directive was limited to the situations of "a Union citizen in a Member State of which he or she is not a national". Amongst others, as can be recalled, in that latter judgment the Court had reasoned that, to the extent that the Directive relates to the 'conditions' governing the exercise of EU citizens' rights to move and reside freely within the territory of the Member States, it could not apply to an EU national residing in his own Member State because, as a principle of international law, the right of a person to reside in the state of which he has the nationality could not be made 'conditional'. These premises, as the Dutch Council of State contended, were difficult to wed with the rights that had been granted to returning EU nationals within their own Member States in *Singh* and *Eind*. Remarkably, as can be recalled, the holdings of *McCarthy* that were now cited to question the continued applicability of *Singh* and *Eind*, had themselves partially been based on similar observations around the prohibition to expel own Member State nationals, 'as a principle of international law', that had been adduced, albeit as side issues, in the latter two judgments.

In addition, and in case of an affirmative answer to this first, more general question, the referring Dutch court also asked what temporal limits could be applied to the assessment of whether an EU national could lay claim to the continued protection of EU law in his own Member State after having resided in another Member State. The Dutch Council of State wanted to know, more precisely, whether there was a "requirement" that such a period of residence had been of "a certain minimum duration" and whether, if so, such a requirement could be met if there had not been a continuous residence, but rather, "a certain frequency of residence, such as during weekly residence at weekends or during regular visits" (*O&B*, paragraph 32).

More specifically, the *O&B* case concerned the situations of Mr. O. and Mr. B. Mr. O., first, was a Nigerian national who sought to rely on EU free movement law to claim a right to reside with his Dutch national spouse in the Netherlands. Mr. O's Dutch spouse had regularly spent time with Mr. O "in the form of holidays" in Spain. Mr. B., second, was a Moroccan national who similarly sought to rely on EU free movement law to claim residence rights with his Dutch national spouse in the Netherlands after that Dutch spouse had, over the course of a two-year period, regularly spent the weekend in Belgium where Mr. B. resided at the time. During that two-year time period, the couple had not yet been married. Their marriage was contracted afterwards when Mr. O. had already returned to Morocco as his further residence in Belgium had been denied. Mr. O. had moved from Morocco to the Netherlands to reside with his spouse two years later. In the context of these circumstances, the Dutch Council of State indicated, with reference to *Singh* and *Eind* in combination with the Court's more recent holdings in *McCarthy*, that it had "doubts" on whether and how to apply the premises deriving from the former two judgments to the settings at hand (Ibid., paragraph 30).

The CJEU started with elaborate considerations on how to combine the dicta it had put forward in *McCarthy* and reinforced in subsequent case law, with the holdings advanced earlier in *Singh* and *Eind*. As a first point, it reiterated, as above, the reinvigorated 'derived rights rule', according to which EU law does not "confer any autonomous right on third-country nationals" but only "rights derived from the exercise of freedom of movement by a Union citizen" (Ibid., paragraph 36). To that effect, the Court invoked *Iida*, *Ymeraga* and *Alopka*. On that basis, it then held that it followed "from a literal, systematic and teleological interpretation of Directive 2004/38" that the Directive established such a "derived right of residence for third-country nationals who are family members of a Union citizen (…) only where that citizen has exercised his right of freedom of movement by becoming established in a Member State other than the Member State of which he is a national" (Ibid., paragraph 39). To that effect, the Court cited *Metock, Dereci, Iida* and *O&S*. From there, the Court referred back to *McCarthy* to reinforce the premise that, as the subject of the Citizenship Directive concerns the conditions governing the exercise of the right to move and reside freely, it could not govern the situations of Union nationals in their own Member State since, under a principle of international law, a State cannot refuse its own nationals the right to enter and remain in its territory (Ibid., paragraphs 40–42). Accordingly, and "having regard" to the derived rights rule invoked above, the Court held that "Directive 2004/38 is therefore also not intended to confer a derived right of residence on third-country nationals who are family members of a Union citizen residing in the Member State of which that latter is a national" (Ibid., paragraph 43).

Next, the Court moved on to examine whether, since a right of residence could not be derived from the Citizenship Directive, such a right could instead flow directly from primary law, more precisely, from Article 21(1) TFEU (Ibid., paragraph 44). In the context of that examination, the Court also rehearsed the holdings of *Singh* and *Eind* in which it had concluded that "where a Union citizen has resided with a family member who is a third-country national in a Member State other than the Member State of which he is a national for a period exceeding two and a half years and one and a half years respectively (…) that third-country national must, when the Union citizen returns to the Member State of which he is a national, be entitled, under Union law, to a derived right of residence in the latter State". If such a residence right would not be granted, "a worker who is a Union citizen could be discouraged from leaving the Member State of which he is a national (…) simply because of the prospect for that worker of not being able to continue, on returning to his Member State of origin, a way of family life which may have come into being in the host Member State as a result of marriage or family reunification" (Ibid., paragraph 46). Joining together these premises with the above rehearsed, and arguably incongruent, principles advanced in *McCarthy* and other more recent case law, the Court held that it was "necessary to determine whether the case-law resulting from *Singh* and *Eind* is capable of being applied generally to family members of Union citizens who, having availed themselves of the rights conferred on them by Article 21(1) TFEU, resided in a Member State other than that of which they are nationals, before returning to the Member State of origin" (Ibid., paragraph 48). Without any further considerations, it was then submitted that "(t)hat is indeed the case". As its final dictum in that respect, the Court held that "(t)he grant, when a Union citizen returns to the Member State of which he is a national, of a derived right of residence to a third-country national who is a family member of that Union citizen and with whom that citizen has resided (…) seeks to remove the same type of obstacle on leaving the Member State of origin as that referred to (…) above, by guaranteeing that that citizen will be able, in his Member State of origin, to continue the family life which he created or strengthened in the host Member State" (Ibid., paragraph 49). Accordingly, and in other words, the incongruity between the two sets of case law was resolved by assigning the principles formulated in the most recent case law (*McCarthy* and other rulings) to secondary free movement legislation, and moving those of the earlier *Singh* and *Eind* rulings up to the level of Treaty law. In that manner as well, the continued applicability of the *Singh* and *Eind* premises was not only confirmed, these premises also received a legal upgrade to primary law. Whereas *Singh* had been based on both primary and secondary legal provisions, the *Eind* premises had previously related to secondary legislation only.

On the basis of this general re-confirmation, the CJEU then considered the Dutch court's follow-up questions on whether any temporal conditions could be applied to the grant of residence rights to family members of 'returning' nationals. In that respect, the Court first pointed out that Article 21(1) TFEU could not be construed in such a way as to "require that every residence in the host Member State by a Union citizen accompanied by a family member who is a third-country national necessarily confers a derived right of residence on that family member (…) upon the citizen's return". Rather, such a right could only flow from Treaty law where the residence had been "sufficiently genuine" (Ibid., paragraph 51). If a residence in the host Member State had been exercised pursuant to and in conformity with the conditions set out in article 7(1) of the Citizenship Directive, the Court held, such would in principle be "evidence" of the "Union citizen's genuine residence" (Ibid., paragraph 53). In other words, as that specific article sets out, a "genuine residence" would consist of a residence exercised for a period longer than three months by either workers, students or self-employed persons, or by Union citizens having sufficient resources to avoid becoming reliant on social assistance. In reinforcement of these holdings, the Court cited both *Eind* and *Iida*. In addition, further guidance was given by indicating that "short periods of residence such as weekends or holidays spent in a Member State other than that of which the citizen in question is a national, even when considered together" did not satisfy the conditions set out in Article 7 of the Citizenship Directive (Ibid., paragraph 59).

The ***S&G*** case, next, similarly concerned the situation of two third-country national family members of Dutch nationals who claimed residence rights on the basis of EU law in 'return contexts' following from *Singh, Eind* and other cases. The situations of *S&G* differed from *O&B*, however, in that there were minor children involved. More precisely, the first *S* case related to the situation of Ms. S., the third-country national mother-in-law of a Dutch citizen who resided in the Netherlands but regularly travelled to Belgium for employment-related reasons. Ms. S. took care of her grandson, the son of the Dutch citizen-sponsor. The second *G* case related to the situation of Ms. G., a third-country national who was married to a Dutch national with whom she had a daughter. In addition, Ms. G. also had a son who had been received into her and sponsor G's family. As in the *S* case, the Dutch citizen-sponsor in *G* travelled often, even daily, between the Netherlands and Belgium for his work but continued to reside in the Netherlands however. In respect of these situations, the Dutch Council of State had asked, first, whether, as in the above case, the principles set out in *Singh* and *Eind* continued to hold in light of the Court's more recent *McCarthy* decision (*S&G*, paragraph 26). It then questioned whether, if this was the case, the third-country nationals in question could derive residence right on the basis of this case law even if their respective Union citizen sponsors had not previously resided in a Member State other than that of which they hold the nationality (Ibid., paragraph 27). In addition, the referring court also cited the CJEU's holdings in *Carpenter* to the effect that citizens' Treaty right to provide services, read in light of the fundamental right to respect for family life, precluded the refusal of a residence right to a third-country national spouse of a provider of services. It questioned, however, to what extent these conclusions could also extend to Union citizens who did not provide cross-border services, as had been the case in *Carpenter*, but instead moved to another Member State in the context of work-related activities (Ibid., paragraph 28). Finally, with reference to *Zambrano* and *Dereci*, the Dutch Council of State also wanted to know whether any residence rights could accrue to the third-country national family members in question on the basis of Treaty provisions on Union citizenship (Ibid., paragraph 29).

The CJEU started out by repeating the first part of the reasoning it had advanced in *O&B*. More specifically, it revisited the derived rights rule with reference to *McCarthy*, *Dereci* and *Ymeraga*, and repeated, with reference to *O&B*, that the Citizenship Directive does not grant derived rights of residence to third-country national family members "of a Union citizen residing in the Member State of which he is a national" (*S&G*, paragraphs 33–34). Accordingly, a refusal of residence rights to family members such as those in the proceedings at hand was not precluded by that Directive (Ibid., paragraph 35). The second part of *O&B*, in which the Court held that derived residence rights for family members could nevertheless flow from primary law was not referred to however. Instead, the Court moved on to examine the situations presented in *S&G* in light of the principles established in *Carpenter*. As it submitted, "admittedly", the interpretation of the Treaty provisions granting a right to provide services in *Carpenter* was "transposable" to those providing for the freedom of movement of workers (Ibid., paragraph 40). However, as it continued with reference to *Iida*, *Ymeraga* and *Alopka*, the "purpose and justification of such a derived right of residence is based on the fact that a refusal to allow it would be such as to interfere with the exercise of fundamental freedoms guaranteed by the FEU Treaty" (Ibid., paragraph 41). In that regard, "the fact that the third-country national in question takes care of the Union citizens' child may, as is apparent from the judgment in *Carpenter*, be a relevant factor to be taken into account (…) when examining whether the refusal to grant a right of residence to that third-country national may discourage the Union citizen from effectively exercising his rights". However, it was also to be noted that: "The mere fact that it might appear desirable that the child be cared for by the third-country national who is the direct relative in the ascending line of the Union citizen's spouse is not therefore sufficient in itself to constitute such a dissuasive effect." (Ibid., paragraph 43). Ultimately, and once more, it was "for the referring court to determine whether, in each of the situations at issue in the main proceedings, the grant of a derived right of residence to the third-country national in question (…) is necessary to guarantee the citizen's effective exercise of the fundamental freedom guaranteed by Article 45 TFEU" (Ibid. paragraph 42). In light of these considerations, the Court considered it unnecessary to engage with the further questions on the application of the principles established in *Zambrano* and *Dereci* (Ibid., paragraph 45). In all, and as in the above, whilst *O&B* and *S&G* confirmed the continued applicability of *Singh*, *Eind* and *Carpenter*, at the same time, and on account of the Court's imprecise final holdings, these judgments have been faulted for "creating more questions than they solve" (Schoenmaekers & Hoogenboom, 2014). On that basis, they are also expected to "trigger a need for further clarification" by means of follow-up litigation (Ibid., p. 511).

7.7 Conclusion

The above qualitative reviews have provided the study's third and final set of empirical observations. On the basis of this final set of observations, the next chapter will retrace *whether* and *how* reasoning by precedent has strengthened the Court's autonomy in the area of family reunification immigration. It does so by comparing the findings on Member States' interests presented in Chap. 5 with those on the precedent-based discursive interactions numerically charted in Chap. 6 and qualitatively reviewed above. This final analytical chapter shifts the analytical engagement with the observations by joining together the different sets of dynamics observed across the case law record's development, independent of their chronological order, and evaluating their cumulative effects.

References

Primary Sources

EU Law

Council Directive 90/364/EEC on the Right of Residence [1990] O.J. L 180/26.

Council Directive 2003/86/EC on the Right to Family Reunification [2003] O.J. L 251/12.

Directive 2004/38/EC of the European Parliament and of the Council on the Right of Citizens of the Union and their Family Members to Move and Reside Freely within the Territory of the Member States [2004] O.J. L 158/77.

Regulation (EEC) No 1612/68 of the Council on Freedom of Movement for Workers within the Community [1968] O.J. 257.

EU Documents

Communication from the Commission to the European Parliament and the Council on guidance for application of Directive 2003/86/EC on the right to family reunification, COM (2014) 210 (final).

Council of the European Union Press Release 1962nd Council meeting Justice and Home Affairs, Brussels 21 September 2009, 13467/09.

Green Paper on the right to family reunification of third-country nationals living in the European Union (Directive 2003/86/EC), COM (2011) 735 (final).

Report from the Commission to the European Parliament and the Council on the application of Directive 2004/38/EC on the right of citizens of the Union and their family members to move and reside freely within the territory of the Member States, COM (2008) 840 final.

CJEU Case Law

Case C-40/76 *Slavica Kermaschek v Bundesanstalt für Arbeit* [1976] ECR 1669.

Case C-35/82 *Elestina Esselina Christina Morson v State of the Netherlands and Head of the Plaatselijke Politie within the meaning of the Vreemdelingenwet; Sweradjie Jhanjan v State of the Netherlands* [1982] ECR 3723.

Case C-147/87 *Saada Zaoui v Caisse régionale d'assurance maladie de l'Ile-de-France (CRAMIF)* [1987] ECR 5511.

Case C-370/90 *The Queen v Immigration Appeal Tribunal and Surinder Singh, ex parte Secretary of State for Home Department* [1992] ECR I-4265.

Case C-206/91 *Ettien Koua Poirrez v Caisse d'allocations familiales de la région parisienne, substituée par la Caisse d'allocations familiales de la Seine-Saint-Denis* [1992] ECR I-6685.

Case C-64/96 *Land Nordrhein-Westfalen v Kari Uecker and Vera Jacquet v Land Nordrhein-Westfalen* [1992] ECR I-3171.

Case C-184/99 *Grzelczyk v Centre public d'aide sociale d'Ottignies-Louvain-la-Neuve* [2001] ECR I-6193.

Case C-413/99 *Baumbast and R v Secretary of State for the Home Department* [2002] ECR I-7091.

Case C-459/99 *Mouvement contre le racisme, l'antisémitisme et la xénophobie ASBL (MRAX) v Belgian State* [2002] ECR I-6591.

Case C-60/00 *Mary Carpenter v Secretary of State for the Home Department* [2002] ECR I-6279.

Case C-466/00 *Arben Kaba v Secretary of State for the Home Department* [2003] ECR I-2219.

Case C-109/01 *Secretary of State for the Home Department v Hacene Akrich* [2003] ECR I-9607.

Case C-200/02 *Kunqian Catherine Zhu and Man Lavette Chen v Secretary of State for the Home Department* [2004] ECR I-9925.
Case C-157/03 *Commission of the European Communities v Kingdom of Spain* [2005] ECR I-2911.
Case C-503/03 *Commission of the European Communities v Kingdom of Spain* [2006] ECR I-1097.
Case C-540/03 *European Parliament v Council of the European Union* [2006] ECR I-5769.
Case C-1/05 *Yunying Jia v Migrationsverket* [2006] ECR I-00001.
Case C-291/05 *Minister voor Vreemdelingenzaken en Integratie v R. N. G. Eind* [2007] ECR I-10719.
Case C-127/08 *Blaise Baheten Metock and Others v Minister for Justice, Equality and Law Reform* [2008] ECR I-6241.
Case C-578/08 *Rhimou Chakroun v Minister van Buitenlandse Zaken* [2010] ECR I-1893.
Case C-34/09 *Gerardo Ruiz Zambrano v Office national de l'emploi (ONEM)* [2011] ECR I-1177.
Case C-434/09 *Shirley McCarthy v Secretary of State for the Home Department* [2011] ECR I-3375.
Case C-40/11 *Yoshikazu Iida v Stadt Ulm* [2013] OJ C 9/10.
Case C-256/11 *Murat Dereci and Others v Bundesministerium für Inneres* [2011] ECR I-11315.
Case C-356/11 & C-357/11 *O and S v Maahanmuuttovirasto and Maahanmuuttovirasto v L* [2013] OJ C 26/19.
Case C-86/12 *Adzo Domenyo Alokpa and Others v Ministre du Travail, de l'Emploi et de l'Immigration* [2013] OJ C 344/21.
Case C-87/12 *Kreshnik Ymeraga and Others v Ministre du Travail, de l'Emploi et de l'Immigration* [2013] OJ C 225/44.
Case C-456/12 *O. v Minister voor Immigratie, Integratie en Asiel and Minister voor Immigratie, Integratie en Asiel v B. Reference for a preliminary ruling: Raad van State—Netherlands* [2014] OJ C135/5.
Case C-457/12 *S. v Minister voor Immigratie, Integratie en Asiel and Minister voor Immigratie, Integratie en Asiel v G.* [2014] OJ C135/5.

Other Sources

Belgian Government, Federal Public Service Foreign Affairs (2009). Written Observation of the Belgian Government on the preliminary reference C-34/09 (Ruiz Zambrano), on file with the author (in French).
Former Council Official (2014). Speaking at an expert seminar organised by the Centre for European Policy Studies, CEPS, Brussels, 14 February 2014.

Government of the Netherlands (2011). *Position paper—The Dutch Standpoint on EU Migration Policy.* On File with the Author.

Report for the Hearing in Case (C-370/90) *Singh*, on file with the author (in English).

Report for the Hearing in Case (C-200/02) *Zhu & Chen*, on file with the author (in English).

Report for the Hearing in Case (C-291/05) *Eind*, on file with the author (in Dutch).

Report for the Hearing in Case (C-540/03) *EPvCouncil*, on file with the author (in Dutch).

Report for the Hearing in Case (C-1/05) *Jia*, on file with the author (in Swedish).

Report for the Hearing in Case (C-578/08) *Chakroun*, on file with the author (in Dutch).

Report for the Hearing in Case (C-34/09) *Zambrano*, on file with the author (in French).

Report for the Hearing in Case (C-434/09) *McCarthy*, on file with the AUTHOR (in English).

Report for the Hearing in Case (C-256/11) *Dereci*, on file with the author (in German).

Report for the Hearing in Case (C-356/11 & C-357/11) *O&S*, on file with the author (in Finnish).

Tweede Kamer der Staten-Generaal. (2010). Brief van de Minister van justitie aan de Voorzitter van de Tweede Kamer der Staten-Generaal. Vergaderjaar 2009–2010, 32175 Nr. 8.

Tweede Kamer der Staten-Generaal. (2011). Brief van de Minister voor immigratie en asiel aan de Voorzitter van de Tweede Kamer der Staten-Generaal. Vergaderjaar 2010–2011, 19637 Nr. 1408.

Literature

Acierno, S. (2003). The *Carpenter* Judgment: Fundamental Rights and the Limits of the Community Legal Order. *European Law Review, 28*(3), 398–407.

Adam, S., & Van Elsuwege, P. (2012). Citizenship Rights and the Federal Balance between the European Union and its Member States: Comment on *Dereci*. *European Law Review, 37*(2), 176–190.

Barrett, G. (2003). Family Matters: European Community Law and Third-Country Family Members. *Common Market Law Review, 40*(2), 369–421.

Bierbach, J. (2008). Case Note on *Eind*. *European Constitutional Law Review, 4*, 344–362.

Bonjour, S., & Vink, M. (2013). When Europeanization Backfires: The Normalization of European Migration Politics. *Acta Politica, 48*(4), 389–407.

Cambien, N. (2012). *EU Citizenship and the ECJ: Why Care About Primary Carers?* Paper presented at the UACES annual conference, 3–5 September 2012, Passau.

Currie, S. (2009). Accelerated Justice or a Step Too Far? Residence Rights of Non-EU Family Members and the Court's Ruling in Metock. *European Law Review, 34*(2), 310–326.

Dawson, M. (2014). How Does the European Court of Justice Reason? A Review Essay on the Legal Reasoning of the European Court of Justice. *European Law Journal, 20*(3), 423–435.

De Somer, M. (2012). Enhanced Competences for the European Court of Justice: "Re-shuffling" the Dynamics of EU Migration Policy-Making? *LSE Migration Studies Unit Working Papers*, No. 2012/01. London: London School of Economics and Political Science.

Fernhout, R., & Wever, R. (2011). Follow-up of the Case Law of the Court of Justice of the European Union. Thematic. Report 2010–2011. *European Network on Free Movement of Workers within the European Union*. Nijmegen: University of Nijmegen, Centre for Migration Law.

Guild, E., Peers, S., & Tomkin, J. (2014). *The EU Citizenship Directive: A Commentary*. Oxford: Oxford University Press.

Hailbronner, K., & Thym, D. (2011). Comment on *Zambrano*. *Common Market Law Review, 48*, 1253–1270.

Hardy, J. (2012). The Objective of Directive 2003/86 Is to Promote the Family Reunification of Third Country Nationals. *European Journal of Migration and Law, 14*, 439–452.

Hofstotter, B. (2005). A Cascade of Rights, or Who Shall Care For little Catherine? Some Reflections on the Chen Case. *European Law Review, 30*(4), 548–558.

Iglesias Sanchez, S. (2012). The Court and the Charter: The Impact of the Entry into Force of the Lisbon Treaty on the ECJ's Approach to Fundamental Rights. *Common Market Law Review, 49*(5), 1565–1612.

Lansbergen, A., & Miller, N. (2011). European Citizenship Rights in Internal Situations: An Ambiguous Revolution? Case note on *Ruiz Zambrano*. *European Constitutional Law Review, 7*, 287–307.

Legomsky, S. (2011). Rationing Family Values in Europe and America: An Immigration Tug of War between States and Their Supra-National Associations. *Georgetown Immigration Law Journal, 25*, 807–858.

Lenaerts, K. (2011). 'Civis europaeus sum': From the Cross-border Link to the Status of Citizen of the Union. *Online Journal on Free Movement of Workers within the European Union, 3*, 6–18.

Lenaerts, K. (2015). EU Citizenship and the European Court of Justice's 'Stone-by-Stone' Approach. *International Comparative Jurisprudence, 1*, 1–10.

Mancini, J. M., & Finlay, G. (2008). 'Citizenship Matters': Lessons From the Irish Citizenship Referendum. *American Quarterly, 60*(3), 575–599.

Menz, G. (2011). Stopping, Shaping and Moulding Europe: Two-Level Games, Non-State Actors and the Europeanization of Migration Policies. *Journal of Common Market Studies, 49*(2), 437–462.

Olivier, B., & Reestman, J. H. (2007). Case Note on *Jia*. *European Constitutional Law Review, 3*, 463–475.

Peers, S. (2009). Free Movement, Immigration Control and Constitutional Conflict. *European Constitutional Law Review, 5*, 173–196.

Schiltz, C. (2005). Akrich: A Clear Delimitation without Limits. *Maastricht Journal of European and Comparative Law, 12*(3), 241–252.

Schmidt, S. (2014). Judicial Europeanisation: The Case of in Ireland. *West European Politics, 37*(4), 769–785.

Schoenmaekers, S., & Hoogenboom, A. (2014). *Singh* and *Carpenter* Revisited: Some Progress but no Final Clarity. *Maastricht Journal of European and Comparative Law, 21*(3), 494–513.

Shuibhne, N. (2011). Seven Questions for Seven Paragraphs. *European Law Review, 36*(2), 161–162.

Spaventa, E. (2005). Case Note on *Akrich*. *Common Market Law Review, 42*, 225–239.

Strik, T. (2011). *Besluitvorming over asiel- en migratierichtlijnen. De wisselwerking tussen nationaal en Europees niveau*. Den Haag: Boom Juridische uitgevers.

Tryfonidou, A. (2007). Jia or "Carpenter II": The Edge of Reason. *European Law Review, 32*(6), 908–918.

Tryfonidou, A. (2009). Family Reunification Rights of (Migrant) Union Citizens: Towards a More Liberal Approach. *European Law Journal, 15*(5), 634–653.

Van der Mei, A. P. (2003). Residence and the Evolving Notion of European Union Citizenship. Comments on *Baumbast v Secretary of State for Home Department*, 17 September 2002 (Case C-143/99). *European Journal of Migration and Law, 5*, 419–433.

Van Elsuwege, P., & Kochenov, D. (2011). On the Limits of Judicial Intervention: EU Citizenship and Family Reunification Rights. *European Journal of Migration and Law, 13*(4), 443–466.

Watson, P. (1993). Free Movement of Workers: A One-Way Ticket? *Industrial Law Journal, 22*(1), 68–77.

White, R. (2004). Conflicting Competences: Free Movement Rules and Immigration Laws. *European Law Review, 29*(3), 385–396.

CHAPTER 8

Precedents and Judicial Politics: Analytical Findings

8.1 Introduction

Has reasoning by precedent strengthened the Court's autonomy in the sensitive area of family reunification and, if so, how? In what follows, this final analytical chapter reviews *whether* autonomous judicial outcomes were engendered, that is, outcomes which move beyond Member States' political preferences and, if so, to what extent such outcomes were supported by the Court's recourse to precedent-based reasoning. The chapter first reviews the findings on Member States' political preferences as examined in Chap. 5 in light of the outcomes of the Court's decisions as recorded in Chap. 7 in order to answer the first sub-question. Next, the chapter looks at *how* these outcomes were supported by precedent-based discursive strategies.

8.2 Judicial Autonomy

8.2.1 Member State Preferences

As emerged from the analyses of Member States' interest articulations during the negotiations on EU family reunification law as conducted in Chap. 5, government representatives were especially watchful, and held the strongest sovereignty concerns, in respect of the clauses regulating the personal scope of the family reunion instruments to be established. Or,

M. De Somer, *Precedents and Judicial Politics in EU Immigration Law*, European Administrative Governance,
https://doi.org/10.1007/978-3-319-93982-7_8

political contention especially surrounded those clauses defining the categories of persons which would be covered by the new rules. Amongst others, Member States voiced fears around the high financial consequences which could result if broad categories of persons, and hence family reunion situations, would be covered. Similarly, governments also referred to concerns about their ability to continue taking their national immigration reception capacity into account. Across the board, as emerged, concerns mostly surrounded the precise immigration control discretion that would be retained at national level depending on the precise personal scope delineation of the new EU legal provisions. The more inclusive the latter, the more family reunification situations and, hence, entry claims of foreigners that would be lifted out of the sphere of exclusive domestic immigration control to instead become governed by EU law. Conversely, the more narrow the latter, the fewer the categories of persons, and hence numbers of family reunification situations that would henceforth fall to be treated by EU-level rules.

The particular personal scope sensitivity translated, more specifically, in high degrees of contestation around, first, the clauses and provisions governing which categories of persons could qualify either as 'sponsor' or as 'joining family member' for the purpose of being covered by the new family reunion rules. Second, much debate also surrounded the clauses laying down the conditions or requirements which Member States could set to the eligibility to these statuses and the grounds on which Member States could justify individuals' exclusion from the remit of the new instruments. These two sets of interrelated personal scope sensitivities are considered in turn.

To begin with, in respect of the first observation, Member States sought to provide for a narrow reach of the definitions of 'sponsor' or 'family member' by first, and most straightforwardly, excluding certain categories of individuals from the definitions' premises. For instance, and most notably, national delegations systematically and vehemently opposed Commission attempts at extending the definitions of sponsors in such a way as to also cover the family reunification situations of 'static' EU nationals (or, nationals not making use of EU free movement rights). Amongst others, and in line with the above, concerns were voiced around the considerable increase in the numbers of 'third-country nationals admitted' which such a personal scope extension to static EU nationals would bring about and, in connection, the large expansion of EU competences that this would entail. In addition, much attention went out to making sure that the respective definitions were described with high levels of detail so that minimum flexibility would attach to them and they would not allow for reading more categories of persons in them than those specifically provided for. To that purpose, national delegations for instance made efforts to ensure that the concepts of joining spouse or registered partner were clearly delineated, and that the provisions on joining children specified that such children were to be underage or dependent on the sponsor and, in any event, not married. Furthermore, much debate also surrounded which categories of relatives would be covered within the category of core family members (in respect of which the instruments provided for more stringent legal obligations) and which family members would, instead, be covered under the label of extended family members (in respect of which Member States' obligations were more lenient). For instance, whereas the Commission's original proposals had included ascending relatives within the clauses on core family members, over the course of the different Council debates this category of family members was moved into the clauses governing family reunion with extended relatives in relation to which Member States were merely to 'facilitate' entry (in the context of free movement legislation), or the admission of which 'could be' (instead of, 'had to' be) authorised (in the context of immigration law).

In respect of the second site of personal scope concerns identified, i.e., the conditional requirements which could be set on the qualification to the statuses of sponsor or family member, Member States resorted to opposite drafting techniques. That is, where the definitions governing eligibility to the instruments' scope were set out with much attention to detail, the provisions governing the conditions that could be set to such eligibility were instead drafted in an ambivalent, generalizable language. The policy preferences underpinning this contrasting drafting technique were the same however. By phrasing the conditional requirements (most centrally, housing, health insurance and 'sufficient' or 'stable' resources conditions) in ambiguous, multi-interpretable terms, Member States sought to widen the grounds on which access to the new EU rights could be refused, and hence by means of which the categories of individuals able to lay claim to the new rights could be reduced. In addition, in the context of the Family Reunification Directive, further barriers to such rights were erected in the format of supplementary integration requirements and through options to apply extended waiting periods. In all, on the basis of these efforts, Member States wanted to ensure that the new EU rights would not come to accrue to more categories of individuals than those politically envisaged and, accordingly, that the reach of EU competences would not come to embed more immigration situations than those specifically agreed to.

8.2.2 *Judicial Outcomes*

As emerged from the subsequent analyses (Chaps. 6 and 7), the judicial outcomes that were cumulatively engendered over the years have not shown a deference to these political preferences. Instead, in small but certain steps, the Court counteracted what was politically envisaged. The categories of individuals entitled to benefit from EU family reunion rights have, over the course of different judgments, been expanded significantly. Conversely, the leeway that Member States had counted on having created through vague, multi-interpretable conditional requirements has, also over the course of different judgments, been significantly curtailed.

Whereas the first jurisprudential developments reviewed (those of the 1970s and 1980s), generated outcomes which arguably remained close to dominant governmental concerns (e.g., through the creation and reinforcement of the 'internal rule' or the 'derived rights rule'), the image changed as from the early 1990s onwards. The 1992 *Singh* judgment, to begin with, extended the reach of family reunion rights to also cover the situations of home nationals, resident in their own Member State after such nationals returned from having exercised free movement rights in another Member State. The *Eind* judgment further expanded on these conclusions by setting out, first, that the EU family reunion provisions which could be claimed in nationals' home State in such 'returnee' contexts also accrued to family members which had not yet enjoyed a right of residence prior to the first move and, second, that EU law protection did not end when the sponsoring EU national stopped meeting the requirements governing qualification to the scope of secondary free movement law (i.e., in the case at hand, when the sponsor stopped being economically active or did not possess 'sufficient resources'). Whereas the 2003 *Akrich* judgment originally appeared to curtail the *Singh* premises by establishing that they could not be relied on to rectify previously unlawful stays, the later overruling of this *Akrich* conclusion in the 2008 *Metock* ruling only further extended the types of situations, and categories of persons, which could lay claim to EU family reunion law within their home Member States. In *Metock*, the Court also further reinforced that the relevant provisions also applied to contexts of family 'formation'. Most recently, in the 2014 *O&B* judgement, the Court has further specified the conditions governing access to the rights deriving from *Singh* (and *Eind* and *Metock*), amongst others, by laying down temporal requirements. At the same time however, the continued applicability of these premises was reinforced and the Court also grounded them more firmly within primary, Treaty law provisions.

As a further set of outcomes, in the 2002 *Baumbast* ruling, the Court came to hold that joining children can continue deriving rights from EU law also beyond the exercise of the sponsor's original free movement rights. Furthermore, such children can, in turn, act as sponsors for family reunification with their parents. In that manner, *Baumbast* in fact extended the personal scope of EU family reunion provisions to persons two steps removed from the individual who enjoyed the first set of free movement rights. Two years later, in *Zhu & Chen*, the Court similarly held that a young child could act as a sponsor for the purpose of reunion with an ascendant relative. In addition, in the latter judgment the Court also established that, for the purposes of meeting the conditional requirements set to the access to such family reunion rights, a child did not need to personally hold the required 'sufficient resources'. Instead, such resources could also be adduced by the ascendant family member in respect of whom family reunification was sought. These propositions were further reinforced in the recent, 2013 *Alopka* judgment where the Court rehearsed that no conditions as to the origin of resources could be instated in the context of reviewing whether a minor citizen sponsor meets the sufficient resources requirement.

A further dismantling of the barriers which Member States can set on EU family reunion rights was effected through a series of Court conclusions on the grounds on which exclusion from the legislation's scope can be justified (most centrally, public policy, health or security considerations). For instance, in its 2002 *MRAX* decision the Court ruled that Belgium could not rely on public policy, health or security considerations to justify the refusal of entry and residence rights to third-country national family members of moving Union citizens on the grounds that these family members did not, or no longer, possess the requisite identity documents or valid visa. Similar premises were also upheld in *Commission v Spain* (C-503/03) as well as, at a later stage, in *Metock*.

Comparable category-broadening and conditionality-limiting outcomes were also registered in the context of the Family Reunification

Directive. Whereas the first Court dicta on this instrument, in the 2006 *EPvCouncil* case, did not—at face value—seem to encroach on the leeway which the Directive left to Member States, the outcomes engendered thereafter, and on the basis of a further application of these first dicta, were very different. To begin with, in its 2010 *Chakroun* decision, the Court firmly established, in analogy to *Metock*, that the legislation applied to both situations of family reunification strictly speaking as well as to contexts of family formation (i.e., contexts where family ties were formed only after the sponsor's move). Moreover, the Court also firmly pronounced itself on the 'stable resources' requirement inscribed in the Directive. In spite of Member States' efforts during the negotiation stages to phrase this conditional requirement in flexible terms so that it would provide manoeuvrability during the implementation stages, the Court's holdings came to *de facto* neutralise any such space for manoeuvre. Most importantly, the Court stated that the said requirement could in any event not be applied in a manner that would not take the individual circumstances of each particular case into account. In the proceedings at hand, and on the basis of this statement, the use of a standard reference income below which all requests for family reunification were refused was found to be in breach of EU law. These premises were further rehearsed in the 2012 *O&S* case where the Court also came to hold that the Directive's personal scope extended to family situations involving a static, home national. Although, as expressly laid down in the Directive's Article 3(3), the instrument's provisions were not to 'apply to members of the family of a Union citizen', the Court stated that their application could nevertheless not be excluded 'solely because a minor Union citizen was also part of the families concerned'.

A final, and remarkable set of personal scope-extending outcomes was engendered through the application of Treaty law provisions to situations otherwise outside of the personal scope of secondary law. In the 2002 *Carpenter* case, the Court for instance established that although the individuals in the case at hand could not derive family reunion rights from secondary EU free movement of services law because the sponsoring EU national remained resident within his home State, such family reunion rights could nevertheless not be denied to him in light of the higher-order right to freedom of services enshrined in Treaty law. Recently, in the 2014 *S&G* case, these premises were transposed to the situations of EU nationals who, whilst continuing to reside within their home Member State, travelled back and forth between their own State and another Member

State for work purposes (instead of, as in *Carpenter*, in the context of providing services). As the Court came to hold, its *Carpenter* dicta also applied to Treaty provisions on the freedom to work and, accordingly, whilst the individuals in the case at hand were not covered by secondary free movement law, the national court was to nevertheless examine whether family reunion rights could not be denied to them in light of Treaty law. Similarly ground-breaking were the judicial outcomes generated through the Court's application of Treaty provisions on EU citizenship. In the 2002 *Baumbast* case, the Court found, in addition to the conclusions referred to above, that an EU national could continue to derive residence rights in another Member State also after his employment activities in that state had come to an end. Whilst no longer covered by the scope of secondary free movement legislation, such rights nevertheless continued to accrue to him directly on the basis of Article 18 EC (now Article 21 TFEU). In spite of questions to that effect, the Court did not attach further family reunion rights to these findings for the time being. In *Zhu & Chen* however, the EU judiciary would come to hold that, to the extent that a minor EU national was found to derive residence rights directly from Treaty provisions on Union citizenship, on the basis of these same provisions, a derived right of residence accrued to that EU national's parent and primary carer. Recently, in the 2011 *Zambrano* ruling, the Court derived similar conclusions from the EU citizenship provisions enshrined in Article 20 TFEU in circumstances where there had not been a previous exercise of free movement rights (as in *Baumbast*) and where, instead, the EU nationals concerned resided within their state of nationality (unlike in *Zhu & Chen*). Additionally, besides an ancillary right of residence, the primary carer-family member concerned was also found to derive employment rights from the Treaty rights which accrued to his EU national children. The *Zambrano* premises were qualified as relating to 'exceptional situations' only in the context of the numerous follow-up judgments that ensued (*McCarthy, Dereci, Iida, O&S, Ymeraga, Alopka*). To date however, and as will be returned to in the below, these premises have not been overruled, nor fundamentally undermined.

8.3 Precedents and Judicial Interlocutors

In line with the study's theoretical expectations, these far-reaching, autonomous judicial outcomes, and their slow but certain sequencing over time, did not surface at random. Instead, as emerges from the analytical observations of Chap. 7, they were strongly supported by repeated, precedent-based discursive interactions between the Court and its external interlocutors. In the below, following the structure of the study's theoretical propositions, the analytical observations on these interactions and the different sets of autonomy-leveraging effects they embedded are considered, first, in respect of the Court's judicial interlocutors (litigant parties and national courts), as is the subject of this subsection, and next, in respect of the Court's non-judicial interlocutors (Member States).

8.3.1 Cue-Taking

First, in respect of its judicial interlocutors, that is, litigants and national courts, the Court's strategic reverence to preceding case law enabled it to emit clear(er) signals and guidelines as to the weight that it attached to certain arguments or standards rather than to others. That is, by repeatedly reinforcing certain dicta rather than others, the Court was able to signpost which dicta it considered most important in the context of interpreting EU family reunion provisions.

As was observed, and in line with the study's theoretical expectations, litigant parties and national courts were keen to take cues from these signals in order to maximize the effectiveness of their own submissions. Litigants, first, clearly took cues from the Court's dicta, and the repeated reinforcement thereof, in the assessment of their chances of winning a dispute on the basis of EU law as well as in respect of which lines of reasoning to strategically put forward for that purpose. More precisely, in order to maximize their chances of securing a favourable outcome, litigants sought to advance what they considered the most effective argumentative strategies within the court room. This usually implied presenting their arguments within the discursive frames through which the Court had articulated its prior decisions, putting forward considerations that were deemed important in earlier proceedings and, generally, demonstrating expert knowledge of the law and its correct (prior) interpretation. National courts, from their part, also took cues from the Court's holdings when assessing which types of claims required (additional) examination by Luxembourg, and which argumentative elements or lines of reasoning were to be considered further in that respect. In presenting their questions, and also with a view to maximizing the efficiency of their interactions with the EU judiciary, they similarly oriented their submissions around the Court's prior argumentation. Generally, whenever litigants or national courts adopted premises stemming from earlier CJEU decisions in the context of their own submissions this entailed, even if only implicitly, a reinforcement of those CJEU premises by these actors. In addition, each new claim or question that, on account of such cue-taking, was anchored in earlier CJEU holdings provided the EU judiciary, anew, with an opportunity to further construct these holdings.

Whereas cue-taking practices of this kind were not prevalently observable in the earliest phase of the jurisprudence (the case law of the 1970s and 1980s), as arguably little jurisprudential material or Court-signalling was available to take cues from, the image changed as from the early 1990s onwards. The questions arising in the 1992 *Singh* case for instance were premised on the Court's earlier dicta in *Morson & Jhanjan* and the repeated reinforcement of these dicta in the cases that had followed afterwards. More precisely, Mr. Singh (or his lawyer) had based his legal claims on the Court's earlier 'internal rule' holdings according to which Community law provisions "may be invoked only where the case in question comes within the area to which Community law applies". On that basis he had argued that, following an *a contrario* interpretation of this dictum, once a case comes within the area of Community law it was open to Community nationals to invoke EU law provisions also against their own, home State. The *Carpenter* claims, next, were premised in part on the rights-extending conclusions which the Court had arrived at in *Singh*. In *Baumbast*, third, rights claims and questions were raised, amongst others, on the basis of the 'effet utile' arguments that the Court had advanced and reinforced over earlier lines of case law, amongst them *Singh* and *Carpenter*.

These cue-taking practices continued as the case law moved into the 2000s. As emerged clearly from both the quantitative and qualitative observations, the Court's dicta in *Singh, Carpenter* and *Baumbast* would in fact strongly condition the premises of the questions and claims that arose before Luxembourg in this next phase. For instance, and to begin with, the questions raised in *Akrich* were explicitly presented by the referring national court as a request for 'further guidance' on the application of the Court's dicta in *Singh*. The *Akrich* proceedings had also emerged on the basis of *Singh*-related rights claims. *Akrich* (and on that basis also *Singh*) was to then set the stakes for the claims and questions in the later *Jia* case, and afterwards, for those arising in the context of *Metock*. *Singh* also defined the premises of the *Eind* case, and most recently, those of the *O&B* ruling. The *Carpenter* ruling, next, prompted similarly long-lasting and numerous cue-taking practices. The Court's dicta in *Carpenter* were for instance taken up on by the European Parliament in presenting its claims in the *EPvCouncil* case. More precisely, the EP referred to the fundamental rights' holdings which the Court had advanced in *Carpenter* and reinforced, amongst others, in *Akrich*, to strengthen its contention that several of the Family Reunification Directive's provisions were incompatible with EU fundamental rights standards. *EPvCouncil* was to then set in motion the follow-up claims and questions that underpinned the *Chakroun* judgment. More recently, the *Carpenter* ruling provided the basis for the claims and questions arising in *S&G*. *Baumbast*, third, was to provide the groundworks for the claims and questions which arrived before Luxembourg in *Zhu & Chen*. More in particular, in *Zhu & Chen* the referring national court asked whether, as the litigant parties had claimed, the Court's argumentation in *Baumbast* could be transposed to also cover the situation of a minor EU national where there had not previously been any exercise of free movement rights and whether, in follow up, such a minor EU national's mother could in turn lay claim to ancillary residence rights. The Court's affirmative answer to these questions, and the reasoning adduced to present them, was, next, to set the stage for the recent *Zambrano* proceedings.

With time, and through sequencing, these cue-taking practices grew ever more refined and dense as the Court's body of dicta to take cues from also grew larger and more refined. For instance, whilst the parameters of the *Metock* case were clearly premised on the Court's dicta in *Akrich*, at the same time and through *Akrich*, they were also conditioned by the arguments that had been adduced further downstream in *Singh*. In addition, the '*Singh-Akrich*' discourses also became cross-pollinated with prior dicta on 'effet utile' and fundamental rights that had been advanced in *Carpenter*, *MRAX*, *Baumbast* etc. As another example, whilst the claims and questions of *Eind* clearly followed on from *Singh*, the *Eind* proceedings additionally raised questions which were premised on the Court's reasoning in *Baumbast* and in *Zhu & Chen*. More specifically, whilst the referring court wanted to know first, as had been claimed by the applicants, whether the *Singh* parameters could also be extended to situations where the sponsor was no longer economically active and where the family member had not enjoyed a right of residence in the home State prior to the sponsor's first move, it also asked, taking cues from *Baumbast* and *Zhu & Chen*, 'what significance' for the answers to these questions was to be attached to the EU national's right to free movement as provided for under Treaty law.

Such cumulative, 'snowballing' argumentative dynamics became ever more prevalent and visible the more time passed and the more decisions were rendered premised on earlier Court dicta (which were themselves potentially conditioned by even earlier ones). In the most recent phase reviewed, that is, the case law following from the 2011 *Zambrano* ruling, the sequences of arguments and standards adhered to ever more clearly derived from prior CJEU-articulated arguments. *Zambrano*, to begin with, arose out of rights claims, and connected questions, that had been structured by *Zhu & Chen* (and to that extent, by *Baumbast*). The Court's *Zambrano* holdings, in turn, prompted a host of follow-up questions which, next, continued shaping further cue-taking by litigants and national courts in a line of case law extending from *McCarthy* and *Dereci*, over *Iida* and *O&S* up to *Ymeraga* and *Alopka*. By the time the case law arrived at *Alopka* the Court's holdings on the 'genuine enjoyment of the substance' of EU citizenship rights, around which these developments turned, had grown so large, through the incremental effects of repeated follow-up claims and questions, that they came to comprise nine full lines.[1] As before as well, these precedent-based lines of reasoning on the 'substance of the rights' doctrine did not remain embedded exclusively within the lines or types of case law within which they had originally emerged. Rather, they would intertwine with and/or start to influence other sets of discursive developments. In the recent *S&G* case for instance three related claims,

[1] More precisely, in *Alopka* (paragraph 32), the 'substance of the rights' doctrine was presented in the following lengthy formulation: "Concerning (…) Article 20 TFEU, the Court has held that there are very specific situations in which, despite the fact that the secondary law on the right of residence of third-country nationals does not apply and the Union citizen concerned has not made use of his freedom of movement, a right of residence cannot, exceptionally, without undermining the effectiveness of the Union citizenship that citizen enjoys, be refused to a third-country national who is a family member of his if, as a consequence of refusal, that citizen would be obliged in practice to leave the territory of the European Union altogether, thus denying him the genuine enjoyment of the substance of the rights conferred by virtue of the status of citizen of the European Union".

and connected questions, were referred to Luxembourg of which the first one asked whether the *Eind* and *Singh* premises could be applied to the situation at hand, the second one questioned the same in respect of the Court's *Carpenter* dicta and the third and final question sought clarification, with reference to *Zambrano* and *Dereci*, on the rights that, in that same situation, could be derived from Articles 20 and 21 TFEU.

In short, on the basis of such cyclic cue-taking practices, and their 'increasing returns' effects, self-reinforcing discursive dynamics continuously reproduced themselves within the case law as it evolved. With time, and following increasing returns logics, they created ever larger sequences of structures and arguments to be adhered to in the court room. In that manner, the settings of the disputes arising before Luxembourg, and the discursive frames within which they were articulated and debated, became ever more defined by the premises on which earlier cases had been debated and decided. To the extent that each cue-taking instance from the part of either litigants or national courts additionally entailed, even if only implicitly, a reinforcement of the Court's holdings by those actors, these sequences of arguments also grew ever more resistant to rollback as more time (and reinforcements) went by and they started carrying an ever stronger weight of prior approval.

8.3.2 Steering Through Precedent

As also emerged from the analyses, the incremental argumentative structuring prompted by these cue-taking processes did not evolve at random. Rather, the step-by-step developments were to a significant extent steered by the Court's engagement with its earlier case law. Or, just as the different judicial outcomes and their sequencing was not coincidental but instead, as recapped above, structured by iterative cue-taking, this cue-taking itself did not materialize coincidentally but was structured by precedent-based steering efforts or 'cue-giving' from the part of the EU judiciary. Adding one finding to the other, and in short, the observed autonomous judicial outcomes, and their sequencing, were to a large extent defined by the CJEU's forward-looking engagement with precedent.

First, as already indicated above, each new claim or question that, on account of cue-taking practices, was grounded in earlier CJEU dicta provided the EU judiciary, anew, with an opportunity to further set out these dicta. In the context of the new case, the Court could then again make choices in regard of which elements to emphasize over others in order to, in that manner, further prompt the likelihood that certain elements, rather than others, would be taken up by judicial interlocutors in new proceedings. On that basis as well, the Court held a discretion to steer the premises on which the cycle would be reinitiated. In addition, within the context of such general 'increasing returns' dynamics, the Court also had a number of more specific precedent-based mechanisms at its disposal by means of which it could steer the likelihood of cue-taking processes developing from certain cases or dicta rather than from others. That is, by adopting a forward-looking approach to the argumentative choices it made in regard of what types of provisions to emphasize over others, and with what level of detail, the Court held an additional leverage to incentivize the development of certain cue-taking paths rather than that of others. These more specific discursive mechanisms are assessed in the below and connected to the analytical observations.

To begin with, cue-taking practices were prompted especially strongly by CJEU dicta which were set out around broad or imprecise legal provisos. In line with the study's theoretical expectations, in the context of broadly phrased stipulations the Court generally enjoyed more interpretative discretion, and also needed to provide more guidance in the format of judge-made rules and their correct further application. Accordingly, to the extent that the Court chose, within the parameters of the questions posed, to ground its reasoning within imprecise, broad provisos rather than in strictly defined ones, it could strengthen the likelihood that further cue-taking from the part of private litigants and/or national courts would ensue. Second, cue-taking also strongly arose from Court dicta around hierarchically high-ranked norms; in the context of EU law, Treaty-based norms. This ties in, first, with the above observation, in that highest-order Treaty provisions are usually, by their very design, described with high levels of generality so that their application to a broad set of circumstances is secured. Furthermore, private litigants were also documented to be especially likely to take strategic cues from dicta around highest-order, Treaty provisions as this provided opportunities to infuse their own claims and submissions with the highest-order, normative weight attaching to such provisions. Accordingly, and as in the above, to the extent that the Court chose, within the parameters of the questions posed, to anchor its reasoning in Treaty-law stipulations rather than in secondary legislation, it could further stimulate the development of follow-up cue-taking practices.

In addition, a discursive discretion to incentivize or dis-incentivize cue-taking by litigants or national courts also accrued to the Court on the basis of how it chose to engage with its own prior dicta. The Court's discretion in respect of its own dicta, arguably, and in line with the theoretical expectations, even exceeded the leeway it enjoyed in respect of which type of legal provisions to emphasize over others. First, as follows from the above, to the extent that the Court chose, in the context of follow-up case law, to reinforce its dicta around broad and/or highest-order legal norms rather than the holdings which it adduced in respect of precise and/or secondary legislation, it could further incite or prolong the cue-taking following from the first set of dicta. Furthermore, the Court also enjoyed a discursive leeway in respect of the generality or, conversely, level of detail with which it described its dicta or referred back to them in the context of subsequent proceedings. That is, to the extent that the Court chose to phrase its holdings in general, programmatic terms rather than in very precise, narrow ones, it held a discretion to cast a wider rather than a more narrow net in regard of the types of disputative settings to which these holdings could be found to apply. Accordingly, by making conscious choices in regard of the level of detail with which it described its dicta, the Court could either compress or enlarge the categories of litigants that would be able to find strategic opportunities in them in the context of their own situations. Similarly, to the extent that these dicta could be connected to various types of on-the-ground legal disputes, rather than being confined to very specific circumstances only, they were also more likely to prompt requests for further guidance from the part of domestic courts. In the context of such follow-up litigation and questions, the Court then held a further discretion to either continue equivocating in respect of the precise contours and ramifications to be drawn from prior broad statements, or instead start delineating them over the course of new decisions. Such delineating, as the final mechanism, could be done either more or less gradually, so as to either more or less gradually reduce the cue-taking appeal of the holdings in question.

In light of these considerations, it can for instance be remarked that the strong precedent value, and the parallel long-lasting and premise-defining effects of the Court's 1990s dicta in the *Singh, Carpenter* and *Baumbast* rulings was not coincidental. All three rulings which, with the benefit of hindsight, provided the argumentative groundworks for much case law to follow, were premised on broad and/or Treaty-based provisos. In addition, in all three of them the Court pronounced itself on questions in regard of which, arguably, EU law provided little to no precise stipulations. Furthermore, in all three of them, the Court also grounded its holdings within broad, Treaty provisions but then refrained from defining the precise ramifications of these holdings beyond the precise factual constellation at hand, creating, in that manner, many opportunities for follow-up legal claims and engendering, in parallel, a strong demand for further clarification.

In the context of these follow-up claims and questions, the Court was then presented with new opportunities to continue setting out these earlier, broad holdings. Within the new contexts, it again held a discretion to emphasize certain elements rather than others and to do so using an either more or less generalist formulation. As emerged clearly from the analytical observations, the continued cue-taking effects engendered by *Singh, Carpenter* and *Baumbast* derived, to a large extent, from the Court's continued equivocation on the precise implications to be taken from these decisions and where to draw the contours. Furthermore, to the extent that the Court engaged with these earlier decisions, it also tended to stress the elements and holdings connected to broad and/or Treaty-based provisos in those decisions rather than, for instance, the considerations it had upheld in respect of secondary legislation. *Singh* was for instance invoked, shortly after its rendering, in *Carpenter* to reinforce the broad 'effet utile' considerations which the Court had advanced in that ruling. *Carpenter* was then similarly re-cited by the Court, also shortly after its rendering, and even in contexts materially unrelated to the facts which had given rise to the *Carpenter* proceedings, to rehearse the fundamental rights-related arguments which had been put forward in that ruling and the connection between such Treaty-based fundamental rights standards and equally broad 'effet utile' considerations (see *MRAX, Commission v Spain (C-157/03), Commission v Spain (C-503/03), Akrich*). *Baumbast*, third, was most often re-invoked by the Court in relation to the dicta which it had advanced in that ruling around Treaty-based EU citizenship provisions or around 'effet utile' considerations which it had also reinforced in that context (see *Zhu & Chen* or *Eind*). In this manner, the Court reinforced and prolonged the cue-taking appeal connected to these dicta.

Similar dynamics can also be highlighted at later stages, for instance, in respect of the more recent *Zambrano* ruling and the numerous follow-up claims and questions triggered by that ruling. As can be remarked, like the Court's *Singh, Carpenter* and *Baumbast* holdings, the dicta in *Zambrano* were anchored in broad, Treaty-based provisos on EU citizenship, which were described at high levels of generality and which opened up many questions (from the perspective of domestic courts) or opportunities (from the perspective of private litigants). However, and different from the prior *Singh*, *Carpenter* and *Baumbast* developments, the Court's further engagement with its dicta in *Zambrano* has been directed towards confining the statements adduced in that judgment. The cue-taking potential of these original dicta, however, has proven to be so large that, in spite of the Court's confining efforts (in *McCarthy, Dereci, Iida, O&S, Ymeraga* and *Alopka*), questions and claims premised on *Zambrano* continued arriving in Luxembourg. In addition, it can also be remarked that, whilst clearly narrowing down their scope, the Court did not overturn the central premises of *Zambrano*, nor did it fundamentally undermine them. Similarly, it has, in spite of the numerous follow-up claims and questions, also refrained from providing definitive closure in regard of their precise scope and implications (amongst others, by setting out baseline standards but leaving the final assessments to national courts). In that manner, the door has been left open for continued cue-taking practices to emerge and, on that basis, further opportunities to continue constructing these holdings to present themselves.

8.4 Precedents and Member States

8.4.1 Cue-Taking

Member States, when interacting with the Court, were found to get dragged into the above described discursive interactions between the Court and its judicial interlocutors. In addition, and in line with the theoretical expectations, Member States could also be found to take cues from prior Court dicta, and the progressive reinforcement thereof, when submitting their written observations to Luxembourg. In so doing, they at times even adopted premises from Court holdings in cases to which they had been the losing party.

As in the above, such cue-taking from the part of Member States was not prevalently observable during the earliest stages of the case law's development (1970s–1980s), arguably, again, as little jurisprudential material was available to take cues from. The image changed, however, as from the 1990s onwards. In the context of the *Carpenter* proceedings for instance, the UK government, against which the *Carpenter* claims were directed, argued—with explicit reference to *Singh* to which it had been the losing party—that Mr. Carpenter could not derive any residence rights in the UK from EU law as he was a British citizen and, hence, such rights were guaranteed to him in any event under domestic UK law. In spite of these arguments, as documented, the UK was nevertheless to find itself ruled against. At a later point in time, the Court's reasoning in *Carpenter* was then taken up by the Irish government in the written observations it submitted in *Zhu & Chen*. More specifically, the Irish government came to argue, on the basis of *Carpenter*, that as Mr. Carpenter had not been able to derive any rights on the basis of secondary EU legislation in his county of birth (instead such rights had been found to accrue to him on the basis of Treaty law), baby Catherine, in the *Zhu & Chen* case, could similarly not lay claim to any such secondary rights. The UK government which also intervened in *Zhu & Chen* drew on the Court's reasoning in *Baumbast*, to which it had also been the losing party, to argue that unlike the children in *Baumbast*, baby Catherine would not be deterred from exercising free movement rights if her mother were not granted residence rights within the UK. In addition, the UK also took more general cues from earlier CJEU fundamental rights-related dicta to contend that "whilst it was well established that fundamental rights form an integral part of the general principles of law whose observance the Court ensures", it was also clear that these rights could not "have the effect of extending the scope of the Treaty" (Report for the Hearing, *Zhu & Chen*, paragraph 101).

Such cue-taking from the part of Member States could also be observed in the later stages of the case law's development. In the 2006 *EPvCouncil* case for instance, the Council used the fundamental rights holdings the Court had advanced in *Carpenter* as a basis from which to question the Court's ability to review the contested provisos in abstract terms, i.e., without information on how exactly they would be implemented at national level. It referred to that effect, more precisely, to the sections of *Carpenter* in which the Court had emphasized the need to take specific circumstances of individual situations into account when assessing the obligations deriving from fundamental rights protection standards. More recently, in the context of *Zambrano*, the Belgian government based its submissions on the holdings which the Court had advanced in *Zhu & Chen, Baumbast, Singh* and *Carpenter*. This was done with a view to distinguishing, as much as possible, the circumstances that had given rise to these rights-extending rulings, from those at issue in *Zambrano*. For instance, the Belgian government contended that, different from the circumstances in *Zambrano*, both the *Zhu & Chen* and *Baumbast* cases had dealt 'clearly and exclusively' with the situations of Union citizens residing in a Member State other than that of which they held the nationality. Nevertheless, as documented, the Court's conclusions in *Zambrano* would significantly extend the scope and rights-expanding implications of both *Zhu & Chen* and *Baumbast* and sanction the Belgian actions at issue. At later stages then, the Court's dicta in *Zambrano* would become the starting point around which Member States oriented their arguments for a narrow interpretation of the new 'substance of the rights' doctrine introduced in that judgment. For instance, in *Dereci*, the eight governments which intervened argued that the principles laid down in *Zambrano* applied to 'very exceptional situations' only and that in any case 'the events which gave rise to the proceedings' in *Dereci* 'differed substantially' from those which had been at hand in *Zambrano*. Similarly, in *O&S* Member States held that the *Zambrano* principles related to 'altogether exceptional situations' only and, accordingly, could not be applied to the new proceedings at hand. In that light, Member States also drew attention to the fact that, different from the *Zambrano* case, the mothers of the children in *O&S* already held a right of residence and, in addition, that the third-country nationals in respect of which a right to remain was sought were not the children's biological fathers.

As outlined in the theoretical section, two interrelated reasons account for such *prima facie* counterintuitive behaviour. First, Member State governments are known to tend to prioritize the immediate material impact of legal decisions over the potential long-term effects of the Court's jurisprudence. Accordingly, when intervening before the Court, governments also tend to find that the short-term benefits to be gained from winning the dispute at hand are more important than the smaller chances of scoring a moral victory by openly challenging preceding CJEU statements. As a result, when submitting written observations, they will seek first and foremost to promote their chances of winning the case at hand. Often, and as the second reason, this will imply engaging in a 'battle by proxy', that is, presenting their arguments in a language and style recognized by the Court or rooted in lines of reasoning that were considered important in earlier decisions. Accordingly, in all, when intervening before the Court, rather than openly challenging prior Court rulings, Member States will use prior rulings as a point of departure from which to argue for a narrow interpretation or on the basis of which to distinguish the settings of the new case from those that underpinned prior unfavourable Court conclusions.

In the long run, however, such tactical adaptions to the legal rules of the game end up strengthening the Court's influence, rather than Member States' ability to call the tune. First, as clearly emerged from the analytical observations, the CJEU's judges inherently enjoy a privileged position within the court room as they get to decide what is or is not relevant and, accordingly, what weight is to be attached to Member States' arguments (whether or not grounded in prior Court statements). Second, and following dynamics similar to the discursive interactions with judicial interlocutors described above, to the extent that prior Court-constructed rules start shaping their own arguments, Members States are also left implicitly internalizing these rules in slow, incremental ways. In addition, and similarly in line with the above dynamics, inasmuch as Member States' arguments are shaped by previous Court-enunciated rules, this further strengthens the extent to which the argumentative settings of the case file overall are premised on prior Court holdings. This then further contributes to the leeway afforded to the CJEU to continue engaging with its prior dicta, emphasizing certain elements rather than others in order to, on that basis, steer the likelihood that certain of these elements, rather than others, will reappear before its bench.

8.4.2 Camouflaging Through Precedent

Reasoning by precedent was also registered to hold a number of additional advantages for the Court in the context of its interactions with Member States. To begin with, in general terms, to the extent that the precedent-based cue-taking dynamics between the CJEU and national courts as well as litigants strengthened well-functioning relations between the CJEU and these judicial interlocutors, this also reinforced the perception of the Court's activities taking place within a legally technical, judicial environment only and, by implication, of its decisions flowing from legally technical, neutral rules exclusively. This then alleviated the potential for political actors to claim that decisions had been motivated by non-legal, political considerations. In addition, it also strengthened the likelihood that Member States would feel compelled to adapt to the legal rules of the game when intervening before Luxembourg, reinforcing the above described discursive dynamics. Beyond these general observations, adherence to precedent also held a number of further, more specific strategic advantages for the Court.

First, by making strategic use of precedent-based reasoning the Court was able to be experimental in constructing its case law. More specifically, by adopting a forward-looking approach and for instance setting out new rights-extending conclusions in a general, open-ended manner, the Court could, as described above, strengthen the likelihood that follow-up claims and questions would arise before its bench. At the same time, the use of such an open-ended, indeterminate language also afforded flexibility to, in the context of such follow-up claims, either expand on the earlier holdings or, conversely, limit their contours depending on the levels of political antagonism registered. In other words, on the basis of such discursive practices, the Court enjoyed a strategic leeway to, in politically sensitive contexts, first launch 'trial balloons' in order to get a feel of the potential resistance. Clear illustrations of such strategic precedent-based practices were for instance found in the context of *Zambrano* and the follow-up proceedings prompted by that decision. Whilst *Zambrano* set off alarms in several European capitals, Member States' reactions eventually remained contained as, shortly after, in the context of *McCarthy* the Court seemed to indicate that the *Zambrano* outcome was limited to the precise circumstances that had given rise to that case. By additionally indicating that the holdings of *Zambrano* were 'specific in character' (in *Dereci*) or related to 'very specific situations only' (in *Iida*) the CJEU was able to further defuse the heightened state of political alert that had been triggered by the first ruling.

Second, and as a connected technique, to the extent that precedent-based reasoning enabled the Court to construct its decisions gradually, by means of step-by-step developments, it also provided the Court with a strategic advantage to set out the potentially politically sensitive implications attaching to its rulings in similarly slow, incremental ways. In that manner, the exposure of these implications could be deferred to later stages when it was possible to present them as derivations of pre-existing rules.

In one of the standard moves registered in that respect, the Court would for instance first set out what would later become key doctrinal principles as side issues in cases that essentially revolved around other premises. As an example, early on in *Singh*, the Court observed, largely in passing, that Mrs. Singh's right to reside in the UK as a British citizen was in any event guaranteed to her because 'as a principle of international law' a State could not expel its own nationals. The Court's conclusions in *Singh*, however, centred on different premises (inter alia, 'effet utile'-related considerations). The observation returned in the 2007 *Eind* case, again however, parenthetically. In the 2011 *McCarthy* decision on the other hand, the Court extensively engaged with these prior observations to conclude that, since the rights of nationals to reside in their state of nationality cannot—under a principle of international law—be made conditional, the Citizenship Directive (which includes conditionality clauses) could not be found to apply to the situations of nationals residing in their own Member State. In the recent *O&B* case then, the Court came to hold that, since secondary legislation could not be found to apply to the situations of nationals residing in their own state (on account of the said 'principle of international law'), the protection which accrued to 'returning' EU nationals in their home Member State had to be interpreted as flowing directly from Treaty law.

Another deferring discursive technique consisted of setting out what would become doctrinally important principles centrally rather than in passing, but to then establish a reason as to why the principle did not apply to the case at hand. The principle was created but since no material consequences attached to it, it did not incite political reactions. At later points in time however, it could be used as a basis from which to reach different, potentially politically sensitive conclusions which could then, similar to the above technique, be presented as flowing from pre-existent rules. Accordingly, in some cases where Member States were found to win the battle, the long-term ramifications of these cases would at later times cause them to lose the war. A telling example of such tactical precedent-based reasoning could be observed in the discourses the CJEU advanced in *EPvCouncil* and the ramifications that were later attached to these discourses in the *Chakroun* case. In *EPvCouncil* the Court had centred its argumentation around fundamental rights principles (which, as can be recalled, were themselves presented as deriving from prior fundamental rights dicta in *Carpenter* and *Akrich*). Ultimately however, these fundamental rights principles were found to not be in the balance in the case at hand given that the contested provisions did not 'expressly or impliedly' authorise Member States to act in a manner that would run counter to fundamental rights protection standards. When applied to a factual review of Member States' actions in the later *Chakroun* case however, the Court used these earlier fundamental rights holdings to support the politically sensitive conclusion that the minimum income-level requirement applied by the Netherlands breached the legal obligations flowing from the Family Reunification Directive.

As also emerged from the analyses however, these camouflaging, precedent-based techniques did not always yield the expected results. In spite of their careful grounding in pre-established judicial materials, the outcomes of for instance *Metock* or those of the above mentioned *Chakroun* ruling incited strong political reactions. Both judgments triggered several political discussions at both EU level as in national fora of which the tone was very anti-CJEU. Amongst others, government officials looked for ways in which to contain, as much as possible, the intrusions which the Court's scope-extending decisions were felt to have made into domestic immigration control capacities. In that light, the heightened state of political alert registered after the 2011 *Zambrano* decision (which was rendered only a few years after *Metock* and *Chakroun*) can at least in part be seen as also deriving from the already sensitive climate engendered by the latter two rulings. Whilst *Zambrano* established yet another scope-extending outcome, the grounds on which this outcome was based, however, were, as registered, sufficiently flexible to allow for backtracking readjustments over the course of follow-up case law.

After *Zambrano* (and *Metock* and *Chakroun*), the Court indeed appeared to retrench in respect of the further rights-extending outcomes that could be attached to the new 'substance of the rights' doctrine. At the same time however, the Court did not cut back in its reliance on strategic precedent-based techniques. Rather, if anything, it stepped up its efforts in that respect. As registered in both the quantitative and qualitative findings, the post-*Zambrano* period was one in which the incidence of precedent-based developments proved to be most intense.

Whilst in *McCarthy*, the first case rendered after *Zambrano*, the Court appeared to indicate that the ramifications of the latter judgment were limited in scope, it did not move beyond providing mere indications. In that manner, ambiguity continued surrounding the exact scope and implications of the 'substance of the rights' doctrine and the door was left open for a host of further claims and questions to arise. In addition, in spite of the generally 'rationalising' outcome of *McCarthy*, the reasoning in which this outcome was anchored moved back and forth between similarly more 'rationalising' dicta and, on the other hand, dicta from which arguably further rights-extending outcomes could be derived. For instance, in respect of the first category, the Court reinstated the 'derived rights rule' as constructed in its earliest case law and according to which the rights conferred on family members of Union nationals are not autonomous rights but rights derived through their status as members of the family. As an example of the second category of more liberal dicta, the Court invoked *Metock* to reiterate that the aim of secondary free movement law is to 'facilitate the exercise of the primary and individual right to move and reside freely within the territory of the Member States'. Similarly mixed discursive structures also reappeared in the Court's reasoning on the numerous follow-up claims and questions that, on account of the sustained ambiguity, continued arriving before Luxembourg. For instance, whilst *Dereci* provided, like *McCarthy*, indications that the application of the new 'substance of the rights doctrine' was limited in scope, the judgment did not offer definitive closure either and was at the same time, also like *McCarthy*, filled with rhetoric (inter alia, fundamental rights premises) that could easily be used to arrive at different conclusions. Further mixed discursive trends could also be observed in the additional cases which, for the same reasons, continued arriving before Luxembourg (*Iida, O&S, Ymeraga* and *Alopka*).

On the whole, whilst the Court continuously indicated that the implications of the *Zambrano* premises were limited in scope, the premises themselves were never explicitly challenged or revoked. Rather, and in line with the study's overall findings, they were used as points of departure from which litigants filed new claims and on the basis of which domestic courts articulated new questions. In that manner, these premises also became ever more embedded within shared judicial hermeneutics and, on that basis, ever more part of the canon of discursive standards to be adhered to in the court room. At the same time, whilst Member States voiced objections to the state of affairs outside of the court room, when submitting written observations to Luxembourg they similarly grounded their claims within the premises of *Zambrano* (or those of the follow-up rulings) from which they then argued for a narrow interpretation and/or sought to distinguish the new settings at hand from those that had underpinned the prior cases. On that basis however, to the extent that the prior Court-constructed rules started shaping their own arguments, Member States were left implicitly internalizing these rules in slow, step-by-step ways. In any event, should the Court apply the *Zambrano* principles in more extensive ways in the context of future case law, it will be much more difficult to counter the disliked principles, which by now have gained ever more traction within the judicial discursive environment, than it would have been when *Zambrano* was first rendered. This is precisely how, with time and through cumulative effects, precedents create outcomes that stick.

8.5 Conclusion

In all, the above analytical findings provide strong support for the expectation that reasoning by precedent allows the Court to strengthen its interpretative autonomy. Over time, on the basis of slow but certain developments, the Court was able to engender outcomes that clearly moved beyond what Member States' had intended. Where Member States were found to favour a minimally inclusive personal scope to be attached to EU family reunification law, the incremental outcomes attaching to the Court's case law moved in the opposite direction. CJEU decisions have, cumulatively, (i) expanded the categories of persons entitled to access EU family reunion rights, as well as (ii) limited the room for manoeuvre which Member States had counted on having created during Council negotiations.

The observations of autonomous Court behaviour however, and in line with the theoretical expectations, could only be observed over time. In fact, when reviewed in the short run, the Court was at times found to issue more prudent judgments. The implications of such more prudent judgments, however, were usually short-lived or would eventually turn out to be yet another building block on the road towards further scope-expanding outcomes. Generally, by adopting a forward-looking approach to the manner in which its discourses would function as precedents in later rulings, the Court was able to steer the long-term argumentative development of its case law, as well as the discursive climate within which its decisions were received and appraised by judicial interlocutors (litigants and national courts) and Member States (non-judicial interlocutors). The final, concluding chapter reflects on the broader relevance of these findings, their generalizability and their limitations. On that basis, avenues for further research are suggested.

References

Case C-35/82 *Elestina Esselina Christina Morson v State of the Netherlands and Head of the Plaatselijke Politie within the meaning of the Vreemdelingenwet; Sweradjie Jhanjan v State of the Netherlands* [1982] ECR 3723.

Case C-370/90 *The Queen v Immigration Appeal Tribunal and Surinder Singh, ex parte Secretary of State for Home Department* [1992] ECR I-4265.

Case C-413/99 *Baumbast and R v Secretary of State for the Home Department* [2002] ECR I-7091.

Case C-60/00 *Mary Carpenter v Secretary of State for the Home Department* [2002] ECR I-6279.
Case C-459/99 *Mouvement contre le racisme, l'antisémitisme et la xénophobie ASBL (MRAX) v Belgian State* [2002] ECR I-6591.
Case C-109/01 *Secretary of State for the Home Department v Hacene Akrich* [2003] ECR I-9607.
Case C-200/02 *Kunqian Catherine Zhu and Man Lavette Chen v Secretary of State for the Home Department* [2004] ECR I-9925.
Case C-157/03 *Commission of the European Communities v Kingdom of Spain* [2005] ECR I-2911.
Case C-503/03 *Commission of the European Communities v Kingdom of Spain* [2006] ECR I-1097.
Case C-540/03 *European Parliament v Council of the European Union* [2006] ECR I-5769.
Case C-1/05 *Yunying Jia v Migrationsverket* [2006] ECR I-00001.
Case C-291/05 *Minister voor Vreemdelingenzaken en Integratie v R. N. G. Eind* [2007] ECR I-10719.
Case C-127/08 *Blaise Baheten Metock and Others v Minister for Justice, Equality and Law Reform* [2008] ECR I-6241.
Case C-578/08 *Rhimou Chakroun v Minister van Buitenlandse Zaken* [2010] ECR I-1893.
Case C-34/09 *Gerardo Ruiz Zambrano v Office national de l'emploi (ONEM)* [2011] ECR I-1177.
Case C-434/09 *Shirley McCarthy v Secretary of State for the Home Department* [2011] ECR I-3375.
Case C-256/11 *Murat Dereci and Others v Bundesministerium für Inneres* [2011] ECR I-11315.
Case C-40/11 *Yoshikazu Iida v Stadt Ulm* [2013] OJ C 9/10.
Case C-356/11 & C-357/11 *O and S v Maahanmuuttovirasto and Maahanmuuttovirasto v L* [2013] OJ C 26/19.
Case C-86/12 *Adzo Domenyo Alokpa and Others v Ministre du Travail, de l'Emploi et de l'Immigration* [2013] OJ C 344/21.
Case C-87/12 *Kreshnik Ymeraga and Others v Ministre du Travail, de l'Emploi et de l'Immigration* [2013] OJ C 225/44.
Case C-456/12 *O. v Minister voor Immigratie, Integratie en Asiel and Minister voor Immigratie, Integratie en Asiel v B. Reference for a preliminary ruling: Raad van State—Netherlands* [2014] OJ C135/5.
Case C-457/12 *S. v Minister voor Immigratie, Integratie en Asiel and Minister voor Immigratie, Integratie en Asiel v G.* [2014] OJ C135/5.

CHAPTER 9

Conclusions and Suggestions for Further Research

9.1 The Court of Justice and European Integration

What do the above findings on CJEU autonomy, strengthened through precedent, mean for debates on the Court's role in processes of European integration? Whilst based on a single issue area, they do point at a generally strong CJEU capacity to move EU legislation beyond Member States' political preferences. As can be recalled, family reunification immigration law, on account of the sovereignty-sensitive implications attached to it, is a highly politicized issue area. On that basis, it also constitutes an unlikely or 'least-likely' case for observing a strong, or strengthened judicial autonomy as political vigilance over Court rulings that depart from preferred policy options can be expected to be high. In that light as well, if the Court generally stays close to dominant political preferences, it should have been especially prone (or obliged) to do so in an area as sensitive as this one. Whilst, of course, findings based on one area of law (albeit, embedding multiple sets of case law) cannot guarantee that the strategic use of precedents provides the Court with the same degree of autonomy in the context of all of its activities, in light of the issue area's sensitive nature, it can reasonably be inferred that such findings are likely to similarly transpire in other issue areas where conditions are similar or more favourable (that is, less politicized).

M. De Somer, *Precedents and Judicial Politics in EU Immigration Law*, European Administrative Governance,
https://doi.org/10.1007/978-3-319-93982-7_9

However, and if one central finding is to be taken from the study, such CJEU autonomy could only be observed over time. When observed in the short run, rulings moved back and forth between sometimes more autonomous outcomes and, at other times, more politically prudent results. This observation which—as observed in the introduction—is commonly found across both legal scholarship and political science on the Court, in fact defined the study's starting premises.

Building on prior understandings on these typically wavering dynamics from across both disciplines, and joining them together, the study advanced a number of interconnected hypotheses on how and why a step-by-step, sometimes wavering development of its case law strengthens the Court's interpretative autonomy in the long run. On that basis as well, the analysis was able to move beyond the empirical hurdles set by this idiosyncratic, fluctuating behaviour which, as documented in the first chapter, have long hindered judicial politics' literature as analysts can advance evidence in support of either Court autonomy or, instead, judicial deference, depending on the rulings they select for review. As documented in the present study, when observed over time, the wavering picture gives way for a clear image. In what follows the study's key findings are recapped. A next and third section considers their limitations and, on that basis, suggests avenues for further research.

9.2 Precedents and Judicial Politics: Key Findings

As traced at the beginning of the study, competing conceptions on whether, or the extent to which the CJEU enjoys an interpretative autonomy relative to the preferences of EU Member States have long occupied academic debates on the Court's role. In spite of three decades of sustained academic engagements, competing conceptions on the CJEU's autonomy continue to claim the attention of the field. In light of this sustained contestation, a meaningful engagement with questions on *how* the Court's autonomy was leveraged necessarily required an evaluation of *whether* autonomous Court behaviour could be registered to begin with.

For this purpose, the study started out by mapping Member States' dominant political preferences as articulated during the drafting stages on EU family reunification law. On this basis the study retrieved an *ex ante* benchmark against which to assess, in the subsequent analyses, *whether* the Court was able to develop judicially autonomous decisions, i.e., decisions that are independent from the identified dominant preferences.

As emerged from this exercise, Member States were especially watchful, and held the strongest sovereignty concerns in respect of those clauses regulating the categories of persons that would be covered by the new EU rules. Put differently, political contention especially surrounded the personal scope of the family reunion instruments to be established. Amongst others, national governments voiced fears around the high financial consequences which could result if broad categories of persons, and hence family reunion situations, would be covered by the new provisions. Similarly, governments also referred to concerns about their ability to continue taking their national immigration reception capacity into account. Across the board, as emerged, concerns mostly surrounded the immigration control discretion that would be retained at national level depending on the precise personal scope delineation of the new EU provisions. The more inclusive the latter, the more family reunification situations and hence, entry claims of foreigners, that would be lifted out of the sphere of exclusive domestic immigration control to instead become governed by EU law. Conversely, the more narrow the latter, the fewer the categories of persons, and hence numbers of family reunion situations, that would henceforth fall to be treated by EU law.

As was documented in the next sets of analyses, the judicial outcomes engendered over the years did not defer to Member States' political concerns around the legislation's personal scope. Instead, the Court's case law significantly widened the categories of persons able to lay claim to EU family reunion provisions and, on that basis, the number of immigration situations falling within the scope of EU law.

In line with the study's theoretical expectations, the key explanans for these observed judicial outcomes was found to reside, centrally, in the Court's forward-looking engagement with precedent-based discourses and in the legitimating as well as camouflaging effects deriving from such precedents over time. The workings and long-term effects of reasoning by precedent were examined in the context of the Court's interactions with, first, its judicial interlocutors, that is, national courts and private litigants and, second, in the context of its interactions with the EU Member States.

9.2.1 *Precedents and Judicial Interlocutors*

First, adherence to precedent was found to provide the Court with opportunities to strengthen smooth, well-functioning relations with domestic courts and litigants and, on that basis, the likelihood that its decisions would be positively received by these judicial interlocutors. As a second finding, by means of repeated precedent-based discursive interactions with its judicial interlocutors, the Court was also found to, with time, hold an ever larger discretion to influence the argumentative parameters underpinning its jurisprudence.

First, precedent-based practices provided the Court with a means to emit clear(er) signals regarding the weight and authority it attached to certain arguments or standards rather than to others. That is, by repeatedly reinforcing certain dicta rather than others, the Court was able to signpost which dicta it considered most important. Both private litigants as well as domestic courts adopted cues from these signals in order to maximize the effectiveness of their own legal strategies. Litigants, first, were found to be especially keen to take up on Court dicta when these dicta opened up opportunities to extend favourable EU law provisions to their own legal claims. In addition, when putting forward such claims, litigants tended to use the Court's prior reasoning as the basic template upon which they modelled their own arguments and discourses. Domestic courts, second, used the Court's dicta as points of orientation to filter out which legal questions required further clarification and, accordingly, further consideration by Luxembourg. In so doing, parallel to litigants' discursive strategies, national tribunals could also be found to discursively model their questions on the parameters of prior CJEU discourses. In line with the theoretical expectations, each new claim or question that arose before the Court's bench in follow-up to one of its earlier decisions provided the EU judiciary anew with an opportunity to further construct the earlier holdings. In the context of the new case, the Court could again make choices regarding which elements to emphasize over others so as to increase the likelihood that some of these elements, rather than others, would reappear before its bench. With time, self-reinforcing discursive structures were found to continuously reproduce themselves within the case law record as it evolved. In addition, to the extent that each cue-taking instance from the part of either litigators or national courts entailed, even if only implicitly, a reinforcement of the Court's holdings by those actors, these sequences of arguments also grew ever more resistant to roll-back as more time (and reinforcements) went by and they started carrying an ever stronger weight of prior approval. With time, 'lock in dynamics' could be observed as some of the standards and arguments repeatedly advanced acquired a taken-for-granted status which rendered their further explicit citation superfluous. Instead, such locked-in precedents then evolved in the building blocks which would dictate the premises of new precedent-based interactions. On that basis, and in the long run, the Court could shape, not only the disputative settings of the litigation likely to come before it in the near future, but also—more widely—the larger discursive frameworks in which this litigation was embedded and through which its decisions were received and appraised.

In respect of the second finding, by adopting a forward-looking approach to its dicta and the manner in which they would come to function as precedents, the Court held a leeway to steer the argumentative direction taken by the above described self-reinforcing discursive processes. To begin with, as already observed, each new claim or question that reappeared before the Court's bench in follow-up to one of its prior holdings, provided the EU judiciary with a new opportunity to construct its holdings. In the context of the new case, the Court could then again make choices in regard of which elements to emphasize over others so as to prompt the likelihood that certain elements, rather than others, would be taken up on by judicial interlocutors in new series of adjudicating activities. Furthermore, within the context of such 'increasing returns' dynamics, the Court also had a number of more specific discursive mechanisms at its disposal by means of which it could influence the likelihood of cue-taking processes developing from certain cases or dicta rather than from others. That is, by making conscious strategic choices in regard of which types of legal provisions to emphasize over others, and with what level of detail, the Court held an additional leverage to incentivize the development of certain cue-taking paths rather than that of others.

To begin with, cue-taking was prompted especially strongly by CJEU dicta which were set out around broad or imprecise legal provisos. In line with the study's theoretical expectations, in the context of broadly phrased legal stipulations the Court generally enjoyed more interpretative discretion, as well as needed to provide more guidance in the format of judge-made rules. Accordingly, to the extent that the Court chose, within the parameters of the questions posed, to ground its reasoning within imprecise, broad provisos rather than in strictly defined ones, it could strengthen the likelihood that further cue-taking from the part of litigants and/or national courts would ensue. Second, cue-taking practices also strongly arose from Court dicta around Treaty-based legal norms. This ties in with the above observation in that such highest-order, Treaty-based norms are usually described at high levels of generality so that their application to a broad set of circumstances is secured. Furthermore, litigants were found to be especially likely to take strategic cues from CJEU holdings around Treaty norms as this provided opportunities to infuse their own rights claims and submissions with the highest-order, normative weight attaching to such provisions. Accordingly, to the extent that the Court could or chose to, within the parameters of the questions posed, anchor its reasoning in Treaty-law stipulations rather than in additionally enacted, secondary legislation, it was able to further stimulate the development of cue-taking practices.

In addition, a discursive discretion to incentivize or dis-incentivize cue-taking by litigants or national courts also accrued to the Court on the basis of how it chose to engage with its own prior holdings. The Court's discretion in respect of its own holdings arguably even exceeded the leeway it enjoyed in respect of which type of legal provisions to emphasize over others. First, as follows from the above, to the extent that the Court chose, in the context of follow-up case law, to reinforce its dicta around broad or highest-order legal norms rather than the holdings it had adduced in respect of secondary legislation, it could further incite or prolong the cue-taking appeal following from the first set of dicta. Furthermore, the Court also enjoyed a discursive leeway in respect of the generality or, conversely, level of detail with which it described its dicta or referred back to them in the context of subsequent proceedings. That is, to the extent that the Court chose to phrase its holdings in general, programmatic terms rather than in precise, narrow ones, it held a discretion to cast a wider, rather than a more narrow, net in regard of the types of disputative settings to which these holdings could be found to apply. In the context of follow-up litigation, the Court then held a further discretion to either continue equivocating in respect of the precise contours and ramifications to be drawn from prior broad statements, or instead to start delineating them over the course of new lines of case law. Such delineating, as the final mechanism, could be done either more or less gradually, so as to either more or less gradually reduce the cue-taking appeal of the holdings in question.

9.2.2 *Precedents and EU Member States*

Member States were found to get dragged into the precedent-based interactions between the Court and its judicial interlocutors. Whilst political objections to the state of affairs could be registered outside of the court room, when intervening before the Luxembourg bench, national governments also took cues from the premises of prior Court decisions, even from decisions to which they had previously been opposed or to which they had originally been the losing party. Similar to the discursive dynamics taking place in the context of the CJEU's interactions with litigants and domestic courts, Member States sought in this manner to advance the most effective legal strategies with a view to, on that basis, promote their chances of winning the dispute at hand. As was also documented in prior studies, when intervening before the Court, national governments were found to prioritize the short-term benefits to be gained from winning the legal dispute at hand over the smaller chances of scoring a moral victory by openly challenging prior Court statements.

In the long run however, such tactical adaptations to the legal rules of the game ended up strengthening the Court's influence, rather than Member States' ability to call the tune. First, inasmuch as governments inscribed their claims and arguments within the discourses underpinning the precedent-based interactions taking place between the Court and its judicial interlocutors, these dynamics were strengthened and the leeway they provided to the Court to continue engaging with its own prior dicta was enlarged. Second, and similar to the discursive socialisation processes registered within the context of the Court's interactions with judicial interlocutors, to the extent that prior Court-constructed rules incrementally shaped their own arguments, Member States, in the context of their legal submissions, were found to, in slow but certain ways, internalize ever more Court-articulated dicta.

As a further set of autonomy-strengthening effects, precedent-based reasoning was also registered to provide the Court with a number of mechanisms by means of which it could camouflage the possibly politically sensitive implications attaching to its decisions. Amongst others, by adopting a forward-looking approach to its discursive choices and their precedent value, the Court could be experimental in setting out its dicta and, more importantly, their political implications. For instance, by putting forward new premises in a broad, open-ended phrasing, the Court could launch trial balloons in order to get a feel of the levels of political resistance to be expected. Depending on the first reactions, the Court could then, over the next lines of case law, either continue expanding on the first set of premises or, instead, retrench by introducing limitations or conditional requirements so that potential political antagonism would be defused. Another, connected technique consisted of setting out statements in a piece-by-piece manner over the course of several lines of case law so that the possible political implications attaching to these statements could be exposed in similarly slow, incremental ways or deferred to later points in time when it was possible to present them as derivations of pre-existing rules. For such purposes, the Court could for instance be found to first introduce what were later to become key doctrinal principles as side issues in cases essentially revolving around other premises. Or, as a related move, the Court sometimes established what were later to become doctrinally important principles centrally, rather than in passing, but then established a reason as to why the principle did not apply to the case at hand. The principle was created but since no material consequences attached to it, it did not incite political responses. By the time the political implications were revealed in full however, the Court's dicta on which they were grounded had acquired, through repeated reinforcements, ever more traction within the judicial discursive environment and were, on that basis, much more resistant to rollback. Accordingly, in some cases where Member States were found to win the battle, the long-term ramifications of these cases generally led them to lose the war.

9.3 Limitations and Suggestions for Further Research

It should be clear that, in spite of these findings, precedent-based reasoning does not render the Court omnipotent either. In what follows, three sets of limitations that apply to the study's results are highlighted. Against the background of these considerations, avenues for further research are suggested.

A first limitation relates to the observation that the study's premises and findings only provide insights into the Court's autonomy, that is, its ability to render decisions independent from dominant political preferences. The findings do not shed light on what happens to these autonomous outcomes once they leave the court room. Put differently, the findings do not speak for the effectiveness of the Court's decisions, that is, the extent to which they also command respect and compliance on the ground. On that basis, they only shed light on part of the picture that is the Court's overall authority which, as advanced by Staton and Moore (2011), can be seen as consisting of the sum of its autonomy and effectiveness.

A more complete understanding of the Court's authority, and as a first suggestion for continued research, can be expected to derive from interlinking the current research agenda with recent enquiries into the reception of, and engagement with, the Court's rulings by the actors at the receiving end of those rulings, that is, private parties, domestic courts and governments' executive or administrative branches. Recent research into the reception of the CJEU's decisions by domestic tribunals can for instance be referred to in this context (Mayoral, 2016; Dyevre, 2016; De Witte, Mayoral, Jaremba, Wind, & Podstawa, 2016). Fruitful links are also expected to derive from joining the current study's findings with recent enquiries into the reception of, and compliance with, Court decisions by national administrative or executive bodies (Blauberger, 2014; Schmidt, 2014; Martinsen, 2015). New studies in this direction could for example investigate to what extent a strengthened judicial autonomy feeds into, or instead hampers (if for instance, the Court strays too far from dominant political preferences), the effectiveness of the Court's decisions and, as follows, its authority.

As a second limitation, it should be remarked that in spite of the observed discretion the CJEU enjoys to steer the argumentative development of its case law, at no time does it hold full control or predictive powers over whether the cues it gives will effectively find a response with litigants, domestic courts and/or Member States. Many additional factors, beyond the Court's strategic discursive steering efforts define how and why certain points of law get picked up on by different sets of interlocutors. For litigants, first, differences in resources, legal aid and expertise available to them as well as differences in the rules governing legal standing before domestic tribunals are known to condition the likelihood of certain (categories of) litigants to find opportunities in certain points of EU law (see e.g., the overview by Alter, 2000). In relation to domestic courts, second, elements such as their respective areas of jurisdiction (and whether these areas are to a larger or smaller extent influenced by EU law), rules governing access to their benches and their relative hierarchical position within the domestic legal system have been highlighted as defining an either smaller or greater propensity of national judges to send in requests for clarification through the preliminary reference procedure (Ibid., Vink, Claes, & Arnold, 2009). Similar contextual or circumstantial elements can also be highlighted in respect of the Court's interactions with Member States. Whether or not national governments will intervene before Luxembourg and, on that basis, potentially go along with the discursive repeat games taking place between the Court and its judicial interlocutors depends on factors such as, inter alia, the availability of human and/or organisational resources, the national-level assessment of the influence that can be exerted through written observations or the general levels of litigiousness characterizing domestic societies (Granger, 2004).

In light of these limitations, building bridges between the findings presented in this study and recent research on the Court's interactions with litigants, domestic courts and Member States is expected to provide for further interesting insights. New research projects that can be highlighted in this respect include Mayoral's (2016) review into the factors that shape judicial trust as a principle encouraging cooperation between domestic courts and the CJEU, Dyevre's (2016) application of game theory to frame the conditions under which domestic courts will be more or less likely to accept or, instead, defy the authority of the EU judiciary, and De Witte et al.'s (2016) recent comprehensive assessment of, amongst others, the judicial dialogues taking place between Luxembourg and domestic tribunals. In respect of CJEU interactions with private litigants, examples to mention include recent critical reviews into the locus standi rules governing access of private parties to the Luxembourg bench (Carrera, De Somer, & Petkova, 2012; Carrera & Petkova, 2013). Third, in respect of interactions with Member States, interlinking the present findings with recent research by Dederke and Naurin (2017) on the factors that shape "when and why" national governments will submit written observations to Luxembourg is expected to provide for interesting new insights.

Finally, a third, important limitation to the precedent-based discretion accruing to the Court and, on that basis, to the study's findings, relates, rather than to the Court's interactions with external interlocutors, to its internal workings and dynamics. More specifically, it is probable that the strategic, forward-looking strategies available to the EU judiciary are constrained by the reality that different, future sets of litigation will be decided in different chamber formations manned by different (groups of) judges. As is clear, the Court is not a unitary actor and where a group of judges sitting on a first case may adopt a certain prospective approach it is unlikely to have any guarantee that a next group of judges presented with follow-up claims and questions will continue the line taken or favour the same approach. It is difficult however to retrieve insights on how, or to what extent, the Court's internal workings either facilitate or complicate forward-looking precedent-based practices as information on judges' individual positions or the deliberations taking place in Luxembourg is not publicly available. This is in fact where the study arrives at the "black box" that is the CJEU's internal workings (see Malecki, 2012; Vauchez, 2012; Dawson, 2014).

Insights into the workings and effects of reasoning by precedent would be greatly enhanced if they could include a better understanding of the Court's internal workings and deliberations. Whilst the study identified a series of consistent structures which, cumulatively, culminated in autonomous judicial outcomes, it cannot account for the manner in which the identified, longitudinal patterns were constructed or contemplated on from within, nor can it investigate the manner in which the daily operations of the Court either facilitated such long-term structural processes or, conversely, what factors may be identified as confounding them. Whilst the lack of public sources on these internal processes confounds the retrieval of academic insights on these matters, a number of recent analyses have nevertheless started paving the way towards understandings of this kind by using other, indirect means of obtaining information. They include, to begin with, Vauchez' (2012) evaluations of "commemorative materials" produced within the Court (Festschriften, tributes, eulogies, and jubilees). On the basis of these materials, Vauchez found support for his thesis that socialisation processes taking place amongst the Court's judges helped creating a shared "esprit de corps" which fed into judges' more general ability to maintain a collegial, consistent jurisprudence. As a further line of new research into the Court's internal workings, Malecki (2012) and Zhang, Liu, and Garoupa (2016) have conducted statistical analyses with the aim of retrieving insights from observations of aggregate trends and patterns within Court rulings. Malecki (2012) for instance reviewed data on the participation rates of individual judges against observations of the eventual disposition of cases in order to probe judges' respective degrees of influence on CJEU decisions. As such research further develops, it will be interesting to link its findings with the precedent-based patterns and structures identified in the present study and the autonomous outcomes engendered through these structures in the long run.

References

Alter, K. (2000). The European Union's Legal System and Domestic Policy: Spillover or Backlash? *International Organization, 45*(3), 489–518.

Blauberger, M. (2014). National Responses to European Court Jurisprudence. *West European Politics, 37*(3), 457–474.

Carrera, S., De Somer, M., & Petkova, B. (2012). The European Court of Justice as Fundamental Rights Tribunal: Challenges for the Effective Delivery of Fundamental Rights in the Area of Freedom, Security and Justice. *CEPS Papers in Liberty and Security, No. 49/August 2012*. Brussels: Centre for European Policy Studies.

Carrera, S., & Petkova, B. (2013). The Potential of Civil Society and Human Rights Organizations through Third-party Interventions before the European Courts: The EU's Area of Freedom Security and Justice. In *Judicial Activism at the European Court of Justice Causes, Responses and Solutions* (pp. 211–232). Cheltenham: Edward Elgar Publishing.

Dawson, M. (2014). How Does the European Court of Justice Reason? A Review Essay on the Legal Reasoning of the European Court of Justice. *European Law Journal, 20*(3), 423–435.

Dederke, J., & Naurin, D. (2017). Friends of the Court? Why EU Governments File Observations before the Court of Justice. *European Journal of Political Research, 2017*, 1–16.

De Witte, M., Mayoral, J., Jaremba, U., Wind, M., & Podstawa, K. (2016). *National Courts and EU Law. New Issues, Theories and Methods*. Cheltenham: Edward Elgar Publishing.

Dyevre, A. (2016). Domestic Judicial Defiance and the Authority of International Legal Regimes. *European Journal of Law and Economics, 35*(1), 1–29.

Granger, M.-P. (2004). When Governments Go to Luxembourg …: The Influence of Governments on the Court of Justice. *European Law Review, 29*(1), 3–31.

Malecki, M. (2012). Do ECJ Judges all Speak with the Same Voice? Evidence of Divergent Preferences from the Judgments of Chambers. *Journal of European Public Policy, 19*(1), 59–75.

Martinsen, D. S. (2015). *An Ever More Powerful Court? The Political Constraints of Legal Integration in the European Union*. Oxford: Oxford University Press.

Mayoral, J. (2016). In the CJEU Judges Trust: A New Approach in the Judicial Construction of Europe. *Journal of Common Market Studies, 55*(3), 551–568.

Schmidt, S. (2014). Judicial Europeanisation: The Case of Zambrano in Ireland. *West European Politics, 37*(4), 769–785.

Staton, J., & Moore, W. (2011). Judicial Power in Domestic and International Politics. *International Organization, 65*(3), 553–587.

Vauchez, A. (2012). Keeping the Dream Alive: The European Court of Justice and the Transnational Fabric of Integrationist Jurisprudence. *European Political Science Review, 4*(1), 51–71.

Vink, M., Claes, M., & Arnold, C. (2009). *Explaining the Use of Preliminary References by Domestic Courts in EU Member States: A Mixed-Method Comparative Analysis*. Paper presented at the 11th Biennial Conference of the European Union Studies Association, 24 April 2009, Marina del Rey.

Zhang, A., Liu, J., & Garoupa, N. (2016). Judging in Europe: Do Legal Traditions Matter? *King's College London Law School Research Paper, No. 2016-03*. London: King's College.

Appendix

Table A1 Cases on family reunification before the CJEU (1976–2016)

	Case number	*Name*	*Jurisdiction*	*Legal base*	*Provisions under review*
1	C-40/76	*Kermaschek*	PrelimRef	Free movement	R 1408/71
2	C-35/82	*Morson & Jhanjan*	PrelimRef	Free movement	R 1612/68
3	C-238/83	*Meade*	PrelimRef	Free movement	Art 48 EEC R 1408/71
4	C-267/83	*Diatta v Land Berlin*	PrelimRef	Free movement	R 1612/68
5	C-94/84	*Deak*	PrelimRef	Free movement	R 1408/71 R 1612/68
6	C-131/85	*Gül*	PrelimRef	Free movement	R 1612/68 D 75/363
7	C-147/87	*Zaoui*	PrelimRef	Free movement	R 1408/71 R 1612/68
8	C-297/88 & 197/89	*Dzodzi*	PrelimRef	Free movement	R 1612/68 D 68/630 R 1251/70 D 64/221
9	C-370/90	*Singh*	PrelimRef	Free movement	Art 52 EEC Art 48 EEC D 73/148

(*continued*)

M. De Somer, *Precedents and Judicial Politics in EU Immigration Law*, European Administrative Governance,
https://doi.org/10.1007/978-3-319-93982-7

Table A1 (continued)

	Case number	*Name*	*Jurisdiction*	*Legal base*	*Provisions under review*
10	C-206/91	*Kouia Poirrez*	PrelimRef	Free movement	Art 7 EEC Art 48 EEC R 1612/68 R 1251/70
11	C-243/91	*Taghavi*	PrelimRef	Free movement	R 1408/71 R 2001/83
12	C-64/96	*Uecker & Jacquet*	PrelimRef	Free movement + Citizenship	Art 48 EC Art 8 EC R 1612/68
13	C-356/98	*Kaba I*	PrelimRef	Free movement	Art 48 EEC R 1612/68
14	C-413/99	*Baumbast*	PrelimRef	Free movement + Citizenship	R 1612/68 Art 18 EC
15	C-60/00	*Carpenter*	PrelimRef	Free movement	Art 49 EC D 73/148
16	C-459/99	*MRAX*	PrelimRef	Free movement	D 68/360 D 73/148 D 64/221 R 2317/95
17	C-189/00	*Ruhr*	PrelimRef	Free movement	R 1408/71
18	C-257/00	*Givane & Others*	PrelimRef	Free movement	R 1251/70
19	C-466/00	*Kaba II*	PrelimRef	Free movement	Art 39 EC R 1612/68
20	C-109/01	*Akrich*	PrelimRef	Free movement	Art 39 EC R 1612/68
21	C-200/02	*Zhu & Chen*	PrelimRef	Free movement + Citizenship	D 90/364 D 73/148
22	C-157/03	*Commission v Spain*	Infringement action	Free movement	D 64/221 D 68/360 D 73/148 D 90/365
23	C-503/03	*Commission v Spain*	Infringement action	Free movement	D 64/221
24	C-540/03	*EP v Council*	Annulment action	Immigration law	D 2003/86
25	C-1/05	*Jia*	PrelimRef	Free movement	R 1612/68 D 73/148
26	C-10/05	*Mattern & Cikotic*	PrelimRef	Free movement	R 1612/68
27	C-165/05	*Commission v Luxembourg*	Infringement action	Free movement	R 1612/68

(*continued*)

Table A1 (continued)

	Case number	*Name*	*Jurisdiction*	*Legal base*	*Provisions under review*
28	C-291/05	*Eind*	PrelimRef	Free movement + Citizenship	Art 18 EC R 1612/68
29	C-57/07	*Commission v Luxembourg*	Infringement action	Immigration law	D 2003/86
30	C-87/07	*Commission v Malta*	Infringement action	Immigration Law	D 2003/86 ***Removed***
31	C-91/07	*Commission v Italy*	Infringement action	Immigration law	D 2003/86 ***Removed***
32	C-192/07	*Commission v Germany*	Infringement action	Immigration law	D 2003/86 ***Removed***
33	C-551/07	*Sahin*	PrelimRef	Free movement	D 2004/38
34	C-127/08	*Metock & Others*	PrelimRef	Free movement	D 2004/38
35	C-310/08	*Ibrahim*	PrelimRef	Free movement	R 1612/68 D 2004/38
36	C-578/08	*Chakroun*	PrelimRef	Immigration law	D 2003/86
37	C-34/09	*Zambrano*	PrelimRef	Free movement + Citizenship	D 2004/38 Art 20 TFEU
38	C-247/09	*Xhymshiti*	PrelimRef	Free movement	R 1408/71
39	C-434/09	*McCarthy*	PrelimRef	Free movement + Citizenship	D 2004/38 Art 20 & 21 TFEU
40	C-508/10	*Comm v Netherlands*	Infringement action	Immigration law	D 2003/109
41	C-256/11	*Dereci & Others*	PrelimRef	Free movement + Citizenship + Immigration law	D 2004/38 Art 20 & 21 TFEU D 2003/86
42	C-40/11	*Iida*	PrelimRef	Free movement + Citizenship + Immigration law	D 2004/38 Art 20 TFEU D 2003/109
43	C-83/11	*Rahman*	PrelimRef	Free movement	D 2004/38
44	C-155/11	*Imran*	PrelimRef	Immigration law	D 2003/86 ***Removed***
45	C-356/11 & C-357/11	*O and S*	PrelimRef	Free movement + Citizenship + Immigration law	D 2004/38 Art 20 TFEU D 2003/86
46	C-529/11	*Alarape & Tijani*	PrelimRef	Free movement	D 2004/38 R 1612/68
47	C-45/12	*Hadj Ahmed*	PrelimRef	Free movement	R 1408/71 D 2004/38 Art 18 TFEU

(*continued*)

Table A1 (continued)

	Case number	*Name*	*Jurisdiction*	*Legal base*	*Provisions under review*
48	C-86/12	*Alopka & others*	PrelimRef	Free movement + Citizenship	Art 20 & 21 TFEU D 2004/38
49	C-87/12	*Ymeraga & Others*	PrelimRef	Free movement + Citizenship	D 2004/38 Art 20 TFEU
50	C-423/12	*Reyes*	PrelimRef	Free movement	D 2004/38
51	C-456/12	*O & B*	PrelimRef	Free movement	D 2004/38 Art 21 TFEU
52	C-457/12	*S & G*	PrelimRef	Free movement + Citizenship	D 2004/38
53	C-513/12	*Ayalti*	PrelimRef	Immigration law	D 2003/86 ***Removed***
54	C 138/13	*Dogan*	PrelimRef	Immigration law	D 2003/86
55	C-202/13	*McCarthy & Others*	PrelimRef	Free movement	D 2004/38
56	C-244/13	*Ogieriakhi*	PrelimRef	Free movement	D 2004/38
57	C-338/13	*Noorzia*	PrelimRef	Immigration law	D 2003/86
58	C-469/13	*Tahir*	PrelimRef	Immigration law	D 2003/109
59	C-153/14	*K & A*	PrelimRef	Immigration law	D 2003/86
60	C-165/14	*Rendon Marin*	PrelimRef	Free movement + Citizenship	Art 20 & 21 TFEU D 2004/38
61	C-218/14	*Singh e.a.*	PrelimRef	Free movement	D 2004/38
62	C-304/14	*CS*	PrelimRef	Free movement + Citizenship	Art 20 TFEU D 2004/38
63	C-527/14	*Oruche*	PrelimRef	Immigration law	D 2003/86 ***Removed***
64	C-558/14	*Khachab*	PrelimRef	Immigration law	D 2003/86
65	C-115/15	*Secretary of State for the Home Department v NA*	PrelimRef	Free movement + Citizenship	Art 20 & 21 TFEU D 2004/38
66	C-133/15	*Chavez-Vilchez and Others*	PrelimRef	Free movement + Citizenship	Art 20 TFEU D 2004/38
67	C-165/16	*Lounes*	PrelimRef	Free movement + Citizenship	Art 21 TFEU D 2004/83

Abbreviations: EEC, Treaty establishing the European Economic Community; EC, Treaty establishing the European Community; R, Regulation; D, Directive; TFEU, Treaty on the Functioning of the European Union. 'Provisions under review' refers to the provisions which are the main subject of interpretation in the proceedings. It does not include all legislation referred to in the judgment. As detailed in the main text, the overview only takes account of proceedings involving at least one third-country national. The table is based on information available on 29 December 2017

References

Primary Sources

EU Law

Council Directive 73/148/EEC on the Abolition of Restrictions on Movement and Residence within the Community for Nationals of Member States with regard to Establishment and the Provision of Services [1973] O.J. L 172/14.

Council Directive 75/34/EEC Concerning the Right of Nationals of a Member State to Remain in the Territory of Another Member State after having pursued therein an Activity in a Self-Employed Capacity [1975] O.J. L 14/10.

Council Directive 90/364/EEC on the Right of Residence [1990] O.J. L 180/26.

Council Directive 90/365/EEC on the Right of Residence for Employees and Self-Employed Persons who have ceased their Occupational Activity [1990] O.J. L 180/28.

Council Directive 93/96/EEC on the Right of Residence for Students [1993] O.J. L 317/59.

Council Directive 2001/55/EC on Minimum Standards for giving Temporary Protection in the Event of a Mass Influx of Displaced Persons and on Measures promoting a Balance of Efforts between Member States in receiving such Persons and bearing the Consequences thereof [2001] O.J. L 212/12.

Council Directive 2003/86/EC on the Right to Family Reunification [2003] O.J. L 251/12.

Council Directive 2003/109/EC Concerning the Status of Third-Country Nationals Who are Long-term Residents [2003] O.J. L 16/44.

M. De Somer, *Precedents and Judicial Politics in EU Immigration Law*, European Administrative Governance,
https://doi.org/10.1007/978-3-319-93982-7

Council Directive 2009/50/EC the Conditions of Entry and Residence of Third-country Nationals for the Purposes of Highly Qualified Employment [2009] O.J. L 155/17.
Directive 2004/38/EC of the European Parliament and of the Council on the Right of Citizens of the Union and their Family Members to Move and Reside Freely Within the Territory of the Member States [2004] O.J. L 158/77.
Directive 2008/115/EC of the European Parliament and of the Council on Common Standards and Procedures in Member States for Returning Illegally Staying Third-Country Nationals [2008] O.J. L 348/98.
Directive 2011/95/EU of the European Parliament and of the Council on Standards for the Qualification of Third-country Nationals or Stateless Persons as Beneficiaries of International Protection, for a Uniform Status for Refugees or for Persons Eligible for Subsidiary Protection, and for the Content of the Protection Granted [2011] O.J. L 337/9.
Directive 2013/33/EU of the European Parliament and of the Council Laying Down Standards for the Reception of Applicants for International Protection [2013] O.J. L 180/96.
Regulation (EEC) No 15/61 of the Council on Initial Measures to Bring About Free Movement of Workers within the Community [1961] O.J. 57/1073.
Regulation (EEC) No 38/64 of the Council on the Freedom of Movement for Workers within the Community [1964] O.J. 64/965.
Regulation (EEC) No 1612/68 of the Council on Freedom of Movement for Workers within the Community [1968] O.J. 257.
Regulation (EEC) No 1251/70 of the Commission on the Right of Workers to Remain in the Territory of a Member State after Having Been Employed in that State [1970] O.J. L 142/24.
Regulation (EU) No 604/2013 of the European Parliament and of the Council Establishing the Criteria and Mechanisms for Determining the Member State Responsible for Examining an Application for International Protection Lodged in one of the Member States by a Third-country National or a Stateless Person [2013] O.J. L 180/31.
Resolution on Harmonisation of National Policies on Family Reunification adopted by the Meeting of Immigration Ministers, Ad Hoc Group Immigration [1993] SN 2828/1/93 WGI 1497 REV 1.

EU Documents

Commission Proposal for a Council Act establishing the Convention on rules for the admission of third-country nationals to the Member States, COM (97) 387 (final).
Commission Proposal for a Council Directive on the right to family reunification immigration, COM (1999) 638 (final).

Commission Amended Proposal for a Council Directive on the right to family reunification immigration, COM (2000), 624 (final).
Commission Proposal for a European Parliament and Council Directive on the right of citizens of the Union and their family members to move and reside freely within the territory of the Member States, COM (2001) 257 (final).
Commission Amended Proposal for a Council Directive on the right to family reunification immigration, COM (2002) 225 (final).
Commission Amended Proposal for a European Parliament and Council Directive on the right of citizens of the Union and their family members to move and reside freely within the territory of the Member States, COM (2003) 199 (final).
Common Position (EC) No 6/2004 adopted by the Council on 5 December 2003 with a view to adopting Directive 2004/.../EC of the European Parliament and of the Council of ... on the right of citizens of the Union and their family members to move and reside freely within the territory of the Member States, O.J. C 54/E12.
Communication from the Commission to the European Parliament and the Council on guidance for application of Directive 2003/86/EC on the right to family reunification, COM (2014) 210 (final).
Communication from the Commission to the European Parliament pursuant to the second subparagraph of Article 251 (2) of the EC Treaty concerning the common position of the Council on the adoption of a European Parliament and Council Directive on the right of citizens of the Union and their family members to move and reside freely within the territory of the Member States, SEC/2003/1293 (final).
Council of the European Union Outcome of Proceedings on the Commission proposal for a Convention on rules for the admission of third-country nationals, 6488/98 ADD 1.
Council of the European Union Outcome of Proceedings on the Commission proposal for a Convention on rules for the admission of third-country nationals, 6488/98 ADD 2.
Council of the European Union Outcome of Proceedings on the Proposal for a Council Directive on the right to Family Reunification, 6504/00.
Council of the European Union Note on the Proposal for a Council Directive on Family Reunification, 9738/00.
Council of the European Union Outcome of Proceedings on the Proposal for a Council Directive on Family Reunification, 11122/00.
Council of the European Union Outcome of Proceedings on the Proposal for a Council Directive on Family Reunification, 11524/00
Council of the European Union Outcome of Proceedings on the Amended Proposal for a Council Directive on the right to Family Reunification, 7144/01.
Council of the European Union Note from the Presidency on the Proposal for a Council Directive on the right to Family Reunification, 7145/01.

Council of the European Union Outcome of Proceedings on the Proposal for a Council Directive on the right to Family Reunification, 7612/01.
Council of the European Union Introductory Note from the Council Secretariat on the Amended Proposal for a Council Directive on the right to Family Reunification, 8491/01.
Council of the European Union Outcome of Proceedings on the Proposal for a European Parliament and Council Directive on the right of citizens of the Union and their family members to move and reside freely within the territory of the Member States, 1057/02.
Council of the European Union Outcome of Proceedings on the Amended Proposal for a Council Directive on the right to family reunification, 10857/02.
Council of the European Union Outcome of Proceedings on the Amended Proposal for a Council Directive on the right to family reunification, 11787/02.
Council of the European Union Outcome of Proceedings on the Amended Proposal for a Council Directive on the right to family reunification, 13053/02.
Council of the European Union Outcome of Proceedings on the Amended Proposal for a Council Directive on the right to family reunification, 13053/02.
Council of the European Union Outcome of Proceedings on the Amended Proposal for a Council Directive on the right to family reunification, 13968/02.
Council of the European Union Note from the Presidency on the Examination of Key Issues of the Proposal for a European Parliament and Council Directive on the right of citizens of the Union and their family members to move and reside freely within the territory of the Member States, 13298/02.
Council of the European Union Progress Report on the Proposal for a European Parliament and Council Directive on the right of citizens of the Union and their family members to move and reside freely within the territory of the Member States, 13942/02.
Council of the European Union Outcome of Proceedings on the Amended Proposal for a Council Directive on the right to family reunification, 14272/02.
Council of the European Union Outcome of Proceedings on the Proposal for a European Parliament and Council Directive on the right of citizens of the Union and their family members to move and reside freely within the territory of the Member States, 6147/03.
Council of the European Union Note from the Presidency on the Amended Proposal for a Council Directive on the right to family reunification, 6585/03.
Council of the European Union Draft Minutes of the 2489th meeting of the Council of the European Union Justice, Home Affairs and Civil Protection held in Brussels on 27/28 February 2003, 6906/03.
Council of the European Union Note from the General Secretariat of the Council on the Council Directive on the right to family reunification, 6912/03.

Council of the European Union Progress Report on the Proposal for a European Parliament and Council Directive on the right of citizens of the Union and their family members to move and reside freely within the territory of the Member States, 8675/03.

Council of the European Union Note from the Presidency on the Political Agreement on the Amended Proposal for a European Parliament and Council Directive on the right of citizens of the Union and their family members to move and reside freely within the territory of the Member States, 12218/03.

Council of the European Union Note from the Presidency on Political Agreement on the Amended Proposal for a European Parliament and Council Directive on the right of citizens of the Union and their family members to move and reside freely within the territory of the Member States, 12585/03.

Council of the European Union Draft Statement of the Council's Reasons on the Common Position adopted by the Council with a view to the adoption of a Directive of the European Parliament and of the Council on the right of citizens of the Union and their family members to move and reside freely within the territory of the Member States, 13263/03.

Council of the European Union Press Release 1962nd Council meeting Justice and Home Affairs, Brussels 21 September 2009, 13467/09.

European Parliament Legislative Resolution on the proposal for a Council Directive on the right to family reunification immigration, A5-0201/2000.

European Parliament Report on the Proposal for a European Parliament and Council Directive on the right of citizens of the Union and their family members to move and reside freely within the territory of the Member States, A5-0009/2003.

European Parliament Report on the amended proposal for a Council Directive on the right to family reunification immigration, A5-0086/2003.

European Parliament Legislative Resolution on the Council Common Position with a View to the Adoption of a Directive of the European Parliament and of the Council on the right of citizens of the Union and their family members to move and reside freely within the territory of the Member States, P5_TA(2004)0160.

Green Paper on the right to family reunification of third-country nationals living in the European Union (Directive 2003/86/EC), COM (2011) 735 (final).

Laeken European Council, Conclusions of the Presidency [2001] EU Bulletin 17.12.2001.

Report from the Commission to the European Parliament and the Council on the application of Directive 2004/38/EC on the right of citizens of the Union and their family members to move and reside freely within the territory of the Member States, COM (2008) 840 final.

Tampere European Council, Conclusions of the Presidency [1999] EU Bulletin No. 10/1999.

Cjeu Case Law

Case C-26/62 *NV Algemene Transport- en Expeditie Onderneming van Gend & Loos v Netherlands Inland Revenue Administration* [1963] ECR 13.

Case C-6/64 *Flaminio Costa v E.N.E.L.* [1964] ECR 585.

Case C-57/65 *Alfons Lütticke GmbH v Hauptzollamt Sarrelouis* [1966] ECR 205.

Case C-9/74 *Procureur du Roi v Dassonville* [1974] ECR 837.

Case C-43/75 *Gabrielle Defrenne v Société anonyme belge de navigation aérienne Sabena* [1976] ECR 455.

Case C-40/76 *Slavica Kermaschek v Bundesanstalt für Arbeit* [1976] ECR 1669.

Case C-120/78 *Rewe-Zentral AG v Bundesmonopolverwaltung für Branntwein* [1979] ECR 649.

Case C-35/82 *Elestina Esselina Christina Morson v State of the Netherlands and Head of the Plaatselijke Politie within the meaning of the Vreemdelingenwet; Sweradjie Jhanjan v State of the Netherlands* [1982] ECR 3723.

Case C-238/83 *Caisse d'Allocations Familiales de la Région Parisienne v Mr and Mrs Richard Meade* [1984] ECR 2631.

Case C-267/83 *Aissatou Diatta v Land Berlin* [1985] ECR 567.

Case C-94/84 *Office national de l'emploi v Joszef Deak* [1985] ECR 1873.

Case C-131/85 *Emir Gül v Regierungspräsident Düsseldorf* [1986] ECR 1573.

Case C-147/87 *Saada Zaoui v Caisse régionale d'assurance maladie de l'Ile-de-France (CRAMIF)* [1987] ECR 5511.

Cases C-297/88 & C-197/89 *Massam Dzodzi v Belgian State* [1990] ECR I-3763.

Case C-370/90 *The Queen v Immigration Appeal Tribunal and Surinder Singh, ex parte Secretary of State for Home Department* [1992] ECR I-4265.

Case C-206/91 *Ettien Koua Poirrez v Caisse d'allocations familiales de la région parisienne, substituée par la Caisse d'allocations familiales de la Seine-Saint-Denis* [1992] ECR I-6685.

Case C-243/91 *Belgian State v Noushin Taghavi* [1992] ECR I-4401.

Case C-64/96 *Land Nordrhein-Westfalen v Kari Uecker and Vera Jacquet v Land Nordrhein-Westfalen* [1992] ECR I-3171.

Case C-85/96 *María Martínez Sala v Freistaat Bayern* [1998] ECR I-2691.

Case C-356/98 *Arben Kaba v Secretary of State for the Home Department* [2000] ECR I-2623.

Case C-184/99 *Grzelczyk v Centre public d'aide sociale d'Ottignies-Louvain-la-Neuve* [2001] ECR I-6193.

Case C-413/99 *Baumbast and R v Secretary of State for the Home Department* [2002] ECR I-7091.

Case C-60/00 *Mary Carpenter v Secretary of State for the Home Department* [2002] ECR I-6279.

Case C-459/99 *Mouvement contre le racisme, l'antisémitisme et la xénophobie ASBL (MRAX) v Belgian State* [2002] ECR I-6591.
Case C-189/00 *Urszula Ruhr v Bundesanstalt für Arbeit* [2001] ECR I-8225.
Case C-257/00 *Nani Givane and Others v Secretary of State for the Home Department* [2003] ECR I-345.
Case C-466/00 *Arben Kaba v Secretary of State for the Home Department* [2003] ECR I-2219.
Case C-109/01 *Secretary of State for the Home Department v Hacene Akrich* [2003] ECR I-9607.
Case C-200/02 *Kunqian Catherine Zhu and Man Lavette Chen v Secretary of State for the Home Department* [2004] ECR I-9925.
Case C-157/03 *Commission of the European Communities v Kingdom of Spain* [2005] ECR I-2911.
Case C-503/03 *Commission of the European Communities v Kingdom of Spain* [2006] ECR I-1097.
Case C-540/03 *European Parliament v Council of the European Union* [2006] ECR I-5769.
Case C-1/05 *Yunying Jia v Migrationsverket* [2006] ECR I-00001.
Case C-10/05 *Cynthia Mattern and Hajrudin Cikotic v Ministre du Travail et de l'Emploi* [2006] ECR I-3145.
Case C-165/05 *Commission of the European Communities v Grand Duchy of Luxemburg* [2005] not yet reported.
Case C-291/05 *Minister voor Vreemdelingenzaken en Integratie v R. N. G. Eind* [2007] ECR I-10719.
Case C-57/07 *Commission of the European Communities v Grand Duchy of Luxemburg* [2007] ECR I-183.
Case C-87/07 *Commission v Malta* [2007] OJ C 82.
Case C-91/07 *Commission v Italy* [2007] OJ C 82.
Case C-192/07 *Commission v Germany* [2007] OJ C 117.
Case C-551/07 *Deniz Sahin v Bundesminister für Inneres* [2008] ECR I-10453.
Case C-127/08 *Blaise Baheten Metock and Others v Minister for Justice, Equality and Law Reform* [2008] ECR I-6241.
Case C-310/08 *London Borough of Harrow v Nimco Hassan Ibrahim and Secretary of State for the Home Department* [2010] ECR I-1065.
Case C-578/08 *Rhimou Chakroun v Minister van Buitenlandse Zaken* [2010] ECR I-1893.
Case C-34/09 *Gerardo Ruiz Zambrano v Office national de l'emploi (ONEM)* [2011] ECR I-1177.
Case C-247/09 *Alketa Xhymshiti v Bundesagentur für Arbeit—Familienkasse Lörrach* [2010] ECR I-11845.
Case C-434/09 *Shirley McCarthy v Secretary of State for the Home Department* [2011] ECR I-3375.

Case C-508/10 *European Commission v Kingdom of the Netherlands* [2012] OJ C174/7.
Case C-256/11 *Murat Dereci and Others v Bundesministerium für Inneres* [2011] ECR I-11315.
Case C-40/11 *Yoshikazu Iida v Stadt Ulm* [2013] OJ C 9/10.
Case C-83/11 *Secretary of State for the Home Department v Muhammad Sazzadur Rahman and Others* [2013] OJ C 331/6.
Case C-155/11 *Bibi Mohammad Imran v Minister van Buitenlandse Zaken* [2011] ECR I-0595.
Case C-356/11 & C-357/11 *O and S v Maahanmuuttovirasto and Maahanmuuttovirasto v L* [2013] OJ C 26/19.
Case C-529/11 *Olaitan Ajoke Alarape and Olukayode Azeez Tijani v Secretary of State for the Home Department* [2013] OJ C 225/20.
Case C-45/12 *Office national d'allocations familiales pour travailleurs salariés (ONAFTS) v Radia Hadj Ahmed* [2013] OJ C 225/40.
Case C-86/12 *Adzo Domenyo Alokpa and Others v Ministre du Travail, de l'Emploi et de l'Immigration* [2013] OJ C 344/21.
Case C-87/12 *Kreshnik Ymeraga and Others v Ministre du Travail, de l'Emploi et de l'Immigration* [2013] OJ C 225/44.
Case C-423/12 *Flora May Reyes v Migrationsverket* [2014].
Case C-456/12 *O. v Minister voor Immigratie, Integratie en Asiel and Minister voor Immigratie, Integratie en Asiel v B. Reference for a preliminary ruling: Raad van State—Netherlands* [2014] OJ C135/5.
Case C-457/12 *S. v Minister voor Immigratie, Integratie en Asiel and Minister voor Immigratie, Integratie en Asiel v G.* [2014] OJ C135/5.
Case C-513/12 *Ayalti* [2013] OJ C 63/6.
Case C-138/13 *Naime Dogan v Bundesrepublik Deutschland* [2014] OJ C 315/11.
Case C-202/13 *The Queen, on the application of Sean Ambrose McCarthy and Others v Secretary of State for the Home Department* [2013] OJ C 189/12.
Case C-244/13 *Ewaen Fred Ogieriakhi v Minister for Justice and Equality and Others* [2014] OJ C 315/15.
Case C-338/13 *Marjan Noorzia v Bundesministerin für Inneres* [2014] OJ C 315/18.
Case C-469/13 *Shamim Tahir v Ministero dell'Interno and Questura di Verona* [2014] OJ C 315/22.
Case C-153/14 *Minister van Buitenlandse Zaken v K and A* [2015] ECLI:EU:C:2015:453.
Case C-165/14 *Alfredo Rendón Marín v Administración del Estado* [2016] ECLI:EU:C:2016:675.
Case C-218/14 *Kuldip Singh and Others v Minister for Justice and Equality* [2015] ECLI:EU:C:2015:476.

Case C-304/14 *Secretary of State for the Home Department v CS* [2016] ECLI:EU:C:2016:674.
Case C-527/14 *Ukamaka Mary Jecinta Oruche and Nzubechukwu Emmanuel Oruche v Bundesrepublik Deutschland* ECLI:EU:C:2015:599.
Case C-558/14 *Mimoun Khachab v Subdelegación del Gobierno en Álava* [2016] ECLI:EU:C:2016:285.
Case C-115/15 *Secretary of State for the Home Department v NA* [2016] ECLI:EU:C:2016:487.
Case C-133/15 *Chavez-Vilchez and Others v Raad van bestuur van de Sociale verzekeringsbank and Others* [2017] ECLI:EU:C:2017:354.
Case C-165/16 *Toufik Lounes v Secretary of State for the Home Department* [2017] ECLI:EU:C:2017:862.

Other Sources

Belgian Government, Federal Public Service Foreign Affairs. (2009). Written Observation of the Belgian Government on the preliminary reference C-34/09 (Ruiz Zambrano), on file with the author (in French).
Court of Justice of the European Union. (2017). *Annual Report 2016. The Year in Review.* Retrieved from https://curia.europa.eu/jcms/upload/docs/application/pdf/2017-04/ragp-2016_final_en_web.pdf
Eurostat. (2015). *Residence Permit Statistics.* Retrieved November 11, 2015, from http://ec.europa.eu/eurostat/statistics-explained/index.php/Residence_permits_statistics
Eurostat. (2017). *Residence Permit Statistics.* Retrived December 28, 2017, from http://ec.europa.eu/eurostat/statistics-explained/index.php/Residence_permits_statistics
Former Council Official. (2014). Speaking at an Expert Seminar Organised by the Centre for European Policy Studies, CEPS, Brussels, 14 February 2014.
Government of the Netherlands. (2011). *Position Paper—The Dutch Standpoint on EU Migration Policy.* On file with the author.
Report for the Hearing in Case (C-370/90) *Singh*, on file with the author (in English).
Report for the Hearing in Case (C-200/02) *Zhu & Chen*, on file with the author (in English).
Report for the Hearing in Case (C-291/05) *Eind*, on file with the author (in Dutch).
Report for the Hearing in Case (C-540/03) *EPvCouncil*, on file with the author (in Dutch).
Report for the Hearing in Case (C-1/05) *Jia*, on file with the author (in Swedish).
Report for the Hearing in Case (C-578/08) *Chakroun*, on file with the author (in Dutch).

Report for the Hearing in Case (C-34/09) *Zambrano*, on file with the author (in French).
Report for the Hearing in Case (C-434/09) *McCarthy*, on file with the author (in English).
Report for the Hearing in Case (C-256/11) *Dereci*, on file with the author (in German).
Report for the Hearing in Case (C-356/11 & C-357/11) *O&S*, on file with the author (in Finnish).
Tweede Kamer der Staten-Generaal. (2010). Brief van de Minister van justitie aan de Voorzitter van de Tweede Kamer der Staten-Generaal. Vergaderjaar 2009-2010, 32175 Nr. 8.
Tweede Kamer der Staten-Generaal. (2011). Brief van de Minister voor immigratie en asiel aan de Voorzitter van de Tweede Kamer der Staten-Generaal. Vergaderjaar 2010-2011, 19637 Nr. 1408.

Literature

Acierno, S. (2003). The *Carpenter* Judgment: Fundamental Rights and the Limits of the Community Legal Order. *European Law Review, 28*(3), 398–407.
Adam, S., & Van Elsuwege, P. (2012). Citizenship Rights and the Federal Balance between the European Union and its Member States: Comment on *Dereci*. *European Law Review, 37*(2), 176–190.
Adams, M., De Waele, H., Meeusen, J., & Straetmans, G. (2013). *Judging Europe's Judges: The Legitimacy of the Case Law of the European Court of Justice*. Oxford: Hart Publishing.
Alter, K. (1996). The European Court's Political Power. *West European Politics, 19*(3), 458–487.
Alter, K. (1998). Who are the Masters of the Treaty? European Governments and the European Court of Justice. *International Organization, 25*(1), 125–152.
Alter, K. (2000). The European Union's Legal System and Domestic Policy: Spillover or Backlash? *International Organization, 45*(3), 489–518.
Alter, K. (2001). *Establishing the Supremacy of European Law: The Making of an International Rule of Law in Europe*. Oxford: Oxford University Press.
Alter, K. (2008). Agents or Trustees? International Courts in their Political Context. *European Journal of International Relations, 14*(1), 33–63.
Alter, K. (2009). *The European Court's Political Power*. Oxford: Oxford University Press.
Alter, K., Dehousse, R., & Vanberg, G. (2002). Law, Political Science and EU Legal Studies. An Interdisciplinary Project? *European Union Politics, 3*(1), 113–136.
Alter, K., & Vargas, J. (2000). Explaining Variation in the Use of European Litigation Strategies: European Community Law and British Gender Equality Policy. *Comparative Political Studies, 33*(4), 452–482.

Armstrong, A. (1998). Legal Integration: Theorizing the Legal Dimension of European Integration. *Journal of Common Market Studies, 36*(2), 156–174.
Arnull, A. (1993). Owning up to Fallibility: Precedent and the Court of Justice. *Common Market Law Review, 30*(2), 247–266.
Arnull, A. (2008). The Americanization of EU Law Scholarship. In A. Arnull, P. Eeckhout, & T. Tridimas (Eds.), *Continuity and Change in EU Law: Essays in Honour of Sir Francis Jacobs* (pp. 415–431). Oxford: Oxford University Press.
Bankowski, Z., MacCormick, N., Morawski, L., & Ruiz Miguel, A. (1997). Rationales for Precedent. In N. MacCormick & R. Summers (Eds.), *Interpreting Precedents: A Comparative Study* (pp. 481–503). Aldershot: Ashgate Publishing.
Barceló, J. (1997). Precedent in European Community Law. In N. MacCormick & R. Summers (Eds.), *Interpreting Precedents: A Comparative Study* (pp. 407–436). Aldershot: Ashgate Publishing.
Barnard, C., & Odudu, O. (2009). *The Outer Limits of European Union Law*. Portland, OR: Hart Publishing.
Barrett, G. (2003). Family Matters: European Community Law and Third-Country Family Members. *Common Market Law Review, 40*(2), 369–421.
Beck, G. (2012). *The Legal Reasoning of the Court of Justice of the EU*. Oxford: Hart Publishing.
Bengoetxea, J. (1993). *The Legal Reasoning of the European Court of Justice*. Oxford: Claredon Press.
Bengoetxea, J., MacCormick, N., & Moral Soriano, L. (2001). Integration and Integrity in the Legal Reasoning of the European Court of Justice. In G. de Búrca & J. Weiler (Eds.), *The European Court of Justice* (pp. 43–85). Oxford: Oxford University Press.
Bernard, N. (1996). Discrimination and Free Movement in EC Law. *International and Comparative Law Quarterly, 45*(1), 82–108.
Bierbach, J. (2008). Case Note on *Eind*. *European Constitutional Law Review, 4*, 344–362.
Blauberger, M. (2012). With Luxembourg in Mind...The Remaking of National Policies in the Face of ECJ Jurisprudence. *Journal of European Public Policy, 19*(1), 109–126.
Blauberger, M. (2014). National Responses to European Court Jurisprudence. *West European Politics, 37*(3), 457–474.
Blauberger, M., & Weiss, M. (2013). 'If You Can't Beat Me, Join Me!' How the Commission Pushed and Pulled Member States into Legislating Defence Procurement. *Journal of European Public Policy, 20*(8), 1120–1138.
Block, L. (2015). Regulating Membership: Explaining Restriction and Stratification of Family Migration in Europe. *Journal of Family Issues, 36*(11), 1433–1452.
Bobek, M. (2013). Of Feasibility and Silent Elephants: The Legitimacy of the Court of Justice through the Eyes of National Courts. In I. M. Adams, H. de

Waele, J. Meeusen, & G. Straetmans (Eds.), *Judging Europe's Judges—The Legitimacy of the Case Law of the European Court of Justice* (pp. 197–234). Oxford: Hart Publishing.

Bonjour, S., & Vink, M. (2013). When Europeanization Backfires: The Normalization of European Migration Politics. *Acta Politica, 48*(4), 389–407.

Börzel, T. (2006). Participation through Law Enforcement. *Comparative Political Studies, 39*(1), 128–152.

Burley, A.-M., & Mattli, W. (1993). Europe before the Court: A Political Theory of Legal Integration. *International Organization, 47*(1), 41–76.

Cambien, N. (2012). *EU Citizenship and the ECJ: Why Care About Primary Carers?* Paper presented at the UACES annual conference, 3–5 September 2012, Passau.

Carens, J. (2003). Who Should Get in? The Ethics of Immigration Admissions. *Ethics & International Affairs, 17*(1), 95–110.

Carrera, S., De Somer, M., & Petkova, B. (2012). The European Court of Justice as Fundamental Rights Tribunal: Challenges for the Effective Delivery of Fundamental Rights in the Area of Freedom, Security and Justice. *CEPS Papers in Liberty and Security, No. 49/August 2012.* Brussels: Centre for European Policy Studies.

Carrera, S., & Petkova, B. (2013). The Potential of Civil Society and Human Rights Organizations through Third-Party Interventions before the European Courts: The EU's Area of Freedom Security and Justice. In *Judicial Activism at the European Court of Justice Causes, Responses and Solutions* (pp. 211–232). Cheltenham: Edward Elgar Publishing.

Carruba, C. (2005). Courts and Compliance in International Regulatory Regimes. *The Journal of Politics, 67*(3), 669–689.

Carruba, C., Gabel, M., & Hankla, C. (2008). Judicial Behavior under Political Constraints: Evidence from the European Court of Justice. *American Political Science Review, 102*(4), 435–452.

Carruba, J., Gabel, M., & Hankla, C. (2012). Understanding the Role of the European Court of Justice in European Integration. *American Political Science Review, 106*(1), 214–223.

Carrubba, C., & Murrah, L. (2005). Legal Integration and the Use of the Preliminary Ruling Process in the European Union. *International Organization, 59*(2), 399–418.

Chalmers, D., & Chaves, M. (2012). The Reference Points of EU Judicial Politics. *Journal of European Public Policy, 19*(1), 25–42.

Cholewinski, R. (2002). Family Reunification and Conditions Placed on Family Members: Dismantling a Fundamental Human Right. *European Journal of Migration and Law, 4*(3), 271–290.

Cichowski, R. (1998). Integrating the Environment. *Journal of European Public Policy, 5*(3), 387–405.

Cichowski, R. (2001). Judicial Rulemaking and the Institutionalization of EU Sex Equality Policy. In A. Stone Sweet, W. Sandholtz, & N. Fligstein (Eds.), *The Institutionalization of Europe*. Oxford: Oxford University Press.

Cichowski, R. (2004). Women's Rights, the European Court, and Supranational Constitutionalism. *Law & Society Review, 38*(3), 489–512.

Cichowski, R. (2007). *The European Court and Civil Society: Litigation, Mobilization and Governance*. Cambridge: Cambridge University Press.

Conant, L. (2002). *Justice Contained: Law and Politics in the European Union*. Ithaca, NY: Cornell University Press.

Conway, G. (2012). *The Limits of Legal Reasoning and the European Court of Justice*. Cambridge: Cambridge University Press.

Costello, C. (2014). Article 33—Family and Professional Life. In S. Peers, T. Hervey, J. Kenner, & A. Ward (Eds.), *The EU Charter of Fundamental Rights: A Commentary* (pp. 891–925). Oxford: Hart Publishing.

Creswell, J., & Clark, V. (2010). *Designing and Conducting Mixed Methods Research*. Thousand Oaks, CA: SAGE Publications.

Currie, S. (2009). Accelerated Justice or a Step Too Far? Residence Rights of Non-EU Family Members and the Court's Ruling in *Metock*. *European Law Review, 34*(2), 310–326.

Davies, G. (2012). Activism Relocated. The Self-restraint of the European Court of Justice in its National Context. *Journal of European Public Policy, 19*(1), 76–91.

Davies, G. (2016). The European Union Legislature as an Agent of the European Court of Justice. *Journal of Common Market Studies, 54*(4), 1–16.

Dawson, M. (2014). How Does the European Court of Justice Reason? A Review Essay on the Legal Reasoning of the European Court of Justice. *European Law Journal, 20*(3), 423–435.

De Búrca, G. (2001). Introduction. In G. de Búrca & J. Weiler (Eds.), *The European Court of Justice* (pp. 1–8). Oxford: Oxford University Press.

De Búrca, G. (2005). Rethinking Law in Neofunctionalist Theory. *Journal of European Public Policy, 12*(2), 310–326.

Dederke, J., & Naurin, D. (2017). Friends of the Court? Why EU Governments File Observations before the Court of Justice. *European Journal of Political Research, 2017*, 1–16.

Derlén, M., & Lindholm, J. (2014). Goodbye *van Gend en Loos*, Hello *Bosman*? Using Network Analysis to Measure the Importance of Individual CJEU Judgments. *European Law Journal, 20*(5), 667–687.

De Somer, M. (2012). Enhanced Competences for the European Court of Justice: "Re-shuffling" the Dynamics of EU Migration Policy-Making? *LSE Migration Studies Unit Working Papers, No. 2012/01*. London: London School of Economics and Political Science.

De Somer, M., & Vink, M. (2015). 'Precedent' and Fundamental Rights in the CJEU's Case Law on Family Reunification Immigration. *European Integration online Papers, 19*, 1–33.

De Witte, M., Dawson, M., & Muir, E. (2013). *Judicial Activism at the European Court of Justice Causes, Responses and Solutions.* Cheltenham: Edward Elgar Publishing.

De Witte, M., Mayoral, J., Jaremba, U., Wind, M., & Podstawa, K. (2016). *National Courts and EU Law. New Issues, Theories and Methods.* Cheltenham: Edward Elgar Publishing.

Dyevre, A. (2010). Unifying the Field of Comparative Judicial Politics: Towards a General Theory of Judicial Behavior. *European Political Science Review, 2*(2), 297–327.

Dyevre, A. (2016). Domestic Judicial Defiance and the Authority of International Legal Regimes. *European Journal of Law and Economics, 35*(1), 1–29.

Eisele, K. (2014). *The External Dimension of the EU's Migration Policy. Different Legal Positions of Third-Country Nationals in the EU: A Comparative Perspective.* Leiden: Martinus Nijhoff Publishers.

Fernhout, R., & Wever, R. (2011). Follow-up of the Case Law of the Court of Justice of the European Union. Thematic Report 2010–2011. In *European Network on Free Movement of Workers Within the European Union.* Nijmegen: University of Nijmegen, Centre for Migration Law.

Fetzer, J. (2012). Public Opinion and Populism. In M. Rosenblum & D. Tichenor (Eds.), *The Oxford Handbook of the Politics of International Migration* (pp. 301–323). Oxford: Oxford University Press.

Fligstein, N., & Stone Sweet, A. (2002). Constructing Polities and Markets: An Institutionalist Account of European Integration. *American Journal of Sociology, 107*(5), 1206–1243.

Fowler, J., & Jeon, S. (2008). The Authority of Supreme Court Precedent. *Social Networks, 30*, 16–30.

Freeman, P., Hansen, R., & Leal, D. (2013). *Immigration and Public Opinion in Liberal Democracies.* New York: Routledge.

Garrett, G. (1992). International Cooperation and Institutional Choice: The European Community's Internal Market. *International Organization, 46*(2), 533–560.

Garrett, G. (1995). The Politics of Legal Integration in the European Union. *International Organization, 49*(1), 171–181.

Garrett, G., Kelemen, R. D., & Schulz, H. (1998). The European Court of Justice, National Governments, and Legal Integration in the European Union. *International Organization, 52*(1), 149–176.

Garrett, G., & Weingast, B. (1993). Ideas, Interests and Institutions: Constructing the European Community's Internal Market. In J. Goldstein & R. Keohane

(Eds.), *Ideas and Foreign Policy: Beliefs, Institutions, and Political Change* (pp. 173–206). Ithaca, NY: Cornell University Press.

Geddes, A. (2003). *The Politics of Migration and Immigration in Europe*. London: SAGE Publications.

George, A., & Bennett, A. (2005). *Case Studies and Theory Development in the Social Sciences*. Cambridge, MA: MIT Press.

Gerring, J. (2007). *Case Study Research: Principles and Practices*. Cambridge: Cambridge University Press.

Goedings, S. (2006). *Labor Migration in an Integrating Europe. National Migration Policies and the Free Movement of Workers, 1950–1968*. Den Haag: Sdu Uitgevers.

Golding, M. (1984). *Legal Reasoning*. New York: Knopf.

Goldner-Lang, I. (2018, January 24). Towards 'Judicial Passivism' in EU Migration and Asylum Law? Preliminary Thoughts for the Final Plenary Session of the 2018 Odysseus Conference. *Blogpost on EU Immigration and Asylum Law and Policy*. Retrieved from http://eumigrationlawblog.eu/towards-judicial-passivism-in-eu-migration-and-asylum-law-preliminary-thoughts-for-the-final-plenary-session-of-the-2018-odysseus-conference/

Granger, M.-P. (2004). When Governments Go to Luxembourg…: The Influence of Governments on the Court of Justice. *European Law Review, 29*(1), 3–31.

Groenendijk, K. (2009). Forty Years of Free Movement of Workers: Has It Been A Success and Why? In P. Minderhoud & N. Trimikliniotis (Eds.), *Rethinking the Free Movement of Workers: The European Challenges Ahead* (pp. 11–23). Nijmegen: Wolf Legal Publishers.

Groenendijk, K. (2011). Pre-departure Integration Strategies in the European Union: Integration or Immigration Policy? *European Journal of Migration and Law, 13*, 1–30.

Guild, E. (2009). Free Movement of Workers: From Third Country National to Citizen of the Union. In P. Minderhoud & N. Trimikliniotis (Eds.), *Rethinking the Free Movement of Workers: The European Challenges Ahead* (pp. 25–38). Nijmegen: Wolf Legal Publishers.

Guild, E., & Niessen, J. (1996). *The Developing Immigration and Asylum Policies of the European Union. Adopted Conventions, Resolutions, Recommendations, Decisions and Conclusions*. The Hague: Kluwer Law International.

Guild, E., Peers, S., & Tomkin, J. (2014). *The EU Citizenship Directive: A Commentary*. Oxford: Oxford University Press.

Haas, E. (1958). *The Uniting of Europe*. Stanford, CA: Stanford University Press.

Hailbronner, K., & Thym, D. (2011). Comment on *Zambrano*. *Common Market Law Review, 48*, 1253–1270.

Hanf, D. (2011). 'Reverse Discrimination' in EU Law: Constitutional Aberration, Constitutional Necessity, or Judicial Choice? *Maastricht Journal of European and Comparative Law, 18*, 29–61.

Hardy, J. (2012). The Objective of Directive 2003/86 Is to Promote the Family Reunification of Third Country Nationals. *European Journal of Migration and Law, 14*, 439–452.

Hart, H. L. A. (1994). *The Concept of Law*. Oxford: Clarendon Press.

Hedemann-Robinson, M. (1996). Third-Country Nationals, European Union Citizenship and Free Movement of Persons: A Time for Bridges rather than Divisions. *Yearbook of European Law, 16*(1), 321–362.

Hedemann-Robinson, M. (1998). From Object to Subject?: Non-EC Nationals and the Draft Proposal of the Commission for a Council Act Establishing the Rules for the Admission of Third Country Nationals to the Member States. *Yearbook of European Law, 18*(1), 289–335.

Hofstotter, B. (2005). A Cascade of Rights, or Who shall Care for Little Catherine? Some Reflections on the Chen Case. *European Law Review, 30*(4), 548–558.

Iglesias Sanchez, S. (2012). The Court and the Charter: The Impact of the Entry into Force of the Lisbon Treaty on the ECJ's Approach to Fundamental Rights. *Common Market Law Review, 49*(5), 1565–1612.

Itzcovich, G. (2009). The Interpretation of Community Law by the European Court of Justice. *German Law Journal, 10*(5), 537–560.

Jacob, M. (2014). *Precedents and Case-based Reasoning in the European Court of Justice: Unfinished Business*. New York: Cambridge University Press.

Joerges, C. (1996). Taking the Law Seriously: On Political Science and the Role of Law in the Process of European Integration. *European Law Journal, 2*(2), 105–135.

Joppke, C. (1998a). Immigration Challenges the Nation-State. In C. Joppke (Ed.), *Challenge to the Nation-State. Immigration in Western Europe and the United States* (pp. 5–48). New York: Oxford University Press.

Joppke, C. (1998b). Why Liberal States Accept Unwanted Immigration. *World Politics, 50*(2), 266–293.

Joppke, C. (1999). *Immigration and the Nation-State. The United States, Germany and Great Britain*. Oxford: Oxford University Press.

Joppke, C. (2001). The Legal-domestic Sources of Immigrant Rights: The United States, Germany and the European Union. *Comparative Political Studies, 34*, 339–366.

Jupille, J. (2004). *Procedural Politics: Issues, Influence and Institutional Choice in the European Union*. Cambridge: Cambridge University Press.

Kagan, R. (2007). Globalization and Legal Change: The 'Americanization' of European Law? *Regulation & Governance, 1*(2), 99–120.

Kelemen, D. (2003). The EU Rights Revolution: Adversial Legalism and European Integration. In T. Börzel & R. Cichowski (Eds.), *The State of the European Union* (pp. 221–235). Oxford: Oxford University Press.

Kelemen, D. (2006). Suing for Europe: Adversial Legalism and European Governance. *Comparative Political Studies, 39*(1), 101–127.

Kelemen, D. (2011). *Eurolegalism: The Transformation of Law and Regulation in the European Union*. Cambridge, MA: Harvard University Press.

Komarek, J. (2009). Precedent and Judicial Lawmaking in Supreme Courts: The Court of Justice Compared to the US Supreme Court and the French Cour de Cassation. In C. Barnard & O. Odudu (Eds.), *Cambridge Yearbook of European Legal Studies* (Vol. 11, pp. 399–434). Oxford: Hart Publishing.

Komarek, J. (2013). Reasoning with Previous Decisions: Beyond the Doctrine of Precedent. *American Journal of Comparative Law, 61*(1), 149–171.

Labayle, H., & De Bruycker, P. (2012). Impact de la jurisprudence de la CEJ et la CEDH en matière d'asile et d'immigration. *Étude Parlement Européen, DG des Politiques Internes*.

Lahav, G. (1997). International Versus National Constraints in Family-Reunification Migration Policy. *Global Governance, 3*(3), 349–372.

Lansbergen, A., & Miller, N. (2011). European Citizenship Rights in Internal Situations: An Ambiguous Revolution? Case note on *Ruiz Zambrano*. *European Constitutional Law Review, 7*, 287–307.

Lasser, M. D. S.-O.-L.'. E. (2009). *Judicial Deliberations: A Comparative Analysis of Judicial Transparency and Legitimacy*. Oxford: Oxford University Press.

Legomsky, S. (2011). Rationing Family Values in Europe and America: An Immigration Tug of War between States and their Supra-National Associations. *Georgetown Immigration Law Journal, 25*, 807–858.

Lenaerts, K. (1990). Constitutionalism and the Many Faces of Federalism. *American Journal of Comparative Law, 38*(2), 205–263.

Lenaerts, K. (1992). Some Thoughts about the Interaction Between Judges and Politicians. *Yearbook of European Law, 12*(1), 1–34.

Lenaerts, K. (2011). 'Civis europaeus sum': From the Cross-border Link to the Status of Citizen of the Union. *Online Journal on Free Movement of Workers within the European Union, 3*, 6–18.

Lenaerts, K. (2015). EU Citizenship and the European Court of Justice's 'Stone-by-Stone' Approach. *International Comparative Jurisprudence, 1*, 1–10.

Levy, J. (2008). Case Studies: Types, Designs and Logics of Inference. *Conflict Management and Peace Science, 25*(1), 1–18.

Lupu, Y., & Voeten, E. (2012). Precedent in International Courts: A Network Analysis of Case Citations by the European Court of Human Rights. *British Journal of Political Science, 42*(2), 413–439.

MacCormick, N., & Summers, R. (1997). *Interpreting Precedents: A Comparative Study*. Aldershot: Ashgate Publishing.

Maduro, M. P. (2007). Interpreting European Law: Judicial Adjudication in a Context of Constitutional Pluralism. *European Journal of Legal Studies, 1*(2), 1–21.

Majone, G. (2001). Two Logics of Delegation. Agency and Fiduciary Relations in EU Governance. *European Union Politics, 2*(1), 103–122.

Malecki, M. (2012). Do ECJ Judges All Speak with the Same Voice? Evidence of Divergent Preferences from the Judgments of Chambers. *Journal of European Public Policy, 19*(1), 59–75.
Mancini, G. F. (1989). The Making of a Constitution for Europe. *Common Market Law Review, 26*, 595–614.
Mancini, J. M., & Finlay, G. (2008). 'Citizenship Matters': Lessons From the Irish Citizenship Referendum. *American Quarterly, 60*(3), 575–599.
Martinsen, D. S. (2011). Judicial Policy-Making and Europeanization: The Proportionality of National Control and Administrative Discretion. *Journal of European Public Policy, 18*(7), 944–961.
Martinsen, D. S. (2015). *An Ever More Powerful Court? The Political Constraints of Legal Integration in the European Union*. Oxford: Oxford University Press.
Mattli, W., & Slaughter, A.-M. (1995). Law and Politics in the European Union: A Reply to Garrett. *International Organization, 49*(1), 183–190.
Mattli, W., & Slaughter, A.-M. (1998). Revisiting the European Court of Justice. *International Organization, 52*(1), 177–209.
Mayoral, J. (2016). In the CJEU Judges Trust: A New Approach in the Judicial Construction of Europe. *Journal of Common Market Studies, 55*(3), 551–568.
McCown, M. (2003). The European Parliament before the Bench: ECJ Precedent and EP Litigation Strategies. *Journal of European Public Policy, 10*(6), 974–995.
Menz, G. (2011). Stopping, Shaping and Moulding Europe: Two-Level Games, Non-State Actors and the Europeanization of Migration Policies. *Journal of Common Market Studies, 49*(2), 437–462.
Messina, A. (2007). *The Logics and Politics of Post-WWII Immigration to Western Europe*. Cambridge: Cambridge University Press.
Moravcsik, A. (1993). Preferences and Power in the European Community: A Liberal Intergovernmentalist Approach. *Journal of Common Market Studies, 31*(4), 473–524.
Neergaard, U., & Wind, M. (2012). Studying the EU in Legal and Political Sciences Scholarship. In U. Neergaard & R. Nielsen (Eds.), *European Legal Method: In a Multi-level EU Legal Order* (pp. 263–292). Copenhagen: Djof Publishing.
Nugent, N. (2010). *The Government and Politics of the European Union*. Basingstoke: Palgrave Macmillan.
Nyikos, S. (2003). The Preliminary Reference Process: National Court Implementation, Changing Opportunity Structures and Litigant Desistment. *European Union Politics, 4*(4), 397–419.
Nyikos, S. (2006). Strategic Interaction Among Courts within the Preliminary Reference Process—Stage 1: National Court Preemptive Opinions. *European Journal of Political Research, 45*(4), 527–550.
Olivier, B., & Reestman, J. H. (2007). Case Note on *Jia*. *European Constitutional Law Review, 3*, 463–475.

Peers, S. (1998). Building Fortress Europe: The Development of EU Migration Law. *Common Market Law Review, 35*, 1235–1272.

Peers, S. (2009). Free Movement, Immigration Control and Constitutional Conflict. *European Constitutional Law Review, 5*, 173–196.

Peers, S. (2011). *EU Justice and Home Affairs Law*. Oxford: Oxford University Press.

Peers, S., & Rogers, N. (2006). *EU Immigration and Asylum Law: Text and Commentary*. Leiden: Martinus Nijhoff Publishers.

Pelc, K. (2014). The Politics of Precedent in International Law: A Social Network Application. *American Political Science Review, 108*(3), 547–564.

Pierson, P. (1996). The Path to European Integration: A Historical Institutionalist Perspective. *Comparative Political Studies, 29*(2), 123–163.

Pierson, P. (2000). Increasing Returns, Path Dependence, and the Study of Politics. *The American Political Science Review, 94*(2), 251–267.

Pitarkis, J.-Y., & Tridimas, G. (2003). Joint Dynamics of Legal and Economic Integration in the European Union. *European Journal of Law and Economics, 16*(3), 357–368.

Pollack, M. (1997a). Delegation, Agency, and Agenda Setting in the European Community. *International Organization, 51*(1), 99–134.

Pollack, M. (1997b). Representing Diffuse Interests in EC Policy-Making. *Journal of European Public Policy, 4*(4), 572–590.

Pollack, M. (2002). Learning from the Americanists (Again): Theory and Method in the Study of Delegation. *West European Politics, 25*(1), 200–219.

Pollack, M. (2003). *The Engines of European Integration: Delegation, Agency and Agenda-Setting in the EU*. Oxford: Oxford University Press.

Pollack, M. (2013). The New EU Legal History: What's New, What's Missing? *American University International Law Review, 28*(5), 1257–1310.

Rasmussen, H. (1986). *On Law and Policy in the European Court of Justice: A Comparative Study in Judicial Policymaking*. Dordrecht: Martinus Nijhoff Publishers.

Schain, M. (2006). The Extreme-Right and Immigration Policy-Making: Measuring Direct and Indirect Effects. *West European Politics, 29*(2), 270–289.

Scharpf, F. (1988). The Joint-Decision Trap: Lessons from German Federalism and European Integration. *Public Administration, 66*(Autumn), 239–278.

Scharpf, F. (2012). Perpetual Momentum: Directed and Unconstrained? *Journal of European Public Policy, 19*(1), 127–139.

Schauer, F. (1987). Precedent. *Stanford Law Review, 39*, 571–605.

Schepel, H., & Wesseling, R. (1997). The Legal Community: Judges, Lawyers, Officials and Clerks in the Writing of Europe. *European Law Journal, 3*(2), 165–188.

Schiltz, C. (2005). Akrich: A Clear Delimitation without Limits. *Maastricht Journal of European and Comparative Law, 12*(3), 241–252.

Schimmelfennig, F. (2006). Competition and Community: Constitutional Courts, Rhetorical Action, and the Institutionalization of Human Rights in the European Union. *Journal of European Public Policy, 16*(8), 1247–1264.

Schmidt, S. (1998). *Following up on Judicial Politics: How the European Commission Uses the Court of Justice to Pressure the Member States.* Paper prepared for the Annual Meeting of the American Political Science Association, 3–6 September, Boston, MA.

Schmidt, S. (2000). Only an Agenda-Setter? The European Commission's Political Power over the Council of Ministers. *European Union Politics, 1*(37), 37–61.

Schmidt, S. (2012). Who Cares about Nationality? The Path-dependent Case Law of the ECJ from Goods to Citizens. *Journal of European Public Policy, 19*(1), 8–24.

Schmidt, S. (2014). Judicial Europeanisation: The Case of Zambrano in Ireland. *West European Politics, 37*(4), 769–785.

Schoenmaekers, S., & Hoogenboom, A. (2014). *Singh* and *Carpenter* Revisited: Some Progress but no Final Clarity. *Maastricht Journal of European and Comparative Law, 21*(3), 494–513.

Schweitzer, R. (2015). A Stratified Right to Family Life? On the Logic(s) and Legitimacy of Granting Differential Access to Family Reunification for Third-Country Nationals Living within the EU. *Journal of Ethnic and Migration Studies, 41*(13), 2130–2148.

Shapiro, M. (1980). Comparative Law and Comparative Politics. *Southern California Law Review, 53*, 357–543.

Shapiro, M. (2008). Law and Politics: The Problem of Boundaries. In K. Whittington, D. Kelemen, & G. Caldeira (Eds.), *The Oxford Handbook of Law and Politics* (pp. 767–774). Oxford: Oxford University Press.

Shapiro, M., & Stone Sweet, A. (2002). *On Law, Politics, and Judicialization.* Oxford: Oxford University Press.

Shaw, J. (2011). Concluding Thoughts—Rottmann in Context. In J. Shaw (Ed.), *Has the European Court of Justice Challenged Member State Sovereignty in Nationality Law?* EUI Working Paper, RSCAS, 2011/62. Florence: European University Institute.

Shuibhne, N. (2010). The Resilience of EU Market Citizenship. *Common Market Law Review, 47*(6), 1597–1628.

Shuibhne, N. (2011). Seven Questions for Seven Paragraphs. *European Law Review, 36*(2), 161–162.

Slepcevic, R. (2009). The Judicial Enforcement of EU Law through National Courts: Possibilities and Limits. *Journal of European Public Policy, 16*(3), 378–394.

Spaventa, E. (2005). Case Note on *Akrich. Common Market Law Review, 42*, 225–239.

Spaventa, E. (2008). Seeing the Wood Despite the Trees? On the Scope of Union Citizenship and Its Constitutional Effects. *Common Market Law Review, 45*, 13–45.
Stalford, H. (2012). *Children and the European Union: Rights, Welfare and Accountability*. London: Hart Publishing.
Stalford, H. (2015). The CRC in Litigation Under EU Law. In T. Liefaard & J. Doek (Eds.), *Litigating the Rights of the Child: The UN Convention on the Rights of the Child in Domestic and International Jurisprudence* (pp. 211–230). Dordrecht: Springer.
Staton, J., & Moore, W. (2011). Judicial Power in Domestic and International Politics. *International Organization, 65*(3), 553–587.
Staver, A. (2013). Free Movement and the Fragmentation of Family Reunification Rights. *European Journal of Migration and Law, 15*, 69–89.
Stein, E. (1981). Lawyers, Judges, and the Making of a Transnational Constitution. *American Journal of International Law, 75*(1), 1–27.
Stone Sweet, A. (2000). *Governing with Judges: Constitutional Politics in Europe*. Oxford: Oxford University Press.
Stone Sweet, A. (2004). *The Judicial Construction of Europe*. Oxford: Oxford University Press.
Stone Sweet, A. (2010). The European Court of Justice and the Judicialization of EU Governance. *Living Reviews in European Governance, 5*(2), 1–50.
Stone Sweet, A., & Brunell, T. (1998). Constructing a Supranational Constitution: Dispute Resolution and Governance in the European Community. *American Political Science Review, 92*(1), 63–81.
Stone Sweet, A., & Brunell, T. (2012). The European Court of Justice, State Noncompliance, and the Politics of Override. *American Political Science Review., 106*(1), 204–213.
Stone Sweet, A., & Caporaso, J. (1998). From Free Trade to Supranational Polity: The European Court and Integration. In W. Sandholtz & A. Stone Sweet (Eds.), *European Integration and Supranational Governance* (pp. 92–134). Oxford: Oxford University Press.
Stone Sweet, A., & Sandholtz, W. (1997). European Integration and Supranational Governance. *Journal of European Public Policy, 4*(3), 297–317.
Stone Sweet, A., & Stranz, K. (2012). Rights Adjudication and Constitutional Pluralism in Germany and Europe. *Journal of European Public Policy, 19*(1), 92–108.
Strik, T. (2011). *Besluitvorming over asiel- en migratierichtlijnen. De wisselwerking tussen nationaal en Europees niveau*. Den Haag: Boom Juridische uitgevers.
Tallberg, J. (2000a). The Anatomy of Autonomy. An Institutional Account of Variation in Supranational Influence. *Journal of Common Market Studies, 38*(5), 843–864.

Tallberg, J. (2000b). Supranational Influence in EU Enforcement. *Journal of European Public Policy, 7*(1), 104–121.
Tallberg, J. (2002). Delegation to Supranational Institutions: Why, How and with What Consequences? *West European Politics, 25*(1), 23–46.
Tomkin, J. (2009). The Worker, The Citizen, Their Families and the Court of Justice: Tales of Free Movement from Luxembourg. In P. Minderhoud & N. Trimikliniotis (Eds.), *Rethinking the Free Movement of Workers: The European Challenges Ahead* (pp. 39–59). Nijmegen: Wolf Legal Publishers.
Tridimas, G., & Tridimas, T. (2004). National Courts and the European Court of Justice: A Public Choice Analysis of the Preliminary Reference Procedure. *International Review of Law and Economics, 24*(2), 125–145.
Tridimas, T. (2012). Precedent and the Court of Justice: A Jurisprudence of Doubt? In J. Dickson & P. Eleftheriadis (Eds.), *Philosophical Foundations of European Union Law* (pp. 307–330). Oxford: Oxford University Press.
Tryfonidou, A. (2007). Jia or "Carpenter II": The Edge of Reason. *European Law Review, 32*(6), 908–918.
Tryfonidou, A. (2008). Reverse Discrimination in Purely Internal Situations: An Incongruity in a Citizens' Europe. *Legal Issues of Economic Integration, 35*(1), 43–67.
Tryfonidou, A. (2009). Family Reunification Rights of (Migrant) Union Citizens: Towards a More Liberal Approach. *European Law Journal, 15*(5), 634–653.
Tsebelis, G., & Garrett, G. (2001). The Institutional Foundations of Intergovernmentalism and Supranationalism in the European Union. *International Organization, 55*(2), 357–390.
Van der Mei, A. P. (2003). Residence and the Evolving Notion of European Union Citizenship. Comments on *Baumbast v Secretary of State for Home Department*, 17 September 2002 (Case C-143/99). *European Journal of Migration and Law, 5*, 419–433.
Van Elsuwege, P., & Kochenov, D. (2011). On the Limits of Judicial Intervention: EU Citizenship and Family Reunification Rights. *European Journal of Migration and Law, 13*(4), 443–466.
Vauchez, A. (2012). Keeping the Dream Alive: The European Court of Justice and the Transnational Fabric of Integrationist Jurisprudence. *European Political Science Review, 4*(1), 51–71.
Vick, D. (2004). Interdisciplinarity and the Discipline of Law. *Journal of Law and Society, 31*(2), 163–193.
Vink, M., Claes, M., & Arnold, C. (2009). *Explaining the Use of Preliminary References by Domestic Courts in EU Member States: A Mixed-Method Comparative Analysis.* Paper presented at the 11th Biennial Conference of the European Union Studies Association, 24 April 2009, Marina del Rey.
Walter, A. (2008). *Reverse Discrimination and Family Reunification.* Nijmegen: Wolf Legal Publishers.

Wasserfallen, F. (2010). The Judiciary as Legislator? How the European Court of Justice Shapes Policy-Making in the European Union. *Journal of European Public Policy, 17*(8), 1128–1146.

Watson, P. (1993). Free Movement of Workers: A One-way Ticket? *Industrial Law Journal, 22*(1), 68–77.

Weiler, J. (1981). The Community System: The Dual Character of Supranationalism. In F. Jacobs (Ed.), *Yearbook of European Law* (pp. 267–280). Oxford: Oxford University Press.

Weiler, J. (1982). Community, Member States and European Integration: Is the Law Relevant? *Journal of Common Market Studies, 21*(1), 39–56.

Weiler, J. (1991). The Transformation of Europe. *Yale Law Journal, 100*, 2403–2483.

Weiler, J. (1994). A Quiet Revolution. The European Court of Justice and Its Interlocutors. *Comparative Political Studies, 26*(4), 510–534.

White, R. (2004). Conflicting Competences: Free Movement Rules and Immigration Law. *European Law Review, 29*(3), 385–396.

Wincott, D. (1995). The Role of Law or the Rule of the Court of Justice? An Institutionalist Account of Judicial Politics in the European Community. *Journal of European Public Policy, 2*(4), 583–602.

Zhang, A., Liu, J., & Garoupa, N. (2016). Judging in Europe: Do Legal Traditions Matter? *King's College London Law School Research Paper*, No. 2016-03. London: King's College.

Index[1]

A
Absolute citation scores, 154, 155, 156, 158, 159, 161
Action for annulment, 99, 232
Advocate General (AG), 47, 212
Ahmed case, 327
Akrich case, 167, 174, 185, 191, 201–209, 218, 220–226, 230, 231, 233, 235, 259, 290, 295, 296, 301, 307
Alarape & Tijani case, 327
Alopka case, 168, 174, 218, 261–275, 279, 291, 293, 297, 297n1, 302, 309
Article 8 ECHR, 97, 123, 188, 196, 204, 211, 214, 235, 236, 241, 245
Article 18 EC, 195, 197, 210, 213, 216, 222, 293
Article 20 TFEU, 96, 130, 247, 248, 257, 258, 270, 272, 273, 293, 297n1
Article 21 TFEU, 195, 210, 251, 254, 260, 262, 272, 273, 293
Ayalti case, 328

B
Baumbast case, 166, 167, 174, 180, 194, 195, 198–201, 210–217, 219, 221, 244, 246, 248, 250, 291, 293, 295–297, 300–304

C
Carpenter case, 162, 166, 167, 174, 180, 185, 186, 188–194, 198–201, 204–208, 212, 216, 217, 221, 226, 230, 233–235, 246, 250, 278–280, 292, 293, 295, 296, 298, 300–303, 307
Cassis de Dijon case, 14, 17, 18, 21, 22

[1] Note: Page numbers followed by 'n' refer to notes.

M. De Somer, *Precedents and Judicial Politics in EU Immigration Law*, European Administrative Governance,
https://doi.org/10.1007/978-3-319-93982-7

Chakroun case, 168, 174, 201, 232–244, 267–269, 292, 296, 307, 308
Charter of Fundamental Rights of the European Union, 32, 211, 259
Chavez Vilchez case, 328
Children's rights, 97, 98, 195, 196, 198, 199, 233, 235, 244, 245, 268, 270
Citizenship
  Belgian, 244, 247, 249
  citizenship rights, 251, 271, 297
  European Union, 77, 92, 93, 96–97, 99, 180–200, 210, 211, 250, 251, 258, 271, 293, 297, 301
  Finnish, 264, 265
  Irish, 209, 211, 217, 218, 252
  United Kingdom (UK), 186, 252, 255, 306
Citizenship Directive, 36, 94, 110, 112–119, 121, 123, 124, 141, 194, 224, 231, 243, 244, 247, 252–254, 257, 258, 261, 262, 265, 270–274, 276–279, 307
Commission v Germany case, 163, 327
Commission v Italy case, 163, 327
Commission v Luxembourg (C-57/07) case, 163, 327
Commission v Luxembourg (C-165/05) case, 163
Commission v Malta case, 163, 327
Commission v Netherlands case, 163, 327
Commission v Spain (C-157/03) case, 162, 167, 191, 193, 226, 301, 326
Commission v Spain (C-503/03) case, 163, 167, 191, 193, 206, 226, 291, 301, 326
Common market, 16, 17, 42, 108, 178
Compliance, 17, 31, 36, 37, 43, 74, 78, 197, 198, 230, 270, 320, 321
Conditional requirements, 111, 122, 125, 135, 137, 138, 142, 143, 239, 268, 289–292, 319
Conditions, 28, 34, 35, 39, 42, 49, 73, 76, 90, 92–95, 111, 114–117, 121, 122, 126, 127, 133–135, 137, 138, 141–143, 180, 181, 183, 187, 196–200, 204–208, 210, 213–215, 220, 221, 223, 224, 227, 228, 231–236, 239, 240, 242, 243, 245, 246, 253, 257, 260, 269, 272–274, 276–278, 288, 289, 291, 295, 313, 321, 322
Constitutionalization
  of EU law, 14, 80
  narrative, 13, 16, 18
  process, 18
Contextualist
  legal literature, 6, 13, 19, 51
  legal scholarship, 11–16, 23, 32, 48, 74
COREPER, 124
Costa v Enel case, 12, 19, 40, 78, 79
Council
  EU, 231, 269, 289
  European, 109, 115, 124–127, 131, 234
Court
  authority, 13, 17, 18, 23–24, 26, 27, 41, 63, 74, 76, 79, 80, 316, 320, 321
  autonomy, 1, 4, 7, 18, 21, 22, 29, 34, 35, 38, 39, 48–50, 75, 76, 81, 84, 89, 90, 107, 108, 151, 175, 280, 287, 313, 314, 320
  behaviour, 3, 4, 6, 29, 47, 49, 152, 169, 310, 314
  discretion, 34, 71, 77, 299, 300, 316–318, 322
  effectiveness, 14, 23, 79, 242, 320, 321
  leeway, 7, 15, 85, 185, 193, 205, 300, 306, 317–319
  role, 1, 3–6, 11–54, 75, 152, 153, 313, 314

CS case, 328
Cue-giving, 83, 298
Cue-taking, 68, 69, 72, 83, 84, 110, 186, 211, 212, 216, 219, 234, 235, 251, 294–305, 316–318

D
Deak case, 98n2, 162, 325
Delegation, 22, 24–25, 27n1, 34, 35, 76, 111, 113, 115–119, 125–127, 131–133, 135–137, 139, 140, 142, 233, 240, 261, 273, 288, 289
  literature, 22, 39
Dereci case, 2, 163, 168, 174, 232, 244–267, 270, 271, 276, 278, 279, 293, 297, 298, 302, 304, 306, 309, 327
Derived rights, 175–180, 186, 189, 195, 197, 198, 210–212, 215–217, 223, 228, 230, 245, 246, 254, 255, 258, 261, 262, 265, 270, 272, 275–279, 292, 293, 303, 308
Diatta case, 162, 325
Discourse, 6, 20, 53, 54, 65, 69, 82, 99, 152, 156, 160, 166, 167, 169, 174, 216, 226, 249–251, 269, 296, 307, 310, 315, 316, 319
Discrimination, 22, 39, 43, 49, 77, 108, 180
Discursive
  interactions, 54, 66n2, 73, 152, 173, 175, 280, 294, 302, 305, 316
  processes, 82, 317, 319
  socialisation, 82, 319
Dogan case, 328
Domestic courts, 23, 30, 69, 71, 74, 174, 252, 300, 302, 309, 315, 316, 319, 321, 322
Dzodzi case, 162, 178, 325

E
Effet utile, 93, 180–200, 211, 216, 229, 295, 296, 301, 306
Eind case, 166–168, 174, 185, 191, 193, 200, 201, 209–232, 253, 262, 263, 274–278, 280, 290, 291, 296, 298, 301, 307, 327
Employment rights, 94, 179, 195, 198, 248, 250, 293
EP v Council case, 163, 168, 174, 191, 201, 206, 232–243, 292, 296, 303, 307, 326
EU immigration law, 5, 90, 92–96, 99, 110, 119–140, 168, 201, 232, 269
European Commission (EC), 16, 46
European Convention of Human Rights (ECHR), 97, 98, 131, 183, 188, 196, 204, 211, 214, 229, 233–236, 239, 241, 245, 259–261, 264, 271
European Court of Human Rights (ECtHR), 66n2, 68, 123, 135, 154, 188, 214, 235, 236
European integration
  history of, 45
  processes, 1–2, 11–54, 313
European Parliament (EP), 33, 64, 99, 109, 112, 114–119, 123–124, 134, 139, 206, 232–236, 296
Ex ante benchmark, 5, 7, 51, 107, 314

F
Family reunification
  case law, 98–100
  directive, 94, 95, 99n3, 110, 120–143, 227, 229, 232, 233, 238, 242, 243, 257, 267, 269–271, 289, 291, 296, 307
  law, 4, 7, 92–98, 107, 126, 143, 179, 310, 314
  provisions, 94, 96

Free movement
case law, 232, 254
law, 92–94, 96, 98, 99, 99n3, 110–119, 121, 142, 168, 176, 178, 181, 184, 192, 194, 195, 197, 198, 201, 203, 207, 209, 222, 224, 229, 230, 243, 252, 255, 262, 263, 265, 274, 275, 290, 293
provisions, 178, 196, 205
rights, 93, 96, 111, 112n1, 121, 128, 129, 177, 181, 182, 184, 195, 201–203, 205–207, 209–212, 214, 218–223, 225, 245, 246, 256, 258, 260, 262, 264, 265, 270, 288, 290, 291, 293, 296, 297, 303, 309
of services, 292
of workers, 220
Fundamental rights, 93, 96–98, 135, 180–200, 204–206, 211, 214–217, 232–237, 241, 245, 251, 259–261, 264, 267–269, 271, 273, 278, 296, 301, 303, 307, 309

G
General principles of EU law, 37, 72, 97, 98, 134, 190, 192, 232, 261
Givane case, 162, 326
Grand theory, 6, 15, 40, 48, 153
Grzelczyk case, 36, 197
Gül case, 98n2, 162, 325

H
Hermeneutics, 68, 309
Human rights, 13, 97, 211, 233

I
Ibrahim case, 163, 327
Iida case, 164, 168, 174, 218, 232, 261–276, 278, 279, 293, 297, 302, 306, 309, 327
Immigration control, 91, 113, 115, 141, 192, 204, 222, 225, 228, 230, 288, 308, 315
Imran case, 163, 327
Increasing returns, 69, 185, 190, 298, 299, 317
Individual rights, 12, 14, 32, 143, 240, 253, 268
Infringement
actions, 99, 99n3
procedures, 26, 33, 99n3
Interdisciplinary, 52, 53
research, 52, 52n2
Intergovernmentalism, 18, 42, 46, 52, 75, 119, 120
Internal rule, 175–200, 228, 245, 254, 290, 295
Inward
citation scores, 154, 155, 156, 159–161, 167, 176, 180, 185, 191, 200, 201, 206, 218
scores, 155, 158–161, 165–168, 175, 178, 180, 185, 191, 193, 201, 218, 232
Ius soli, 209, 217, 244, 249

J
Jia case, 163, 167, 174, 201–209, 222–224, 296, 326
Judicial
autonomy, 1, 4, 7, 18, 21, 22, 29, 34, 35, 39, 48–50, 76, 81, 82, 84, 89, 90, 107–110, 151, 175, 280, 287–293, 313, 314, 320, 321
dialogue, 322

interlocutors, 67–73, 152, 174, 294–302, 305, 310, 315–319, 321
leeway, 1, 319
outcomes, 1, 7, 26, 51, 246, 287, 290–294, 298, 308, 315, 323
reasoning, 53, 65, 75, 77, 81, 296, 303, 309, 316

K

Kaba case, 162, 185, 326
Kaba II case, 162, 167, 185, 326
K&A case, 328
Kermaschek case, 5, 92, 94, 161, 162, 166, 167, 174, 175
Khachab case, 328
Koua Poirrez case, 162, 167, 178, 179

L

Least-likely case, 4, 89–92, 313
Legal
  certainty, 63
  exegesis, 54
  reasoning, 53, 54, 64, 65, 66n2, 70, 81, 182, 193, 205, 212, 220, 221, 225, 228, 249, 250, 252, 255, 260, 262, 263, 271, 287, 295, 296, 299, 303, 304, 306, 307, 309, 310, 315–317, 319, 320, 323
  scholarship, 1–3, 11, 12, 18, 23, 32, 48, 51–54, 63, 65, 73–75, 314
  theory, 7, 61–63, 70, 76
Legitimacy, 2, 15, 17, 30, 37, 64–66, 66n2, 74–76, 82, 90, 130, 181, 188, 197, 204
Lisbon Treaty, 32, 92
Litigants, 19, 25, 30, 37, 41, 42, 65–69, 72, 74, 78, 82–84, 153, 174, 185, 252, 294–302, 305, 309, 310, 315–319, 321, 322
Longitudinal, 6, 42, 44, 65, 66, 73, 98n2, 151, 152, 169, 323
Lounes case, 328
Lütticke case, 40

M

Maastricht Treaty, 96, 179
McCarthy and Others case, 277, 328
McCarthy case, 2, 163, 174, 185, 232, 244–263, 265, 270, 274–276, 278, 279, 293, 297, 302, 306–309, 327
Martinez Sala case, 77, 96
Mattern & Cikotic case, 163, 326
Meade case, 162, 325
Member States' interests, 5, 7, 20, 21, 23, 90, 107–143, 175, 280, 287
Metock case, 166–168, 174, 193, 201, 206, 209–232, 241, 243, 244, 252, 253, 258, 262, 265, 276, 290–292, 296, 308, 309
Minister for Justice
  Dutch, 242
  Irish, 224, 226
Mixed methods, 5, 6, 32, 50, 153
Morson & Jhanjan case, 96, 162, 166, 167, 175, 177–183, 228, 246, 295, 325
MRAX case, 162, 167, 174, 180, 191–193, 200, 201, 205, 221, 226, 230, 291, 296, 301, 326

N

NA case, 328
National courts, 14, 19, 23, 24, 30, 38, 41, 65–69, 72, 83, 84, 152, 174, 198, 221, 223, 237, 260, 266, 293–302, 305, 310, 315–318
  See also Domestic courts

National governments
Austrian government, 192
Belgian government, 245–247, 249, 303
Danish government, 219–221, 223
Dutch government, 219–221, 238, 239, 241–243, 265
Finnish government, 265
French government, 17, 111, 131
German government, 196, 197, 221, 265
Greek government, 131
Irish government, 212–216, 245, 303
Italian government, 78, 265
Polish government, 245, 265
Spanish government, 193
Swedish government, 131
UK government, 181–184, 186, 196, 197, 204, 212, 214–216, 223, 302, 303
Negotiations, 7, 25, 36, 51, 94, 95, 109–111, 113, 128, 129, 133, 140, 229, 233, 234, 242, 287, 292, 310
Neofunctionalism, 28, 42, 46
Non-compliance, 24, 43–46, 49, 90
Non-discrimination, 139, 178, 179, 192, 233, 251, 270
Non-judicial interlocutors, 74–82, 294, 310
Noorzia case, 328

O

O&B case, 164, 166, 168, 175, 185, 232, 274–280, 291, 296, 307, 328
O&S case, 164, 168, 174, 232, 261–274, 276, 292, 293, 297, 302, 304, 309, 327
Observational equivalence, 5, 22, 29, 35, 39, 40, 43, 45–47, 49–51, 107, 108
Ogieriakhi case, 328
Oruche case, 328
Outward
citation scores, 154, 155, 156, 158–161, 165
scores, 154, 155, 156, 158, 160, 161, 165–168, 201, 218, 232, 274

P

Paradigm, 16, 27, 29, 40, 52, 82, 244–274
Partner, 113–118, 122, 126, 130, 136, 243, 289
Path-dependency, 65, 69
Patterns, 4, 6, 7, 62, 63, 66, 69, 73, 113, 125, 152, 160, 165–169, 173–175, 177, 180, 182, 185, 323
Personal scope, 110–113, 115, 118, 120, 124, 126, 128, 129, 133, 140–143, 175, 269, 287–289, 291, 292, 310, 315
Political
preferences, 4, 5, 7, 16, 34, 46, 107, 287, 290, 313, 314, 320, 321
science, 1–4, 6, 7, 11, 12, 15, 16, 18, 21, 23, 25, 29, 30, 35, 51–54, 52n2, 64–66, 73, 74, 76, 78, 90, 314
weight, 108, 109
Precedent
effect, 2, 6, 7, 99, 152
value, 66, 100, 167, 168, 193, 201, 300, 319
weight, 71
Preliminary reference, 14, 19, 25, 26, 30, 32, 40–43, 45, 67, 92, 99, 251, 321
Presidency (of the Council), 115, 127
Primary
law, 96–98, 190, 200, 205, 244, 245, 254, 262, 263, 276, 277, 279
provisions, 178

See also Treaty, law; Treaty, provisions
Primary carer, 98, 195, 196, 198, 199, 210–212, 216, 217, 250, 263, 273, 293
Principal-Agent, 25, 27, 28, 33–35
Proportionality, 37, 123, 134, 188, 190, 192, 197, 198, 200, 215, 230

Q
Qualitative
  analysis, 26, 166–168
  orientations, 5, 6, 50, 153
  research, 29–39, 47, 49
  scholarship, 6, 12, 38, 48, 153
Quantitative
  analysis, 25, 173
  orientations, 5, 6, 50, 153
  research, 29, 48, 49
  scholarship, 40, 49

R
Rahman case, 164, 327
Rational anticipation, 22, 29, 49
Regulation 1612/68/EEC, 93, 94, 111, 112, 121, 225, 226
Relative citation scores, 154–159, 162–164
Rendon Marin case, 328
Repeat game(s), 2, 78, 252, 321
Report for the hearing, 174, 174n1, 181, 182, 211, 212, 214, 219, 234, 245, 257, 303
Residence rights, 37, 77, 114, 115, 118, 122, 125, 181, 182, 187, 190, 194–200, 202, 204, 205, 207, 211, 213–217, 219–221, 223, 225, 229, 230, 244–248, 250, 252–254, 256–259, 261–267, 271–273, 275–279, 290, 291, 293, 296, 297, 297n1, 303, 304
Returnee(s), 184, 189, 191, 202, 204, 219, 290
Reverse discrimination, 96, 128–130, 178, 225, 228, 229
Reyes case, 164, 328
Right to family life, 97, 190, 192, 196, 206, 217, 233, 235, 236, 245
Ruhr case, 98n2, 162, 177, 326
Rule of law, 62, 63, 75

S
Sahin case, 163, 327
Same-sex, 113, 114, 116, 122, 132, 136
S&G case, 164, 166, 168, 175, 185, 191, 274–280, 292, 296, 297, 328
Secondary
  law, 96, 183, 190, 197, 198, 200, 205, 213, 214, 257, 262, 263, 265, 271, 273, 292, 297n1, 309
  legislation, 17, 36, 93–95, 181, 187, 190, 210, 212, 215, 221, 247, 250, 269, 277, 293, 299–301, 303, 307, 318
  provisions, 96, 210, 277
Selective case sampling, 6, 49–51, 152
Self-citation
  observations, 5, 153, 161, 167–169, 180
  patterns, 160, 175
  practices, 5, 92, 100, 101
  scores, 154n2, 169
  structures, 5, 156, 161–169, 173, 174
Side issue, 77, 220, 253, 274, 306, 320
Singh and others case, 328
Singh case, 162, 166–168, 174, 180–191, 194, 198–206, 218–220, 222, 230, 246, 253, 274–278, 280, 290, 291, 295–298, 300–303, 306, 325
Social
  assistance, 122, 139, 198, 215, 218, 220, 238, 278
  security, 77, 175, 176, 242

Social network analysis, 154, 154n2
Societal interest
groups, 26, 31, 38
litigation, 26, 32, 69, 72, 74
Sovereignty-sensitive, 4, 37, 92, 313
Spouse, 94, 111, 113–116, 118, 122, 131, 136, 142, 175–177, 179, 181–184, 186–189, 192, 194, 202, 203, 205–207, 209, 214, 222–224, 226, 227, 229, 254, 255, 257, 262, 264, 267, 275, 278, 279, 289
Stare decisis, 61
Static EU citizens, 121, 125, 128, 129, 131
Strategic Committee on Immigration, Frontiers and Asylum, The (SCIFA), 124, 125
Substance of rights' doctrine, 250–252, 254–256, 258, 260, 262–265, 267, 273, 274, 297, 297n1, 304, 308, 309
Supranational
governance, 14, 25, 41
level, 14, 26, 27n1

T
Taghavi case, 162, 176, 254, 326
Tahir case, 328
Tampere Council, 121
Third-country national, 38, 92, 94–96, 98, 98n2, 99n3, 118, 120, 121, 125, 126, 129, 137, 138, 142, 175–177, 179, 186, 191–194, 203, 205–207, 210, 216, 218, 219, 223–225, 227, 230, 243, 248, 256–259, 261–268, 270–273, 275–279, 288, 291, 297n1, 304, 328
family member, 38, 92, 94, 95, 118, 119, 125, 127, 138, 142, 175, 176, 179, 192, 193, 206, 207, 210, 211, 219, 223, 225, 227, 230, 243, 256, 258, 260, 262, 263, 265, 267, 271, 273, 276–279, 289, 291, 297n1
Time horizons, 3, 24, 79, 81n3
Treaty
law, 71, 72, 190, 191, 195, 205, 207, 210, 212, 217, 246, 261, 262, 277, 291–293, 297, 299, 303, 307, 315
provisions, 71, 96, 99, 178, 179, 183, 189–191, 195, 198, 205, 210, 215, 216, 219, 222, 223, 246, 250, 255, 258, 262, 263, 270, 272, 279, 291–293, 299, 301
Trial balloons, 78, 249, 306, 319

U
Uecker & Jacquet case, 162, 167, 179, 228, 326

V
Van Gend en Loos case, 12, 19, 40

W
Written observations, 13, 26, 32, 40, 44–46, 51, 80, 108, 109, 174, 181, 184, 192, 196, 219, 224, 238, 245, 246, 257, 259, 265, 302–304, 309, 322

X
Xhymshiti case, 163, 327

Y
Ymeraga case, 164, 168, 174, 261–275, 279, 293, 297, 302, 309, 328

Z

Zambrano case, 2, 38, 163, 166, 168, 174, 200, 218, 244–263, 247n6, 265, 266, 270, 271, 274, 279, 293, 296–298, 301–304, 306, 308, 309, 327
Zaoui case, 162, 167, 176, 178, 179, 325
Zhu & Chen case, 162, 166, 167, 174, 200, 201, 209–232, 244–248, 250, 255, 262, 263, 272, 273, 291, 293, 296, 297, 301, 303, 304, 326

The manufacturer's authorised representative in the EU is Springer Nature Customer Service Centre GmbH, Europaplatz 3, 69115 Heidelberg, Germany. If you have any concerns regarding our products, please contact ProductSafety@springernature.com

Printed and bound by CPI Group (UK) Ltd, Croydon, CR0 4YY
05/10/2026
02228128-0013